D1558282

Detroit Monographs in Musicology/Studies in Music, No. 25

Editor
J. Bunker Clark
University of Kansas

Vistas of American Music

Essays and Compositions in Honor of
William K. Kearns

Edited by
Susan L. Porter and John Graziano

HARMONIE PARK PRESS
Warren, Michigan
1999

Frontispiece:
William K. Kearns

Copyright ©1999 by Harmonie Park Press

Printed and bound in the United States of America
Published by
Harmonie Park Press
23630 Pinewood
Warren, Michigan 48091

Editor, J. Bunker Clark
Book Design and Typesetting, Leslie DeGrassi and Larry Worster

Library of Congress Cataloging-in-Publication Data

Vistas of American music : essays and compositions in honor of William
  K. Kearns / edited by Susan L. Porter and John Graziano.
        p.   cm. -- (Detroit monographs in musicology/Studies in music
; no. 25)
  Includes bibliographical references and index.
  ISBN 0-089990-088-7
  1. Music--United States--History and criticism. I. Kearns,
William, 1928- . II. Porter, Susan L., 1941- . III. Graziano,
John Michael. IV. Series.
ML200.1.V57   1999
780'.973--dc21   99-19347

Contents

Illustrations

FIGURES

GRAPHS

CHART

TABLES

Foreword

William Kearns is a man of many musical interests, but his greatest passion has been his exploration of, and involvement with, the multi-faceted nature of American music. He has examined the life and works of Horatio Parker, one of the major composers of the second New England School, and has investigated various aspects of American popular music as well as folk music and cowboy songs of the West. Among the papers he has delivered and published over the years are "A Study of the Rural Music of the Appalachian Region and Its Impact on American Popular Culture," "From the Cotton Field to the Concert Hall: The Black Spiritual in America," "Jimmie Rodgers's Many-Hewed Blue Yodels," "Horatio Parker's Oratorios: A Measure of the Changing Genre at the Turn of the Twentieth Century," "From Black to White: A Hillbilly Version of Gussie Davis's 'The Fatal Wedding'," and "'Will She Ever Return'? A Study in the Esthetics of a Popular American Song." During his long academic career, Bill has also been active as a professional French horn player, an instructor of brass instruments, and an educator *par excellence*.

This volume's celebratory essays and compositions are offered as a tribute to our good friend, mentor, and colleague, William Kearns. They are all concerned with aspects of American music that have interested Bill throughout his career. The essays offer a panoply of topics, ranging from eighteenth-century tunebooks and social dances, through nineteenth-century composers and merchants, to America's international connections in the twentieth century. Several essays address specific genres, such as college song books, periodical and music publishers, research problems in American music, and native American music. Finally, the compositions are intended to allow Bill the pleasure of music-making.

—John Graziano

Editor's Note

When Susan L. Porter asked me to be a contributor to a festschrift in honor of William Kearns, I readily agreed. Susan singlehandedly conceived and gathered the essays and compositions for this volume. Soon after she began to edit the submissions, Susan was stricken with an illness that would eventually take her life. After her first encounter with her illness, she and I agreed that if she was unable to continue or complete the editorial task, I would take over for her. I have attempted to remain true to her original vision.

—J.G.

1

William Kearns's Contribution to American Music

Robert R. Fink

William Kearns was born on 17 January 1928 in Wilmington, Ohio. He graduated from Wilmington High School in 1945 and served in the United States Army from 1946 to 1948 as a Staff Sergeant in the 36th Regimental Band in Germany. He returned home and attended Wilmington College (1948-50) before enrolling at Ohio State University, where he received a Bachelor of Science degree, *summa cum laude*, with a major in music education in 1952, and a Master of Arts in music theory and composition in 1954. Bill completed a Ph.D in musicology with a major in music history and minors in philosophy and music theory at the University of Illinois in 1965.

Between 1952 and 1965, he held professional positions in the Columbus, Ohio public schools, at Friends' University in Wichita, Kansas, and at Ohio State University, where he was first an instructor and then an assistant professor of music, teaching French horn and other brass instruments, music appreciation and music literature, and serving as conductor of various ensembles. During this time he also performed as hornist with the Wichita Symphony Orchestra, the Columbus Orchestra, and the Wheeling (West Virginia) Symphony Orchestra.

Bill Kearns was appointed to the faculty of the College of Music at the University of Colorado in 1965 to initiate a graduate program in music history and to teach French horn. He was very successful in both of these endeavors. A good number of young horn students developed their talents under his tutelage and have entered the profession as teachers and performers, and the graduate music history program at the university has prospered, furnishing exceptionally well-trained and highly qualified professors for important positions at universities across the nation.

William Kearns was promoted to associate professor in 1967 and professor in 1970. He chaired the College's Music History Division from 1966 to 1976 and the Academic Area from 1979 to 1981. In 1981 I appointed him Associate Dean for Graduate Studies in Music; he was enormously effective in this position. Under his guidance the graduate program flourished, reaching a total enrollment of over 200. During his tenure as dean, countless graduate students related to me his selfless devotion to their education as administrator, teacher, advisor, colleague, and friend. His normal workday was frequently stretched to meet the needs of students, and Bill's genuine interest in students and support of their work has become a legend within the College. The respect and admiration that students and colleagues had for his work as an administrator was nothing short of spectacular and quite unusual in these days when it is more fashionable to revile administrators than to praise them.

In 1985, Bill decided it was time to devote all his energies to his first loves, teaching and research. His many contributions as a distinguished scholar in the field of American music will be documented elsewhere in this festschrift, but it should be noted that he has also been a masterful teacher and a caring mentor for hundreds of music students during his career. Recently, when he was nominated for a Presidential Teaching Scholar Award at the University of Colorado, a number of students wrote letters of support that include the following statements:

> As a teacher he has an excellent reputation among students, not because his classes are undemanding (au contraire!), but because he is so personable, positive, and enthusiastic that students find themselves interested in the subject in spite of themselves. He even makes subjects like music esthetics come alive. His inspirational teaching was largely responsible for my decision to choose American music as my professional area of specialization [Linda G. Davenport].

> Besides being an excellent teacher, Dr. Kearns is also personally interested in his students. He asked me about my plan of study and became actively involved in guiding me in a more interesting and productive direction. Not only does he willingly give of his time upon students' requests, but he personally suggests that students arrange conferences to discuss their program, thoughts, ideas, and/or feelings about the progress of their particular course of study [Sheryl Mueller].

> Inspiring ideas, constructive criticism, and professional support characterize my dissertation meetings with Professor Kearns. His impeccable credentials and voluminous knowledge make sessions valuable mid-thesis motivations. Most often I leave the interviews feeling that thirty years of concentrated work will still leave me far behind him. And yet, he convinces me that my ideas are interesting and my progress is worthy of praise. In an environment where publication demands often cause scholars to become self-involved, he distinguishes himself by treating my writing, whether well-developed or in its embryonic state, as important. His approach to students is a unique blend of professional integrity and sincere interest in the individual [Kay Norton].

When post-tenure reviews were instituted at the University of Colorado in 1984, Bill's faculty colleagues summarized his accomplishments in the following statement:

> For the entire time of his tenure, Professor Kearns has been remarkably productive in scholarship, teaching and in service. He presently holds the position of Associate Dean for Graduate Studies in the College of Music. Under his leadership during the past three years, a higher degree of communication among graduate students through the Graduate Student Council, newsletters, symposia and colloquia has become evident. He has moved toward establishing a greater uniformity of standards and achievement among the various graduate degrees. New courses, clearer definition of requirements and two new degree programs have been initiated. Faculty and students in the College have looked to Professor Kearns over the years for enlightened leadership, first in establishing the Ph.D in musicology and as chair of the Music History Division, and then as chair of the Academic Area. Professor Kearns is highly esteemed as an outstanding teacher, both in general history and literature courses for undergraduates and courses in his specialties: American music—art, popular and folk—and music esthetics. He has been and is very active as a graduate committee member and has directed many Ph.D. dissertations. Professor Kearns' scholarship has been focused in American music. His curriculum vitae lists numerous articles, monographs and papers over many years and he has served as editor of the Sonneck Society Bulletin. He has written both a biography and bio-bibliography of American art music composer Horatio Parker. The Post-Tenure Review Committee believes that Professor Kearns has given many years of outstanding service to the College, to the University and to the profession as a scholar, teacher and administrator, and that he will continue to make equally important contributions in the future in the roles he chooses to fill.

In the spring of 1988, Bill came to me with a proposal to bring the American Music Research Center (AMRC) to the University of Colorado. He had been collecting research materials in the field of American music for years and served as curator of the Ben Gray Lumpkin Colorado Folkmusic Collection and the Early Country Music Collection, housed in the Music Library at the University of Colorado. Bill and his colleague, Professor Karl Kroeger, Head of the Music Library and himself a well known and frequently published Americanist, had been contacted by Sister Mary Dominic Ray, the Director-Founder of the American Music Research Center at Dominican College in San Rafael, California, to see if we might be interested in acquiring the Center. The AMRC had outgrown its environment at Dominican College and Sister Mary's failing health made it impossible for her to continue to bear its responsibilities. The Center had been awarded a special citation at a recent national meeting of the Sonneck Society for American Music and had a sterling reputation. Bill informed me that AMRC encompassed books and music from the seventeenth through the twentieth centuries with extraordinary strength in eighteenth- and nineteenth-century tunebooks and ballad operas. Needless to say, he convinced me that we should obtain the AMRC, and we proceeded to negotiate with Dominican College for ownership of the Center. The Music Library had been building collections in American music over the years and they fit very well with the holdings of AMRC. In the fall of 1988, an agreement was reached whereby the University of Colorado would purchase the American Music Research Center, its materials and equipment and its endowment. Bill received a large grant from the University of Colorado Humanities Special Purchase Fund to help with the funding, and additional support was provided by the President, Chancellor, and Vice Chancellor for Academic Affairs of the university. Once the AMRC was moved to Boulder, Professor Kearns was appointed director and Professor Kroeger curator of the collection.

Since the acquisition of the Center, Bill has succeeded in attracting over $200,000 in donated materials to expand its holdings. Undergraduate and graduate students have gained exceptional benefit from working with its materials, and faculty members from Colorado universities, institutions in the region, and across the nation, have investigated its richness. In addition, the Center has sponsored concerts of American music, funded research fellowships, published a bulletin and, in general, established itself as a vital part of the life of the College.

William Kearns has now retired as director of the American Music Research Center but he has continued as a Senior Research Fellow. His impact on the College of Music, the University of Colorado, and American music is immeasurable and deeply appreciated. He is a remarkable man who has made significant contributions as a scholar, teacher, and administrator. This festschrift will stand as a lasting tribute to the immensely positive effect that this dedicated, able, and humane person has had on the lives of students and colleagues and to the quest for knowledge that his life has signified, and that is the heart of the university experience.

2

Doctoral Programs in Music Education:
A Personal Reminiscence

Allen P. Britton

This personal account of my encounter with the need to obtain a doctor's degree is intended to show the opposite side of the doctoral coin, so to speak. Instead of dealing with general problems of philosophy, curriculum, and the like, I propose to describe how a particular doctoral program impinged upon my life as a school music teacher, leading me along pathways I had never dreamed of following. It seemed to me at the time that fellow students in the doctoral program considered themselves to be involuntary participants in an educational endeavor designed by others and possessing little relationship to their needs and aspirations. Nevertheless, if music was to prosper in the academic world, wiser heads than ours had come to understand that we had to adapt to general customs of that world. Doctor's degrees represented the last step in a process that had begun with instituting bachelor's and master's degrees.

The first time that the subject of doctoral work in music education was presented to me in a manner that got my attention was in December 1941, when Robert Guy Buzzard, then president of Eastern Illinois State Teachers College at Charleston, called me in for a conference. At the time I was a new instructor of music and English in the EISTC Training Schools, having just joined the faculty in October after teaching in the public schools of Griffith, Indiana. The conference was brief. He told me I was doing fine as the high school band director, but he wanted me to know that he could not promote me to the rank of assistant professor until I got a doctor's degree.

Doctor's degree? I had heard of such things. I remembered my pal Bruce Bowman telling me, back in high school days, that his father had just completed a doctorate at

Teachers College, Columbia University. I remembered how, in the midst of my trumpet lessons at the University of Illinois, Raymond F. Dvorak had fulminated against doctoral candidates who sent him questionnaires, all of which he threw in the wastebasket. Ray felt that such people were seeking to earn degrees based on the knowledge and experience of others, his in particular, and he wasn't about to cooperate in anything like that. I also remembered, strangely enough, that Ray, in an avuncular mood, once advised me to consider going away somewhere after I graduated and getting a doctor's degree. It was the coming thing, he thought. But I didn't pay much attention. The idea was too remote to consider seriously.

After leaving President Buzzard's office that cold winter day, I talked the matter over with a faculty colleague, Robert A. Warner, conductor of the college orchestra and holder of a master's degree from the Eastman School of Music. He too would need a doctor's degree in order to get promoted. We made inquiries and found that, in our region of the country, only the Universities of Iowa and Michigan offered doctoral work in music. There was, of course, Teachers College of Columbia University, but we considered it too far away and also, perhaps, too remote in its educational philosophy. Many of the questionnaires Dvorak used to complain about came from there.

Bob decided to take the summer session at the University of Iowa in order to check out the doctoral program chaired by the redoubtable Phillip G. Clapp, under whom Leo Dvorak, chairman of our music department at Charleston, had earned his own Ph.D. I, on the other hand, decided to try the University of Michigan in Ann Arbor. Michigan, in fact, was the only school that replied to my inquiries. I received two letters from there. The first contained a brief acknowledgement of my own letter to the registrar's office and a Graduate School bulletin that outlined several programs leading to the Doctor of Education degree with various options in music. After applying for admission, I received a second letter from Michigan, dated 2 May 1942, and signed by Clifford Woody, chairman of the committee on graduate study in education.

"I am glad to know of your interest," he began, and continued with a detailed account of the intricacies involved in combining practical musical studies with studies of a purely academic nature. He suggested, however, that all could be readily resolved. He explained that the Doctor of Education degree, abbreviated Ed.D. at Michigan, was available in four programs, three of them under the direct jurisdiction of the School of Education. These allowed varying amounts of course work in music, from thirty-two to sixty-four of the required total of seventy-two semester hours. In the fourth, he wrote, "the degree is offered where the major part of the program is in the field of specialization with only a few hours in Education. If you desire to work for the Ed.D. with major emphasis on Music, then you should write to Mr. Glenn D. McGeoch of the School of Music. In fact, I have just called him concerning your case and he suggests that were it at all possible for you to have a conference with him or with him and me that this would lead to most satisfactory arrangements. As a result of this we might have to take the deliberations up with the Dean of the Graduate School before speaking with certainty."

These communications impressed me. I detected in them a relaxed academic confidence that could only be found at a school that was very sure of itself. The University of Illinois, where I earned my B.Sc. in instrumental music, and my M.A. in education and English (there being no graduate work in music at Illinois at that time) was a tough school, where half the first year class regularly flunked out, and where a general spirit of "Do you really think yourself capable of the work?" prevailed at all levels. The tone of the letters from Michigan seemed to assume that any one who applied must be fully capable of undertaking all the work required. Michigan sent me a notice of admission, and I'll always remember what President Buzzard said when I told him. "Good! You can always sell a Michigan degree." The phraseology shocked me at the time, but I learned soon enough that there was considerable truth in it.

So, in the summer of 1942, my wife Veronica and I moved from Charleston to Ann Arbor to begin work on an Ed.D. in music. Professor Woody, my official adviser, smiling reassuringly, scratched on a yellow sheet of paper the numbers of two advanced seminars in the history of education given by Professor Claude Eggertsen, and two seminars in educational psychology given by Professor W. Clark Trow. "You'll need these seminars to pass your prelims in education," Woody informed me. "The rest of your work will be in music. Go over to see what Professor McGeoch wants you to take this summer." About this time I began to fall in love with Ann Arbor and its university.

Professor McGeoch wanted me to take three courses in the department of musicology, of which he was chairman. The term "musicology" was used at Michigan to encompass courses in music acceptable for credit toward degrees granted by the Horace H. Rackham School of Graduate Studies (M.A., Ed.D., and Ph.D.). The School of Music at Michigan, then as now, maintained its own graduate division, which offered the degree Master of Music. By means of this juxtaposition, some work in music education, music theory, and music history came under the rubric of musicology and could be taken for Rackham credit. At that time Rackham would not approve any course in the actual making of music, nor in composition, nor in the practical aspects of teaching music. Philosophical ruminations were O.K., but Bill Revelli's course in "band technics" never did get approved for Rackham credit.

At any rate, I spent a glorious and grade-wise very successful summer taking courses entitled "Music in the Eighteenth Century," "The Teaching of Music Literature," both brilliantly taught by McGeoch himself, and "The Tone Poem," taught by McGeoch's assistant Leonard Gregory. Oh yes, out of love for blowing the horn and also to keep a firm anchor embedded in what I then thought of as the real world, I spent the one o'clock hour each day of the summer session playing B-flat cornet in Revelli's summer band.

Invigorated marvelously, I went back that fall to Charleston and my high school choir, band, orchestra, and English classes. The Warners and the Brittons jointly employed a private tutor in German in anticipation of doctoral language requirements. After one summer at the University of Iowa, Bob had decided to continue his advanced work at Michigan. Both of us, however, were soon taken off by the U. S. Army. Bob was sent to the South Pacific, where he served in many of the combat areas and so was able eventually and with justice to get out of service about a year sooner than I did. My own military career was spent mostly in the state of Illinois at Fort Sheridan and Camp Ellis, playing for dances at service clubs, and finally, after the war was over, in Michigan at Camp Custer in the military police guarding 30,000 German prisoners and practicing my

German, which I had continued to improve while still at Camp Ellis by taking an Army correspondence course.

When I knew that I was about to be discharged, I wrote to President Buzzard, inquiring about further leave in order to take up fulltime studies at Michigan. He replied that he was granting me sabbatical leave at half salary and that I could take all the time needed to complete the work. He proved to be even better than his word. While I studied at Michigan, he regularly granted me promotions of one kind or another. He made me conductor of the college band. He kept raising the salary I would earn upon return. He promoted me to the rank of assistant professor and then associate professor. He gave me two extensions of leave as, each year, I decided to stay another year.

Camp Custer was about eighty miles from Ann Arbor, so I wrote to Professor McGeoch requesting an interview to discuss coming back to the University and resuming doctoral studies. He never replied. Rather, I received a letter from Professor Raymond A. Kendall, setting a time and place for such an interview. I learned later that Dean Earl V. Moore of the School of Music, a man of considerable academic vision and a leading force in the National Association of Schools of Music, had concluded that doctorates would be much in demand after the War. In order to offer convincing doctoral degrees, he thought, he had to have appropriate faculty, so he had employed two men with doctorates: Kendall, as chairman of the musicology department, and John H. Lowell, as chairman of the theory department. Kendall's doctorate was from Cornell University, obtained under the tutelage of the great musicologist Otto Kinkeldey. Lowell's degree had been earned at the Eastman School of Music under Allen Irving McHose, author of *Contrapuntal Harmonic Techniques of the Eighteenth Century*, the harmony textbook that exerted so much influence on beginning theory instruction in music departments across the nation.

Moore's new appointments achieved the purposes for which they were intended, but they also caused immediate and lasting pain within the school. McGeoch told me later that he had learned of Kendall's appointment to succeed him as chairman of musicology only when he read it in the *Ann Arbor News*. Another longtime member of the faculty, Louise Cuyler, was similarly replaced as chairman of the theory department. She had served with the USO in the South Pacific throughout the war, returning from such patriotic duties to find a Ph.D. in her former position. This so startled her that she enrolled at once at Eastman in a doctoral program under Charles Warren Fox, which she completed in record time without ever having to take leave from her job at Michigan.

My original interview with Kendall proved to be a little disheartening. I had come to Ann Arbor effectively disguised as a Technical Sergeant in the Military Police. We met in his office on the eighth floor of Burton Memorial Tower. A Mrs. Kilpatrick of the Executive Board of the Metropolitan Opera Association was visiting him when I arrived, and she took a seat on the other side of the room while we talked. It soon turned out that Kendall had a poor view of "bandmasters who think they need a doctor's degree," as he bluntly put it. His remark did not intimidate me. (Men in uniform tend to think of civilians as a lower order of beings—at any rate, they are never ready to take unwelcome suggestions from them.) I replied, with what I considered to be casual dignity, that the University of Michigan was guaranteeing the readmission of all servicemen, that whether I succeeded after I got back was a matter to be settled later, and that we should proceed with the business of deciding my summer electives. Kendall was a little taken aback, particularly, I think, because of the presence of the distinguished lady from New York. At any rate, he made no further protest regarding my return, but he did ask me to prepare a statement describing what I hoped to accomplish in doctoral studies.

This I did back at the barracks at Camp Custer, sending it on to Veronica, who was in Chicago, for typing. The next time I saw Kendall he seemed a changed man. As I came to discover, he was a brilliant scholar and writer, a man full of gusto and abreast of all current musical matters. At any rate, my statement had apparently won him over. Maybe it was the actual sense of the basic argument: that there was a gap now dividing the world of practical musicians and teachers from that of musicologists and psychologists, and that there would be an academic demand for those who could bridge that gap.

From then on, it has been mostly peaches and cream for me at Michigan and in life. I had in fact entered an environment in which I felt comfortable, intellectually and musically, where I found myself in a sea of music and musicians on the one hand, scholarship and scholars on the other, able to indulge my love of music and of learning to my heart's content and to enjoy the company of marvelous musicians and scholars of all kinds. This was veritably a delicious artistic stew, one in which I have been so fortunate as to spend the remainder of my life. My conscious but rarely expressed purpose from then on has been to reconcile the worlds of music and professional education with the world of music education. I have sought always to make music education more musical and more scholarly. I have never doubted for a minute that these were the highest of aims and that pursuing them would be the way to live the best possible life.

In retrospect, I realize how lucky I was to be the only student that summer of 1946 who possessed a master's degree in a field other than music. Scholarly knowhow acquired at Illinois gave me an advantage over the other students at Michigan, most of whom had backgrounds entirely in music and who didn't really know how to find things in libraries, take competent notes, and prepare scholarly papers.

How large an advantage I possessed was brought home to me very vividly that summer. As surprises go, about the biggest in my life occurred at the end of the sixth week of the session. Moore had secured Otto Kinkeldey, Kendall's mentor, as a visiting professor. Kinkeldey had just retired as director of the library at Cornell, where he also held the first American chair in musicology. He was scheduled to teach two seminars, "Introduction to Graduate Study" and "Seminar in Musicology." Kendall signed me up for the first, meant for beginners, instead of the second, meant for advanced researchers. Despite his contentment with my statement, he obviously still lacked confidence in bandmasters. As things turned out, Kinkeldey's engagement was for only the first six weeks of an eight-week session, and, on the day of his final lecture to the thirty-five registrants of the combined classes, they were joined by several members of the faculty, including Moore, Kendall, and Lowell.

Kinkeldey concluded his lecture with compliments for all the students, saying that everyone had worked hard and made great progress. So, he said, he was going to give everyone a "B," except, he continued, for one student who was far in advance of the rest and had done work of so superior a nature ("Who can this genius be?" went through my mind), that he was going to give that student the only "A." "I am referring, of course," he smiled, "to Mr. Britton."

I felt myself sinking right through the eight floors of concrete. Apparently the rigorous scholarly preparation I had received at Illinois set me apart in Kinkeldey's mind. But I couldn't argue the matter with him that day. After such beatification, no one at Michigan ever gave me anything but an "A," except Louise Cuyler, always of an independent mind, who hadn't attended that final seminar anyway. (She was off for a long weekend at Eastman in pursuit of her own doctoral degree.) She gave me a "B+" in the course I was taking from her, "Twentieth Century Musical Styles and Idioms."

That summer I also took a course from Theodore Heger, "Advanced Studies in the History of Music," in which I found that what really mattered in the history of music was now considered by musicologists to begin with the Greeks. The greatest achievements in music came during the Middle Ages and the Renaissance, and what transpired thereafter, except possibly for what Haydn, Mozart, and Beethoven accomplished, largely represented deterioration in the art of music. I sensed that Heger didn't believe a word of this himself, only feeling an obligation to report the current state of thinking in the field.

For the next two years, I took equal doses of courses in educational theory and psychology, music education, music theory, and music history. I enjoyed all of it, believing that a broad view of education and music would enable me to function more effectively. Many of my fellow students were of a different opinion, tending to resent work in fields they considered of little interest. As a result, many of the music educators then enrolled dropped out of the program.

Having passed German and French in early 1947, in 1948 I was admitted to candidacy for both the Ed.D. in music and the Ph.D. in musicology. So I had my choice. The Ed.D was a better degree for jobs in teacher's colleges and departments of education in general, but the Ph.D. was the better degree by ancient repute and could be sold, in President Buzzard's language, in universities. I chose the Ph.D., and, as things turned out, that was the fortunate choice for me.

Fortune smiled later on in another regard: the choice of a dissertation topic. In private conversation with Kinkeldey during the summer of 1946, we had agreed that the American factory band would be a marvelous subject for investigation. A year later, however, when prelims were passed, Dean Moore called me in for a talk. He was keeping a close eye on the doctoral program. He asked about my dissertation plans and reacted negatively, indeed, to the thought of such a subject as factory bands. However, Kendall, who as Kinkeldey's student was more positive toward American subjects, was able to save the day, satisfying Moore and me, too, by suggesting a study of the musical instructions found in early American tunebooks, the textbooks of our eighteenth-century singing schools. Elaborate musical instructions typically appear as introductions to the musical contents of these works. So it happened that my dissertation appeared under the strange title "Theoretical Introductions in American Tunebooks to 1800."[1]

1. (Ann Arbor: University Microfilms, 1950). The bibliography of tunebooks in the dissertation has recently been published, considerably augmented, under the title *American Sacred Music Imprints, 1698-1810: A Bibliography*, by Allen Perdue Britton, Irving Lowens, and completed by Richard Crawford (Worcester, Mass: American Antiquarian Society, 1990).

Why such a title and subject could penetrate the walls of prejudice that existed with regard to the fields of education itself, music education particularly, and American music as distinguished from European music, can perhaps be accounted for as follows: I accepted Kendall's suggestion that I borrow the general type of subject matter from a famous English scholar, John Stainer,[2] proposing in effect to do for early American music what he had done fifty years earlier for English music. Furthermore, the tunebooks to be studied constituted the first musical publications on Anglo-American soil, and they contained the works of the earliest Anglo-American school of composers. Although these composers were almost entirely unschooled and their music of a simple folklike style, it indeed was the sacred choral music of the immediate descendents of the Pilgrims and Puritans. Furthermore, practically all of the compilers of the tunebooks were singing-school masters. In short, the tunebooks represented the very beginning of music education in this country.

Almost by chance, I had found a subject of inarguable historical significance. I believe, also, that the subject was so far removed in time and style from anything else known to the typical musicologist and professional educator that no one could object to it without danger of putting himself in the position either of seeming an ignoramus or, at the least, of lacking a proper respect for the accomplishments of our Puritan ancestors.

There were still additional considerations of significant weight. Oscar Sonneck, the revered founder of American musicology, had already published a history of our earliest concert life as well as a bibliography of our earliest secular music.[3] In prefatory remarks to his history of concert life, he had remarked wistfully that his sources (colonial newspapers) contained many more references to singing schools than they did to concerts. Who could object to filling in the gaps admittedly left by Sonneck himself?

Having approved the topic, Kendall took leave of absence and went out to the University of Southern California as dean of the School of Music. This also turned out to be lucky for me. John H. Lowell, who had replaced Louise Cuyler as chairman of the theory department, was appointed chairman of my doctoral committee in Kendall's absence. Always well disposed toward me anyway, he evinced no inclination to argue with anything that I proposed. As a theorist, he was entirely sympathetic to theoretical introductions.

I was also very fortunate in the other committee members. By the time I was ready to show them chapters, Louise Cuyler had attained a position of genuine authority on the music of the Catholic Church. The music of the Calvinist churches in America was unfamiliar to her and became a matter of special interest, although I think she never took its quality very seriously. Claude Eggertsen was already recognized as an authority in the history of American education. He had published a seminar paper I had written for him

2. John Stainer, "On the Musical Introductions Found in Certain Metrical Psalters," *Proceedings of the Musical Association* 27 (13 November 1900): 1-50.

3. Oscar G. T. Sonneck, *Bibliography of Early Secular American Music (18th Century)* (1905), revised and enlarged by William Treat Upton (Washington: Library of Congress, 1945; reprint, New York: Da Capo, 1964). See also Sonneck's *Early Concert-Life in America (1731-1800)* (Leipzig: Breitkopf und Härtel, 1907; reprint, New York: Da Capo, 1978).

that dealt with the shape notes used in some of the tunebooks.[4] David Mattern, chairman of the music education department, was eager to support any music educator seeking respectability amongst musicological types. Lewis G. Vander Velde, chairman of the history department in the College of Literature, Science, and the Arts, was a brilliant and creative scholar who seemed to be very sympathetic to the project from the start.

I shall always be thankful to the federal government for the help provided through the G.I. Bill, which paid for tuition, supplies, textbooks, and living expenses; it even allowed me to accept a generous stipend associated with a Rackham pre-doctoral fellowship. In addition, Veronica worked throughout my enrollment as secretary to Dean Wells Bennett of the School of Architecture and Design (and we both learned a little about "deaning"). Such financial support allowed me to complete degree requirements in three years and avoided the difficulties associated with going back to work prior to completion of the dissertation. Doing so, in the case of many of my fellow students in the program, actually ended their degree attempts.

During the last full semester (spring 1949) as a student at Michigan, while my dissertation was being typed, an event occurred that was to change the whole course of my life in ways that I could never have dreamed. One day David Mattern asked me to come in to see him. He wanted to know if I might be interested in a position at Michigan that would involve responsibility for instrumental student-teaching assignments and supervision, for the instrumental methods course that was co-requisite with student teaching, and, at the doctoral level, for the seminars in historical and quantitative research.

Up to that point, the thought had never occurred to me that I would not return to Charleston, where the rank of associate professor with tenure awaited me, together with the conductorship of the college band, and a salary of $4,000. Michigan offered me $6,000 for an assistant professorship without tenure. I never hesitated a minute, although I did make an unsuccessful attempt to bargain for a tenured appointment. In those days, the School of Music did not make firm commitments until the state legislature had approved the University budget appropriation. I could not resign from Charleston until the legislature acted. As soon as that occurred, I called President Buzzard. We had a difficult conversation. He felt bad, he said, and he asked a rhetorical question—why should the big schools be able to afford to pay more than the little schools? Little schools need good teachers too, he went on, but, of course, he said he would release me, and, of course, Illinois state law required that I pay back the sabbatical salary. Doing so salved my conscience a little. Charleston was a wonderful place. Leo Dvorak and Robert Buzzard had shown me nothing but kindness. They had opened for me the possibility of teaching at the college level, something I had fervently wished for but had absolutely no idea how to attain.

So now I had to turn from working for a doctoral degree to directing a doctoral program. I had to start thinking about whys and wherefores. Up to that point I had accepted uncritically all the various requirements imposed on me by advisers. I realized

---

4. Allen P. Britton, "The Original Shape-Note Tune Books," *Studies in the History of American Education,* ed. Claude Eggertsen (Ann Arbor: University of Michigan School of Education, 1947), 117-23.

that little of what I studied had any relationship to the actual problems of teaching or conducting, but I assumed that the broadened education somehow would enable me to do a better job. If so, why and how could that be? Should future students at Michigan take studies similar to mine or should sharp revisions be made?

Marguerite V. Hood, David Mattern, and I began weekly meetings to consider these questions. We had to confront several facts over which we had little or no control. It was clear that doctoral program requirements had been imposed on music education rather than arising from needs felt by members of the profession. Such imposition stemmed from the biases of faculty members then in control of programs. Each tended to demand what had been demanded of him. For example, although there was little written in French or German that an American music educator had to know, Ph.D. programs continued to require some mastery of these or other foreign languages. We eventually decided not to try to change such requirements but, rather, to go along with the basic requirements of doctoral programs in general and especially those in music. We came to consider that their value resided in the fact that they were common to other programs and that, in fulfilling them, music educators could join a grander academic club. In doing so, it seemed to us that music educators might be in a better position to advance the general cause of music education. Thus, we decided to allow students in music education to spend most of their time studying subjects other than music education.

In my own atypical case, of a total of sixty-four graduate semester hours of course work taken at Illinois and Michigan, thirty-four hours were in the fields of music history, composition, and theory; twelve were in English; fourteen were in professional education; and only twelve hours were in music education proper. These totals do not include the dissertation, for which no credit was given at Michigan. Whether or not such preparation was most appropriate for a professor-of-music-education-to-be must remain a question, of course, but a question that still needs discussion. I had taken the M.A. in education and English at Illinois only because there was no graduate program in music. However valuable doing so had proven in my case, we could not expect to find such preparation typical of most applicants. We tried to design programs that would be appropriate for the actual students we hoped to have.

We retained the joint Ed.D. programs with the School of Education. These programs were welcomed by students who had done previous graduate work in schools or departments of education. In those days, the Ed.D. was the preferred degree in many schools, and our graduates with this degree proved to be as sought after as others. But the majority of students entering Michigan had graduated from conservatories and schools of music. We designed a Ph.D. program for them. This was based on the master's degree in music, of course, and was intended to prepare students to teach college-level music education courses and to be capable of handling undergraduate courses in music history and music theory. Although many of our students were accomplished conductors of collegiate bands, orchestras, and choirs, and many were already teachers of piano, violin, or other instruments, we could make little or no provision for their advanced education in such fields. Later on, after we had introduced and had established the principle of giving graduate credit "for a little fiddlin'," in the parlance of the dean of the Graduate

School, our students were allowed to substitute performance for either history or theory. This was in line with our efforts to keep the purely musical requirements as high as possible.

For the major field we devised four seminars, one each in curriculum, administration, scientific research, and historical research. Marguerite Hood took charge of the first two, and I the last. Marguerite was already a complete master of her subjects, but mine were new in the world of music, and I had to prepare them from scratch. We had difficulty finding on the campus a course in elementary statistics needed to prepare for the seminar in scientific research. One semester, I even tried to teach it myself. There is today somewhere in this land a brilliantly successful music educator who goes into shock just a little bit whenever the term "standard deviation" is mentioned.

As for dissertations, we resolved to be as flexible as possible, allowing students to pick their own topics. The more than 100 dissertations accepted over the past fifty years or so at the University of Michigan are evenly divided with regard to their scientific or historical nature, and the variety of topics treated is gratifyingly diverse. Our aim was to see to it that all students actually graduated within a finite length of time, and so far as I can remember, no student was held up on account of disagreements among committee members. The actual content of a doctoral dissertation is not as important, in my opinion, as the fact that the dissertation is well planned, thoroughly researched, and written up in good literary style.

Thus, to summarize, the doctoral program was calculated to provide advanced work in the major field and work basically equivalent to that required for the master's degree in the minor fields. Minor fields for the Ph.D. were at first restricted to history and theory; later on, in addition to performance, other fields were permitted upon request if the student was prepared to do graduate work in them. All work was validated by taking "examinations preliminary to candidacy"—the fearsome "prelims."

The encompassing idea was to prepare students at a high level in the minor and major fields, and, via the dissertation requirements, to turn each of them into the world's greatest authority in one highly specialized area. As a rule of thumb, the Ed.D. dissertation was allowed to be a relatively modest document, requiring approximately the equivalent of one full-time semester to prepare. The Ph.D. dissertation, which was to be the report of an entirely original investigation, required the equivalent of one full year of work. On the other hand, the Ed.D. required the completion of seventy-two semester hours of graduate credit, including credit earned in connection with the master's degree; there were at that time no specific credit hour requirements for the Ph.D. Later, after someone in the bursar's office noticed that some degrees had been granted to students who had registered for hardly any course work at all, a fee requirement was introduced guaranteeing that students would make a minimum contribution to the University's financial needs. During my own career as a chairman of dissertation committees, I watched over the preparation of fifty-two doctoral dissertations, a few for the Ed.D., but most for the Ph.D. In general, it should be said, in terms of heft, quality, and originality, I cannot distinguish between the two types of dissertation. Mostly, it seems, students chose one degree or another because of the difference in language requirements, two for the Ph.D., only one for the Ed.D. Regardless, all produced works of the highest quality.

So this is how one who still thinks of himself as a high school bandmaster got to be a college professor and eventually dean, and as a collateral consequence met a larger number of marvelous people than he might have otherwise, and was able to assume many significant responsibilities, none of which he had anticipated. My career, and I suspect that of many others as well, seems in retrospect to have been the result of pure happenstance, except that I never forgot William James's comforting advice: "Let no youth have any anxiety about the upshot of his education. . . . If he keep faithfully busy each hour of the working day, . . . he can with perfect certainty count on waking up some fine morning to find himself one of the competent ones of his generation."[5] Although I did what I had to do every day, as best I could, I was hardly ever able to see what the future might bring.

But what of doctoral degrees now? Are they as good as they should be? What should they be like? Some answers to these questions have already been given, or implied, in what has been said above. However, it may not be amiss to review some of the general considerations that pertain.

Never forgetting, at our peril, that music always occupies an equivocable place in formal educational establishments, we are required to justify ourselves continually, to prove over and over again that we belong in the system. Since it is a tricky matter to justify music as music, except to musicians, generally we are forced to justify it to others on the basis of its ancillary values, of which, thank God, it possesses many. Doing so, however, requires that we talk in the language of the educated world. Acquiring doctoral degrees, provided too much specialization is avoided, helps us to do that.

We should remember that music education, as a field, must always remain a minor field both of music and of education. We can think of it as a major field when describing curriculums in college catalogs, but we should never delude ourselves regarding its relation to music as such and education in general. Without attention to the pure values of the musical sound itself, we hardly have a field at all. On many occasions, I have thought it necessary to remind colleagues that, in fact, what we call music education exists only in the upper and graduate divisions of colleges and universities. High-school bandmasters think of themselves as conductors and have to remind themselves that they are also music educators. Grade-school teachers properly consider themselves teachers of music, not of music education.

The doctoral degree, structured so as to require extensive command of the basic fields of music and of professional education, enables the music educator better to engage in mutual dialogue, not only with colleagues in music and education, but with a larger world as well. Such ability may well prove to be of significant value in advancing an individual career and in enhancing the status of music and of music education in the eyes of the world. Most importantly, it provides inner riches of incalculable value for all those who attain to its rights and privileges.

---

5. William James, *Talks to Teachers on Psychology, and to Students on Some of Life's Ideals* (New York: Henry Holt, 1899), 78 (in 1915 ed.).

3
Soliloquoy
for Horn Alone

(To Sophia and William Kearns)

Charles Eakin

4

Hezekiah Cantelo, an Eighteenth-Century Dance Collector in British-Occupied New York

Kate Van Winkle Keller

There will always be commercial opportunities for those who judge the winds of fashion correctly. Beginning in the eighteenth century in England, it became fashionable to collect and perform tunes and songs from or about distant and exotic places, a trend that was to reach full bloom with Romanticism in the nineteenth century. To London society in the 1780s, both Scotland and America qualified as exotic and thus were very fashionable, even though bitter conflicts with both lands continued to occupy the nation.

In 1782, before the war with the "rebels" was even over, an opera called *The Fair American* played at Drury Lane with great success. In 1785, London music publisher John Welcker released a collection of dances created by the master at King's Theatre in Covent Garden. The Hon. Earl Winterton and his Countess headed the list of subscribers. Along with minuets named for Winterton's family and friends, the collection included "The

I wish to thank Charles Cyril Hendrickson for his help in interpreting Cantelo's dances. Ginger Hildebrand offered excellent comments on the music as fiddle tunes, and Raoul F. Camus guided me to military resources. In addition to the sources mentioned in the footnotes, the following books were used in preparation of this study: Rodney Atwood, *The Hessians: Mercenaries from Hessen-Kassel in the American Revolution* (Cambridge: Cambridge University Press, 1980); John W. Jackson, *With the British Army in Philadelphia 1777-1778* (San Rafael, Calif.: Presidio Press, 1979); Philip R. N. Katcher, *Encyclopedia of British, Provincial, and German Army Units, 1775-1783.* (Harrisburg, Pa.: Stackpole Books, 1973); George C. McCowen, *British Occupation of Charleston, 1780-82* (Columbia: South Carolina Tricentennial Commission, 1972); William B.Willcox, *Portrait of A General, Sir Henry Clinton in the War of Independence* (New York: Alfred A. Knopf, 1964).

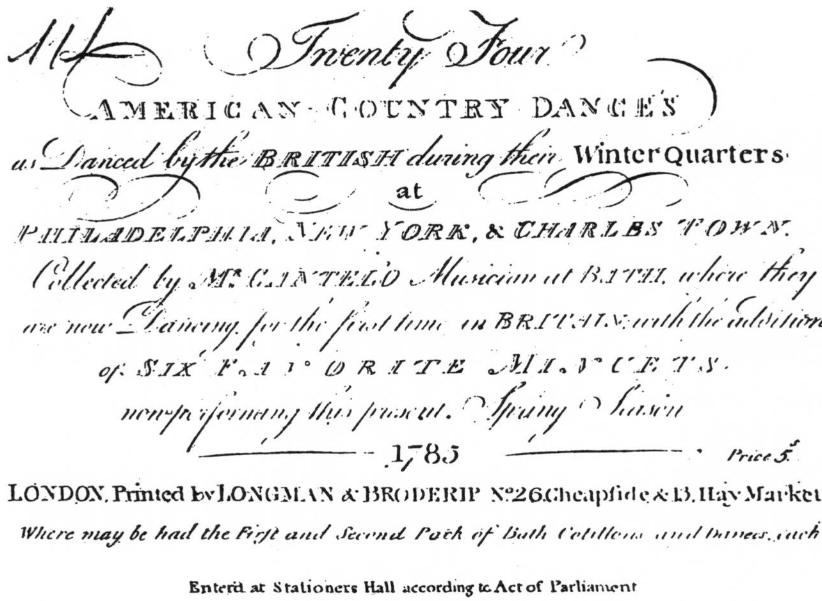

Twenty Four
AMERICAN COUNTRY DANCES
as Danced by the BRITISH during their Winter Quarters
at
PHILADELPHIA, NEW YORK, & CHARLES TOWN.
Collected by Mr. CANTELO Musician at BATH, where they
are now Dancing for the first time in BRITAIN, with the addition
of SIX FAVORITE MINUETS
now performing this present Spring Season
1785 Price 5/
LONDON. Printed by LONGMAN & BRODERIP No. 26 Cheapside & 13 Hay Market.
Where may be had the First and Second Book of Bath Cotillons and Dances, each
Enter'd at Stationers Hall according to Act of Parliament

Figure 4.1. Title page of *Twenty four American Dances* (London, 1785). Courtesy Clements Library, University of Michigan. Other copies of the book are located at the Library Company of Philadelphia, the British Library, the Bodleian Library, and the Kongelige Bibliotek in Denmark.

Americans Cotilion," "Independance Cotilion," "The Washington Country Dance," and "The American Ladies Country Dance" (all titles *sic.*). [1] The same year, Longman and Broderip capitalized on the same opportunity, releasing *Twenty Four American Country Dances as Danced by the British during their Winter Quarters at Philadelphia, New York, & Charles Town. Collected by Mr. Cantelo Musician at Bath, where they are now dancing for the first time in Britain, with the addition of Six Favorite Minuets now performing this present Spring Season* (see fig. 4.1).[2]

Oscar Sonneck included this book in his *Bibliography of Early Secular American Music,* presumably on the basis of the contents being "American."[3] He apparently

1. *The Fair American,* with music by Thomas Carter and libretto by Frederick Pilon, opened at Drury Lane 18 May 1782. *Thirty two new Minuets, Cotillions, Country-Dances, Allemands and Hornpipes for the Year 1785, with Figures by James Fishar, First-Dancer & Ballett-Master for Ten Years at the Kings Theatre* (London: John Welcker, [1785]), 11-12, 16.

2. Not wasting an opportunity, the publisher included an advertisement for other collections of "Bath" dances on the cover. But his price of five shillings was significantly higher than contemporary dance books of similar size. Most twelve-page yearly collections of twenty-four country dances cost six pence, and a 100-page volume of dances, three shillings sixpence. This may be an indication that the book was produced in a more expensive limited edition.

3. Oscar George Theodore Sonneck, *A Bibliography of Early Secular American Music (18th Century),* revised and enlarged by William Treat Upton (1945; reprint, New York: Da Capo, 1964), 97-98.

accepted the title page at face value and added without further documentation the comment that the author was "with the British Army in Philadelphia, New York and Charles Town."

Hezekiah Cantelo (1750s-1811) was a versatile English musician. He played the trumpet, bassoon, flageolet, oboe, and the bagpipes. Member of a large musical family, Cantelo lived in Bath, a lively resort city where music and dancing were as important as politics. He traveled to London regularly to perform at theaters, festivals, and pleasure gardens, and to perform in the band of music of the First Regiment of Foot Guards.[4] The collection of American country dances, his only known book, was published the year that he was admitted to the prestigious Royal Society of Musicians.

Sonneck's listing the book in his bibliography of American imprints gave it an importance with which dance historians have long been uncomfortable. While it is true that no specifically "American" quality that can be seen in the country dances known to American residents in this period, there was a repertory of popular dances in circulation.[5] These appear over and over again in manuscript dance collections from the 1780s and 1790s, and printed American tune collections from the 1790s and early 1800s. Dances set to such British tunes as "Fisher's Hornpipe," "Allemand Swiss," "Successful Campaign," "College Hornpipe," "Flowers of Edinburgh," "Sweet Richard," "Saint Patrick's Day in the Morning," and "Rural Felicity" were among the most popular. Although to the non-dancer they seem to be a random succession of repetitive figures, many country dances have an integrity of figures, tune, and/or title. Often the same tune/title/dance combinations can be found in both American and British manuscript and published sources.[6]

Except for one dance and four tunes, the contents of Cantelo's book has little in common with known American sources. In a comparison of the figures and titles of 2,800 dances collected or published in America before 1810, Cantelo's dances stand alone. Most are longer, they have different tunes, different titles, and their figure sequences are different. Four have alternate finishing figures, which is unusual even in English dance collections. While most of the terms employed in describing the figures are the same, the frequent use of the term "gallop" is also unusual and seldom appears in American dances.

In order to explain this apparent contradiction and to determine whether these dances can be called "American" at all, a thorough analysis of Cantelo's book is necessary. Table 4.1 lists the contents with salient facts about each piece.

The book is organized into two main sections. Pages 1-24 contain melodies, bass lines, and figures of twenty-four country dances; pages 24-31 contain melodies and bass

4. Philip H. Highfill and others, *A Biographical Dictionary of Actors, Actresses, Musicians, Dancers, Managers, and Other Stage Personnel in London, 1660-1800*, vol. 2 (Carbondale: Southern Illinois University Press, 1973), 38-40.

5. Robert Keller, *Dance Figures Index: American Country Dances, 1730-1810* (Sandy Hook, Conn.: Hendrickson Group, 1989); Kate Van Winkle Keller, "A Bibliography of Eighteenth-Century American Social Dance," *Country Dance and Song* 18 (spring 1988): 9-22.

6. Kate Van Winkle Keller, "Selected American Country Dances and Their English Sources," *Music in Colonial Massachusetts, 1630-1820*, vol. 1: *Music in Public Places* (Boston: Colonial Society of Massachusetts, 1980), 14-73.

Table 4.1. Contents of *Twenty Four American Country Dances*

Title (punctuation and spelling original) *Title References*	*Source*	*Key*	*Time*	*Style*	*Range*	*Phrases*	*Am. Relevance**
The Hamiltonian—Lady Amelia Murray's Choice. Lt. Gen. Sir Robt. Hamilton	(by the Honr. C. G.)	A	6/8	jig	c'-a"	8.8.8	tMil?
The Monckton—British White Feathers. Lt. Col. Henry Monckton or Lt. Gen. Robert Monckton	(Hon: C. G.)	D	6/8	jig	a-a"	8.8.8	tMil; mMS
Lady George Murray's Reel	(Hon: C. G.)	D	C	strath	c'-b"	4.4.4.4	---
La Buona Figuiliola—Lady Jean Murray's Dance Published in Philadelphia, by Willig (1795-1797)	(From Piccini)	C	2/4	march	c'-a"	8.8.8.8	t&m in Sheet
The Fair Emigrant or Mrs. Dawsons delight	(Hon: C. G.)	D	6/8	jig	b-b"	4.4.4	tCiv?
General Abercromby's Reel or the Light Bob Lt. Col. Robert Abercrombie (1740-1827); "Light Bob" refers to officer of Grenadier battalion	(Hon: C. G.)	G	C	strath	g-b"	4.4.4.4	tMil
The Walton William Walton, merchant	(Capt W.)	G	2/4	march	g-b"	8.8.16	tCiv
Mrs. Lt. Col: Johnsons Reel Rebecca Franks married Col. Henry Johnson (1748-1835).	(Hon: C. G.)	A	C	strath	a-a"	4.4.4.4	tCiv/Mil
La Belle Frene	(Austrian Dance)	A	2/4	march	e'-a"	8.8.16.8	---
Mrs. S. Douglas' Reel— Danced with Prince William Hon: C. G. in New York	(Royal Navy) (Hon: C. G.)	D	C	strath	a-a"	4.4.4.4	tCiv/Mil
Capt. Oakes's Whim— Sir Hildebrand Oakes (33d. Regt.) (1754-1822)	(33d. Regt.)	D	2/4	march	d'-a"	8.8.8.8.8	tMil;mMS
The Belles about the Flatbush—(a Village on Long Island so called) New York battle	---	D	2/4	march	a-a"	16.16	tPlace;mMS
La Belle Annette.	---	D	2/4	march	a-b"	8.8.8	---
The Yager Horn Jaeger troops from Hesse-Cassel used bugle horns	---	D	2/4	march	d'-b"	8.8.8.8	mMSS
How Imperfect is Expression Title used with tune in American manuscripts	(Capt. O)	D	2/4	march	a-a"	8.8.8	mMS
The Heredetary Prince Name of Münchhausen's regiment	---	D	2/4	march	d'-b"	8.8.8	tMil

Title / Title References	Source	Key	Time	Style	Range	Phrases	Am. Relevance*
Laurel Hill / Estate in Philadelphia	--	B♭	2/4	march	a'-b♭"	8.8.16	tPlace
The Munichausen / Col. F. E. von Münchhausen aide to Gen. William Howe	--	B♭	2/4	march	f'-b♭"	8.8.8.8.8	tMil;m&dMS
The Monmouth—or the Victory / Monmouth, New Jersey battle	--	B♭	C	march	g-b♭"	4.4.4	tPlace
The St. George	(Capt. Baker's Choice)	F	3/8	waltz	c'-b♭"	8.8.8	--
L'Escapade		B♭	2/4	march	c'-b♭"	8.8.8	--
The Brandewine / Brandywine, Pennsylvania battle	--	B♭	2/4	march	b♭-b♭"	8.8.8.8	tPlace
The Donop—Lady Mary Murray's Fantaisie / Count von Donop, commanded at Flatbush, killed later	--	F	2/4	march	e'-b♭"	8.8.8	tMil
The Anspacher / Anspach Jaegers, Hessian troops	--	G	3/4 [=3/8]	waltz	d'-a"	8.8	tMil
MINUETS							
Lady Louisa Lenox's Minuet	(Cantelo)	C	3/4	minuet	g'-c"	16.16	--
Mr. Dawsons New Minuet / Master of the Ceremonies, New Rooms at Bath	(Cantelo)	F	3/4	minuet	f'-b♭"	8.8	--
Miss Cornish's Minuet / James Cornish, oboist, family of Bath	(Cantelo)	F	3/4	minuet	c'-a"	8.16	--
Miss Wroughtons Minuet / ?Wife of Richard Wroughton, actor from Bath	(Cantelo)	C	3/4	minuet	g'-c"	8.16	--
Mr. Greville's Minuet / ?[H.F.?] Greville, actor	--	E	3/4	minuet	e'-c"	8.8	--
The Hon'ble Col. Cosmo Gordon's Minuet	[Cosmo Gordon?]	D	3/4	minuet	g'-a"	14.20	see essay

*Explanation of codes: t = title, m = music, d = dance figures. Civ = civilian name connection; Mil = military name connection; MS (MSS) = appears in American manuscript collection(s); Place = location in America.

lines for six minuets. By selecting the format of twenty-four dances, Cantelo followed current fashion for annual collections of English country dances. However, the layout of one dance to a page and the use of tunes with bass lines were more typical of collections of Scottish dances. Other aspects of the book, as we will see, also invoke Scotland, an additional play to the fashion of the day.

The Music

Musically, the country dance section falls into three parts, suggesting that Cantelo collected from three sources. The first has a distinctly Scottish flavor in titles, attributed composer, and some tunes and dances. The second and third sections are more varied; music in the second group being all in the key of D, the easiest key for fiddles, flutes, and fifes, and the last group is in B-flat or F, better for oboe or clarinet.

Atypically for dance music, much of the music was conceived for a small chamber ensemble rather that a fiddle alone. The last strain of "The Fair Emigrant" comprises two statement/answer motives: the bass is tacit on the statement but comes in on the answers which are marked "vio:." The rests on the second beats in the last phrase of "The Donop" give a dynamic richness unusual in dance music. A few pieces, with full chords in the bass, are more appropriate for violin and keyboard. These are "Capt. Oakes's Whim," "How Imperfect is Expression," "The Monmouth," and "L'Escapade." There are bowing marks on many melody lines, and dynamics such as "pia" and "for" in a number of the pieces. In most cases these appear to be instructions to the musicians rather than abbreviated scoring or solo-versus-ensemble contrasts.

Perhaps catering to amateur musicians, eleven of the country dance tunes lie in the range of the violin in first position, the rest straying only briefly to b''-flat or b'', the minuets' highest notes being c'''. On the other hand, many of the bass lines are lively and interesting, particularly in the minuet section, a change from the quite ordinary bass lines in other dance collections. Although there are brief chromatic phrases in "The Walton," "Laurel Hill," and "The Monmouth," the general harmonic structure of most pieces is simple. Except for a single phrase in "The Munichausen," the entire collection is in the major mode.

The title of the first piece honors two Scots and its composition is credited to the Honorable Cosmo Gordon, evidently a nobleman and amateur musician who wrote six other country dances tunes and the last minuet (see fig. 4.2). Except for the minuet, Gordon's tunes all appear near the beginning of the book. They are all somewhat unpolished and formulaic. The bass lines occasionally create awkward intervals, parallel octaves, fifths, and other dissonances with the melodies.

Four of Gordon's tunes are strathspey reels, a unique and fairly recent Scottish fiddle tune genre that from all evidence was unknown to American musicians.[7] The strathspey was usually in common time, had many dotted rhythms and a distinctive cadential rhythm, was often in the minor mode, and often included the so-called "Scotch snap"

---

7. "Maggie Lauder" is the only tune of this nature that was widely known in the last quarter of the eighteenth century in America, and was more of a Scots measure than a strathspey, lacking the distinctive cadential rhythm of the latter. The history of the strathspey is complex. See George S. Emmerson, *A Social History of Scottish Dance* (Montreal: McGill-Queen's University Press, 1972), 173-76.

Figure 4.2. The Honorable Cosmo Gordon, Third Regiment of Guards. Courtesy Print Collection, Lewis Walpole Library, Yale University.

that Niel Gow's strong bowing technique had popularized. Gordon's strathspey reels have some of these attributes, but not all. Two are noticeably lacking: his strathspey tunes are all in major and there are no "Scotch snap" rhythms. In addition, the introduction of triplets in "Mrs. Lt. Col: Johnsons Reel" is particularly curious. While Gordon's tunes employ some Scottish elements, they seem somewhat more eclectic.

Once past the Gordon pieces, the music improves considerably. The remaining country dance tunes are from several sources, some traditional, some composed, and some arranged from other music. Most are in duple time.

The minuet section is quite a different story. Four of the minuets, two each in the keys of C and F, are by Cantelo and are well-crafted and orchestrally conceived. Another well-written minuet in E has no attribution. These all appear to be named for musicians or theater personalities in Bath. Instrumentation cues (for "corni" or "flute") are indicated in two, and three have simple dynamics markings ("pia," "for," "cres"). The final minuet, probably written by Gordon, is less sophisticated. It is unbalanced, formulaic, and sounds like a student's exercise in minuet writing.

The Eighteenth-Century Ballroom

Upon entering an eighteenth-century ballroom in New York or Philadelphia, or even in Bath, where Cantelo claimed that his minuets and country dances were being performed, the first impression was of formal deportment, erect bodies, and presentational movements. Moving with carefully chosen step combinations phrased to the music, dancers had to be keenly aware of the audience that surrounded them. Among the gentry and upper classes of this period, dancing was a structured activity, one that supported and advanced social, political, and professional careers.

Dances performed included elite couple dances like the minuet and the allemand, and individually choreographed solos and duos to hornpipes, gigues, gavottes, and other tunes. Group dances included composed English country dances, French contredanses, cotillions, and improvised three- and four-handed reels.[8] Cantelo included two of these

---

8. Kate Van Winkle Keller, *"If the Company Can Do It!": Technique in Eighteenth-Century American Social Dance* (Sandy Hook, Conn.: Hendrickson Group, 1991), 6-13.

forms in his book: country dances and minuets. His title page claims that the country dances were performed in America and had recently been introduced in Bath. He makes no such claim for the minuets, suggesting rather that they were simply the latest dances from Bath, adding, for commercial appeal, a high fashion note to the more exotic "American" dances.

The Minuet

Minuets were couple dances—elite pieces in which a gentleman and his partner performed alone on the floor while the company watched. Minuet music was written in 3/4 time, but was played and danced with a specific step in units of six counts or two measures. Minuet tunes were written in phrases of even numbers of measures, usually eight, ten, or twelve. While the step had to be performed on even two-measure phrases, the routine itself could begin and end at any point in the music, a freedom of performance that enhanced its adaptability to many ballroom circumstances. It was the musicians' job to play the requested tune as many times as necessary to accomodate the dancers' honors, routine, and exit from the floor. Still, judging from the enormous number of named minuet tunes that were published, many dancers probably worked out their routines to specific tunes, and many composers gained patronage for writing them.

For over one hundred years, the dance remained the same, flexible within a rigid design. Notation was unnecessary. After the opening honors, a lead-in pattern brought the dancers to the opposite corners of a square, facing each other. From the corners, the dancers traced Z's on the floor, moving sideways to the adjacent corner, forward diagonally through the center and past each other to the opposite corner, then sideways again to complete the Z. As each Z-track was performed, the dancers either passed each other without touching, or took hands in the center and turned by the right, the left, and finally both hands. The man controlled the sequence of moves and signaled his partner with his own arm movements and the management of his hat. The dance was completed with honors to the company and partner.

English Country Dance

In English country dances many couples participated, forming lines, partner facing partner, and performing figures in groups of four or six dancers. The country dance was a form with many options of figures and steps. Although it was not a rustic dance by any means, it could be danced with simple steps in a carefree manner or with practiced step combinations. Because its identity lay principally in the patterns and the music, fashionable dancers could introduce new steps and modifications of the figures at will without jeopardizing the basic dance. It was this flexibility that ensured its long popularity as a genre of social dancing.

The music, the occasion, and the skill of the participants determined appropriate deportment and style of movement. The couple at the top of the set usually selected the dance to be performed and told the manager or master of the ceremonies the title of their choice. He then informed the musicians who were expected to know the appropriate music or find it in a recently published book. A dance consisted of a tune and a specific set of figures that were repeated many times in the course of its performance. The top couple danced the figures with the second and third couples. At the repetition, the first couple then danced the same sequence of figures with the next couples in the line. Once the other dancers had seen how the figures were to be done, when their turn came they were ready to join in.

The figures were not complex: hand turns, setting to partners, leads up or down the set, circles, or hands-across. What made the dance physically and aesthetically pleasing was the match of figures to music and the selection of steps chosen by the leading couple. They might select a series of energetic gavotte hops, or the gentler *pas de bourrée,* depending on who else was in their set. It would not be appropriate to select a complicated new dance and complex step sequences if an elderly officer and his wife were also in the set. But if all the dancers were young and agile and their commanding officers were watching, it would be important to perform well and appear to have had recent lessons in the art of dancing. Such skills were highly regarded and could make the difference between gaining early promotion or being assigned to distant guard duty.

Cantelo's Dances

Cantelo's dances are typical of country dances of this period. From the early 1700s, French dance technique (the actual movement and the deportment of the body and the feet) was the basis of cultivated dance in England and America. But specific steps were seldom given in dance directions which usually specified only the figures such as "lead down the middle," or "1st and 2nd couple right and left."[9] The appearance of the setting step called rigadoon in "How Imperfect Is Expression," "Laurel Hill," and "L'Escapade," and the *pirouette* in "The St. George" gives helpful performance information.

Turns from the German couple dance called the *Allemand* became fashionable in the 1770s. Two of the most common were one with an interlaced side-by-side handhold and another with a turn under the arm. Nine dances in this collection include allemand turns, although which kind is not specified. Only two of these have German titles: "The Donop" and "The Anspacher."

There are other features among Cantelo's dances that stand out as well. The country dances associated with the four strathspey tunes, "Lady George Murray's Reel," "General Abercromby's Reel," "Mrs. Lt. Col: Johnsons Reel," and "Mrs. S. Douglas' Reel," share several figures unique to themselves. Each has an alternate final figure, an easier option in case the dancers cannot perform the more difficult figure of the "hey on opposite sides."[10] Although this kind of substitution was undoubtedly common practice on the dance floor, alternate figures were seldom recorded in print.

The other feature of these dances is the set-and-turn corner-then-partner. Like the hey this figure was close kin to the traditional Scottish reel. Variations of this figure are

---

9. Ibid.,14-20.

10. A hey is the English term for the figure known in Scotland as a reel. There are many ways to perform a hey or reel; they all involve several dancers weaving in and out among each other. For the heys in Cantelo's book, the active dancers cross to the opposite side, and the dancers in each minor set then perform simultaneous interwoven figures-of-eight for three, along the sides, each starting from a different position in the track.

found in English dances, as in "swing partners, swing corners" in "La Belle Frene" and "The Heredetary Prince," but it was particularly popular in Scottish country dances.

Overall, three styles of dance can be distinguished. First and most prominent are the four Scottish dances with their distinctive and deliberate tunes. Much solo footing, gallops down the center, and many turns indicate active dances. Similar in flavor is a second group with somewhat less strong Scottish connections: "The Hamiltonian," "The Monckton," "The Fair Emigrant," "The St. George," and "The Donop."

Another group features quieter leads, settings, balances, and allemand turns. Among these are "The Walton," "Capt. Oakes's Whim," "La Belle Annette," "How Imperfect Is Expression," "Laurel Hill," "L'Escapade," and "The Brandewine." It is interesting that the designation on "La Belle Frene" that it is an "Austrian Dance" appears to apply only to the music. Although the dance shares figures with two German-titled dances, "The Yager Horn" and "The Heredetary Prince," there is nothing that distinguishes it significantly from these or from the rest of the dances in the collection.

Most of the dance descriptions are worded as commands to the dancers rather than descriptions of the figures. Six specifically direct the dancers to turn or set to "your partner." Only in the first two dances of the collection, which are themselves nearly identical, and "The Brandewine" do descriptive phrases appear. The first figure in "The Monckton" is completely descriptive: "First Lady foots it to the 2d genn and turns him to the right." In "La Buona Figuiliola" the same basic figure is given as a command: "First Cu: foot it with 2d lady & turn." The method of recording dances as commands gives an immediacy to the figures and suggests that Cantelo received the material from a teacher rather than by observation on the floor.

As in the music, there are a few errors in some dances, indication that the collector was not dance-knowledgeable. The figure "right hands across to the right round" in "Mrs. Lt. Col: Johnsons Reel," "The St. George," and "The Anspacher" surely should be "to the left" as it is correctly given in "Lady George Murray's Reel" (see fig. 4.3).

Based on our present understanding of dance figures of this period, it appears that some of the dances do not fit their music symmetrically as one would expect. Several require unusual phrase repetitions, such as AABBC ("The Monkton"), AABBCD ("La Buona Figuiliola"), ABCCD ("General Abercromby's Reel"), and so forth. The figures for "Laurel Hill" and "The Fair Emigrant" are much too long for their tunes. This suggests that figures may have been omitted, or that some are included in print that were not originally part of the dance.

Cantelo's Titles

Titles of tunes and dances were frequently used to flatter social superiors, to demonstrate loyalty to a person or cause, and occasionally to make a joke, satirical remark, or political statement. Sometimes these were simply jests or toasts for an evening. The *New York Weekly Journal* (January 26) reported on a private party held in honor of the Prince of Wales's birthday in 1736, at which two American-composed country dances were performed:

Figure 4.3. "Lady George Murray's Reel." Courtesy Clements Library, University of Michigan.

> It was celebrated at the Black Horse in a most elegant and genteel manner. . . . The ball began with French dances. And then the company proceeded to country dances, upon which Mrs. Norris led up two new country dances made upon the occasion; the first of which was called, *The Prince of Wales,* and the second, *The Princess of Saxe-Gotha,* in honour of the day.

Mrs. Norris may have jotted down her figures and tune selection on the blank back of a discarded playing card; she left no permanent record of her creations. Another example of the political use of country dances appeared in the foreign news section of the *Massachusetts Spy* on 13 March 1777, taken from a London paper of 1 November 1776.

> In the country dances published for 1777, there is one called "Lord Howe's jigg;" in which there is a "cross over change hands, turn your partner, foot it on both sides," and other movements admirably depictive (says a correspondent) of the present war in America.[11]

The Marquis de Chastellux attended a ball in Philadelphia in 1780 and noted his impression in his diary. He too saw politics in action on the ballroom floor. The dances he listed have often been cited by historians as being the most common in the period.

---

11. The dance appeared in *Twenty Four Country Dances for the Year 1777* (London: Chas. & Saml. Thompson, [1776]), 59. The actual wording is "Hey on your own side ÷ hands 6 round ÷ all six foot it and change sides the same back again ÷ cross over and right and left ÷"

> . . . like the "toasts" we drink at table, [the dances] have marked connection with
> politics; one is called "the success of the campaign," another "Burgoyne's defeat,"
> and a third, "Clinton's retreat."[12]

Of these, "Successful Campaign," the least specifically topical, was an English country dance first published in 1764. It came to America with tune, title, and dance intact, and was exceedingly popular throughout the colonies from the 1770s through the 1790s.[13] The latter two dances were probably ephemeral as no other reference to them has been found. Despite Chastellux's generalization, dances with very specific political references were unusual and atypical of the general repertory. It appears that most of the dances that Cantelo collected fall into this ephemeral category, and may have been created for specific companies or occasions. Some are so esoteric that their significance will probably remain hidden from all but the intimate circle into which they were introduced.

The places mentioned in Cantelo's collection are the easiest to interpret. Flatbush, Monmouth, and Brandywine were the locations of battles on Long Island, in New Jersey, and in Pennsylvania, respectively. "The Walton" may have been named for leading New York merchant William Walton, whose lavish home was known for the "splendor of its hospitalities."[14]

Cantelo should have known that the British officers did not like their Hessian counterparts, but his titles of "The Yager Horn," "The Heredetary Prince," "The Munichausen," "The Donop," and "The Anspacher" refer to Hessian units or officers who were in the British service in America.

Somewhat more unexpected are the apparent references to the enemy, America's French allies, in the titles of "La Belle Frene," "La Belle Annette," and "L'Escapade." However, French was the international language of the time and they may simply have been oblique topical references, or in the case of "La Belle Frene" ("Pretty Oak Tree"), perhaps puns.

Several Scottish and English officers active in America are honored,[15] but it is hard to understand how a nearly forgotten Italian opera by Niccolò Piccini, the Ladies Murray, a group of Scottish strathspeys, and the Honorable Cosmo Gordon fit into the American military theater. It is very odd that there are no dances in honor of the principal officers and social leaders such as Howe, Clinton, André, Cornwallis, DeLancey, or Arnold.

Some of the dance titles apparently refer to such specific local people and places that it is only by luck that the historian discovers them. One of these is "Mrs. Lt. Col: Johnsons Reel," on a fiddle strathspey attributed to Gordon. The Mrs. Johnson in question was probably Rebecca Franks, daughter of a prominent Loyalist family of Philadelphia. Lt. Col. Sir Henry Johnson (1748-1835) may have been present at a ball

---

12. Marquis de Chastellux, *Travels in North America in the Years 1780, 1781 and 1782*, trans. Howard C. Rice, Jr., vol. 1 (Chapel Hill: University of North Carolina Press, 1963), 177.

13. See Charles Cyril Hendrickson and Kate Van Winkle Keller, *Social Dances from the American Revolution* (Sandy Hook, Conn.: Hendrickson Group, 1992), 17-18, 46-47.

14. James Grant Wilson, *Memorial History of the City of New York* (New York: New-York History Co., 1892), 305.

15. Sir Robert Hamilton, Henry Monckton, Sir Robert Abercromby, and the wives of Sir Henry Johnson and S. Douglas.

held at Christmas time in New York in 1781. Perhaps Cantelo and Gordon were there too. The headstrong girl caused enough of a stir that it was reported in several colonial newspapers:

> A person who lately ran away from New York brings intelligence, that a splendid ball was given in that city a few weeks since by a number of British officers. Sir Henry Clinton had for a partner the celebrated Miss Franks, late of Philadelphia; as his Excellency had to open the ball, in leading out his partner, he desired the musician to play the old martial tune of - Britons strike home! "Indeed, may it please your Excellency," said the young lady, "I think if he was to play Britons go home: it would be much more pertinent and suitable to the present time." Sir Henry was much disconcerted, and could scarcely make a shift to get over the severity of the repartee; however, the next morning he complained to the lady's father of her rudeness to him. "Indeed, Sir Henry, rejoined the old man, she is a saucy girl, and if you will dance with her, you must e'en put up with her jokes."[16]

Johnson must have been impressed with the strong-willed American. He married her shortly afterward.

Two other titles were explained only through a chance browse in a collection of diary and letter excerpts. Rebecca Rawle Shoemaker lost her country estate of Laurel Hill when the British evacuated Philadelphia. It may have been the scene of British parties and thus commemorated in the dance "Laurel Hill," set to a good duple tune. The family fled to New York, and Mrs. Shoemaker was present at the grand ball honoring the Queen's birthday attended by Prince William Henry, third son of George III and future King William IV. In this era of social hierarchy and royal privilege, there was a great discussion before the ball as to who should dance the opening minuet. Rebecca recorded the decision and a name:

> It was settled that the prince should dance two minuets, but they must be with married ladies, and the first in rank must be complimented. The two first were B. Elliott and Friend Smith. The latter had not danced in public for twenty years. They both declined. Some other ladies next in course could not dance minuet. He danced the first with the wife of Capt. Douglass of the Navy, lately married, a pretty woman about 30. . . .[17]

Cantelo may have honored this moment in history by applying the title "Mrs. S. Douglas' Reel (Royal Navy)" to another strathspey tune attributed to Gordon. Again the question arises: were Cantelo and Gordon present at this event? Were these officers and their new wives friends of Gordon?

The Honorable Cosmo Gordon

Although there is no dedication or mention of Gordon on the title page, the arrangement of the contents suggests that Cantelo's primary goal was to flatter the nobleman whose tunes are clustered at the front of the book, and whose amateurish

---

16. [Hartford] *Connecticut Courant*, 22 January 1782.

17. Elizabeth Evans, *Weathering the Storm* (New York: Paragon House, 1989), 299-300.

Cauld Kail in Aberdeen.

162 * There 's cauld kail in Aberdeen, And castocks in stra _ bo _

Lively

_ gie; Gin I hae but a bony lass, Ye're welcome to your Cogie, And

ye may sit up a' the night; And drink till it be braid day light;Gie

me a lass baith clean and tight, To dance the Reel of Bogie.

In Cotillons the French excel;
John Bull, in Countra-dances;
The Spaniards dance Fandangos well,
Mynheer an All' mande prances:
In Fourfome Reels the Scots delight,
The Threesome maist dance wondrous _
But Twasome ding a' out o' sight, (light;
  Danc'd to the Reel of Bogie.

Come, Lads, and view your Partners well,
Wale each a blythsome Rogie;
I'll tak this Lassie to mysel,
She seems sae keen and vogie:
Now, Piper lad, bang up the Spring;
The Countra fashion is the thing,
To prie their mou's e're we begin
  To dance the Reel of Bogie.

Now ilka lad has got a lass,
Save yon auld doited Fogie,
And ta'en a fling upo' the grass,
As they do in Stra'bogie.
But a' the lasses look sae fain,
We canna think ourfel's to hain;
For they maun hae their Come-again
  To dance the Reel of Bogie.

Now a' the lads hae done their best,
Like true men of Stra'bogie;
We'll stop a while and tak a rest,
And tipple out a Cogie:
Come now, my lads, & tak your glass,
And try ilk other to surpass,
In wishing health to every lass
  To dance the Reel of Bogie

Figure 4.4. "Cauld Kail in Aberdeen," James Johnson, *The Scots Musical Museum . . . humbly dedicated to the Society of Antiquaries of Scotland*, vol. 2 (Edinburgh, 1788), 170.

minuet closes the collection. No evidence of their relationship has emerged, but on the face of it, it would appear that, at the very least, Gordon was Cantelo's patron.

Positive identification of Gordon is unclear at this time. Two Scots of that name and rank were prominent in the 1780s. The first is Cosmo Alexander (1743-1827), who became fourth Duke of Gordon in 1752. Gordon served in the Army and was promoted to colonel in 1780 at the same ceremony as several other Scots whose family names appear in this collection. There is no official evidence that he served in America. He loved music, and had a superb musician in his household, his butler, fiddler William Marshall, whom Burns called "the first composer of strathspeys of the age."[18] The lyrics of a song attributed to Gordon, "Cauld Kail in Aberdeen," suggest that he was a knowledgeable dance enthusiast as well (see fig. 4.4).

While Cosmo, the Duke of Gordon, did not come to America, another Gordon did come, and he stayed five years. In the fall of 1777, Cosmo Gordon, brother of the Earl of Aberdeen, sailed for New York with a large contingent of recruits for General Howe's army. After considerable delay, he finally reached America, and served with the Third Regiment of Guards in the New York area until his return to England in 1782.[19] In the fall of 1783, the London *Public Advertiser* reported a duel between the Hon. Col. Cosmo Gordon and a colleague, Colonel Thomas of the First Regiment of Guards in which Thomas was killed.[20] The dispute stemmed from an incident following a battle at Springfield, New Jersey in June of 1780. Thomas had accused Gordon of cowardice; Gordon had been tried by a court martial in New York and acquitted.[21] When they returned to England at the end of 1782, Gordon challenged Thomas to a duel. For nine months Thomas refused to meet him. They finally fought on September 4, Thomas died the next day, and on the 8th, Gordon was convicted of willful murder. If this Gordon was Cantelo's patron, his reputation was apparently strong enough to negate the public effect of this judgement.

The American Connection?

Thus far, except for about half of the titles and the possibility that both Cantelo and Gordon were in New York during the occupation, there is little about the collection that appears to have much to do with America. But there are some hints that at least some of these tunes and at least one dance were actually known on this side of the Atlantic. "The Munichausen" is one. This same combination of dance and tune appears in no other

---

18. George S. Emmerson, *Rantin' Pipe and Tremblin' String, a History of Scottish Dance Music* (Montreal: McGill-Queen's University Press, 1971), 67-69; *Dictionary of National Biography*, s.v. "Alexander, Cosmo."

19. My thanks to Dr. Mary Jane Corry, who located several references to Gordon's trip in *The New-York Gazette and the Weekly Mercury* (particularly 22 December 1777) while reading that paper for the project *The Performing Arts in Colonial American Newspapers, 1690-1783*.

20. September 8 and 9.

21. The principals were newsworthy beyond the confines of New York. The Charleston *Royal Gazette* of 26-29 December 1781 published a statement of Thomas's accusation that suggests that the argument was taking place in the public prints in London as well as in New York and was of interest to the garrison in South Carolina as well.

Caft down 2 Cut up again lead down the middle up again.& caft off —
fet to your partner— fet to 2d Lady—fet to partner—fet to 1st Lady—
Hands 4 round at bottom—Right & Left at Top—

Figure 4.5. "The Munichausen." Courtesy Clements Library, University of Michigan.

English source, but was copied into two American manuscripts as "The Dutchess of Brunswick" (see fig. 4.5).[22]

Cantelo's title refers to Col. Friedrich von Münchhausen (1753-95), who was in America with the Regiment Landgraf from August 1776 to June 1778. He served on Howe's staff as translator for the allied armies.[23] His Hessian employer was the Duke of Brunswick-Lünenberg, who was married to Augusta, a sister of George III. She became Duchess of Brunswick when her husband inherited his father's realm in 1780. Somehow, this tune and dance crossed the lines and was known to American dancers with the different but related title.

Further searching for concordances reveals that while no other dances from this collection can be found, four more of Cantelo's tunes were known by American musicians. "Capt. Oakes's Whim" appeared in Silas Dickinson's manuscript band book

---

22. Aaron Thompson, "A Table of Time" (manuscript commonplace book made while serving in New Jersey in 1777), 51 (Yale University Library [Sterling]); George Bush, "A New Collection of Songs" (manuscript begun in Sunbury, Pennsylvania in 1779), 20 (Historical Society of Delaware). The dances in the latter collection were realized and published in Charles Cyril Hendrickson and Kate Van Winkle Keller, *Social Dances*.

23. Friedrich von Münchhausen, *At General Howe's Side, 1776-1778*, trans. Ernest Kipping (Monmouth Beach, N.J.: Philip Freneau Press, 1974), 4. This regiment was also known as "The Hereditary Prince."

(ca. 1800) as "Oakes Whim."[24] This title probably commemorated Sir Hildebrand Oakes (1754-1822), who accompanied his regiment to America in December of 1775, and was made Captain in 1776.[25] Fiddler Eleazer Cary of Mansfield, Connecticut, wrote out the tune Cantelo called "The Monckton or the British White Feathers," using its alternate title and adding a note that it was a country dance tune.[26] The tune itself is derived from an earlier English country dance tune called "Fete Champetre" or "Warley Common."[27]

John Turner, another Connecticut fiddler, collected two of Cantelo's tunes consecutively on one page: "How Imperfect Is Expression," for which Turner had no title, and "Belles about the Flat Bush" that he called "The New York Assembly" (see fig. 4.6 a-b).[28] Turner may have learned both from John Griffiths, a dancing master who taught dancing in New York City in the 1780s and 1790s and who taught in Norwich in 1788.[29]

Sources of other tunes are varied. "The Yager Horn," a piece based on familiar calls of the instrument used by the Hessian mounted troops, can be found in British and American music collections of the 1790-1810 period as "The Bugle Horn." It may have been a familiar German dance tune. "La Buona Figuiliola" is taken from the overture to Niccolò Piccini's opera, *La buona figliuola* (1760), that was loosely based on the story from Samuel Richardson's *Pamela.* The popular overture was published in Philadelphia in the 1790s.

None of the remaining tunes can be found in American sources. For "The Monmouth, or the Victory," Cantelo borrowed the entire tune, but not the dance, of "The Victory" from a collection printed in London in 1780. He kept the original title and added a topical one, and added a third strain to the melody, probably to make it fit his dance.[30] Of the tunes with French titles, it is interesting to find Cantelo's "L'Escapade" as "Caledonian Beauty," printed twice in a collection made in Glasgow.[31] Two dances are in 3/8, the meter of the *dreher,* a German couple dance that was evolving into the waltz. One of these, as might be expected, is called "The Anspacher" after a Hessian regiment that served in America; the other, surprisingly, "The St. George," after the patron saint of

24. Silas Dickinson, "Silas Dickinson's Book" (manuscript copybook made in Amherst, Massachusetts, ca. 1800), 127 (New York Public Library, Research Library for the Performing Arts).

25. *Dictionary of National Biography*, s.v. "Oakes, Hildebrand."

26. Eleazer Cary, "Eleazer Cary's Book, A Storrs, scribe" (manuscript copybook made in Mansfield, Connecticut, 1797), 6 (Connecticut Historical Society).

27. *Longman and Broderip's Compleat Collection of 200 Favorite Country Dances*, vol. 2 (London: [Longman and Broderip], [1781]), 82, 91.

28. John Turner, "John Turner's Liber" (manuscript commonplace book begun in Norwich, Connecticut in 1788), 56 (Connecticut Historical Society).

29. Kate Van Winkle Keller, "John Griffiths, 18th-century Itinerant Dancing Master and His Influence on Traditional Social Dance in New England," *The Dublin Seminar for New England Folklife, Annual Proceedings, 1984. Itinerancy in New England and New York* (Boston: Boston University, 1986), 96-97.

30. *Thompson's Compleat Collection of 200 Favourite Country Dances*, [vol. 4] (London, Saml. Ann & Peter Thompson, [1780]), 9.

31. [James Aird], *A Selection of Scotch, English, Irish and Foreign Airs*, vol. 4 (Glasgow: A. Macgoun, [ca. 1796]), 14, 33.

Hands acrofs and back again, caft off 2 couple, up again, turn partners
half round, and back again, lead down 2 couple, turn your partners, lead
up again, and caft off ———

Figure 4.6a. "The Belles about the Flat Bush." Courtesy Clements Library, University of Michigan. Obvious errors in the cadence of the first strain and the eighth measure of the B strain suggest that the final plates were not proofread before the volume was printed.

Figure 4.6b. John Turner untitled manuscript ["How Imperfect is Expression"] and "The New York Assembly." Courtesy Connecticut Historical Society. Note that "The New York Assembly" is Cantelo's "The Belles about the Flat Bush," but with correct half-cadences and a slightly varied final two measures.

England. Cantelo's associated dance figures for the latter include a specific French movement, *la pirouette,* and the English "gallop."[32]

Conclusion

Although Cantelo certainly capitalized on the "American" connections in his book, the dances were probably not American in the strictest sense. They were probably not devised by Americans nor were they among the common repertory in American ballrooms. But some of them may have come from America. As the title page claims, Cantelo probably collected dances that had been created by members of the British occupation forces in America; these would have been dances intended for the entertainment and diversion of the officers and their Loyalist guests during the winter seasons. Eighteen of the pieces have either titles, music, or tunes relating to people, places, or events that happened in America; some of these are so esoteric that only those on the scene could have known their relevance. There may be others that have eluded our search.

Whether Cantelo actually collected the material in America is not clear. The British army spent the winters from 1776 to 1782 in New York, finally evacuating in November of 1783. Occupation forces held Philadelphia for the winter of 1777-78 and Charleston from 1780-82. Cantelo worked at Drury Lane during the season of 1778-79, but no other record of his employment in London or in Bath between 1779 and 1784 has been found. He might well have been in America, or he may have collected the dances in Bath from officers or musicians who served in America.

He was a member of the band of music for the First Regiment of Foot Guards. The regiment itself did not leave England, but fifteen men were selected from each of the 64 companies of household infantry and combined into a brigade of Guards that did come, possibly including a band.[33] A band might also have been sent with Prince William Henry, who arrived in New York on 24 September 1781, a few weeks before Cornwallis's surrender at Yorktown. The Prince stayed through the summer of 1782.[34] Although there is no concrete supporting evidence, it is possible that both Cantelo and Gordon were in New York at the same time. During winter quarters they would have had ample time to become acquainted with the local social scene and develop the collection together. Since all the occupation forces eventually convened in New York, Cantelo could have observed and collected pieces attributed to the winter seasons in Philadelphia and Charleston.

With the addition of his own "favorite minuets now performing this present spring season," Cantelo's book thus became self-promotion, a paean to his patron and his

32. Based on present knowledge, a gallop in 3/8 time is an awkward move. More work is needed to interpret this dance accurately.

33. An advertisement in the London *Public Advertiser* suggests that Cantelo's skills would be in demand even in peacetime: "MUSICIANS Wanted immediately to go abroad, two horns and two clarinet players. Apply at No. 26 Cheapside and No. 13 Haymarket between this and Monday next; after that Time it will not do" (9 December 1785). It is interesting to note that this address is that of Longman & Broderip, publisher of Cantelo's book.

34. Philip Ziegler, *King William IV* (New York: Harper & Row, 1973), 33-42; Thomas Jefferson Wertenbaker, *Father Knickerbocker Rebels, New York City during the Revolution* (New York: Charles Scribner's Sons, 1948), 200-02.

friends, and a commemorative volume on two themes—country dances from exotic America and minuets from fashionable Bath. Produced by a noble Scottish patron and amateur composer, an English musician and composer who was seeking admission to the Royal Society of Musicians, and a major music publishing house in London, it was a combination quite likely to succeed.

5

Early American Psalmody and the Core Repertory: A Perspective

Daniel C. L. Jones

During the colonial and early national eras in America, psalmody—the custom of singing sacred texts[1]—was an enormously important part of the cultural life of the Protestant, particularly Congregationalist, sub-culture concentrated in the New England region.[2] Practiced in a variety of circumstances—daily as well as on Sunday, at home as well as in church, privately as well as congregationally—it was a ritualized proclamation of this sub-culture's interpretation of Christian doctrine. Through this ritual, mere words were intensified by poetic imagery and given heightened emotional content through musical intonation and perhaps elaboration, generating synergistic power and reinforcing cultural solidarity when performed collectively. For a thorough appreciation of this prominent early American sub-culture, some understanding of psalmody is essential.

In addition to its cultural significance, psalmody has been an attractive topic for research in early American cultural history, due to its accessible and circumscribed historical record. A sizable proportion of the sacred music of this era appeared in print and has thus been largely preserved for the examination of modern scholars. The volume of

---

1. By convention, the term psalmody has been used to refer both to the custom of singing sacred texts and to the repertory of musical settings used for such activity. With regard to this period, it is also used to refer to the singing of all sacred texts, hymns as well as paraphrased psalms. For the sacred vocal music tradition since the early nineteenth century, the term hymnody is generally applied.

2. A useful discussion of religious demographics in America during this time can be found in Edwin Scott Gaustad, *Historical Atlas of Religion in America* (New York: Harper & Row, 1962), 1-36.

pieces and publications—estimated at about 7,500 different pieces in roughly 500 editions[3]—is large enough to represent a significant cultural artifact and yet sufficiently limited to be manageable. As a result, the combined efforts of many scholars, particularly in the decades since World War II, have been able to bring the published record of American psalmody under virtually complete bibliographic control.[4] Richard Crawford's *Core Repertory of Early American Psalmody*[5] represents a milestone in American psalmody scholarship. Published in 1984, it was one of the first studies to deal with the repertory of American psalmody comprehensively and, at the same time, directly (i.e., at the level of individual pieces). Completion of the project was a phenomenal accomplishment, representing years of gathering and tallying massive amounts of data. Moreover, as Nym Cooke pointed out in his review of the published version,[6] the extensive introductory materials to the edition represent scholarship at its finest, combining meticulous thoroughness with insightful interpretation and commentary. Since its publication, the *Core Repertory* has proven to be an invaluable tool for many scholars, including the present author, researching in this field. The design of the *Core Repertory* is remarkably uncomplicated. Utilizing number of appearances in print as the sole criterion for selection, it consists of "representative versions of the 101 sacred pieces most often printed in America between 1698 and 1810."[7] The objectivity of this plan is very attractive, for it provides "one measure of the musical preferences of an earlier age"[8] in strictly quantifiable terms. The result is a corpus of very manageable proportions well-suited to musical and particularly statistical analysis.

Not long after the appearance of the *Core Repertory,* I began a several-year study of the life and music of one early American psalmodist, Elias Mann (1750-1825). My research revealed that Mann was a well-respected musician in his own time and that his

---

3. Richard Crawford and D. W. Krummel "Early American Music Printing and Publishing," in William L. Joyce et al, eds., *Printing and Society in Early America* (Worcester: American Antiquarian Society, 1983) report the number to be 473. In a later study, Nym Cooke, "American Psalmodists in Contact and Collaboration, 1770-1820," 2 vols. (Ph.D. dissertation, University of Michigan, 1990), 1:xlii, reports approximately 550.

4. The most recent and prominent evidence of this bibliographic control is Allen P. Britton, Irving Lowens, and Richard Crawford, *American Sacred Music Imprints, 1698-1810: A Bibliography* (Worcester, Mass.: American Antiquarian Society, 1990), which documents and details the contents of all known pre-1811 American sacred music publications.

5. Richard Crawford, ed., *The Core Repertory of Early American Psalmody,* Recent Researches in American Music, 11-12 (Madison, Wisc.: A-R Editions, 1984).

6. *American Music,* 4 no. 3 (fall 1986): 337-49.

7. Crawford, *Core Repertory,* ix. The first sacred music printed in the English-speaking American colonies appeared in 1698 in the ninth edition of the so-called "Bay Psalm Book." See Richard G. Appel, *The Music of the Bay Psalm Book,* I.S.A.M. Monographs, 5 (Brooklyn: Institute for Studies in American Music, 1975). A stylistic watershed in American religious music occurred around 1810, a culmination of reform impulses which had begun around 1790. Aspects of this reform movement will be discussed later in this article. Also see *The New Grove Dictionary of American Music* (1986), s.v. "Psalmody," by Richard Crawford, 642.

8. Crawford, *Core Repertory,* ix.

music was in general well-crafted, expressive, and, in some respects, exceptional.[9] A comparison of publication statistics on Mann's sacred compositions with those on Core Repertory pieces, however, shows a disturbingly sizable disparity: Mann's two most "popular" sacred tunes, in Core Repertory terms, were his NO. 5 and NO. 6, each printed twelve times; the Core Repertory tune with the least number of American printings, Amos Bull's PSALM 46, was printed in this country forty-four times while, at the high end of the scale, the eminent PSALM 100 received 226 American printings.[10] This disparity provoked in me—beyond the naturally-arising, defensive indignation of one who has delved and advocated a particular subject—the desire to explore further the nature of the Core Repertory and its portrayal of sacred music in early America.

The following discussion offers insights gleaned from that exploration. A mixture of respect and fear compels me to preface with a few disclaimers. First, I mean no discredit to Crawford nor to any of his scholarly work. He is widely recognized as a—if not *the*—foremost expert in the field of American psalmody. And indeed, as the reader will discover, I do not hesitate to draw frequently upon his scholarship throughout this article. Also, I make no claims to be entirely original in issues or points of view. Many of the ideas presented here are well known to scholars in the field of American psalmody and are included in an effort to make this article useful to the non-expert in the field. Finally, I do not intend to defend or champion the music of Elias Mann. I have done enough of that elsewhere (see note 9), and here Mann's music is used merely to exemplify certain points. What I do hope to accomplish is to provide a type of addendum to the Core Repertory, one which encourages its user to investigate certain aspects of its contents, explore various circumstances of the Core Repertory period that helped shape and define its ultimate contents, and reflect on its depiction of this important component of early American cultural life.

My contention is that the Core Repertory, by its very design, presents a limited and even somewhat distorted portrayal of American psalmody. I suggest that two factors, in conjunction, are primarily responsible for this misrepresentation. First is the criterion used for inclusion in the Core Repertory, the number of times a particular piece was printed, for the dimensions, character, and significance of music printing changed so radically over the course of the Core Repertory period that its equability in gauging the entire time span is questionable. The second factor involves the concept of musical preference. Human preference—individual or cultural, musical or otherwise—is always shaped by a number of influences, many of which may have no immediate connection to the intrinsic merit of the favored or neglected items. As a result, a record of musical preference may be, in fact, more of an account of the impact of non-musical values. In addition, such values and the preferences that reflect them are certainly not static, but change over time and space. As a result, an attempt to summarize the preferences of a

9. For a summary presentation of Mann's life and music, see my article "Elias Mann: Reform-Era Massachusetts Psalmodist," *American Music* 11, no. 1 (spring 1993): 54-89. For more in-depth discussion, see my dissertation, "Elias Mann (1750-1825): Massachusetts Composer, Compiler, and Singing Master," 2 vols. (University of Colorado, 1991).

10. Crawford, *Core Repertory*, lxxvii-lxviii, table 2.

sizable time/space span according to a single criterion can overlook relatively short-term or tangential, but nonetheless significant, episodes in a tradition. The following discussion will explore these points in more detail, suggest some alternate ideas for assessing the tradition of American psalmody, and offer a case in point.

*   *   *

During the Core Repertory period, New England (as well as the rest of English-speaking America) underwent extensive change. During this roughly 110-year span, its population grew by a factor of more than sixteen, from approximately 90,000 to nearly 1,500,000.[11] More consequential from a cultural perspective were the robust economic and industrial development and the evolution of societal convictions and ideals, both religious and secular. Naturally, such growth and change had considerable impact on customs as central to the cultural life of this region as psalmody. Over the course of this period, its music was transformed from a primarily functional, relatively simple, tradition-bound folk medium entirely of European origin to a thriving creative and commercial forum, dominated by indigenous composers and entrepreneurs, and consisting of a comparatively vast repertory which included many elaborate and expressive composed settings.

In light of this transformation, it is useful in examining the contents of the Core Repertory and exploring its formative influences to distinguish subdivisions in the overall period represented. Thus, in the preface to the *Core Repertory* (p. x), Crawford identifies and briefly discusses "Three Stages of America Tunebook Publishing": I. 1698-1760; II. 1761-1790; and III. 1791-1810. Utilizing this framework, table 5.1 presents an estimate of the number of printings each of the Core Repertory pieces received during each of the three stages, assembled from information presented in the "Tune Biographies."[12]

---

11. Figures from Evarts B. Greene and Virginia D. Harrington, *American Population before the Census of 1790* (1932; reprint, Gloucester, Mass.: Peter Smith, 1966), 4, and U.S. Department of Commerce, Bureau of the Census, *Historical Statistics of the United States, Colonial Times to 1970*, Bicentennial Edition (Washington, 1975), part 1, 24-37.

12. For these tune biographies, see Crawford, *Core Repertory*, xxii-lxvi. Exact reconstruction of publication records is often not possible from the information given in the tune biographies. In many instances, no doubt to make extensive amounts of information suitably concise, incomplete data are given and generalizations are made with indefinite language such as "including . . . and others" (see, for example, the biographies for COLCHESTER and DALSTON). Also, in many cases a particular tune appeared in more than two editions of the same title, for which the abbreviated notation "ff" has been used (see, for example, the biographies for BATH, BRIDGEWATER, and BRISTOL).

When discrepancies occur between the total number of American printings a tune received—as reported in the second paragraph of the biography and summarized in appendix 3, table 2 (pp. lxxvii-lxxviii)—and the number tallied from information given in the tune biography, the estimated number of printings for one or more stages has been adjusted so that the sum of the three stages agrees with the reported total. In most instances, such adjustments are slight. For ten tunes, however, the discrepancy accounts for ten percent or more of the total printings: BANGOR, BROMSGROVE, COLCHESTER, DALSTON, DENMARK, DUNSTAN, LISBON, LITTLE MARLBOROUGH, ST. MARTIN'S, and WELLS. In most of these cases, reasonably complete publication records are given in the tune biographies for two of the stages, substantiating the estimate for the third.

Remarkable here is the increase in the total number of printings of Core Repertory pieces across the three stages. This proliferation becomes even more striking when one takes into account the decreasing number of years represented by each successive stage and thus considers the rate at which sacred music in print was being produced: during Stage I, printings of Core Repertory tunes averaged just over five per year; during Stage II, roughly sixty-three per year; and during Stage III, approximately 246 per year. This geometric increase was a direct result of the beginning, around 1760 in this country, of tunebook production as a commercial enterprise and the phenomenal growth of this industry from the 1780s on.[13] The impact of this dynamic industry is a primary factor in shaping the "Core Repertory view" of American psalmody. Totals for Stages II and III combined—that together make up less than half of the Core Repertory time period—account for over ninety-five percent of all printed appearances of the Core Repertory pieces. In Stage III alone, eighty-four of these 101 pieces received fifty percent or more of their printings pieces, and forty-three received seventy-five percent or more. In other words, the Core Repertory consists primarily of sacred pieces that were "preferred" by music publishers during the years represented by Stages II and especially III.

To take an opposite view of the same issue, because appearances in print is the criterion used, the Core Repertory cannot accurately document that portion of this tradition that was carried on in oral practice. And, while most historical accounts of American psalmody tend to place great emphasis on the beginnings of the singing-school movement around 1720 and the ascension of "Regular Singing," evidence suggests that oral practice remained a, and in some places *the*, principal mode for the preservation and dissemination of sacred music throughout much of the eighteenth century—i.e., through much of the Core Repertory period. This was especially true in more rural areas where lack of resources, the inertia of entrenched tradition, and esthetic convictions all served to protect oral practices. One point of evidence to support this assertion is the fact that wordbooks, containing sacred texts but no music, were by far more common than tunebooks that included music.[14] Further confirmation comes from local records that discuss efforts to reform psalmody practices and implement note reading. Paul Osterhout, for example, offers "accounts from four central Connecticut communities" to support his conjecture that "note reading played little if any role there in congregational singing until probably the last third of the eighteenth century."[15] Available information on the Northampton area in western Massachusetts similarly suggests that performance of sacred music by note reading may have begun there as early as the mid 1730s, but did not take hold as a regular practice until at least the mid to late 1760s, and even then may have

13. For more on this advent, see Crawford and Krummel, "Early American Music Printing and Publishing" (which deals with both sacred and secular music), and Britton, Lowens, and Crawford, *American Sacred Music Imprints*, 26-42.

14. See Britton, Lowens, and Crawford, *American Sacred Music Imprints*, 1. Nicholas Temperley, in reference to both English and American psalmody, further corroborates and specifies this point: "The great majority of psalm books in the English American tradition had no music at all (perhaps 80% of the surviving editions up to 1800)"—*New Grove Dictionary of American Music*, s.v. "Psalms, metrical," 647.

15. Paul R. Osterhout, "Note Reading and Regular Singing in Eighteenth-Century New England," *American Music* 4, no. 2 (summer 1986): 130.

Table 5.1. Estimated Number of Printings of Individual Core Repertory Pieces
during Each of the Three Stages of the Core Repertory
Estimated Number of Printings (Percentage of Tune Total)

CR No.	Tune Name	Stage I (1698-1760)		Stage II (1761-1790)		Stage III (1791-1810)		Tune Total
1	Adeste Fidelis	0	(0%)	0	(0%)	48	(100%)	48
2	All Saints	0	(0%)	34	(59%)	24	(41%)	58
3	Amherst	0	(0%)	21	(28%)	53	(72%)	74
4	Amsterdam	0	(0%)	16	(33%)	32	(67%)	48
5	Angels Hymn	0	(0%)	24	(33%)	49	(67%)	73
6	Anthem for Easter	0	(0%)	1	(2%)	45	(98%)	46
7	Aylesbury	0	(0%)	41	(31.5%)	89	(68.5%)	130
8	Bangor	0	(0%)	32	(29%)	78	(71%)	110
9	Bath	1	(1%)	39	(43%)	50	(56%)	90
10	Bedford	0	(0%)	29	(35%)	54	(65%)	83
11	Bethesda	0	(0%)	14	(28%)	36	(72%)	50
12	Bridgewater	0	(0%)	22	(22%)	77	(78%)	99
13	Bristol	0	(0%)	15	(19%)	64	(81%)	79
14	Bromsgrove	1	(2%)	36	(59%)	24	(39%)	61
15	Brookfield	0	(0%)	30	(34%)	58	(66%)	88
16	Buckingham	0	(0%)	28	(38%)	46	(62%)	74
17	Burford	2	(4%)	22	(49%)	21	(47%)	45
18	Calvary	0	(0%)	10	(22%)	36	(78%)	46
19	Canterbury	30	(33.33%)	30	(33.33%)	30	(33.33%)	90
20	Chester	0	(0%)	20	(36%)	36	(64%)	56
21	Christmas	0	(0%)	1	(2%)	51	(98%)	52
22	Colchester	1	(1%)	35	(36.5%)	60	(62.5%)	96
23	Coleshill	1	(2%)	13	(29%)	31	(69%)	45
24	Coronation	0	(0%)	0	(0%)	47	(100%)	47
25	Dalston	0	(0%)	24	(34%)	47	(66%)	71
26	Denmark	0	(0%)	8	(9%)	85	(91%)	93
27	Dunstan	0	(0%)	2	(4%)	52	(96%)	54
28	Dying Christian	0	(0%)	1	(2%)	45	(98%)	46
29	Enfield	0	(0%)	2	(3.5%)	55	(96.5%)	57
30	Funeral Thought	0	(0%)	32	(34%)	63	(66%)	95
31	Greenfield	0	(0%)	20	(19%)	83	(81%)	103
32	Greenwich	0	(0%)	9	(11%)	73	(89%)	82
33	Habakkuk	0	(0%)	6	(11%)	49	(89%)	55
34	Hartford	0	(0%)	18	(39%)	28	(61%)	46
35	Hotham	0	(0%)	1	(2%)	58	(98%)	59
36	Irish	0	(0%)	12	(15%)	70	(85%)	82
37	Isle of Wight	11	(18%)	26	(42%)	25	(40%)	62
38	Jordan	0	(0%)	3	(4%)	68	(96%)	71
39	Judgment	0	(0%)	6	(12.5%)	42	(87.5%)	48
40	Kingsbridge	0	(0%)	24	(47%)	27	(53%)	51
41	Landaff	2	(2.5%)	39	(46.5%)	43	(51%)	84
42	Lebanon	0	(0%)	11	(23%)	37	(77%)	48
43	Lenox	0	(0%)	18	(17%)	87	(83%)	105
44	Lisbon	0	(0%)	4	(6%)	61	(94%)	65
45	Little Marlborough	0	(0%)	35	(26%)	100	(74%)	135
46	London New	17	(32.5%)	18	(35%)	17	(32.5%)	52
47	Majesty	0	(0%)	11	(15%)	64	(85%)	75
48	Maryland	0	(0%)	19	(32%)	41	(68%)	60
49	Mear	5	(4%)	25	(21%)	91	(75%)	121
50	Middletown	0	(0%)	15	(23%)	49	(77%)	64

CR No.	Tune Name	Stage I (1698-1760)		Stage II (1761-1790)		Stage III (1791-1810)		Tune Total
51	Milford	0	(0%)	16	(23.5%)	52	(76.5%)	68
52	Montague	0	(0%)	15	(25%)	45	(75%)	60
53	Montgomery	0	(0%)	1	(2%)	54	(98%)	55
54	Morning Hymn	0	(0%)	29	(64%)	16	(36%)	45
55	New Jerusalem	0	(0%)	0	(0%)	52	(100%)	52
56	Newbury	0	(0%)	28	(53%)	25	(47%)	53
57	Newton	0	(0%)	1	(2%)	60	(98%)	61
58	Norwich	0	(0%)	26	(31%)	59	(69%)	85
59	Ocean	0	(0%)	5	(7%)	71	(93%)	76
60	Plymouth	0	(0%)	40	(40%)	60	(60%)	100
61	Portsmouth	12	(22.5%)	31	(58.5%)	10	(19%)	53
62	Portsmouth	0	(0%)	4	(8.5%)	43	(91.5%)	47
63	Portugal	0	(0%)	0	(0%)	54	(100%)	54
64	Psalm 25	0	(0%)	9	(20%)	37	(80%)	46
65	Psalm 33	0	(0%)	22	(49%)	23	(51%)	45
66	Psalm 34	0	(0%)	33	(29%)	82	(71%)	115
67	Psalm 46	0	(0%)	14	(32%)	30	(68%)	44
68	Psalm 100 [Old]	34	(15%)	56	(25%)	136	(60%)	226
69	Psalm 100 [New]	15	(29%)	17	(33%)	20	(38%)	52
70	Psalm 136	0	(0%)	15	(31%)	34	(69%)	49
71	Psalm 148	30	(59%)	19	(37%)	2	(4%)	51
72	Psalm 149	12	(10%)	46	(38%)	63	(52%)	121
73	Putney	0	(0%)	27	(39%)	42	(61%)	69
74	Rainbow	0	(0%)	15	(29%)	36	(71%)	51
75	Rochester	0	(0%)	35	(42%)	48	(58%)	83
76	Russia	0	(0%)	4	(6%)	64	(94%)	68
77	St. Anne	1	(1%)	36	(41%)	51	(58%)	88
78	St. David's	31	(54.5%)	19	(33.5%)	7	(12%)	57
79	St. George's	0	(0%)	9	(20%)	37	(80%)	46
80	St. Helen's	0	(0%)	28	(39%)	43	(61%)	71
81	St. James	17	(30%)	23	(40%)	17	(30%)	57
82	St. Martin's	1	(1%)	33	(24%)	103	(75%)	137
83	St. Thomas	0	(0%)	10	(20%)	41	(80%)	51
84	Sherburne	0	(0%)	16	(20%)	63	(80%)	79
85	Southwell	31	(61%)	15	(29%)	5	(10%)	51
86	Stafford	0	(0%)	19	(22%)	66	(78%)	85
87	Standish	14	(25%)	25	(45%)	17	(30%)	56
88	Suffield	0	(0%)	18	(29.5%)	43	(70.5%)	61
89	Sutton	0	(0%)	24	(39%)	37	(61%)	61
90	Sutton	0	(0%)	0	(0%)	45	(100%)	45
91	Virginia	0	(0%)	19	(21%)	73	(79%)	92
92	Walsall	0	(0%)	19	(33%)	39	(67%)	58
93	Wantage	0	(0%)	27	(40%)	41	(60%)	68
94	Wells	0	(0%)	45	(28%)	115	(72%)	16
95	Weston Favel	0	(0%)	18	(39%)	28	(61%)	46
96	Winchester	0	(0%)	16	(31%)	36	(69%)	52
97	Windham	0	(0%)	6	(9%)	59	(91%)	65
98	Windsor	34	(29%)	33	(27.5%)	52	(43.5%)	119
99	Winter	0	(0%)	9	(17%)	43	(83%)	52
100	Worcester	0	(0%)	16	(26%)	45	(74%)	61
101	York	30	(52.5%)	17	(30%)	10	(17.5%)	57
Stage Total (Percentage of overall total)		333	(4.5%)	1910	(26.5%)	4933	(69%)	7176

lapsed into disuse again until the mid 1790s.[16] The Core Repertory criterion is based upon our present cultural viewpoint—corporate and mass market economics—wherein popularity is equated with numbers of units produced and sold. But in oral tradition, popularity is more a personal and group value associated with an object or action by ritual importance and merely by repetition.

Similarly, by its design, the Core Repertory cannot represent two other significant modes of circulation: manuscript and European publications. Scholarship on manuscript sources is necessarily more fragmentary and speculative than that on published sources. Nonetheless, the little evidence that exists suggests that manuscript transmission probably played a significant role in American psalmody. Nym Cooke, for example, offers some wonderful hypothetical scenarios, supported by anecdotal accounts in personal papers and memoirs, and suggests that "a tune could make its way far and wide, through an extensive network of musical contacts, before it reached print."[17] While it is impossible to know precisely the extent to which European collections of sacred music actually circulated in America, there is no doubt that they did. Before American publications with music were produced—i.e., before Stage I—imported European collections such as the Ainsworth psalter,[18] the Ravenscroft psalter,[19] and the psalters of John Playford[20] served as the only printed sources of sacred music for English-speaking colonists. Editions of the Bay Psalm Book prior to the ninth referred users to "neere fourty common tunes; as they are collected . . . by Tho[mas] Ravenscroft" and in "our english psalm books."[21] During Stage I, the few American publications with sacred music produced drew directly upon such English collections. Irving Lowens, for example, has shown that the music included in the Bay Psalm Book, ninth edition, is identical to that found in various editions of John Playford's *Brief Introduction to the Skill of Musick* (London, 1658),[22] and that the vast majority of the musical settings included in John Tufts's *An Introduction to the Singing of Psalm-Tunes* (Boston, 1721) and Thomas Walter's *The Grounds and Rules of Musick Explained* (Boston, 1721) were taken from Playford's *Whole Book of Psalms* (London, 1677).[23] Even during Stage II, as American sacred music publications began to appear in

---

16. See my dissertation, 1:34-39, for a summary account of information on the development of psalmody in the Northampton area.

17. Cooke, "American Psalmodists," 1:171-76. See pp. ix-x and 87 for further comments and sources relevant to this topic.

18. *The Book of Psalmes: Englished both in Prose and Metre* (Amsterdam, 1612). See Waldo Selden Pratt, *The Music of the Pilgrims* (1921; reprint, New York: Russell & Russell, 1971).

19. Thomas Ravenscroft, *The Whole Booke of Psalmes: With the Hymns* (London, 1621).

20. See Nicholas Temperley, "John Playford and the Metrical Psalms," *Journal of the American Musicological Society* 25, no. 3 (fall 1972): 331-78. Also see Karl Kroeger, "Introduction," in *The Complete Works of William Billings*, 4 vols. (Boston: American Musicological Society and the Colonial Society of Massachusetts, 1977-90), 1:xx-xxii.

21. Quoted in Appel, 2-3.

22. Irving Lowens, "The Bay Psalm Book in 17th-Century New England," in *Music and Musicians in Early America* (New York: Norton, 1964), 33-35.

23. Irving Lowens, "John Tuft's *Introduction to the Singing of Psalm-Tunes* (1721-1744): The First American Music Textbook," in ibid., 51-53.

more significant numbers, the presence of English tunebooks was still felt strongly. To cite but two examples, Crawford notes in his preface to the reprint edition of James Lyon's *Urania* (Philadelphia, 1761), that the title page, tune repertory, and theoretical introduction of *Urania* reveal its direct indebtedness to as many as ten different English sources.[24] Karl Kroeger likewise indicates that when William Billings created his landmark *New-England Psalm-Singer* (Boston, 1770), his sources for materials in the theoretical introduction included five English tunebooks.[25] While the actual dissemination in print of English psalm tunes in America may have taken place more through American publications than English ones, it is clear that American psalmody was directly and indirectly influenced by English collections throughout much of the Core Repertory period.

The existence and apparent significance of these alternate modes of circulation undermine the Core Repertory's validity as the sole gauge by which to assess American psalmody. While the influences of these alternate modes are largely unquantifiable, it seems plausible to suggest that their importance was in inverse relationship to the growth of the tunebook industry. In other words, they probably played significant roles in shaping this tradition during (as well as before) Stage I, decreasingly so during Stages II and particularly III. Were we able to fully appraise their contributions and incorporate this information into our picture of American psalmody, we would probably find that two general repertories would appear more prominent: tunes of European origin, especially more traditional ones, and tunes popular on a local basis, especially outside of large urban centers.

To return to our consideration of the tunebook industry's influence on the Core Repertory, ramifications of changing philosophies, methods, and circumstances of tunebook production as the industry developed had significant impacts on the ultimate content of the Core Repertory. During Stage I, the music presented in the relatively few American collections produced was made up primarily of tunes already commonly sung in public worship. Thus, in terms of repertory, the American tunebook during this time was primarily a servant of tradition. (To some extent, then, the repertory of sacred music printed during Stage I *does* reflect the influence of oral practice in this tradition.) But as of about 1760, the objective and repertory of American collections began to change. The compiler took on a more influential role "as a representative of the singing public, canvassing available repertories and choosing pieces according to his own musical taste and his idea of public preference."[26]

During the 1780s, the introduction of typographical printing and professional publishers to the field of sacred music publishing further altered the concept of a

---

24. James Lyon, *Urania* (reprint, New York: Da Capo, 1974), with new preface by Richard Crawford, viii-x. In the same preface (p. i), Crawford cites another American tunebook from this time heavily indebted to English sources for its contents, Josiah Flagg's *A Collection of the Best Psalm Tunes* (Boston, 1764).

25. Kroeger, *Complete Works of William Billings*, 1:xxxv.

26. Britton, Lowens, and Crawford, *American Sacred Music Imprints*, 5.

tunebook into a mass market commodity.[27] The act of compiling became geared primarily to market demands, and astute businessmen such as Worcester printer-publisher Isaiah Thomas soon hit upon the formula for commercial success. Two traits found in all "formula" tunebooks, such as Thomas's *Worcester Collection*, were an eclectic mix of forms and styles and an emphasis on familiar works.[28] Furthermore, the shift during this time from copperplate printing to the use of movable type transformed the meaning of "a printing," the very basis of the Core Repertory criterion.[29] One result was that tunebooks could be produced more cheaply and, therefore, made more affordable. A second result was larger press runs. Once engraved, a copper plate could be reused, thus encouraging smaller press runs at first with the option of printing more later. A setting of movable type, on the other hand, was lost after a press run as the type was redistributed. "Since typesetting was a considerable part of the cost, the larger the press run, the more cheaply a copy of a book could be produced. . . . Therefore, the economic advantage of typographical printing lay in volume."[30]

One other late eighteenth-century change in this industry also affected patterns of publication. As early as 1770, a few enterprising American composers, most notably William Billings and Andrew Law, had begun to seek legal protection for their compositions.[31] In 1790, the first Federal law was passed which allowed music to be copyrighted as a book.[32] One result, because official permission at the national level was

27. For information pertaining to these advents and particular printer-publishers important in the sacred music field, see Richard J. Wolfe, *Early American Music Engraving and Printing* (Urbana: University of Illinois Press, 1980), chaps. 2 and 3; Crawford and Krummel, "Early American Music Printing and Publishing," 186-227; Britton, Lowens, and Crawford, *American Sacred Music Imprints,* 29-39; Karl Kroeger, "Isaiah Thomas as a Music Publisher," *Proceedings of the American Antiquarian Society* 86 (October 1976): 321-41; and Paul R. Osterhout, "Andrew Wright: Northampton Music Printer," *American Music* 1, no. 4 (winter 1983): 5-26.

28. For a detailed study of the *Worcester Collection*, see Karl D. Kroeger, "The Worcester Collection of Sacred Harmony and Sacred Music in America, 1786-1803" (Ph.D. diss., Brown University, 1976). Britton, Lowens, and Crawford, *American Sacred Music Imprints,* 7, lists eight collections from the 1780s that were based on this formula, each running several editions, and notes that "between 1790 and 1810, no fewer than fifty American books of sacred music followed [this] pattern."

29. For statistics on this shift, see Crawford and Krummel, "Early American Music Printing and Publishing," 196, table 2, reprinted in Britton, Lowens, and Crawford, *American Sacred Music Imprints,* 36, table B.

30. Britton, Lowens, and Crawford, *American Sacred Music Imprints,* 37.

31. See David P. McKay and Richard Crawford, *William Billings of Boston: Eigtheenth-Century Composer* (Princeton: Princeton University Press, 1975), 221-30, and Irving Lowens, "Andrew Law and the Pirates," in *Music and Musicians in Early America,* 58-88, for discussions of efforts by these two composers to obtain copyright protection.

32. The Federal Act of 31 May 1790 states that:
the author and authors of any map, chart, book or books already printed within these United States . . . shall have the sole right and liberty of printing, reprinting, publishing and vending such map, chart, book or books, for the term of fourteen years from the recording the title thereof in the clerk's office. . . . And that the author and authors of any map, chart, book or books already made and composed, and not printed or published, or that shall hereafter be made and composed . . . shall have [the same rights for the same time span]. . . . And if, at the expiration of the said term, the author or authors, of any of them, be living, and a citizen or citizens of these United States, or resident therein, the same exclusive rights shall be continued to him or them, his or their executors,

now required for reproduction, was a significant reduction in the reprinting of tunes composed after 1790 in subsequently compiled collections.[33]

The combination of these developments in the American tunebook industry resulted in, on the one hand, a tremendous increase in the quantity of publications, especially as of the mid 1780s. During each of the last three decades of the Core Repertory period, the number of tunebook editions issued in America approximately doubled from the previous decade: twenty during the 1770s; fifty-eight during the 1780s; 107 during the 1790s; and 222 during the 1800s.[34] (As we have seen, this increase is also evident at the level of individual pieces, as reflected in the stage totals of table 5.1.) At the same time, the dominance of "formula" tunebooks and the enactment of federal copyright legislation served to prevent newer pieces from gaining significant exposure. Together, these conditions resulted in only a tiny fraction of tunes first published in America after 1790 making it into the Core Repertory: "of the 6,000 new compositions published during this period, only five are in the present core repertory."[35]

Graph 5.1 is an attempt to summarize and represent visually many of the points discussed thus far. Decades of the overall Core Repertory period are on the horizontal axis, and the vertical dotted lines divide the graph space into the three stages. When presented in this manner, the increasing time compression across the three stages becomes clear. The "TP" line represents the percentage of total printings of Core Repertory tunes occurring during each stage, taken from the stage totals in table 1: 0.1 percent at the outset (7/7176);[36] 4.5 percent (333/7176) by the end of Stage I; 26.5 percent (1910/7176) during Stage II; and 69 percent (4933/7176) during Stage III. The "E" line represents the percentage of Core Repertory tunes that first entered into print in American publications during each stage: 6.9 percent at the outset (7/101); 22.8 percent (23/101) by the end of Stage I; 72.3 percent (73/101) during Stage II, and 4.9 percent (5/101) during Stage III.[37]

The combined result of these two patterns has much to do with the overall character of the Core Repertory. While the tunebook industry continued to grow geometrically throughout the Core Repertory period (reflected in the "TP" line), the proportion of the

---

administrators or assigns, for the further term of fourteen years: Provided, he or they shall cause the title thereof to be a second time recorded and published in the same manner. [*Copyright Enactments: Laws Passed in the United States since 1783 Relating to Copyright* (Washington: Copyright Office, Library of Congress, 1973), 22.]

33. Crawford notes the effect of this legislation on Billings's tunes first published in his last tunebook: "It was no coincidence that the circulation of music in *The Continental Harmony* (1794), the only one of Billings's tunebooks published after the Federal copyright law was passed, was by far the smallest of any of his tunebooks." "William Billings [1746-1800] and American Psalmody: A Study of Musical Dissemination," in Crawford, *The American Musical Landscape* (Berkeley: University of California Press, 1993), 110-11.

34. Crawford and Krummel, "Early American Music Printing and Publishing," 191, table 1.

35. Crawford, *Core Repertory*, x. The five tunes are: ADESTE FIDELIS, CORONATION, NEW JERUSALEM, PORTUGAL, and SUTTON (no. 90).

36. Seven of the tunes in the Bay Psalm Book, ninth edition, are included in the Core Repertory.

37. Figures from Crawford, *Core Repertory*, x.

Graph 5.1
Correlation of: 1) Percent of CR Tunes Entering into Print Each Stage,
2) Percent of Overall CR Prints Occurring Each Stage

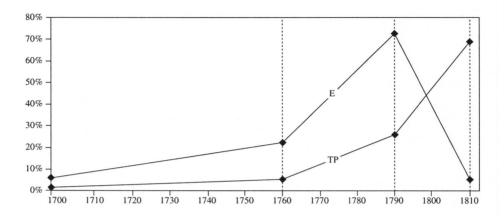

Core Repertory tunes first appearing in print in American publications peaked dramatically during Stage II and then fell off sharply during Stage III. The interaction of these two patterns points to the central importance of Stage II in establishing the Core Repertory view of American psalmody. On the one hand, this stage represents the beginning of the defining growth in the pattern used as the criterion for acceptance into this historically select group. At the same time, it represents by far the greatest source for Core Repertory music and the virtual closing of the Core Repertory to new input.

* * *

At various points during the Core Repertory period, musics of different origin and style were introduced into American psalmody. Crawford identifies four basic types of pieces discernible in the Core Repertory: 1) English and French "common" tunes of the sixteenth and seventeenth centuries; 2) English parish tunes of the eighteenth century; 3) English Methodist-inspired pieces of the mid-eighteenth century and later; and 4) American compositions by New Englanders working from 1770 on.[38] Thus, another useful approach for considering the contents of the Core Repertory and its portrayal of American psalmody is to chart the "preferences," measured in Core Repertory terms, for these various types of sacred music across the three stages. Table 5.2 presents estimates of the number of printings (data from table 5.1) that each of Crawford's four types, with two of his categories modified slightly so as to be more inclusive,[39] received during each of the three stages.

---

38. Ibid., xi.

39. Category 1 has been expanded from "English and French" to "European" so as to include tunes such as IRISH, WINCHESTER, and YORK, which may have originated from elsewhere in Europe. In category 4, the stipulation "from 1770 on" has been omitted to include one apparently American tune in the Core Repertory, PSALM 100 [NEW], first published in the 1720s.

**Table 5.2. Estimated Printings of Tune Types among Core Repertory Pieces during
Each of the Three Stages of the Core Repertory Period**

Estimated Number of Printings (Percentage of Tune Type Total)
{Percentage of Stage Total}

Tune Type	Stage I (1698-1760)		Stage II (1761-90)		Stage III (1791-1810)		Tune Type Total	
16th-/17th-cent. common[40]	271	(25.5%) {81.5%}	347	(32.5%) {18%}	452	(42%) {9%}	1070	{15%}
English 18th-cent. parish[41]	47	(2%) {14%}	923	(34%) {48%}	1745	(64%) {35.5%}	2715	{38%}
English Methodist-inspired[42]	0	(0%) {0%}	110	(14%) {6%}	654	(86%) {13.5%}	764	{10.5%}
American[43]	15	(1%) {4.5%}	530	(20%) {28%}	2082	(79%) {42%}	2627	{36.5%}
Stage Total	333		1910		4933		7176	

Looking first to patterns within tune type (parenthetical percentages, reading across), once again the growth of the tunebook industry is evident in the growing percentages across the three stages. The one significant aberration in this pattern lies in the sixteenth- and seventeenth-century common tunes, which show a much slower rate of increase than the other three categories. Somewhat more important are the data within stages (braced percentages, reading down), for here we get a picture of the comparative "popularity" of the various types during each stage and during the Core Repertory period as a whole. Clearly, and not surprisingly, Stage I is far and away dominated by sixteenth- and seventeenth-century common tunes. Beginning with Stage II, however, we find distinct changes in tune-type popularity. The traditional tunes drop radically in relative popularity with English parish and American tunes virtually exploding onto the scene, and a small

---

40. The fourteen Core Repertory tunes considered here to be in this category are ANGELS HYMN, CANTERBURY, COLESHILL, LANDAFF, LONDON NEW, PSALM 100 [OLD], PSALM 148, ST. DAVID'S, ST. JAMES, SOUTHWELL, STANDISH, WINCHESTER, WINDSOR, and YORK.

41. The thirty-two Core Repertory tunes considered here to be in this category are ALL SAINTS, AYLESBURY, BANGOR, BATH, BEDFORD, BROMSGROVE, BUCKINGHAM, BURFORD, COLCHESTER, DALSTON, FUNERAL THOUGHT, IRISH, ISLE OF WIGHT, LITTLE MARLBOROUGH, MEAR, MILFORD, NEWBURY, NEWTON, PLYMOUTH, PORTSMOUTH (no. 61), PSALM 34, PSALM 149, PUTNEY, ROCHESTER, ST. ANNE, ST. HELEN'S, ST. MARTIN'S, ST. THOMAS, WALSALL, WANTAGE, WELLS, and WESTON FAVEL.

42. The fourteen Core Repertory tunes considered here to be in this category are ADESTE FIDELIS, AMSTERDAM, BETHESDA, CHRISTMAS, DENMARK, DUNSTAN, THE DYING CHRISTIAN, HABAKKUK, HOTHAM, KINGSBRIDGE, PORTSMOUTH (no. 62), PORTUGAL, ST. GEORGE'S, and SUTTON (no. 89).

43. The forty-one Core Repertory tunes considered here to be in this category are AMHERST, ANTHEM FOR EASTER, BRIDGEWATER, BRISTOL, BROOKFIELD, CALVARY, CHESTER, CORONATION, ENFIELD, GREENFIELD, GREENWICH, HARTFORD, JORDAN, JUDGMENT, LEBANON, LENOX, LISBON, MAJESTY, MARYLAND, MIDDLETOWN, MONTAGUE, MONTGOMERY, MORNING HYMN, NEW JERUSALEM, NORWICH, OCEAN, PSALM 25, PSALM 33, PSALM 46, PSALM 100 [NEW], PSALM 136, RAINBOW, RUSSIA, SHERBURNE, STAFFORD, SUFFIELD, SUTTON (no. 90), VIRGINIA, WINDHAM, WINTER, and WORCESTER.

Graph 5.2
Tune Types Across Periods

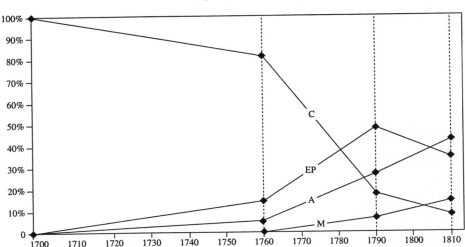

but notable introduction of English Methodist-inspired pieces. Stage III continues these basic trends with a few changes: English parish tunes fall off noticeably, surpassed by American tunes for "most popular,"[44] and Methodist-inspired pieces gain in popularity and overtake slightly common tunes. Graph 5.2 represents these data visually: the "C" line represents common tunes; the "EP" line represents English parish tunes; the "M" line represents English Methodist-inspired tunes; and the "A" line represents American tunes.

In exploring the causes behind these patterns of preference, we are interested both in the introduction of new types at certain points and in the philosophical and tangible sanctioning or disregard for current types. This second factor involves, in addition to patterns in the tunebook industry discussed above, influences from a combination of religious and secular value systems. A useful framework for considering these influences is provided by a recognition of the "Centaurian" nature of sacred music. On the one hand, it is obligated to a larger, "higher" aim as an adjunct to the overall worship ritual. As such, it must remain subordinate to the ultimate objective: the message of God. It should enhance but not interfere with nor distract from the primary vehicle for this message, which in Western culture has always been the sacred text. Simplicity of musical setting, particularly of rhythm and texture, is paramount. On the other hand, music is a "lower," human activity undertaken and enjoyed for its own sake. From this viewpoint, physical and emotional expression, competence, and creativity are completely valid and

---

44. It appears that American tunes accounted for a much larger proportion of the overall repertory printed in American tunebooks during Stage III than the data in table 5.2 indicate. In another source —"'Ancient Music' and the Europeanizing of American Psalmody, 1800-1810," in Richard Crawford, R. Allen Lott, and Carol Oja, eds., *A Celebration of American Music: Words and Music in Honor of H. Wiley Hitchcock* (Ann Arbor: University of Michigan Press, 1990), 227, table 1, and 229, table 2—Crawford presents comparative data on American versus non-American tunes for all sacred pieces printed in American publications during Stages II and III, not just Core Repertory tunes. These figures indicate that during Stage III, and especially during 1790-1805, American tunes outdistanced all non-American tunes (not just parish style) by a significantly greater margin than that shown in table 5.2 here.

valuable pursuits. During the Core Repertory period, as throughout the history of human existence, the balance between these aims for sacred music shifted more than once, and with it the preference for musical style.

As table 5.2 and graph 5.2 indicate, the vast majority of the repertory of sacred music printed in American publications during Stage I was comprised of common tunes of European origin. Rhythmically uniform and unembellished, completely homophonic in texture, the stateliness and simplicity of this style make it ideal sacred music for congregational singing. Its lack of distinct rhythmic profile also makes it versatile, as any text with the correct number of syllables per line can be easily substituted without creating prosody problems. YORK and STANDISH from the Core Repertory provide good examples of this style. During (and before) Stage I, two basic factors served to sanction this tune type. The first was ideological: an emphasis on the worship function of psalmody. The very basis of early colonial culture in New England was Calvinist-based theology, which regarded congregational psalm singing as a centrally important ritual, but musical elaboration in this context as morally corrupting. The second was more circumstantial: the constraints of oral practice. As suggested above, despite the fact that sacred music was being printed in America since 1698, oral practice remained a significant mode of circulation and preservation throughout much of the eighteenth century. In this mode, the inertia of tradition and limits of memory capacity naturally favor well-known and relatively unadorned music. Together, these two factors served to restrict both the repertory size and the style of sacred music during this time.

Even within this confining context, however, shifts in the aims for sacred music did occur. In the so called "Usual Way" or "Old Way" of singing, musical expression and creativity were pursued as passing and ornamental tones were added, extemporaneously on an individual basis, to the primary melodic line.[45] By around 1720, desire among some church leaders to regularize performance practice—as well as to increase the current repertory of sacred music—resulted in the instigation of a reform movement that advocated the implementation of music literacy.[46] The primary vehicle for this reform was the singing school: group instruction in music led by a "singing master." Integral also was a new type of book, the so-called tunebook, which included a selection of pieces plus an instructional preface which addressed basic rudiments of music theory and perhaps vocal production. That the initial impulse of this reform represented a shift back toward religiously-based, conservative esthetic goals was reflected in the fact that two of the first American tunebooks were created by clergymen: Reverend John Tufts's *An Introduction to the Singing of Psalm Tunes* and Reverend Thomas Walter's *The Grounds and Rules of Musick Explained*.[47] Accordingly, singing schools and tunebooks at this point served primarily to reinforce sanctioning of the traditional, common-tune style.

45. For more on the development and characteristics of this style, see Nicholas Temperley, "The Old Way of Singing: Its Origin and Development," *Journal of the American Musicological Society* 34, no. 3 (fall 1981): 511-44.

46. Two useful accounts offering different viewpoints of this reform and the controversy over oral versus written practice can be found in McKay and Crawford, *William Billings of Boston*, 9-20, and Gilbert Chase, *America's Music: From the Pilgrims to the Present*, 3d ed. (Urbana: University of Illinois Press, 1987), 19-37.

47. For more on Tufts's *Introduction*, see Lowens, "John Tufts's *Introduction to the Singing of Psalm-Tunes*," 39-57.

By the end of Stage I, parish-style tunes had begun to augment this traditional repertory. Three English Core Repertory tunes considered here to be of this newer type began appearing in American publications during the mid-1720s,[48] and each had accrued significant "popularity" by 1760. By this time, several other Core Repertory tunes of this type had also appeared at least once in American publications. Still, these appearances account for only one-third of the English parish tunes represented in the Core Repertory; the remaining two-thirds first entered into print in American publications during Stage II. In other words, while English parish tunes made some appearance in American tunebooks during Stage I, their greatest influx was during Stage II. Table 5.2 and graph 5.2 are somewhat misleading in representing the introduction of American tunes during Stage I, for only one anonymous but apparently American tune accounts for all Core Repertory printings of this tune type during this time.[49] The real arrival of substantial numbers of American tunes in print was not until well into Stage II, beginning in the 1770s and especially during the 1780s.[50]

During Stage II, the singing-school tradition became a new outlet for pursuing musical goals, fostering the growth of parish-style repertory of both English and American provenance. As abilities and confidence of singing masters and pupils increased, they both naturally sought more complex and interesting music. The creative results were the introduction and cultivation of more elaborate styles of sacred music and the rise of choirs, trained singers separated from the congregation. By the mid-eighteenth century in England, enterprising country singing masters had begun to compose their own musical settings. As noted above, tunebooks and tunes created by such individuals had begun to circulate in America before the end of Stage I. In post-Revolution peace time, with the English models before them, increasing numbers of ambitious American singing masters composed and published their own settings during the latter half of Stage II. In both countries, with little to no formal training and largely without the aid of a keyboard instrument, these composers reinterpreted and adapted materials and methods according to their own abilities, needs, and tastes, "rediscovering" (not in a historically conscious sense, of course) techniques of composition reaching back to the Renaissance and even Medieval periods. The parish style that resulted was, on the one hand, far simpler and rougher than professionally-composed music of this era. Mid-phrase open-fifth sonorities, "incorrect" part-writing, clashing harmonies, and awkward prosody were not uncommon.[51] But this style also exhibited a spirit of invention and its own expressive nuances. Compared to the common-tune style, melodic lines were ornamented and

---

48. ISLE OF WIGHT, PORTSMOUTH (no. 61), and PSALM 149 were all included in Tufts's *Introduction*, 5th ed. (Boston, 1726).

49. The first known publication of PSALM 100 [NEW] was in an earlier edition of Tufts's *Introduction* (3d ed., 1723). Its composer is unknown, but is supposed to be American and perhaps Tufts himself. See Lowens, "John Tufts's *Introduction to the Singing of Psalm-Tunes*," 51-55.

50. Only two other American tunes from the Core Repertory appeared in print before 1770: MORNING HYMN and PSALM 33. Both first appeared in James Lyon's *Urania* (Philadelphia, 1761).

51. For further discussion and examples of the development of the parish style, see Nicholas Temperley, *Music of the English Parish Church*, 2 vols. (Cambridge: Cambridge University Press, 1979), 1:141-203, especially 162-65 and 170-76, and Kroeger, *Complete Works of William Billings*, 1:xviii-xxviii.

rhythmic motion was enlivened through the use of varied metric and note-value patterns.[52] A comparison of YORK and STANDISH with the parish-style Core Repertory tunes ALL SAINTS and BANGOR illustrates early stages of such elaboration. It was the realm of textural variety, however, in which country psalmodists showed the greatest ingenuity and daring. The most conspicuous example of such textural innovation was the celebrated fuging tune, which for many epitomizes the parish style, and of which there are many examples in the Core Repertory.[53]

The Methodist-inspired style, though very different from the parish style and springing from different circumstances, shares the same general impulse toward musical appeal and also made a first and significant impact on American psalmody contribution during Stage II. First introduced in England around 1740,[54] a dozen tunes of this type were reprinted in American publications during Stage II, with a handful accruing substantial popularity here by 1790. With the goal of creating a more "popular" style of sacred music, English Methodist composers incorporated traits from contemporary secular music. Pieces in this style often resemble late Baroque/early Classical instrumental trio sonatas or Italianate solo songs. They are simple in texture compared to the parish style, are ornate and elegant in melodic line, have harmonically-oriented bass parts, and often exhibit instrumental formal logic. The Core Repertory tune DENMARK is a good example. While no American psalmodists adopted this style outright, as early as Stage II some did incorporate elements from it into their own compositional techniques; Amos Bull's MIDDLETOWN, a Stage II Core Repertory piece, is an example.[55]

The basic preference patterns established during Stage II were continued into Stage III with no drastic changes. Parish-style works, of both English and American origin, remained the mainstay of the Core Repertory. Not clearly indicated, however, was one more shift, albeit brief in context of the Core Repertory period, in the ideals for sacred music. During the first decade of the nineteenth century, a conservative reform impulse emerged once more as religious leaders sensed in the parish style music that was

---

52. Crawford's discussion of the evolving rhythmic styles in American psalmody (*Core Repertory*, xii-xiii) is largely a description of the developing elaboration in the parish style from the perspective of rhythm. It is also worthy of note that rhythm was one realm in which New England composers developed recognizable "Americanisms" within the parish style. Particularly cultivated was what Crawford has called "declamatory duple" rhythmic motion, based on the steady, pumping motion of continuous, undecorated quarter-notes.

53. See Nicholas Temperley, "Historical Introduction," in Temperley and Charles G. Manns, *Fuging Tunes in the Eighteenth Century* (Detroit: Information Coordinators, 1983), for discussion of the development of the fuging tune in English psalmody. See Irving Lowens, "Origins of the American Fuging-Tune," in *Music and Musicians in Early America*, for discussion of the fuging tune in American psalmody.

54. See Temperley, *Music of the English Parish Church*, 1:204-23, especially 207-13, for discussion of the advent and characteristics of the Methodist style. The two main English sources for Methodist-style pieces reprinted in America were Thomas Butts's *Harmonia sacra* (London, [ca. 1760]), and Martin Madan's so-called Lock Hospital Collection *A Collection of Psalm and Hymn Tunes . . . to be had at the Lock Hospital* (London, 1769).

55. See also my observations on possible Methodist-style influences in the music of Elias Mann in my dissertation, 159, 188, and 199-200. A broad study of Methodist-style influences upon the compositional styles of American composers could prove valuable for understanding changes in indigenous American psalmody in its late stages.

inappropriately secular and complex for worship.[56] Instead, they advocated music that was suitably simple and dignified, what a contemporary singing master and later chronicler of American psalmody, Nathaniel Gould, referred to as "ancient" music.[57] And there was yet another aspect of this shift in ideals. As we have seen with regard to the Methodist-inspired style, European music in a more refined, contemporary idiom had begun to influence American psalmody during Stage II. During the 1790s and 1800s, while some American composers were continuing to develop their craft in the parish style, others, largely as the result of contact with classically-trained emigrant musicians and compositions by European masters of the art, came to question and even condemn their own indigenous music on purely technical grounds.[58] On the one hand, such self-criticism may be viewed as a healthy quest for growth among American composers. Yet the matter of provenance also became an argument in itself, with "progressive" musicians and critics claiming that European music was intrinsically superior to American. As Crawford notes, this "Europeanization" remained merely an "influence" on American psalmody until it was linked to the more radical "reform" advocated by religious leaders, at which point "European" became another label alongside "ancient" used to indicate "proper" music. One result was that, in the last five years of the Core Repertory period, printings of tunes of American provenance declined noticeably, while European tunes, including some in parish style, received a significant boost in popularity.[59] While this shift was certainly a harbinger of the situation to come, within the context of Stage III as a whole the decline in American tunes was not significant enough to negate the increasing majority they enjoyed during the previous two and a half decades; thus, no apparent decline is evident in table 5.2 and graph 5.2. But table 5.2 and graph 5.2 do seem to reflect a slowing in the decline of common tunes during this time, as some of these truly "ancient" pieces enjoyed some revival in pro-reform and reform-influenced collections, as well as the increasing popularity of Methodist-style works.

In sum, based originally entirely on a traditional repertory of common tunes, American psalmody's stylistic breadth began to expand as of mid-Stage I and blossomed during Stage II. More than any other single factor, the singing-school tradition was

---

56. Sidney E. Ahlstrom, *A Religious History of the American People* (New Haven: Yale University Press, 1972), 403-06, attributes the roots of this conservative force in the latter eighteenth century to a split among New England theologians into three factions: the "Old Calvinists" (moderates), "Arminians" (liberals), and the "New Divinity" (conservatives). Ahlstrom connects the rise of the New Divinity to dominance around the turn of the century to the influence of the Second Great Awakening in New England (pp. 415-17).

57. See Crawford, "'Ancient Music' and the Europeanizing of American Psalmody," 225-35.

58. See ibid., 235-37. *The Massachusetts Compiler of Theoretical and Practical Elements of Sacred Vocal Music* (Boston, [1795]), conjointly compiled by Samuel Holyoke, Oliver Holden, and Hans Gram, was heralded as a landmark publication in this regard. This collection not only offered a repertory "chiefly selected or adapted from Modern European Publications" (title page), but also provided the most extensive technical discussion to date of musical theory available to American psalmodists, compiled by the classically-trained emigrant organist Hans Gram, from European theoretical treatises.

59. See Crawford, "'Ancient Music' and the Europeanizing of American Psalmody," 229, table 2. The confusion resulting from mixing "ancient" and "European" as ideals is evident in the fact that of the sixteen tunes that Crawford (n. 19) lists as common to nine devoutly pro-reform collections, at least ten are English parish-style tunes, only one of which (MEAR) received more than one printing during Stage I.

responsible for this expansion. But Stage II also marks the end of this expansion; by 1790, the stylistic breadth of American psalmody was established. These facts again point to the pivotal position of Stage II in forming the Core Repertory view of American psalmody.

As a final perspective on tune type preference, it is useful to inquire how the Core Repertory portrayal of American psalmody would change if the sampling period were abridged to a portion of its present length. Comparisons between individual stages and totals for each tune type in table 5.2 reveal that the total proportions are least like Stage I and most like a blend of Stages II and III. In fact, when figures for Stages II and III are combined—as if the sampling period were limited to the years 1761-1810—the data turn out nearly identical to those of the present entire Core Repertory: 12 percent (799/6843) common tunes; 39 percent (2668/6843) English parish tunes; 11 percent (764/6843) English Methodist-inspired pieces; and 38 percent (2612/6843) American tunes. This fact corroborates the picture that has emerged during the previous examination of patterns in total numbers of tunes printed and in numbers of each type printed across the three stages: the essential preference patterns which characterize the Core Repertory view were established during Stage II and were solidified during Stage III through large numbers of printings with only minor changes in repertory. From the opposite angle, if the Core Repertory sampling period were limited to the years represented by Stage I, the Core Repertory view would look entirely different, with a much smaller and very different body of music represented. This suggests that the present Core Repertory really represents two fairly distinct bodies of sacred music and two eras—one geared toward congregational singing and consisting of simpler, more traditional pieces, the other geared toward the singing-school tradition and choirs, consisting of more elaborate music—and that subdividing the Core Repertory between Stages I and Stage II would provide a truer picture of the musical preferences at a given point.[60]

It is also valuable to ask what the Core Repertory does not seem to accurately represent. First, it seems to underrepresent the importance of the traditional common-style tunes. The Tune Type Total in table 5.2 suggests that they account for only fifteen percent's worth of weight in the overall tradition of American psalmody. But if, as Crawford suggests, the Core Repertory "documents persistence and continuity in a context of change" (*Core Repertory*, ix), these common tunes—perhaps more as symbols than as specific pieces—constitute the backbone of that persistence and continuity. Moreover, the record of their importance has been recorded as much in people's memories and feelings as in print. Second, an enormous amount of new music, largely by American composers, was first published during Stage III ("approximately five times as many new sacred pieces were printed as had appeared in the previous 90 years"—ibid., x) that, due primarily to tunebook industry influences discussed above, remains almost entirely excluded from the Core Repertory. Finally, the Core Repertory does not necessarily represent the "best" of American psalmody. Instead, it is primarily a record of the most

---

60. One could also make a strong case for treating the reform period from 1805 on as a third era. As noted, the musical "preferences" changed rather radically during these final years of the Core Repertory period and, as Crawford notes, "all available evidence . . . indicates that between 1811 and 1820, the pro-European trend continued and that the European pieces in print once again outnumbered the American" ("'Ancient Music' and the Europeanizing of American Psalmody," 228).

commercially successful pieces in American psalmody. And as those of us who live with an economy based on freemarket capitalism will recognize, "preference for" and "success of" a particular commodity are often determined more by production and marketing influences than by intrinsic product merits.

*   *   *

This brings me back to my original impetus for inquiring into the nature of the Core Repertory, the music of Elias Mann, for an example of the effects of influences discussed here on the publication patterns of one sacred composer's works. Mann was a prominent and influential Massachusetts psalmodist active from approximately 1785-1810—that is, from the latter half of Stage II through Stage III. His products as a composer and compiler include roughly fifty published sacred works, many of them sizable, and three tunebooks. His musical career divides neatly into three phases, the first of which was an eight-year period in Worcester. During this time, roughly one-third of Mann's published compositional output first appeared in print, and he most likely served as musical consultant for the first five editions of Isaiah Thomas's *Worcester Collection* (1786-94). Mann spent the next eight or nine years in the relatively small western Massachusetts town of Northampton, where he achieved his career peak in terms of musical output and renown, known locally as "Master Mann." During this time, well over half of his published works appeared for the first time in print, and he produced two of his own tunebooks, *The Northampton Collection*, first and second editions (1797, 1802). For the remainder of his musical career, Mann moved to Boston, apparently in pursuit of new and "progressive" musical influences. There he produced his third tunebook, *The Massachusetts Collection* (1807), published a few remaining sacred works, kept a manuscript containing as many as sixteen additional original pieces, and involved himself in the activities of two pro-reform musical societies.

Throughout his career, Mann's compositional style was essentially parish style, though his works from 1799 begin to exhibit some signs of simplification and Europeanization, particularly in formal types and techniques, rhythmic restraint, and to some degree in melodic character. Similarly, his first two tunebooks are clearly products of a local composer-compiler, intended for singing-school use, whereas the size, repertory, rhetoric, and style of *The Massachusetts Collection* demonstrate significant pro-reform influences and suggest congregational use. His greatest distinction as a composer lies in his cultivation of and excellence in the set-piece form.[61] Set-pieces comprise 44 percent of his overall published output of sacred music and constitute 67 percent of his mature works before reform influences begin to become evident. Perhaps more important is the artistic excellence he achieved in his best set-pieces, that successfully combine convincing setting of the text with unity and complexity of form.[62]

---

61. Set-piece is the term used to denote a through-composed setting of a metrical text, often several verses in length. This distinguishes it from the anthem, which sets a prose text. See also *New Grove Dictionary of American Music*, s.v. "Set-piece," by Richard Crawford.

62. One of Mann's better set-pieces, his No. 12, is presented in full and discussed in detail in my dissertation, 68-70, and appendix 1.

Since Mann composed some truly impressive works and was apparently highly regarded in his own time, the question arises as to why his music achieved only limited success in Core Repertory terms. Several factors related to issues discussed above seem to be at least influential if not directly at cause. One was timing. Mann's first published works appeared in 1786, and roughly 85 percent of his published compositions first appeared after 1790. As noted above, after 1790 the commercial market for psalm tunes was besieged with new products, while tunebook industry practices and copyright protection severely limited the probable impact of any new piece. Another factor was location. Mann's greatest period of success was spent as a local musician in the relatively rural area around Northampton, where the population he and his music reached was relatively small. Yet another factor was his compositional predilection for the set-piece. While this relatively lengthy and complex form may have offered him the greatest personal challenge and satisfaction as a composer, its inherent difficulty and non-utilitarian nature automatically precluded a "popular" status.[63]

In light of such points, it is useful to survey which of Mann's sacred pieces did achieve the greatest "popularity," for influences from issues and circumstances discussed here can be observed in action. Table 5.3 lists Mann's sacred works that received three or more printings.[64]

Table 5.3. Mann's Sacred Works That Received Three or More Total Printings

Tune Name	Number of Printings
No. 5	12
No. 6	12
No. 1	9
No. 2	8
No. 3	8
No. 8	7
No. 30	7
SOLITUDE	6
No. 29	6
No. 12	5
SUPPLEMENT TO DENMARK	4
No. 4	3
DOXOLOGY	3
No. 19	3
No. 21	3
No. 22	3
No. 24	3
No. 27	3
No. 35	3
No. 41	3

63. Core Repertory statistics also support this fact: only two of the 101 works are set-pieces.

64. For a complete record of the printings of Mann's published compositions, see my dissertation, appendix 7.

Seven of these works—NO. 6, NO. 1, NO. 2, NO. 3, SOLITUDE, NO. 12, and DOXOLOGY—received one or more printings in the first five editions of *The Worcester Collection*, for which Mann probably served as musical advisor. In addition, virtually all of Mann's sacred pieces received at least one, and as many as three, printings in his own tunebooks. A few of the pieces in table 5.3 also appeared in three other publications besides *The Worcester Collection* with which Mann very probably had direct affiliation.[65] Thus, while table 5.3 gives a sense of the total amount of published exposure some of Mann's sacred pieces received, an equally valuable perspective is gained by noting which pieces were most often reprinted by other compilers, for this gives us some idea which pieces were "preferred" by others. Table 5.4 lists Mann's sacred works that received three or more printings in publications other than his own tunebooks or those with which he was probably directly affiliated.

Table 5.4. Mann's Sacred Works That Received Three or More Printings
in Publications Other Than His Own Tunebooks or Publications
with Which He Was Directly Affiliated

Tune Name	Number of Printings
NO. 5	8
SOLITUDE	6
NO. 1	4
NO. 2	4
NO. 6	4
NO. 8	4
NO. 29	4
NO. 30	4

These eight pieces fall into two groups which seem to reflect two different spheres of influence. The first group—SOLITUDE, NO. 1, NO. 2, and NO. 6—were first published 1786-91 during Mann's early years in Worcester. Their "popularity" seems to have resulted primarily from the influence of the "formula" approach to tunebook compilation. As well as being a commercially successful tunebook widely used by the public in its own right, *The Worcester Collection* was consulted by several other compilers as a model and tune source for their own collections. Four other publications that were crucial to the published dissemination of these four tunes—Daniel Bayley's *The New Harmony of Zion*, *The Federal Harmony*, *Sacred Harmony*, and Henry Ranlet's *Village Harmony*—were directly influenced by and drew extensively upon *The Worcester Collection*.[66] The importance of 1790 as a watershed may also have been important: only six of Mann's

---

65. These three publications—*The American Musical Magazine*, *The American Musical Miscellany*, and *The Patriotic Gazette*—were printed and published by Northampton printer Andrew Wright. Several circumstances establish close ties between Mann and Wright, most significantly: Andrew and his uncle, Daniel Wright, printed and published Mann's *Northampton Collection*, first and second editions, and Mann's second wife, Asenath, was Daniel's sister and Andrew's aunt.

66. In Kroeger's survey of tunebooks that shared a common repertory with *The Worcester Collection*, all four of these collections ranked in the top ten, with *Federal Harmony* and *Sacred Harmony* occupying the number one and two positions, respectively. See "The Worcester Collection of Sacred Harmony," 510-17, especially table 53.

sacred works appeared in print before 1790, and three of these (SOLITUDE, NO. 1, and NO. 2) are included in table 5.4. The other group comes from the years 1799-1802, as Mann's compositional style began to show reform influences. NO. 5, NO. 8, and NO. 29 are all relatively short works, similar in form and style. In each, the music is divided into two equal-length sections, with the second half repeated. The second half begins with two lines of text set in a duet, moving predominantly in parallel thirds or sixths, then returns to the full four-part texture to close. The relative simplicity of form and texture (compared to a fuging tune, set-piece, or anthem), afforded sufficient interest by the textural and timbral variety (compared to a plain tune) may have struck reform-influenced compilers as a good balance between simplicity and tasteful variety. NO. 30 features a graceful melodic line, with contours consisting largely of triadic outlines and filled-in thirds, set in a smooth rhythmic style of simply embellished iambic motion in triple meter. In short, Mann's most "popular" sacred pieces were those that appeared in *The Worcester Collection* or publications with which Mann had direct contact, appeared in "formula" tunebooks drawing upon *The Worcester Collection*, were first published before the Federal copyright law of 1790, or conformed to the esthetic standards of the reform movement of the early nineteenth century.

*   *   *

The objectivity and quality of the Core Repertory study make it extremely useful and an important contribution to psalmody scholarship. The chosen criterion is simple, sufficiently definable, and meaningful; it is probably the single most representative and feasible gauge for quantifying this cultural tradition. Perhaps more important is the excellence of Crawford's scholarship, combining painstaking thoroughness with extraordinary breadth and depth of insight. Nonetheless, a single criterion can only provide a limited and somewhat biased viewpoint, especially when applied to varied and changing circumstances. In light of issues raised and points discussed here, three adjuncts to the Core Repertory seem important for a more accurate appraisal of early American psalmody. The first is the acknowledgment of other valid and significant, though less quantifiable, expressions of preference in addition to appearances in print. This seems particularly critical for fair representation and understanding of the years before significant growth in the sacred music industry—i.e., before and during Stage I. The second is an appreciation of the dynamism of American psalmody. The repertory and character of this cultural tradition changed direction more than once over the course of the Core Repertory period, particularly during the latter eighteenth and early nineteenth centuries, in response to many influences, non-musical as well as musical. By subdividing the Core Repertory temporally, charting characteristics of the repertory during different stages, and contemplating connections between apparent influences and observed changes in the repertory, one can begin to get a sense of the "life" of this custom.[67] The third is a recognition of the relatively huge but essentially lost body of American sacred

---

67. One could certainly also create regional subdivisions, charting the publication location of each collection (though this would not always correspond to the location of composition or compilation) in which a given tune appeared.

music that first appeared in print after 1790. As the example of Elias Mann testifies, some excellent music was created during this time, representing both the zenith of parish-style psalmody in America and continuing stylistic evolution among American composers of sacred music in response to new influences.[68] Taking these adjunct considerations into account would seem to provide a more inclusive, vital, and representative picture of American psalmody during this period.

---

68. Fortunately, scholarly editions of the sacred works of many lesser known American psalmodists are presently being undertaken. David Warren Steel's edition *Stephen Jenks: Collected Works* is published as vol. 18 of Recent Researches in American Music (Madison, Wisc.: A-R Editions). Karl Kroeger is serving as editor-in-chief for a fifteen-volume series, Music of the New American Nation (New York: Garland, 1996) that includes editions of the sacred music of Samuel Babcock, Supply Belcher, Daniel Belknap, Asahel Benham, Jacob French, Samuel Holyoke, Elias Mann, Joseph Stone, Abraham Wood, and others.

6

Practicality, Patriotism, and Piety: Principal Motivators for Maine Tunebook Compilers, 1794-1830

Linda G. Davenport

At the turn of the nineteenth century, the northeast frontier was a popular destination for young adults from southern New England, particularly Massachusetts, who sought inexpensive land on which to settle. Transportation by sea made Maine, a district of Massachusetts until 1820, particularly accessible and attractive for those without the funds for a long overland journey.

The hardy new residents brought with them the Sabbath worship practices of their New England upbringing. In some areas, they met together in the town meetinghouse for "Divine Service"; in other places, they gathered informally with their neighbors in a schoolhouse, barn, or private home to hear an itinerant preacher. Regardless of the setting, music was an important component of worship.

An earlier version of this essay was read at the annual meeting of the Sonneck Society for American Music in Hampton, Virginia in April 1991, and forms part of my Ph.D. dissertation, "Maine's Sacred Tunebooks, 1800-1830: Divine Song on the Northeast Frontier" (University of Colorado at Boulder, 1991), and my book *Divine Song on the Northeast Frontier: Maine's Sacred Tunebooks, 1800-1830* (Lanham, Md.: Scarecrow Press, 1996). My research in New England was partially funded by two University of Colorado Graduate School Dean's Small Grant Awards. I am grateful to Professor Karl Kroeger, my dissertation advisor, and Professor William Kearns, my pre-dissertation advisor and doctoral committee member, for their suggestions and encouragement during the preparation of this study, and to Nym Cooke and the late Susan L. Porter for their knowledgeable and incisive comments.

Table 6.1. Chronological List of Extant Maine Tunebooks, 1794-1830

Date	Title	Compiler(s)	Publisher	Place of Publication
1794	The Harmony of Maine	Supply Belcher	Isaiah Thomas and E. T. Andrews	Boston
1802	The Oriental Harmony	Abraham Maxim	Henry Ranlet	Exeter, N.H.
1805	The Columbian Harmony	Charles Robbins	Henry Ranlet for the author	Exeter, N.H.
1805	The Northern Harmony	Abraham Maxim	Henry Ranlet for the compiler	Exeter, N.H.
1808	The Northern Harmony/2	Abraham Maxim	Norris and Sawyer	Exeter, N.H.
1813	The Parish Harmony	J. C. Washburn	C. Norris & Co. for the author	Exeter, N.H.
1815	The Chorister's Companion	Edward Hartwell	C. Norris & Co. for the author	Exeter, N.H.
1816	*The Northern Harmony/4	A. Maxim and J. C. Washburn	E. Goodale	Hallowell, Me.
1817	The Hallowell Collection of Sacred Music	[Ezekiel Goodale?]	E. Goodale	Hallowell, Me.
1818	The Temple Harmony	J. C. Washburn	E. Goodale and J. C. Washburn, Esq.	Hallowell, Me.
1819	The Hallowell Coll./2	[Ezekiel Goodale?]	E. Goodale	Hallowell, Me.
1819	*The Northern Harmony/5	Abraham Maxim	E. Goodale	Hallowell, Me.
1820	The Wesleyan Harmony	Henry Little	E. Goodale	Hallowell, Me.
1820	The Temple Harmony/2	J. C. Washburn	Goodale, Glazier & Co.	Hallowell, Me.
1821	The Wesleyan Harmony/2	Henry Little	Goodale, Glazier & Co.	Hallowell, Me.
1821	The Temple Harmony/3	J. C. Washburn	Goodale, Glazier & Co	Hallowell, Me.
1823	The Temple Harmony/4	J. C. Washburn	Goodale, Glazier & Co.	Hallowell, Me.
1824/5?	The Temple Harmony/5	J. C. Washburn	[Goodale, Glazier & Co.]	Hallowell, Me.
1826	The Temple Harmony/6	J. C. Washburn	Glazier & Co.	Hallowell, Me.
1830	Songs of Sion	[Smith Hinkley & Christopher T. Norcross]	Hinkley & Norcross	Charleston, Me.

Second and later editions are indicated by "/2," etc. after the title. An asterisk (*) notes works for which I have located only incomplete copies.

Printed collections called "tunebooks" provided the tunes for the singing, while psalters and hymnals supplied the texts.[1] The tunebooks typically began with several pages of instructions on the fundamentals of music, followed by three- and four-voice unaccompanied choral settings. The publications were used not only in churches but also in singing schools by students learning music reading and choral singing. Table 6.1 lists the extant tunebooks compiled in Maine in the late eighteenth and early nineteenth centuries.

Most of the Maine tunebook compilers, like many other new settlers to the area, were born in Massachusetts proper but moved to the District of Maine[2] in the late eighteenth century. Table 6.2 provides a biographical overview of these psalmodists. They had varied musical backgrounds. Some, like Supply Belcher and Abraham Maxim, are thought to have attended singing schools taught by William Billings.[3] The formal musical training of others, such as Henry Little, may have been negligible or even nonexistent. Most, but not all, were composers who published their own tunes along with those by others. Like many of the better-known Yankee psalmodists, they pursued musical activities as a sideline to other professions, which included farming, teaching, cabinet making, and trading.

Significantly, these compilers lived not in the more cultured, established, southern Maine towns such as Portland, but in burgeoning inland or river towns. Figure 6.1 shows the locations of the towns where they lived when they compiled their collections. Sacred music collections published in Boston or Exeter, New Hampshire, were easily obtained by merchants in the older coastal towns and may have been quite adequate for southern Maine citizens, who were often culturally allied with Massachusetts urban society. Such publications may have been less suitable for those living in small Maine towns on the leading edge of the frontier. My study of the prefaces and repertory of the twenty extant Maine editions published between 1794 and 1830 suggests that practicality, patriotism, and piety motivated the Maine psalmodists to compile them.

A concern for practicality, in particular, is a thread running through many of the prefaces. As recent settlers themselves, the psalmodists recognized that many potential tunebook purchasers in their area were subsistence farmers struggling to make a living. Farming was not easy in Maine with its rocky soil, harsh winters, and short growing season. Neither was cash plentiful; the new settlers frequently bartered their goods and labor with each other. The depiction of the typical "Down Easter" as thrifty may not be an invalid stereotype; out of necessity, Mainers had to be frugal. As a result, several of the Maine compilers sought to provide tunebooks that cost less. In his "advertisement" in

---

1. A single stanza of text was usually printed beneath the music in tunebooks. Additional stanzas were obtained from hymnals or psalters. Since the appropriate meter was indicated above most tunes, any other text of the same meter could be substituted for the printed one. Singers did not necessarily have to refer to tunebooks and wordbooks in tandem, since familiar tunes or texts could be sung from memory.

2. Until Maine statehood was achieved in 1820, the official name of the region was the "District of Maine." To simplify references, however, I will use "Maine" hereafter to refer to both the District of Maine and the State of Maine.

3. Although this supposition may very well be true, it can only be backed up, at present, by circumstantial evidence and hearsay testimony (the latter being a letter written by Abraham's considerably younger brother, John). See Davenport, *Divine Song on the Northeast Frontier*, 82, 84, 314 (n. 19).

Table 6.2. Compilers of Maine Tunebooks, 1794-1830

Compiler	Place of Birth	Occupation	Maine Town	Tunebook(s)
*Supply Belcher (1751-1836)	Mass.	Teacher, justice of the peace, legislative representative, tavern keeper	Farmington (5)	The Harmony of Maine (1794)
*Edward Hartwell (1747-1844)	Mass.	Ferry-boat operator, farmer	Bloomfield (1)	The Chorister's Companion (1815)
Henry Little (1788-1878)	N.H.	Clerk, trader, postmaster	Bucksport (2)	The Wesleyan Harmony, 2 eds. (1820, 1821)
*Abraham Maxim (1773-1829)	Mass.	Teacher, farmer	Turner (7)	The Oriental Harmony (1802); The Northern Harmony, 5 eds. (1805-19)
*Charles Robbins (1782-1842)	Mass.	Cabinetmaker, tavern keeper	Winthrop (8)	The Columbian Harmony (1805)
*Japheth Coombs Washburn (1780-1850)	Mass.	Store owner, trader, justice of the peace, postmaster, legislative representative	China (4)	The Parish Harmony (1813); The Temple Harmony, 7 eds. (1818-27); The Northern Harmony, 4th ed. (1816) (co-compiler with Maxim)
(Possible compilers—not named on title pages)				
Ezekiel Goodale (1780-1828)	Mass.	Publisher	Hallowell (6)	The Hallowell Coll., 2 eds. (1817, 1819)
Smith Hinkley &	?	Clergyman	Charleston (3)	Songs of Sion (1830)
Christopher Norcross	?	Farmer?	Charleston (3)	

* Denotes those who were composers as well as compilers. Numbers next to town names correspond to locations on fig. 1 map.

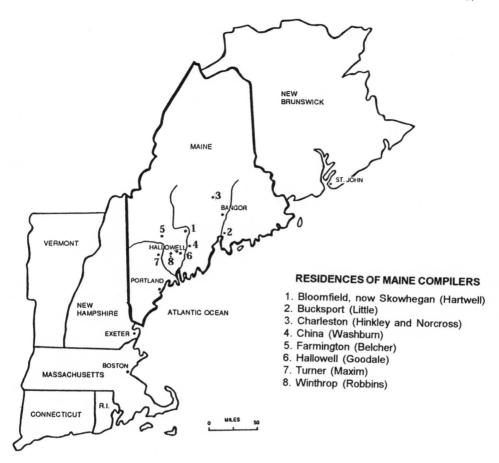

RESIDENCES OF MAINE COMPILERS

1. Bloomfield, now Skowhegan (Hartwell)
2. Bucksport (Little)
3. Charleston (Hinkley and Norcross)
4. China (Washburn)
5. Farmington (Belcher)
6. Hallowell (Goodale)
7. Turner (Maxim)
8. Winthrop (Robbins)

Figure 6.1. Maine and Its Neighbors.

Parish Harmony (1813), store owner Japheth Coombs Washburn noted that the expense of the various large music books in use made it difficult for some societies to purchase them. His smaller and less expensive volume would make it possible for singing schools and societies to be "more generally furnished with Books."[4] At six dollars per dozen, *Parish Harmony* was cheaper than the very popular *Village Harmony,* for example, which sold in Maine for as much as $8.50 per dozen for some editions.[5]

A concern for expense was also expressed by Edward Hartwell, whose *Chorister's Companion* attempted to provide "a greater variety of approved tunes" at more moderate

---

4. Japheth Coombs Washburn, *The Parish Harmony, or Fairfax Collection of Sacred Musick* (Exeter, N.H.: C. Norris & Co. for the author, 1813), [3].

5. For example, an advertisement in the *Hallowell Gazette* 9, no. 40 (2 October 1822): 3, for Hallowell booksellers Goodale, Glazier & Co., lists *The Village Harmony,* 16th ed. (1819), at $8.50 per dozen. Of course, the 350-page *Village Harmony* was considerably larger than the 133-page *Parish Harmony.*

cost.[6] Similarly, Henry Little, who compiled the Methodist-oriented *Wesleyan Harmony* in 1820, hoped, among other things, "to save more than one half of the expense for Singing Books."[7] His prepublication solicitation stated that the price would be just 45 to 50 cents each, depending on the binding selected.[8]

Several Maine psalmodists, then, specifically chose to compile books that were smaller and less expensive than others on the market. No doubt they expected that their potential customer base would be expanded if their collections were within the affordable range for more people. To produce these smaller books, the compilers probably tried to include only pieces that had a reasonable chance of being performed by Maine singers.

One genre they cut back was the anthem, an extended setting of Biblical prose. Anthems were more difficult to compose and perform than simple psalm or hymn tunes. Unlike today, when church choirs frequently perform an anthem as a regular part of the Sunday service, anthems in the early nineteenth century were normally performed only on special occasions such as Thanksgiving, fast days, ordinations, and funerals, or at the exhibition held at the conclusion of a singing school. Perhaps because of the greater demand for psalm and hymn tunes sung in weekly church services, most of the early Maine tunebooks focus on such tunes and include less than a handful of anthems. Several collections include only one.[9] The other genre of extended length, the set-piece, also received only limited space in the Maine tunebooks, probably because of the smaller number of occasions on which such pieces would be performed. Set-pieces are through-composed settings of metrical poetry.

Besides tailoring their smaller collections to the needs of Maine singers, some Maine compilers took into account that singing schools were not as available in the newly-settled areas of Maine as in other areas of New England. Charles Robbins, in his *Columbian Harmony* (1805), purposefully laid down the Rules of Music "in a very plain manner"[10] to assist those without the opportunity of attending singing school. His theoretical introduction, where the rudiments were explained, fills twenty-four pages, making it the longest and most detailed of any found in the Maine tunebooks.

Another aspect of the Maine collections' practicality is their versatility. One of my favorite examples of Yankee versatility, as well as of Down-East thrift, is a traditional New England meal called "Red Flannel Hash," so named because of its red color. This entreé consists of the leftovers of a New England boiled dinner (beets, potatoes, carrots, and cabbage), mashed together and fried for another meal. The boiled vegetables, which are

---

6. Edward Hartwell, *The Chorister's Companion* (Exeter, N.H.: C. Norris & Co. for the Author, 1815), [3].

7. Henry Little, *The Wesleyan Harmony* (Hallowell, Me.: E. Goodale, 1820), [3].

8. *Hallowell Gazette* 7, no. 7 (16 February 1820): 3. Once published, the price was slightly higher ($62\frac{1}{2}$ cents, single), but still on the low side for tunebooks. The selling price was considerably less a few years later (1822 and 1824) when *Wesleyan Harmony* was advertised at $3.50 per dozen, a cost of less than 30 cents a copy. *Hallowell Gazette* 7, no. 24 (14 June 1820): 3; 9, no. 40 (2 October 1822): 3; 11, no. 37 (15 September 1824): 3.

9. Washburn notes in the preface of *The Parish Harmony*, [3], that he had originally planned to include several anthems, but decided that "Psalm Tunes might be more useful in a Book of this size, and equally acceptable to people in general," and consequently included but one anthem (for Thanksgiving).

10. Charles Robbins, *The Columbian Harmony: or, Maine Collection of Church Music* (Exeter, N.H.: Printed at the Music-Press of Henry Ranlet, for the author, 1805), [iii].

used in two different contexts, serve double duty. Similarly, the Maine tunebooks, like most New England collections of the period, were designed for at least two different groups—singing schools and churches. The Maine compilers often noted that no tunes had been included that would be unsuitable for singing in church. Other uses included musical societies and family gatherings.

In addition to choosing pieces appropriate to the various occasions on which they would be sung, the Maine psalmodists, like many other New England compilers, attempted to satisfy a variety of tastes and abilities by including tunes of varying styles and difficulty. Supply Belcher, the compiler of the earliest of the collections, wrote that he had included a number of easy airs for learners and more difficult ones "for the amusement of those who have made some proficiency."[11]

From the earliest to the latest, the Maine tunebooks were oriented to provide something for everyone. Perhaps because tunebooks limited to the pieces of a single composer were less able to achieve this goal, only the two earliest collections, Belcher's *Harmony of Maine* and Maxim's *Oriental Harmony*, were devoted exclusively to tunes composed by their compilers. The later tunebooks all contained pieces by many different composers.

In addition to providing music for various uses and abilities, compilers in general were careful to include tunes for a variety of poetic meters, proportionate to the number of hymns and psalms written in those meters.[12] The Maine compilers were not exceptions in this regard. Washburn noted that the fourth edition of his *Temple Harmony* contained music for all the meters in Watts's *Psalms and Hymns* and Winchell's supplement thereto.[13] Likewise, Little's tunebook contained tunes for all the Particular Meter hymns in the Methodist hymnbook. He had discovered that not all the Methodist hymns could be sung because there were few tunes of the appropriate meters. Perhaps to ensure that sales were not limited to Methodists, though, his title page described the book as "Designed for the Methodist Societies, but proper for all Denominations."[14]

The Maine compilers were not unique in seeking to provide tunebooks suitable for different texts, functions, tastes, and skill levels. Such a goal was shared by most tunebook compilers throughout New England. Although some collections were intended for a

11. Supply Belcher, *The Harmony of Maine* (Boston: Isaiah Thomas and Ebenezer T. Andrews, 1794), [3].

12. This idea is suggested by Richard Crawford in an essay titled "William Billings (1746-1800) and American Psalmody: A Study of Musical Dissemination," in *The American Musical Landscape* (Berkeley: University of California Press, 1993), 146-47. He observes that the nineteen Billings tunes Simeon Jocelin chose to reprint from *The Singing Master's Assistant* for Jocelin's *Chorister's Companion* (1782) represent a balanced cross-section of the meters and styles of declamation found in eighteenth-century Anglo-American psalmody. He proposes that Jocelin chose the tunes (which cover all but one meter in the hymnbook) because they met his need for tunes of various textual meters.

13. Japheth Coombs Washburn, *The Temple Harmony*, 4th ed. (Hallowell, Me.: Goodale, Glazier & Co., 1823), [3].

14. Little, [3], [1]. The tunebook's usefulness to other denominations resided in the fact that a substantial number of its tunes set the usual Common, Short, and Long Meters in which most hymns and psalms were written.

single use,[15] the more common practice was to compile a multi-function work with the potential for sales in greater numbers.

Maine compilers, however, differed from their New England colleagues in the subtle patriotism they displayed by continuing to publish tunes "made in the U.S.A." later than other compilers. Pieces by American composers are found in Maine tunebooks even in the 1820s, well after European pieces had gained ascendancy in most other New England collections.

In the preface to the second edition of his *Northern Harmony* (1808), Abraham Maxim indicated that the additional music he had selected for this expanded edition was "mostly American, from an idea that the European Music, is less agreeable to the American ear, than her own."[16] His is a remarkable statement for 1808, when American sacred choral pieces were considered by many on these shores to be inferior to those by Europeans. Contemporaneous Massachusetts reform collections such as *The Salem Collection* (1805-06) and *The Middlesex Collection* (1807-11) were emphasizing so-called "ancient" tunes by eminent European composers. Richard Crawford has noted that by 1810 even eclectic collections such as *The Village Harmony* contained a core of older, European tunes in a simple style.[17] Meanwhile in Maine, Maxim and his colleagues were continuing to produce tunebooks emphasizing American music.

In tables 6.3 and 6.4, the extant Maine tunebook editions are grouped into five categories, based not only on chronology, but also on similarity of repertory and nationality representation.[18] Each of the first four groups include a smaller percentage of

---

15. The publications of both William Billings and Andrew Law included books intended for a particular purpose and directed toward a specific clientele. For example, Billings's *Music in Miniature* (1779) was a tune supplement containing plain tunes for congregational singing. His *Psalm-Singer's Amusement* (1781), like Law's *Collection of Hymn Tunes* (1783), was intended not for beginners, but specifically for accomplished singers. See David P. McKay and Richard Crawford, *William Billings of Boston: Eighteenth-Century Composer* (Princeton: Princeton University Press, 1975), 110; and Crawford, *Andrew Law, American Psalmodist* (Evanston: Northwestern University Press, 1968), 35.

16. Abraham Maxim, *The Northern Harmony*, 2nd ed. (Exeter, N.H.: Norris & Sawyer, 1808), [2]. The punctuation is as printed in the original.

17. The origins and results of the reform movement are thoroughly discussed in Crawford's essay "'Ancient Music' and the Europeanizing of American Psalmody, 1800-1810," in *A Celebration of American Music: Words and Music in Honor of H. Wiley Hitchcock*, ed. Richard Crawford, R. Allen Lott, and Carol J. Oja (Ann Arbor: University of Michigan Press, 1990), 225-55.

18. The fourth edition of *The Northern Harmony* is actually a transitional work which seems to straddle groups II and III. Its nationality and genre proportions place it within the parameters of group II, but a strong case could also be made for assigning it to group III since eighty-two percent of its tunes are shared with one or more of the group III tunebooks. I know of only two copies (both incomplete) of this edition. The copy at the Essex Institute in Salem, Massachusetts, ends with page 56, but includes the title page, preface, theoretical introduction, and forty-six pages of tunes. The copy at the Newberry Library in Chicago, while lacking a title page and other preliminary matter, encompasses all the music from pages 11 to 242, except 131 to 134. Advertisements imply that the edition originally contained 280 pages.

Even though the fourth and fifth editions of *The Northern Harmony* exist only in incomplete copies, the percentages derived from complete copies (if such could be found) would probably be similar. An 1822 newspaper advertisement for the fifth edition (1819) of *The Northern Harmony* states that it, too, contained 280 pages; the incomplete copy in the Library of Congress ends with page 142 and has several earlier pages missing. Nevertheless, this partial copy not only shares a great many tunes with the contemporaneous editions of *The Temple Harmony* (1818 and 1820), but also has very similar nationality and genre percentages.

Table 6.3. Nationality of Tunes in Extant Maine Tunebooks, 1794-1830

Group	Dates	Books	American Tunes[a]	European Tunes
I	1794-1808	The Harmony of Maine The Oriental Harmony The Columbian Harmony The Northern Harmony The Northern Harmony/2	90-100%	0-9%
II	1813-16	The Parish Harmony The Chorister's Companion *The Northern Harmony/4	54-63%	35-41%
III	1818-20	The Temple Harmony *The Northern Harmony/5 The Temple Harmony/2	47-51%	42-48%
IV	1817-21, 1830[b]	The Hallowell Collection The Hallowell Collection/2 The Wesleyan Harmony The Wesleyan Harmony/2 Songs of Sion	2-7%	63-94%
V	1821-26	The Temple Harmony/3 The Temple Harmony/4 The Temple Harmony/5 The Temple Harmony/6	19-26%	55-65%

*Incomplete copy

a. The combined percentages of American and European tunes do not add up to one hundred percent for all the tunebooks listed because I have not been able to determine the authorship and/or nationality for some tunes, particularly those lacking an attribution. *Songs of Sion* (1830), a group IV tunebook, presents the most problems. Only sixty-eight percent of its tunes have been identified in terms of national origin (see also notes 20 and 33).

b. Although the chronological range of the group IV tunebooks may appear curious, the books have been classified together because they are all reform collections.

American tunes than its predecessor. The movement away from American tunes reaches its apex in the group IV tunebooks, published between 1817 and 1821, and in 1830. While most of these books are contemporaneous with those in group III, they have been assigned to a separate group because they are quite different in content. They feature plain tunes by European composers while severely limiting the number of American tunes and fuging tunes.

Table 6.4. Selected Genres in Extant Maine Tunebooks, 1794-1830

(Not listed here, but comprising a very small percentage of the tunebooks, are anthems and set-pieces.)

Group	Dates	Books	Fuging Tunes	Plain Tunes and Tunes with Extension
I	1794-1808	The Harmony of Maine	26-53%	40-69%
		The Oriental Harmony		
		The Columbian Harmony		
		The Northern Harmony		
		The Northern Harmony/2		
II	1813-16	The Parish Harmony	7-39%	59-80%
		The Chorister's Companion		
		*The Northern Harmony/4		
III	1818-20	The Temple Harmony	17-20%	76-80%
		*The Northern Harmony/5		
		The Temple Harmony/2		
IV	1817-21, 1830	The Hallowell Collection	1-4%	93-97%
		The Hallowell Collection/2		
		The Wesleyan Harmony		
		The Wesleyan Harmony/2		
		Songs of Sion		
V	1821-26	The Temple Harmony/3	1-5%	91-93%
		The Temple Harmony/4		
		The Temple Harmony/5		
		The Temple Harmony/6		

*Incomplete copy

Table 6.3 shows that American tunes predominate in all of the group I and II collections. Even in the group III collections, pieces by American composers constitute just slightly less than half of the repertory. Washburn, compiler of a group III collection, noted in 1818 that in choosing the music, he had not been wholly confined either to American or European writers, but had taken care to select "such as may be useful and pleasing."[19]

Not all the Maine compilers of the late 1810s considered American tunes useful and pleasing. The compilers of the group IV collections, tunebooks in the reform tradition, clearly preferred European tunes; only two percent of the pieces in *The Hallowell*

19. Japheth Coombs Washburn, *The Temple Harmony* (Hallowell, Me.: E. Goodale and J. C. Washburn, 1818), [2].

Collection, for example, are of American provenance.[20] Nevertheless, nearly a fifth or more of the tunes in the later editions of Washburn's *Temple Harmony* (group V) are American. This proportion is much higher than in many other contemporaneous New England tunebooks. In the 1821 edition of *The Village Harmony,* for example, only six percent of the tunes are American. Why did the Maine compilers include so many American tunes after they had become unfashionable in other parts of New England? An obvious answer is that Maine singers must have enjoyed singing them, perhaps unaware of the stigma attached to them in urban areas. Even if they were aware that some authorities considered most American tunes to be crude and harmonically incorrect, they apparently held a different opinion. Many of the Maine settlers had moved to the region precisely because they chafed under the authoritarian restrictiveness of Massachusetts society, and they were to remain independent in their musical preferences for another decade.

The comments of Abraham Maxim imply that blind (or deaf) patriotism was not behind the preference for American tunes. He did not favor them just because they were written by his countrymen, but because they sounded better than European pieces. His statement that European music was "less agreeable" to the American ear than American music is somewhat puzzling. Hymn-tune settings by relatively untrained English parish church musicians were not significantly different from those by untrained American psalmodists. However, both types differed from the harmonizations of European or immigrant American composers trained in European, common-practice harmony. Rural Mainers may have been accustomed to American settings in which the voice parts were conceived as independent lines and were composed successively. Consequently, harmonically-oriented arrangements written by European-trained composers may have sounded strange to their ears.

By 1816, Maxim, perhaps influenced by Washburn, appears to have tempered his opinion somewhat that American tunes necessarily sounded better than European ones, but he apparently still considered many American pieces worthy of publication and performance. In the preface to the fourth edition of *The Northern Harmony,* Maxim and Washburn, joint compilers, make quite a remarkable statement. They note that they had "neither left out nor inserted a single piece of music on account of the age or country in which it was written, persuaded [that?] neither the merit nor demerit of music rests on either of those circumstances."[21] Such an unbiased selection process was very unusual for the time. Most other New England compilers were convinced that European tunes, particularly those of older vintage, were inherently superior to more modern American ones. Maxim's and Washburn's statement, as well as their repertory choices, implied disagreement with that opinion.

---

20. In the two editions of *The Hallowell Collection* and *The Wesleyan Harmony,* American tunes range from just two to seven percent of the whole, while European tunes constitute eighty-three to ninety-four percent. *Songs of Sion* represents the low end of the European range with its sixty-three percent; however, at least some of the tunes for which I have not been able to determine nationality may be of European origin. These tunes amount to thirty-two percent of the collection.

21. Abraham Maxim and Japheth C. Washburn, *The Northern Harmony,* 4th ed. (Hallowell, Me.: E. Goodale, 1816), [2]. The spelling or punctuation may vary slightly from the original because the text of the preface was transcribed from an oral reading over the telephone. (The tunebook is too fragile to be photocopied.) The bracketed word has been supplied; the page is torn where it would have been printed.

A corollary to the Maine compilers' approbation of American tunes was their interest in fuging tunes, largely of American origin, well after they had fallen out of favor in other regions. Fuging tunes are strophic settings containing at least one section in which the voices enter successively, producing textual overlap. While not an American invention, fuging tunes were written in large numbers by American psalmodists in the 1780s and 1790s. Early nineteenth-century reformers deemed them unsuitable for worship, however, largely because of their lively tempo and because their verbal conflict tended to obscure the text. While fuging tunes began to wane in popularity after 1800 in many parts of New England, particularly urban areas, interest in them apparently remained strong in Maine as late as 1820, judging from the number of printings in Maine tunebooks (see table 6.4). Almost a fifth of the tunes in the group III tunebooks (dating from 1818 to 1820) are fuging tunes, compared to one percent or less in other contemporaneous New England collections such as *The Village Harmony* and *Bridgewater Collection.*

Although Maine psalmodists included more fuging tunes in their tunebooks than was customary elsewhere in New England in the mid- to late 1810s, they were not of one mind concerning them, judging from their comments and the genre distribution in their collections. Some compilers, like Hartwell, were opposed to fuging tunes. In his 1815 tunebook, he expressed his aversion to "the volatile and fugeing style which has characterised so much of our modern compositions."[22] Other compilers, like Washburn, may have recognized that many people enjoyed singing fuging tunes outside of church, especially if they were sung less often during worship services. As late as 1818, Washburn noted that he had inserted a number of fuging pieces in *The Temple Harmony* "to render the variety such as to give more general satisfaction."[23]

By 1817 or so, piety and concern about suitable worship music came to the forefront even in Maine as the first Maine reform collections, classified here as group IV, were published. Table 6.3 shows that after 1820 European tunes dominated all the Maine tunebooks. Table 6.4 reveals that plain tunes and tunes with extension—strophic settings without textual overlap—constitute the vast majority of the later repertory.[24] These somewhat simpler tunes were considered more appropriate for worship services by those favoring church music reform. Sentiments similar to those expressed in Massachusetts a decade earlier are apparent in the prefatory material of *The Hallowell Collection* (1817). The compilers note that they have selected simple, dignified tunes by authors of "well-known eminence" while excluding "light and flimsy airs" as "unsuitable for the temple of the Most High."[25] Only four of the tunes (representing two percent of the

---

22. Hartwell, [3]. The quotation uses spelling faithful to the original.

23. Washburn, *The Temple Harmony* (1818), [2].

24. The musical structure of plain tunes is strictly controlled by the meter of the text: one line of text is set to one line of music, with no textual or musical repetition of words or phrases. Plain tunes are not necessarily limited to block chords; each voice can be somewhat melismatic as long as the melismas do not extend the length of the piece beyond a syllabic setting. Tunes with extension are slightly more elaborate settings of a psalm or hymn in which the composer repeats or extends some words or phrases, thus transcending the meter.

25. *The Hallowell Collection of Sacred Music* (Hallowell, Me.: E. Goodale, 1817), iii.

collection) are by Americans.[26] Officers of the Handel Society of Maine, in a printed endorsement, affirm the tunebook's usefulness for reform. They recommend it as a volume "well calculated to improve the musical taste of our country and aid the devotional exercises of our Churches."[27]

The emphasis on music appropriate for worship, clearly stated in *The Hallowell Collection,* was consistent with the interests of clergymen and other community leaders in reversing the trend toward secularization in church music. Choirs, rather than congregations, were doing most of the singing in church at this time, and their desire to demonstrate their musical skill may have been stronger than their desire to enhance worship. Richard Crawford concludes that it was the secularization of psalmody more than any other factor which prompted the reform movement of 1805 and after and the return to older, time-tested pieces in a simple style.[28] Although the reform movement seems to have affected psalmody in Maine about a decade later than in Massachusetts, the circumstances precipitating it were probably similar.

Samuel Gilman's fictionalized account of a New Hampshire choir suggests that the persistence and persuasion of a single choir member who had been exposed to reform sentiments in one of the seaport towns could lead to the introduction of the older, "purer" repertory in a northern New England church.[29] The reform movement may have spread to Maine churches through the influence of individuals whose southern New England contacts familiarized them with the changes taking place in the church music there. The contents of several orations delivered to southern Maine musical societies in the early 1810s suggest that the reform position was adopted in coastal, southern Maine earlier than in central Maine, perhaps partly because of the better access which the port towns had to Boston and other Massachusetts ports.[30]

The last tunebook of the period, *Songs of Sion* (1830),[31] shows a new and different motive for compiling a collection: preservation. The unnamed compilers justify their tunebook's existence as follows:

26. The balance of the collection consists of European pieces (ninety-four percent) and pieces of undetermined nationality (four percent).

27. Ibid.

28. Crawford, "Ancient Music," 232-33.

29. [Samuel Gilman], *Memoirs of a New England Village Choir, with Occasional Reflections* (1829; reprint, New York: Da Capo, 1984), 78-84. In Gilman's tale, Mr. Forehead, a new choir member who had lived for a year in an unnamed seaport town, created dissention in the pews by convincing some, but not all, of the choir members that old, slow, simple tunes such as OLD HUNDRED and ST. MARTIN'S were the only ones worthy of performance. The choir he formerly belonged to in the seaport town had been introduced to "a new and purer taste for sacred music" (p. 78) and now sang no fuging tunes and no tunes of American origin. His efforts in foisting the older European repertory on his new choir initially caused a choir split, but ultimately resulted in a compromise in which the five tunes sung on the Sabbath included two fuging tunes, two of the slow, older tunes, and one different from either (pp. 95-96).

30. Oliver Bray, *An Oration on Music* (Portland, Me.: Arthur Shirley, 1812); Ammi R. Mitchell, *An Address on Sacred Music* (Portland, Me.: Hyde, Lord & Co., 1812).

31. [Smith Hinkley and Christopher T. Norcross], *Songs of Sion: or, Maine Collection of Sacred Music* (Charleston, Me.: Hinkley & Norcross, 1830). No compiler's name appears on the title page, but Hinkley and Norcross are named as the proprietors, as well as the publishers, in the copyright notice. The book was printed by Glazier, Masters & Co. in Hallowell, Maine.

> The numerous complaints made against musical publications, on account of the
> frequent alterations which are made in old and approved pieces of Church Music,
> is the prime cause of this collection being presented to the public. All the ancient
> pieces will be found in their original form, or nearly so, in this work.[32]

Almost all of these "ancient pieces," which comprise about two-thirds of the
collection, are by Europeans of the eighteenth century or earlier. Only about five percent
of the repertory is unquestionably of American origin. *Songs of Sion* is a forerunner of later
Maine retrospective collections such as *Ancient Harmony Revived* (1847 and later) in its
reprinting of unaltered older tunes (albeit European ones).

The practice of publishing "corrected" versions was a product of the "scientific
music" movement of the 1820s. The concept of music as both a science and an art was
particularly fashionable in that era. Older hymn-tune settings, particularly American
ones, were looked down upon because they were not based on principles of musical
"science" (i.e., European common-practice harmony). Newer harmonizations (by Lowell
Mason, Thomas Hastings, and others) that followed these principles were considered
more "scientific." The compilers of *Songs of Sion* were not oblivious to this trend and did
not limit their selection to older tunes. They also included a "considerable number of new
pieces," many of which are unattributed and of unknown nationality. Although the
editors conceded that these pieces "may not be strictly scientific, in every particular," they
believed "they will not be found to deviate essentially."[33] So, while *Songs of Sion* consists
primarily of older tunes in unaltered form, the collection also contains tunes acceptable
to those concerned with the new "scientific" ideals. Like the earlier Maine compilers (and
like successful hymnal editors of any era), the tunebook's editors provided a variety of
music "to please the different tastes of singers generally."[34]

To summarize, Maine psalmodists apparently felt that the many other New England
collections then available were not completely suitable for local use, so they tailored books
specifically for Maine residents. The "advertisements" printed in Maine collections
compiled between 1794 and 1830 reveal a fundamental concern for practicality
throughout the period. Particularly in the early nineteenth century, compilers sought to
hold down costs for new settlers by producing smaller less expensive volumes which could
serve a variety of functions and tastes. Patriotism (perhaps mixed with stubborn
independence) came into play as Maine compilers continued to include American tunes,
especially American fuging tunes, even into the 1820s, well after simpler European tunes
completely dominated other New England collections. Compilers late in the period were
guided by piety as they sought to provide time-tested music to enhance worship and by
an interest in preservation as they reprinted older tunes in unaltered form. Maine
compilers throughout the period produced collections prepared primarily to please
potential Maine purchasers.

---

32. Ibid., [3].

33. Ibid. About a third of the collection is of unknown nationality, since many of the tunes lack an
attribution and have not yet been traced elsewhere. It is possible, and probably likely, that many of the
unattributed tunes are by Americans. Some may be by Maine residents.

34. Ibid.

7

"Children in the Wood": The Odyssey of an Anglo-American Ballad

Susan L. Porter

When I was a child, my sisters and I used to beg our grandmother to sing the song "Babes in the Wood" for us. Despite the protests of our mother, who thought our psyches would be forever damaged, we avidly listened again and again to the tragic history of two little children who were abandoned to die in the woods. As I grew older, the attraction of the song remained, but some questions arose: Who were those lost children? Who first sang their song? My twenty-year search has led me to additional versions of my grandmother's song, to the sixteenth-century English ballad that preceded it, and to stories, poems, books, and musical theater works based on the story.

The tale of two children abandoned in the woods became very popular and was widely circulated during the seventeenth and eighteenth centuries. Its inclusion as a ballad form can be traced to the following entry, found in the Registers of the Stationers' Company in London for 15 October 1595:

> Thomas Millington entred for his copie under th' handes of both the Wardens, a ballad intituled "The Norfolk Gentleman, his Will and Testament, and howe he commytted the keeping of his children to his own brother whoe delte most wickedly with them, and how God plagued him for it."[1]

The unacknowledged author, possibly Millington himself, was later celebrated by Thomas Jernigan (1727-1812), whose verses entitled "On the Author of the ballad called the Children in the Wood" include these lines:

---

1. William Chappell and J. Woodfall Ebsworth, eds., *The Roxburghe Ballads*, 8 vols. (Hertford: Stephen Austin and Sons, 1895), 2:214.

Let me that humble Bard revere
tho' artless be his theme
Who snatch'd the tale to Pity dear
from dark oblivion's stream.

Jernigen identifies the poet's burial site "where Wanton's limpid streamlet flows in Norfolk's rich domain."[2]

The earliest extant printed version of the ballad is found in the Roxburghe Collection of 1640 (fig. 7.1). "The Norfolk Gentleman" contains twenty stanzas of eight lines each in ballad meter (8.6.8.6), and is divided into two parts of ten stanzas each. It is a narrative type, told entirely in the third person, although the narrator speaks directly to the audience at both the beginning and end. The morality pattern is that described by Abrahams and Foss: "Action begins because of a *violation* of law, taboo, or common sense; it is ended by the imposition of an appropriate punishment."[3]

The story begins with the deaths of a Norfolk couple, who leave their small children to the care of the husband's brother. Their will names the children as beneficiaries of their estate and, in the event that the children do not survive, their uncle. The wicked uncle hires two ruffians to murder the children; however, the would-be assassins quarrel and one is killed. The survivor takes the children deep into the woods and, after telling them that he will return with food, abandons them. The children wander about eating blackberries until, finally, they perish. Robin Redbreast covers their bodies with leaves. Thereafter, the uncle suffers dire misfortunes: his cattle die in the fields, his crops fail, his buildings burn, his sons drown, he is jailed for debt and dies in prison. Meanwhile, the hired murderer is apprehended, confesses his role in the dastardly deed, and is hanged. The ballad ends with a stern warning to all estate executors who might be disposed to act as did the wicked uncle.

The ballad may be based on an actual event. Tradition in Norfolk says that the tragedy occurred near Watton in Wayland Wood, popularly called Wailing Wood. William Chappell reported in 1895 that Griston Hall, supposedly the house of the cruel uncle, was still standing and had been at one time decorated with wood carvings, now lost, telling the story of the ballad.[4] On the chimney wall was an inscription: "God Save the Queen. Thomas May, 1597," which Chappell felt might be a reference to the author of the ballad.[5]

Bishop Thomas Percy, the eighteenth-century English antiquary and poet, believed the ballad to be based on a play by Robert Yarrington, dated 1601, in which a young child is "murthered in a wood, by two ruffians, with the consent of his unkle."[6] The ballad and play have many similarities as well as differences, and their close proximity in time may

2. Ibid., 8:854.

3. Roger D. Abrahams and George Foss, *Anglo-American Folksong Style* (Englewood Cliffs, N.J.: Prentice-Hall, 1968), 93.

4. *Roxburghe Ballads*, 2:215.

5. Ibid., 8:853.

6. *Reliques of Ancient English Poetry* (London: George Routlege and Sons, 1857), 479.

[Roxb. Coll. I. 284, 285; III. 586 and 588.]

The Norfolke Gentleman, his last Will and Testament:

And how hee committed the keeping of his children to his owne brother, who dealt most wickedly with them: and how God plagued him for it.

To THE TUNE OF *Rogero.*

Now ponder well, you parents deare,
    The words which I shall write;
A dolefull story you shall heare,
    Which time hath brought to light.   4
A gentleman of good account
    In Norfolke liv'd of late,
Whose wealth and riches did surmount
    Most men of his estate.   8

Figure 7.1. Earliest extant printed version, *The Roxburghe Ballads*, 2:284-85, stanzas 1-6.

Sore sicke he was, and like to die,
   No helpe that he could have;
His wife by him as sicke did lie,
   And both possest one grave.   12
No love between these two was lost,
   Each was to other kinde;
In love they lived, in love they dide,
   And left two babes behinde.   16

The one a fine and pretty boy,
   Not passing three years old;
The next a girle, more young than he,
   And made of beauties' mold.   20
This father left his little sonne,
   As well it doth appeare,
When hee to perfect age should come,
   Three hundred pounds a yeare.   24

And to his little daughter Jane
   Three hundred pounds in gold
To be paid downe at marriage day,
   Which might not be contrould: 28
But if these children chance to die
   Ere they to age should come,
Their uncle should possess this wealth;
   And so the will did runne.   32

"Now, brother," said the dying man,
   "Looke to my children deare;
Be good unto my boy and girle,
   No friends I else have here.   36
To God and you I doe commend
   My children night and day;
But little time, be sure, wee have
   Within this world to stay.   40

"You must be father and mother both,
   And uncle, all in one;
God knowes what will become of them
   When wee are dead and gone!"   44
With that bespake their mother deare,
   "O brother mine!" quoth shee,
"You are the man must bring my babes
   To wealth or misery.   48

Example 1

Figure 7.1, continued.

indicate a common basis in an actual event. The murder of nephews in order to inherit land and titles is all too common in English history. References to robins covering the bodies of the dead are often made by authors contemporary with the origin of the ballad. In John Webster's *The White Devil* (ca. 1612) Cornelia says:

> Call for the Robin-redbreast and the Wren,
> Since o'er the shady groves they hover,
> And with leaves and flowers they cover
> The friendless bodies of unburied men.[7]

Shakespeare wrote in *Cymbeline* (ca. 1609):

> The Ruddock would, with charitable bill—
> Without a monument—bring thee all this;
> Yea, and furr'd moss besides, when flowers are none,
> To winter-ground thy corse.[8]

Michael Drayton (1563-1631) wrote:

> Cov'ring with moss the dead's unclosed eye,
> The little red-breat teacheth charitie.[9]

Several tunes have been used for "The Norfolk Gentleman," commonly known as "Children in the Wood." Most seventeenth-century sources call for the tune *Rogero*, the title being an Anglicized version of the Italian *ruggiero*, and the several extant versions of the tune have in common the fact that they can be set to the standard *ruggiero* bass pattern (ex. 7.1).

Example 7.1. "Rogero."[10]

---

7. *Roxburghe Ballads*, 2:214.

8. Ibid., 8:854.

9. James Orchard Halliwell-Phillips, *Popular Rhymes and Nursery Tales* (London: John Russell Smith, 1849), 162.

10. The tune is from Claude Simpson, *The British Broadside Ballad and Its Music* (New Brunswick, N.J.: Rutgers University Press, 1966), 612.

A different tune is most commonly associated with the eighteenth-century English versions of the ballad. It is also used for other ballads, notably *Chevy Chase* or *Dives and Lazarus*. This tune is found in twenty-two ballad operas from the mid-eighteenth century, including John Gay's *Beggar's Opera* (fig. 7.2).[11] Here the tune is identified as "Now Ponder well, ye Parents dear," the first line of the ballad. The tune accommodates only a stanza of four lines and must thus be used forty times if the entire ballad is to be sung.

AIR XII. Now ponder well, ye Parents dear.

Polly.   *O ponder well ! be not severe ;*
          So save a wretched Wife !
          For on the Rope that hangs my Dear
          Depends poor Polly's Life.

Figure 7.2. Ballad Tune in *The Beggar's Opera*.[12]

"Children in the Wood" was widely known in England and America during the three centuries following its appearance. Joseph Addison, writing in *The Spectator* in 1711, discussed the ballad at length, calling it "one of the Darling Songs of the Common People":

> The Condition, Speech, and Behavior of the dying Parents, with the Age, Innocence and Distress of the Children, are set forth in such tender Circumstances, that it is impossible for a Reader of common Humanity not to be affected with them.[13]

The ballad appeared in dozens of broadsides and chapbooks printed in England, Ireland, Scotland, and the United States, usually without music, but often accompanied

---

11. According to the *National Tune Index*, comp. Kate Van Winkle Keller and Carolyn Rabson (New York: University Music Editions, 1980). The operas are *The Reconciliation* (1790), American; *Marches Day* (1771), Scottish; *Chuck* (1729); *The Author's Farce* (1730); and *The Stage-Coach* (1730)—all Irish. The remaining are English: *The Beggar's Opera, Penelope* (both 1728); *The Jovial Crew, The Wanton Jesuit, Calista, The Generous Freemason* (all 1731); *The Devil to Pay, The Disappointment, The Downfall of Bribery* (all 1732); *The Honest Electors, Lord Blunder's Confession, The State Juggler* (all 1733); *The Old Man Taught Wisdom* (1735); *The False Guardians Outwitted* (1740); *Ragged Uproar* (1754); *The Bow Street Opera* (1773); *The Virgin Unmasked* (1786).

12. John Gay, *The Beggar's Opera* (1728; London: William Heinemann, 1921), 20.

13. Joseph Addison, *The Spectator* (1711-12, 1714), 5 vols., ed. Donald F. Bond (Oxford: Clarendon, 1964), 1:362-63.

by vivid illustrations. The Harvard Library has at least eleven English, Scottish, and Irish broadsides and chapbooks that contain the ballad under various titles.[14] Seven American broadsides appeared between 1768 and 1820. Even young Moravians were acquainted with the ballad; it appeared in a German translation, *Die Kinder im Wald*, published in Lebanon, Pennsylvania, in 1810.[15] It can be found also in ballad collections from the seventeenth century and later, including the Samuel Pepys collection, the Roxburghe collection, and the Bagford collection.

It was also expanded and elaborated on in stories, often with strong emphasis on the moral lessons to be learned from the ballad. In an eighteenth-century chapbook version, *The Most Lamentable and Deplorable History of the Two Children in the Wood*, for example, the retribution visited on the wicked uncle is embroidered:

> Divine vengeance follow'd him; affrighting Dreams terrifying him in his Sleep, and the image of the murther'd children still staring him i' th' Face; and he that egg'd him on to all this wickedness, now in most horrid Shapes appear'd to him, and threat'ning every Moment to destroy him.[16]

In one little masterpiece, written by Clara English and published in Philadelphia in 1803, the children's fate seems, indirectly, to be the fault of the industrial revolution. The story is padded to sixty-three pages by the addition of much extraneous material about the activities of good little children. This version begins slowly, with the boy Edgar relating various stories to his sister Jane. After the death of the children's parents, their uncle takes the children home by way of a workhouse and a textile factory. Both are praised. The workhouse is described as a nice place for orphan children to live and learn while being supported by the other members of a caring community. The history of the English spinning and weaving industry is outlined from its beginning in 1733. Hymns are interspersed throughout the story whenever the children need encouragment. The narrative follows the ballad as far as the blackberry scene; then an old woman finds the children, takes them home, and has them placed in a nice workhouse. The uncle meets with the usual disasters described in gleeful detail. The children inherit the uncle's home, take the old woman to live with them, and all live happily ever after amidst endless moralizing and hymn singing. The actual ballad follows, with the verse describing the death of the children conveniently omitted.[17]

One of the most interesting adaptations of the ballad story is a "musical piece" written by Thomas Morton (1764-1838), with music by Samuel Arnold (1740-1802). Although Arnold is perhaps best remembered today for preparing the first complete edition of the works of Handel, he was also a prolific composer in many genres. He became music director at the Theatre Royal in the Haymarket in 1765 and eventually

---

14. G. Malcolm Laws, Jr., *British Broadside Ballads Traditional in America* (Philadelphia: American Folklore Society, 1957), 290.

15. Ralph Shaw and Joseph Shoemaker, *American Bibliography, 1801-1829* (New York and Metuchen, N.J.: Scarecrow, 1958-71), microform edition, no. S19765.

16. John Ashton, *Chapbooks of the Eighteenth Century* (1882; reprint, New York: Benjamin Blom, 1966), 371.

17. Shaw and Shoemaker, S4165.

wrote the music for more than 100 theatrical productions. One of the most popular of these was *Children in the Wood*, a two-act comic opera which had its London premiere at the Little Theatre in the Haymarket on 1 October 1793. The opera was performed seventy times in its first London season, and the Boston *Federal Orrery* claimed that "no afterpiece, except *The Padlock*, ever brought so much money into English theatres."[18] It arrived in America the next year and the score was published by Benjamin Carr, who had been a student of Arnold in London before moving to the United States. Carr's edition, with an added song and new accompaniments, was first performed in Philadelphia on 24 November 1794. New York critics found the opera abounding in "the purest morality, and the most instructive lessons of disinterested virtue."[19]

The opera plot follows the ballad narrative. The children are left with their uncle while the parents are on a journey. The uncle, thinking the parents dead, orders the children killed. One ruffian turns out to be a hero of sorts: he slays his villainous companion and saves the children, but then he accidentally loses them in the woods. The children lie down to die, but the parents unexpectedly return from their journey, discover their unconscious children covered with leaves, and revive them. The cruel uncle is disposed of, and everyone joins in a finale of

> Have we sav'd this boy and girl
> Is't so understaood, sirs?
> May I hallow now for joy!
> Are we out of the wood, Sirs?

Arnold wrote ten musical numbers for his opera, including an overture; several additional pieces were added by Carr and others. The era had an interest in ballads and ballad tunes, and, even though the popularity of the ballad opera as a genre had faded, a few traditional tunes were still used in most English operas. Arnold was especially interested in English traditional melodies and used them frequently. Several are found in *Children in the Wood*, but only the overture uses the ballad tune associated with the opera's title. The overture is a single movement, with a slow introduction followed by three quicker sections, each in a different tempo. This form can be found in dozens of comic opera overtures. The slow introduction typically presents a popular air, in this case "Children in the Wood," played by a solo instrument (ex. 7.2). Though much ornamented and richly harmonized, the tune is little changed from the *Beggar's Opera* version. The third section of the overture is a rondo, and the final digression presents the complete ballad tune again, this time in duple meter, piano, and staccato (ex. 7.3). The overture also appeared in an arrangement for two German flutes, published in *The Gentleman's Amusement* (1794) by Benjamin Carr.

The ballad, sometimes severely truncated or otherwise altered, survived beyond the eighteenth century, and is found in numerous English and American traditional song collections published in the nineteenth and twentieth centuries. Even in the briefest versions, the essential details remain: the children getting lost while waiting for the

---

18. 9 November 1795. See also Robert S. B. Hoskins, *The Theater Music of Samual Arnold: A Thematic Index* (this publisher, 1998).

19. William Dunlap, *History of the American Theatre,* 2 vols. (New York: Harper, 1832), 1:377.

Example 7.2. Opening from the Overture to the Comic Opera *Children in the Wood* (1793) by Samuel Arnold.[20]

ruffian's return, the eating of blackberries, the weeping at darkness, their deaths in each other's arms, and Robin Redbreast covering them with leaves.

In these later transmissions of the tale, many text alterations occur typical of those found in oral transmission. Not only do the poetic conceits of the cultivated text disappear, but also details of the story change as each singer asserts his or her own understanding of the ballad text. Memory lapses, garbled verse, misunderstanding of words, and even nonsensical rearranging of the events of the story are evident. A recent

20. [Samuel] Arnold, *Children in the Wood: A Comic Opera in Two Acts* (London: Longman & Broderip, 1793), 4.

Example 7.3. Opening from the Overture to the Comic Opera *Children in the Wood* (1793) by Samuel Arnold.[21]

version found in *Folksongs of Florida*,[22] is notorious for many of these alterations. Obvious cases of mishearing are apparent: "furious mood" becomes "curious mode"; "unfrequented wood" is heard as nonsense—"uncreek wintered wood." A line not completely understood has been rationalized: "Yea, fearful fiends did haunt this house" becomes "The awful friend he'd haunters have." Several major variants to the story occur, including the omission, transposition, or addition of entire verses. Finally, the most bizarre transposition of events has the children die first and eat blackberries later.

As with many popular pieces, this ballad also was parodied. In a late nineteenth-century version, the basic plot is intact; however, the uncle makes several humorous attempts to dispose of the children:

> Vhen he looked at the kids, he longed for their gold;
> In damp sheets he laid 'em, 'cos he thought they'd catch cold;
> They both caught the measles, and the whooping cough,
> And he prayed every night that it would take 'em off,
> But they got over that, and all other disease
> Vich kids mostly have—which it didn't him please;
> So to cook the poor babbies, he thought on a plan,
> For their nunky he vos such a vicked old man,
> Their nunky he vos such a hard hearted man.[23]

The tune has undergone some transformation as well. Three versions, transposed to G for easy comparison, serve as illustrations (ex. 7.4).[24] The earliest, found in Chappell,

21. Ibid., 6.

22. Alton C. Morris, *Folksongs of Florida* (Gainesville: University of Florida Press, 1950), 401-06.

23. John Ashton, *Modern Street Ballads* (1888; reprint, New York: Benjamin Blom, 1968), 369-74.

24. William Chappell, *Old English Popular Music, 1855-59*, ed. E. Ellis Woodridge (New York: Jack Brussel, 1961), 92; Bertrand Harris Bronson, *The Traditional Tunes of the Child Ballads*, 4 vols. (Princeton: Princeton University Press, 1959-72), 2:19; Cecil J. Sharp, *English Folk Songs from the Southern Appalachians*, 2 vols. (London: Oxford University Press, 1932), 1:309.

Example 7.4. Tune Variants for *Children in the Wood*.

is almost identical to that found in *The Beggar's Opera*. The later tunes follow the contour of the earlier tune only in a very general way. All are diatonic and hexatonic, with the single scale gap occurring at the seventh step in Chappell and Bronson variants, and at the fourth step in Sharp's version.

The motivic repetition found in the first two measures of Chapell and Bronson is lost in Sharp, and Chappell's unifying motive (meas. 3, 5, 7) is sustained in neither Bronson nor Sharp. The later versions also differ in their omission of Chappell's dotted rhythm (meas. 1, etc.) and their setting of the tune in duple meter. Sharp's version does change to 3/2 meter in its penultimate measure to accommodate the lengthening of the first note. Harmonically, there are significant differences as well. Chappell moves to the dominant at the end of the first line; Bronson and Sharp go to the subdominant and return to the tonic. For the second line, Chappell starts with the subdominant; Bronson and Sharp remain on the tonic and move to the subdominant in the second measure. Thus, a harmonic arch unifies Chappell's tune while the other tunes divide into two distinct phrases harmonically.

In summary, many listeners might find the motivic and rhythmic gracefulness of the eighteenth-century tune, as well as its harmonic unity, more satisfying than the structures of the later variants. Such an evaluation, however, places emphasis on the artistic merit of the tune in its approximately original form rather than those features which enable it to endure in the aural tradition. Whereas Bronson's tune is clearly related to the earlier version, Sharp's digresses to the point where listeners might believe they are hearing nearly another tune.

At the end of the eighteenth century, a second song based on the familiar story of the children in the wood appeared. The opera was at the height of its popularity and the time was propitious to take advantage of public interest in the story. It was first published under the title "Children in the Wood" by Thomas Cahusac and Son sometime between 1794 and 1798.[25] Over a half-century later, William Gardiner (1770-1853) of Leicester took credit for its authorship. Gardiner was a hosiery manufacturer and musical amateur who made himself notorious by compiling hymns, masses, quartets, symphonies, oratorios, and even operas from garbled fragments of Mozart, Haydn, and Beethoven. In his memoirs, Gardiner included the words and music of the song, which he described as follows:

> Another early production of mine was the following little song, from a street cry that much interested the children of Leicester. An itinerant vender [sic] of toys, with a musical and plaintive voice, paraded the streets with two little wax figures in a bower, representing the Babes in the Wood. To this morceau I persuaded Mr. [Thomas] Combe to write some lines, of which I made the song that was published.[26]

In spite of his attempts in larger genres, "Babes in the Wood" is by far the best-known of Gardiner's works—if, indeed, we can credit him for its composition at all. The new song was published about 1798 in the United States in Benjamin Carr's Musical Repository, Philadelphia, as well as by James Hewitt in New York and Joseph Carr in Baltimore (ex. 7.5).

The verse is related to the earlier ballad topically but not stylistically. Its three narrative stanzas (2-4) are based on the central events of the ballad only. In fact, the piece could be called a lyric rather than a ballad for a number of reasons. The relative objectivity of the ballad is replaced by a first-person description of the story, although the speaker is not involved in the action. By selecting the emotional core of the story only and eliminating preceding and subsequent events, the ballad's narrative function has been severely curtailed. The text's emphasis is based entirely on the feeling kindled by the central event of the story. Finally, the use of refrain at the beginning and following each stanza of verse further slows down the action of the central event.

This song is seldom seen in later American versions. The tune is included in *Riley's Flute Melodies*, a two-volume collection published serially from 1814 to 1820 and containing 709 popular melodies of the day.[27] It is entitled "Babes in the Wood" and appears exactly as written in the flute part of the earlier Carr publication. *Riley's Flute Melodies* also contains the first tune under the title "O ponder well," the opening words of the ballad (vol. 2, p. 81). In England the second tune has continued in use to the present day, though it has sometimes been altered in various locales.

Six variants of this second tune appear in ex. 7.6, including the three mentioned above and three later versions from the oral tradition. The verses are set to phrases A and

---

25. *The Children in the Wood, a favorite Ballad, for the Harpsichord or Piano-Forte* (London: Cahusac and Sons, [1794-98]).

26. Gardiner, *Music and Friends*, 3 vols. (London: Longman, Brown, Green, and Longmans; Leicester: Crossley & Clarke, 1853), 3:207.

27. Edward Riley, *Riley's Flute Melodies*, 2 vols. (1816, 1820; reprint, New York: Da Capo, 1973), 2:89.

B, and A returns for the refrain. Phrase A is quite stable among the first four variants, making its opening motive the most memorable feature of the song. The B phrase is more unstable, taking different melodic and harmonic directions in each variant.

The fifth and sixth versions are quite different from the original tune and also from each other. Jenner abandons the ABA structure, favoring instead AA'A", with the first phrase cadencing at the dominant and the remaining two on the tonic. The basic motive of the first four versions is also put aside for an rising octave arpeggio. Once the octave is attained, the range of the singer (the original is in C) possibly necessitated other adjustments in the melody. Copper, by contrast, is a through-composed ABC form, although the opening arppeggiated triad (meas. 1) reappears in the final phrase (meas. 21). The melodic contours of the last two variants contrast with those of the first four; however, similarities in rhythmic patterns and harmonic progression suggest a common source for all.

The poem commonly known as "Babes in the Wood" is widely found in song books, nursery rhyme collections, and in the oral tradition during most of the nineteenth century and well into the twentieth.[28] The earliest versions tend to be in Mother Goose books, but, as latter-day mothers became more concerned about the morbid features of this story, printed versions became fewer. Consequently, the oral tradition (including printed recoveries from that tradition) has carried increasing weight in keeping the story alive. The text below has the most common features of twenty-five versions of "Babes in the Wood" found in print and in the oral tradition from 1846 to 1974:

> O don't you remember a long time ago
> Two poor little babes, whose names I don't know
> Were stolen away one bright summer day
> And lost in the woods, I've heard people say.
>
> And when it was night so sad was their plight
> The moon went down and the stars gave no light
> They sobbed and they sighed and they bitterly cried
> Poor babes in the wood they lay down and died.
>
> And when they were dead, the robin so red
> Brought strawberry leaves and over them spread
> And sang them a song the whole day long
> Poor babes in the woods, poor babes in the wood.

A comparison of this text with the earlier "Children in the Wood" (fig. 7.1) brings out several interesting features. In addition to the story of "Babes in the Wood" being drastically reduced to three, or sometimes four, stanzas, the poetic structure is entirely different. The flowing iambic, ballad meter of "Children" (4, 3, 4, 3 accents per line) is replaced by a less frequent dactyllic, long meter (4 accents per line) in "Babes." The alternating rhyme scheme of "Children" (ABAB) gives way to the repeated end rhymes

---

28. For example, the text can be found in a tiny book titled *A Songbook for Little Children*, published in Newburyport, Mass., (1818) and in another little book published in Philadelphia (1846), extravagantly entitled *The Book of Nursery Rhymes Complete from the Creation of the Earth to the Present Time.*

Example 7.5. Transcription of second song for *Children in the Wood*, ca. 1798.

Sweet Babes in the Wood

A Ballad

Founded on the well known Legend

Price 25 Cents

Rented and Sold at B: Carrs Musical Repository Philadelphia, J: Hewitts New York and J: Carrs Baltimore

Example 7.5, continued.

My dear, you must know—Twas a long time ago
There were two little Children, whose names I don't know
That were stolen away—On a fine Summer's day
And left in the wood as I've heard the folks say.
                         Poor Babes in the wood &c

And when it grew night,—How sad was their plight
The sun it had set, and the moon gave no light
They sobbed and the sigh'd—and bitterly cried
Then the poor little creatures, they laid down and died.
                         Poor Babes in the wood &c

Then a Robin so red—When he saw them lay dead
Brought strawberry leaves and over them spread
And all the day long—The branches among
He plaintively whistled and this was his song.
                         Sweet Babes in the wood &c

Example 7.6. Variants of Second Tune.[29]

29. Sources: for Gardiner see n. 26; Cahusac, n. 25; Carr, ex. 7.5. Mason is found in his *Nursery Rhymes and Country Songs both Tunes and Words from Tradition*, 1878 (London: Metzler, 1909), 22. The song was traditional in Mason's family of Northumberland. Jenner (b. ca. 1837), a native of Kent; collected by Anne Gilchrist about 1907, is found in Roy Palmer, ed., *Everyman's Version of English Country Songs* (London, Melbourne, and Toronto: J. N. Dent, 1979), 106-07. Copper is found in Bob Copper, *A Song for Every Season: A Hundred Years of a Sussex Farming Family* (London: Heinemann, 1971), 198-99.

(AABB; exception, stanza 3, lines 3 and 4) of "Babes," and some internal rhymes (line 3 of all three stanzas; lines 1 and 4, stanza 3).

Even more interesting is a comparison of the later oral-tradition "Babes" text with the published, eighteenth-century version (ex. 7.5). In the latter, the final line of each stanza becomes a lead to a mandatory refrain. Since most later versions do not require a refrain, these final lines round off each stanza. In the last stanza of the composite text, lines 3 and 4 of the eighteenth-century text are condensed into line 3, and a new line, "Poor babes in the woods, poor babes in the wood," is added. Elsewhere, nearly every line of the later composite version has strengthened, simplified, and made more dramatic those lines of the original song.

Let us now turn to the tune and the version of "Babes in the Woods" that I learned from my grandmother (ex. 7.7). All American traditional versions are sung to this same tune with only minor differences. Most singers learned the song in the early twentieth century. Many recall singing it in school. My own grandmother learned it "as a bride" in Michigan about 1901.

Example 7.7. "Babes in the Wood," as sung by Lillie Helen Ingerson.

My dear, don't you know, how a long time a-go Two poor lit-tle chil-dren whose names I don't know

Were sto-len a-way on a bright sum-mer day And left in the woods, So I've heard peo-ple say.

And left in the woods so I've heard peo-ple say.

Six variants of this tune are compared in ex. 7.8. The first four are vocal and from traditional sources. Variants E-1 and E-2 are fiddle tunes. Versions D—my grandmother's variant—and E-1 have an added refrain, which is omitted here. All have been transposed to G major. Five motives, based on contour and intervals, can be found among these variants. Motive *a*, with its upper neighbor and descent of a third, dominates, serving as a head to most of the phrases and spawning two mutations (*a'* = descent of a third; *a''* = upper neighbor and descent of a fourth). The wider leaping *b* motive serves as a consequent to *a* in nearly all cases except variant D, where it substitutes for *a* as the head of the first phrase. Motive *c* and its variants feature a descending countour at the fourth measure cadence, and *d*, an ascending contour, is the closing cadence for the song. An additional motive, *e*, has no contour and is found in variant D at the head of the final phrase. The melody is remarkably stable in all versions. Even E-2, which appears at first to be different from the other variants, harmonizes with them.

The story of the "Babes in the Wood" has been told in poetry, song, and narrative. It became an opera in the eighteenth century and a stage play in the nineteenth; in

Example 7.8. Comparison of tunes from six versions of "Babes in the Woods."[30]

30. Variant A, Vance Randolph, *Ozark Folksongs*, 4 vols. (Columbia: University of Missouri Press, 1980), 1:365 (collected 1929); variant B, Morris, *Folksongs of Florida*, 406-07; variant C, Abrahams and Foss, *Anglo-American Folksong Style*, 121-22 (collected 1965); variant D, Susan Porter, learned from her grandmother, Lillie Helen Ingerson (collected in the 1940s); variants E-1 and E-2, Randolph, 1:368 (collected in 1941).

pantomime form it became a staple item in nineteenth-century English and American theaters, and it is still in use in England in the 1990s. A march, "Babes in the Woods Lancers," by F. Schleichardt, was published in 1880 and performed by B. Moses' Band at the Spanish Fort picnic ground in New Orleans. The story still had enough appeal to be made into a Hollywood movie by William Fox in the 1920s. Cole Porter wrote a song titled "Two Little Babes in the Wood" in 1928, based on the old story but with new words and music. The title of the song has often been used symbolically for novels and plays related only slightly to the story, such as H. G. Wells's novel *Babes in the Darkling Wood* (1940), concerning the beginning of World War II. Today no English Christmas would be complete without its "Babes in the Wood" pantomime, and American grandmothers sing the song to new generations.

The timeless popularity of this simple, pathetic tale transcends any specific tune or bit of poetry. Perhaps because it reflects universal fears of becoming lost, of being separated from family, and of dying, it has remained, in spite of the quaint and morbid aspects of the story, "one of the darling songs of the common people" for nearly four centuries. John Gay expressed some of these feelings about the song in *Shepherd's Week: Sixth Pastoral* (1714) as he described a rustic minstrel:

> Then sad he sang the Children in the Wood:
> Ah! barbarous Uncle, stain'd with infant blood!
> How blackberries they pluck'd in desarts wild,
> And fearless at the glitt'ring faulchion smil'd;
> Their little corps the Robin-redbreast found,
> And strow'd with pious bill the leaves around.
> Ah! gentle birds! If this verse lasts so long,
> Your names shall live forever in my song.[31]

---

31. *Roxburghe Ballads*, 8:854.

8

Mountain Calls
for French horn and piano

To my friend Bill Kearns

Daniel Kingman

Duration 2'15"
Sacramento, April 1993

9

Musical Theater as a Link between Folk and Popular Traditions

Paul F. Wells and Anne Dhu McLucas

Scholars studying twentieth-century folk and popular musics are well aware of the intersections between them, and of the difficulty of drawing clear boundaries between their definitions.[1] It is less usual to think of folk and popular musics of previous centuries as similarly intermixed; we tend to romanticize a "purer" oral tradition that we imagine existed prior to the advent of twentieth century mass communications media. However, from at least the eighteenth century on, such interaction has played an important role in shaping the folk repertory. Print media such as broadsides, songsters, instrumental tutors and tune books, and sheet music have been recognized by modern scholars as contributing to the dissemination of ballads, songs, and fiddle tunes. Less well known is the role that the musical theater has played in providing a link between oral and popular traditions. This relationship between musical theater and folk music has operated in

---

The authors would like to thank the American Antiquarian Society for sponsoring the early stages of Anne McLucas's research with a Petersen Fellowship and Kate Van Winkle Keller for providing several examples and dates. This article originally appeared in the form of papers read at 1987 national meetings of Sonneck Society for American Music, International Association for Popular Music in Pittsburgh, and the 1993 national meeting of the American Folklore Society in Eugene, Oregon.

1. Such problems of definition abound in the twentieth century. Were early hillbilly and race recordings, for instance, folk music or popular music? For purposes of this paper, "folk music," a term that is often used broadly and vaguely, will be confined to music that has passed into oral tradition, with the result that the music and/or text shows traits of multiformity and diffusion in a tradition. For this definition, the test of folk music is that one can find variant versions spread over time and space, showing community acceptance with the freedom for each performer to recreate it in his or her own style.

Popular music is usually made by professionals who are in some sense paid, and it is itself a commodity. Commercial values influence its existence; deliberate promotion for sales and copyright are important factors. For additional exploration of this topic, see McLucas, "The Multi-Layered Concept of 'Folk Song' in American Music: The Case of Jean Ritchie's 'Two Sisters,'" in *Themes and Variations: Writings on Music in Honor of Rulan Chao Pian*, ed. Bell Yung and Joseph S. C. Lam (Cambridge: Harvard University Music Dept., 1994), 212-30.

complex ways over a broad time span, both in this country and in England, Scotland, and Ireland.

Evidence of interaction between folk and theater music in the eighteenth and early nineteenth centuries is plentiful. Perhaps the best-known examples are found in the ballad operas of the early eighteenth century. Tunes that were in currency from a variety of sources—from oral transmission, from printed broadsides, even from well-known Italian operas—were appropriated by ballad opera composers to carry new texts. On the other hand, folk tunes such as "Todlen Hame," "Bonnie Dundee," and "The Broom of Cowdenknowes," and others made popular in ballad operas have been perpetuated in oral tradition. Less well known is a similar phenomenon in later eighteenth-century and early nineteenth-century comic operas, which featured scores that included both folk tunes and tunes composed in imitation of folk style.

The easy intermixture of folk and theater repertory is reflected in the pages of nineteenth-century violin and flute tutors, where pieces from works such as *Blue Beard* and *Oscar and Malvina* sit side-by-side with traditional tunes such as "Soldier's Joy" and "Fisher's Hornpipe." Both types of tunes were obviously regarded as ones that would be familiar to amateur instrumentalists (see fig. 9.1). Likewise, songsters containing the words to theatrical ballads often contain tune directions that indicate a traditional melody. Less frequently encountered, but important, is evidence from autobiographies and diaries in which theatrical personalities recount their experiences with certain tunes, as well as giving information on how they adapted them. In this article, several case studies of interactions between folk and theater music illustrate some of the mechanisms that allowed the mutual influences to thrive in American society of the late eighteenth and early nineteenth centuries.

Case Study No. 1: *The Poor Soldier* and "The Rose Tree"

The Poor Soldier, John O'Keeffe's comic opera of 1783, with a score by William Shield (1748-1829), was staged many times well into the nineteenth century on both sides of the Atlantic. In America it was known to be the favorite theater piece of George Washington; William Dunlap even wrote a sequel to it entitled *Darby's Return,* which used the same characters, many of the same tunes, and incorporated a scene in America which paid homage to George Washington.[2]

As was common at the time, the work was in a constant state of flux, with songs and text added, dropped, and reordered over the course of its life. Numerous editions of both score and libretto were published, and individual songs were frequently anthologized. Shield drew heavily on traditional airs for his settings. In the group of nineteen airs that comprise what seems to be the most stable form of *The Poor Soldier* (and are the ones found in the vocal scores), only four melodies seem to have been composed by Shield. A summary listing of the airs used in *The Poor Soldier,* with brief notes regarding their circulation beyond the opera, is included in appendix 1.

---

2. See Oscar Sonneck, "The Musical Side of Our First President," *New Music Review* 6 (1907): 311-14, 382-85. The libretto for *Darby's Return,* at Yale University Library, is listed in Oscar Sonneck and William Treat Upton, *A Bibliography of Early Secular American Music (18th Century)* (1945; reprint, New York: Da Capo, 1964), 99.

Figure 9.1. Sample pages from *New and Complete Preceptor for the German Flute* [3d ed.?] (Albany, N.Y.: Oliver Steele, [1828-31]). Courtesy the Center for Popular Music, Middle Tennessee State University.

College Hornpipe.

Fisher's Hornpipe.

Durang's Hornpipe.

Du Wier's Hornpipe.

Rickett's Hornpipe.

Figure 9.1, continued.

Without a doubt, the most well-known and enduringly popular of all the airs from *The Poor Soldier* is "The Rose Tree." It is part of the common stock of tunes known in string band revival circles, in a form that differs little from the way it appears in Shield's score for *The Poor Soldier.* That a still-popular tune survived intact in its original form across two centuries is intriguing. Investigation into the history of "Rose Tree" uncovers a tangled and complex tune family. In addition to survival as both an instrumental piece and as a vehicle for numerous songs with little change from Shield's setting, the melody has sprouted several branches, at least two of which have been popularized through intervention of later nineteenth-century stage traditions.

Although Roger Fiske, in his list of "Borrowings 1760-1800,"[3] was unable to trace the melody before *The Poor Soldier,* and suggests that it might have been composed by Shield, it was clearly in circulation in Scotland, and possibly Ireland as well, more than twenty years prior to the 1783 debut of *The Poor Soldier.* The earliest printing of the melody we have is "The Gimblet" in volume 10 of James Oswald's *Caledonian Pocket Companion* (ca. 1760).[4]

The tune next turns up in the first number of James Aird's *Selection of Scotch, English, Irish, and Foreign Airs,* published in Glasgow in 1782.[5] Aird titles it "The Dainty Besom Maker," and a nearly identical setting by this name appears in *A Favourite Collection of Scots Tunes & Highland Airs,* by William McGibbon and James Oswald, published around 1795.[6] The first strain of "Dainty Besom Maker" does not differ significantly from Shield's setting, but the first phrase of the second strain begins on the fourth degree of the scale, rather than the third.

The appearance of the melody under the title "Old Lee Rigg or Rose Tree," in Niel Gow's *Second Collection of Strathspey Reels* [1788], suggests a link with the well-known Scottish tune "Lee Rigg" (also known as "My Ain Kind Dearie"). However, apart from a very general similarity of contour, and a sharing of an AA'/BA' phrase structure, there is no discernible connection between the two tunes.

---

3. Roger Fiske, *English Theatre Music in the Eighteenth Century,* 2d ed. (Oxford: Oxford University Press, 1986), 611-12.

4. Francis O'Neill and Samuel P. Bayard both note the relationship of "The Gimblet" and "Rose Tree." See O'Neill, *Irish Folk Music: A Fascinating Hobby* (Darby, Pa.: Norwood Editions, 1973), 131, and Bayard, *Dance to the Fiddle, March to the Fife: Instrumental Folk Tunes in Pennsylvania* (University Park: Pennsylvania State University Press, 1982), 28.

5. *A Selection of Scotch, English, Irish and Foreign Airs Adapted to the Fife, Violin, or German-Flute,* vol. 1 (Glasgow: James Aird, [1782]). The publication date of the first volume of what was ultimately a six-volume series is often given as "1778." It is so dated in David Johnson's article on Aird in *Music Printing and Publishing,* ed. D. W. Krummel and Stanley Sadie (New York: Norton, 1990), 136. Johnson apparently drew on Frank Kidson's article on Aird that appears in the 5th edition of *Grove's Dictionary of Music and Musicians.* However, Kate Van Winkle Keller has shared with us her unpublished research on Aird, in which she dates the publication of the first volume in 1782, based on the evidence of newspaper advertisements. We have accepted Keller's dating.

6. W[illiam] McGibbon and J[ames] Oswald, and others [*sic*], *A Favourite Collection of Scots Tunes and Highland Airs, etc. for the Violin, German Flute, with a Bass for the Violoncello or Harpsichord* (Glasgow: A. McGoun, [1795]).

The melody may also have been current in Ireland before Shield, as the tune for a song called "Little Mary Cullinan" (or some variant thereof, and often spelled in Irish). Francis O'Neill notes that "Little Mary Cullinan" was written by Munster poet John O'Tuomy, who died in 1775, and thus argues for this as the first use of the melody we now know as "Rose Tree."[7] We have been unable to confirm the existence of this song in print prior to Joyce's 1909 collection.[8]

The popularity of "The Rose Tree" after its use by Shield is easy to track. In addition to frequent printing of O'Keeffe's song, either with or without tune, the air was a staple of instrumental tutors and tunebooks (see list of references in appendix 2). As noted earlier, the melody is currently well known among fiddlers and other musicians, especially revivalists. It is common fare at contradances. The 1983 publications by Miller-Perron and Brody, noted in appendix 2, testify to its place in the current repertory.

The tune was given fresh life when Thomas Moore wrote new lyrics, "I'd Mourn the Hopes That Leave Me," and published it in the fifth number of *Irish Melodies,* around 1815. In early editions of this work, the air is listed as "unknown," though in later editions it carries an indication that the air used is "The Rose Tree." This suggests that the melody was popular enough, and probably in oral tradition, so that Moore knew it without knowing initially where it came from. Moore's song was frequently anthologized in the nineteenth century, though there is no evidence of it passing into oral tradition. The recording by McConnell's Four Leaf Shamrocks of the tune as "Moore's Favorite" suggests a link to "I'd Mourn the Hopes."

A small branch of the tune-family, which may prove to be larger on further investigation, is formed by the use of variants of the melody in the shape-note hymn tradition. What may be the first such use is in a hymn titled "The Rose Tree," published in *Knoxville Harmony* of 1838. A variant of the melody is used for the same text in *Southern Harmony,* indicating that the piece probably enjoyed some circulation. A slightly different variant is used in another piece in *Southern Harmony.* All of these are cited in appendix 2.

Most intriguing, though, are two offshoots of the family which are a bit more distantly related melodically, and which were in turn popularized through later nineteenth-century stage tradition: Samuel P. Bayard, Alan Jabbour, George Pullen Jackson, and Eloise Hubbard Linscott all relate the "Rose Tree" to the famous minstrel melody "Old Zip Coon" and its better known relative "Turkey in the Straw."[9] This is a relationship that is a bit difficult to see, particularly if one has in mind a modern bluegrass rendition of "Turkey in the Straw." However, a comparison of "The Rose Tree" with a very early version of "Zip Coon" reveals many similarities of contour and lends credibility to this hypothesis. (See ex. 9.1 for a comparison of the first strains of Shield's melody and

---

7. Ibid., 130.

8. P[atrick] W[eston] Joyce, ed., *Old Irish Folk Music and Songs: A Collection of 842 Irish Airs and Songs Hitherto Unpublished* (1909; reprint, New York: Cooper Square, 1965).

9. Bayard, 28; Alan Jabbour, notes to *American Fiddle Tunes,* Library of Congress AFS L62 (1971), 32; George Pullen Jackson, *White Spirituals in the Southern Uplands: The Story of the Fasola Folk, Their Songs, Singings, and "Buckwheat Notes"* (1933; reprint, New York: Dover, 1965), 166; Eloise Hubbard Linscott, *Folk Songs of Old New England,* rev. ed. (1939; reprint, Hamden, Conn.: Archon Books, 1962), 334.

Example 9.1. Comparison of "Rose Tree," "Zip Coon," and "My Grandma's Advice."

"Rose Tree" (1783) [original key: B♭]

"Zip Coon" (1834)

"My Grandma's Advice" (1857) [original key: G]

of a setting of "Zip Coon," from an 1834 flute tutor.) "Zip Coon" has a somewhat busier melody than "Rose Tree," and there are numerous differences of detail, but in overall melodic contour and on stressed tones the resemblance is clear. "Turkey in the Straw," of course, is perhaps the most familiar of all American fiddle tunes and has been used for countless parodies. "Zip Coon" has spawned a complex of related fiddle tunes including "Sugar in the Gourd" and "Natchez Under the Hill."[10]

The second major offshoot from "The Rose Tree" is the song known variously as "My Grandmother Lives on Yonder Little Green," "My Grandma's Advice," "Little Johnny Green," or some variant of one of these. This song employs a variant of the first strain of "Rose Tree," sung twice for each verse and then repeated a third time for the refrain. (See ex. 9.1 for the first strain of a typical version.)

"My Grandma's Advice" apparently emerged into popularity in the late 1850s through performances by the Tremaine Family. The cover of the sheet music carries the notation "Sung with great applause by the Tremaine Family," and it also attributes the words and music to "M."[11] The Tremaine Family, a singing family of six members, was part of the wave of Hutchinson Family imitators. Their performances are recorded in New York venues from 1855 through 1862, when it seems that only two brothers remained in the act.[12]

Like the Hutchinsons, the Tremaines apparently reworked older, traditional material on occasion. John Harrington Cox notes that predecessors of the song appear as early as 1795.[13] None of the pre-Tremaine versions he cites have been located, and it is unclear from his notes if they included music or just the lyrics.

---

10. Jabbour, 311-14, discusses this group of tunes at some length, and provides extensive references.

11. Sheet music found at Houghton Library, Harvard University; it is also printed in Lester Levy, *Flashes of Merriment: A Century of Humorous Songs in America, 1805-1905* (Norman: University of Oklahoma Press, 1971), 336.

12. George C. Odell, *Annals of the New York Stage*, 15 vols. (New York: Columbia University Press, 1927-49), 6:498, 508; 7:202, 297, 300, 303, 370, 456, 461, 622; 8:412, 543, 554ff., 684, 692.

13. John Harrington Cox, *Folk Songs of the South* (1925; reprint, New York: Dover, 1967), 469.

"My Grandma's Advice" seems quickly to have acquired the status of an "old familiar song," and has been widely recovered as a folk song in North America. It turns up also in *Sam Henry's Songs of the People*, a collection of songs from Ireland.[14] The geographic spread of collected variants is remarkable: Ohio, West Virginia, Nova Scotia, Massachusetts, Alabama, Iowa, Illinois, Michigan, Pennsylvania, Arkansas, etc.[15] The comments of many singers clearly indicate that it was common musical fare in the second half of the nineteenth century. How much the Tremaine Family, or possibly other professional performers, had to do with popularizing the song is difficult to determine with precision, but given the wide range over which it is known, it seems likely that performances on the stage played a role. A visual representation of the "Rose Tree" family tree appears as fig. 9.2.

To summarize, there seems to have been a melody circulating in both Ireland and Scotland that William Shield adapted for use in *The Poor Soldier*. The air became quite popular through this use both directly via stage performances of an enormously popular work, and indirectly via later anthologizing of the individual song. The melody itself

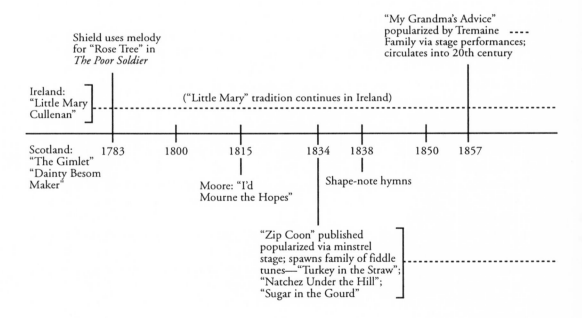

Figure 9.2. "The Rose Tree" and Its Branches.

---

14. *Sam Henry's Songs of the People*, ed. Gale Huntington, rev. Lani Hermann (Athens: University of Georgia Press, 1990), 258.

15. See the list of references in appendix 2 for details on regional folk song collections in which variants appear.

became firmly established as a popular instrumental piece, and remains so to this day. The melody was used by Thomas Moore and by an unknown shape-note hymn writer. Two variants, "Zip Coon" and "My Grandmother," were subsequently popularized via later stage traditions and ultimately also became staples of both vocal and instrumental folk traditions.

Case Study No. 2: "Vilikins and His Dinah"

One of the most remarkable instances of theater/folk interchange is found in the history of the tune which in its stage guise was known as "Vilikins and His Dinah" (see ex. 9.2b). The song emerged as a tune-text combination sometime in the 1840s, the performance vehicle of a popular comic stage performer named Fred Robson, a cockney-speaking character actor at the Olympic Theatre in London. He used it to good effect as the culminating song in Henry Mayhew's farce *The Wandering Minstrel,* and by some combination of his personality, the song's position in the play, and the power of the tune itself, it became a true "hit tune," the refrain of which was quoted in contemporary newspapers and diaries.[16] It was used as a tune direction in songsters and broadsides of the period, and it was borrowed by many other performers.

As in the case of "The Rose Tree," cited above, the "Vilikins and Dinah" tune has predecessors in oral tradition. The earliest tune and title associations with a similar melody is found in "Paddywhack," documented in *The National Tune Index* in many eighteenth-century prints in both Britain and America, and continuing in the oral tradition through the twentieth century.[17] With another set of lyrics, it is found in Beethoven's arrangement of the song "English Bulls, or the Irishman in London," which he did for the Edinburgh publisher George Thomson in 1814.

"Paddywhack" is a double-strained tune in almost all of its eighteenth-century appearances, and shows both *that* characteristic and its ascent to the octave in the first phrase—a trait that keeps it distinct from the later "Vilikins" tune while remaining close to the general outline. Whether Robson picked it up and reworked "Vilikins" from "Paddywhack," or simply came upon a similar contour on his own, we can't really know. As is shown in the comparison of six related tunes in ex. 9.2, there is at least the possibility that a similar tune was known in Ireland as the tune for a traditional version of "Lord Randal" (Child 12) as early as 1848—a date earlier than the first printed versions of the tune with the "Vilikins" text in 1853.

Whatever his source, the "hit" status of "Vilikins" dated from Robson's introduction of it with his own text, a parody of a serious traditional ballad on the tragic love affair of William and Dinah, done in a comic-tragic style with a nonsense refrain of the sort that was popular in the 1830s and 1840s: "singing right tooral-right tooral, right." The song was picked up by fellow actor Sam Cowell, who published it in his *Universal Songster* of

---

16. For a more detailed account of the theatrical history of the song, see Anne Dhu Shapiro [McLucas], "The Tune-Family Concept in British-American Folk-Song Scholarship" (Ph.D. diss., Harvard University, 1975), appendix 4.

17. Kate Van Winkle Keller and Carolyn Rabson, *The National Tune Index: 18th Century Secular Music* (New York: University Music Editions, 1980).

Example 9.2.

a. "Where were you all the day, my own pretty boy" [Lord Randal], P. W. Joyce, *Old Irish Folk Music and Songs* (1909), 394-95, no. 812, as sung by Peggy Cudmore, County Limerick, Ireland, age 12 or 13 years, ca. 1848.

b. "Vilikins and His Dinah, the popular serio-comic ballad as sung by Fred Robson in *The Wandering Minstrel*" (London: Musical Bouquet Office, 1853). Piano/vocal sheet music in key of E-flat.

c. "Dinah," Phillips Barry, Fannie H. Eckstorm, and Mary W. Smyth, *British Ballads from Maine* (New Haven: [n. p.], 1929), 67, as sung by Mrs. Susie Carr Young, Brewer, Me., recorded by George Herzog. Original key, D.

d. "Lord Randal," G. L. Kittredge, "Ballads and Songs," *Journal of American Folklore* 30 (1917): 290, as sung by Eva Warner Case, Missouri, collected by Belden in 1916. Original key, C.

e. "Lord Ronald," Gavin Greig and Alexander Keith, *Last Leaves of Traditional Ballads and Ballad Airs* (Aberdeen: n.p., 1925), 14, as sung by A. Barron, Mains of Whitehill, and T. Roger, Crimond, Scotland, January 1908. Original key, F.

f. "Not Far from Ballston," Folk Legacy FSA-15, side 1 (McLucas's transcription), sung by Lawrence Older, Mt. Pleasant, N. Y., as sung by his father, late nineteenth century. Original key, B-flat.

1856; it made its way to America on Cowell's numerous tours. In the 1850s the tune, both as a song in the original play and in various minstrel show parodies of it, was ubiquitous on the New York stage, and it is often given special mention on the playbills. It is from this period that we can date many of its other printed forms, including its tune-direction for Stephen Foster's election-year satire "The Great Baby Show" of 1856. Medleys, suites, arrangements, and quadrilles based on it by parlor music composers are found, especially in the years 1856-57, which seem to mark the height of its popularity in the American theater. It was used as a tune-direction for singing everything from Mormon hymns to the gold-rush text "Sweet Betsy from Pike," found first in *Put's Golden Songster* of 1858. Possibly from reprinting in twentieth-century anthologies like *American Folksongs* and *Fireside Book of Folksongs,* but even more likely from the recording made by Burl Ives, this seems to be the version known to most Americans in more or less expurgated forms. "Vilikins" continues to be a tune used for parody texts of various sorts; see ex. 9.2f for one such version from Lawrence Older of New York, whose text recounts a disastrous night on the town as recounted by his father, who apparently was the author.

From the compilation of variants of the "Vilikins" tune collected from oral tradition, it is possible to see the way in which the popular theater tune influenced oral tradition, but was, in turn, reshaped by that tradition. The tunes in ex. 9.2, many of them carrying either the "Vilikins" or the "Lord Randal" text, are closest to the original "Vilikins" outline, while those in ex. 9.3 show wider divergence in choice of texts, but especially in the way that the tune, though recognizably related, is reshaped. For example, "The Indian Lass" (see ex. 9.3a) is one of a group of tunes to similar texts that habitually use the sixth degree as an important note in the first and second phrases, creating a slightly different tonal flavor, while still retaining much of the "Vilikins" quality. The third and fourth phrases seem to take off from there, departing from "Vilikins" altogether.

Ex. 9.3b is a setting of the text to the ballad "Henry Martyn," and shows a mixing of the two strong traditions. The usual Henry Martyn tune has an extra phrase to accommodate a line of text after phrase 3; the singer manages this same extra phrase using the "Vilikins" outline." "The Croppy Boy" (ex. 9.3c) shows a condensation of the "Vilikins" contour. The tell-tale opening triad is truncated, but all the important structural tones are there, and by phrase 3 the triad returns. The final phrase is a tonal expansion of the "Vilikins" tune, using the flat seventh as the top of a wonderful downward sweep. Example 3d shows how a singer in the freely declaiming Maine Woods style can magically change the jaunty, parodistic little theater tune to a dramatic one.

Finally, ex. 9.3e-f, actually two parts of one tune, show a singer deliberately linking a longer filling-out of the "Vilikins" contour to accommodate a typical lumbering "Come All Ye" logging-camp text, with its shorter "original" form as a refrain in part 2. As can be seen from the number of notes in ex. 9.3e, the tune accommodates almost a third more syllables than ex. 9.3f, yet they are unmistakably versions of the same tune.

Such examples can be multiplied many times over, but these six show some of the ways in which the oral tradition has worked on the theater tune—modal and rhythmic changes, condensation or expansion of numbers of notes or of range, combination with other tunes, simple juxtaposition of two forms—and through it all a remarkable retention

Example 9.3.

a. "The Indian Lass," Frank Kidson, *Traditional Tunes* (Oxford, 1891), 110, as sung in North Yorkshire, England. Original key, C.

b. "Henry Martyn," *Journal of the Folk Song Society* 2 (1900), as sung by Henry Burstow, Sussex, 1893.

c. "The Croppy Boy," P. W. Joyce, *Old Irish Music and Songs* (Dublin, 1909), no. 300.

d. "Henry Sawyer," Phillips Barry, *Maine Woods Songster* (Cambridge, Mass., 1939), 81, no. 43, as sung by Mr. Harry Peters, Clifton, Maine, (n.d.). Original key, D.

e. "Bold Jack Donahoo," part 1, *Northeast Folklore* 8 (1968): 38-39, transcribed by Norman Cazden.

f. "Bold Jack Donahoo," part 2, same source.

of a basic contour and moments of note-for-note identity that link each example with the "Vilikins" melody.

This overview of the "Paddywhack"/"English Bulls"/"Lord Randal"/"Vilikins and His Dinah"/"Sweet Betsy," etc., tune gives us an appreciation of the fluidity of the musical culture of the nineteenth century. A tune from oral tradition may be dressed up for the concert-hall or salon, or sharpened for a stage-parody, then reabsorbed by oral tradition and virtually reinvented. A strong tune such as "Vilikins and His Dinah" seems not only to survive all of this but also becomes, at the height of its popularity, a magnetic force drawing other tunes into its orbit and in turn being reshaped by their texts and tendencies.

Case Study No. 3: "Hunters of Kentucky"

For insight into some of the mechanisms by which tunes were actually picked up by musicians and spread through theatrical appearances, the case of "The Hunters of Kentucky" is instructive. In the often hilarious account of the travels of actor/manager Sol Smith with a small touring theatrical company in the 1820s, *The Theatrical Apprenticeship of Sol Smith,* he tells of a tour he took in the western towns of New York, in the company of Mr. H. A. Williams, around 1825. After touring Schenectady, Utica, Saratoga Springs, Syracuse, and Auburn, he writes:

> At the latter place my wife and myself withdrew from the company and proceeded to Rochester, where we had been invited by the manager. We performed during the season, and had good benefits. At this place I sung the "Hunters of Kentucky" forty-one nights, and on the last night forgot some of the words, and was prompted from the boxes![18]

"Hunters of Kentucky" was one of the most popular songs of this period. The lyrics were by Samuel Woodworth, a prolific American journalist and playwright of the period, most well-known to popular music lovers as the author of the words to "The Old Oaken Bucket." He published "Hunters of Kentucky" in his *Melodies, Duets, Trios, Songs, and Ballads* of 1826, indicating there that it was originally written for the actor-singer Arthur Keene, active on the New York stage at that time. His tune direction for it was "Miss Bailey," a song from Colman's comic opera *Love Laughs at Locksmiths.* The text was picked up in *Lafayette Songster* of 1829 (p. 16) and in Grigg's *Southern and Western Songster,* a theatrically-oriented songster published in Philadelphia about 1826, where it is listed without tune direction "as sung by Mr. Ludlow, in the New-Orleans and Western Country Theatres."

Sol Smith's career as an actor was inspired by his contact with the traveling theatrical company of the playwright, actor, and impresario Noah Ludlow who, at the end of a long life in American theater, also left us a record of his travels in his *Dramatic Life as I Found It,* published at St. Louis in 1880. Ludlow recounts how in 1822 he first had success with "Hunters of Kentucky" at one of his benefits in New Orleans. According to Ludlow, he was sent the words to Woodworth's song by his brother, who had cut them out of the *New York Mirror,* and Ludlow also used the tune "Miss Bailey," to which, as he put it, "they seemed adapted." He goes on to describe the scene:

> When the night came I found the pit, or parquette, of the theatre crowded full of "river men,"—that is, keel-boat and flat-boat men. There were very few steamboat men. These men were easily known by their linsey-woolsey clothing and blanket coats. As soon as the comedy of the night was over, I dressed myself in a buckskin

---

18. Sol Smith, *The Theatrical Apprenticeship of Sol Smith* (Philadelphia: Carey and Hart, 1846), 95-96.

hunting-shirt and leggins, which I had borrowed of a river man, and with moccasins on my feet, and an old slouched hat on my head, and a rifle on my shoulder, I presented myself before the audience. I was saluted with loud applause of hands and feet, and a prolonged whoop, or howl, such as Indians give when they are especially pleased. I sang the first verse, and these extraordinary manifestations of delight were louder and longer than before; but when I came to the following lines:—

> "But Jackson he was wide awake, and wasn't scared with trifles;
> For well he knew what aim we take with our Kentucky rifles;
> So he marched us down to 'Cyprus Swamp;' the ground was low and mucky;
> There stood 'John Bull,' in martial pomp, but here was old Kentucky."

As I delivered the last five words, I took my old hat off my head, threw it upon the ground, and brought my rifle to the position of taking aim. At that instant came a shout and an Indian yell from the inmates of the pit, and a tremendous applause from other portions of the house, the whole lasting for nearly a minute, and, as Edmund Kean told his wife, after his first great success in London, "the house rose to me!" The whole pit was standing up and shouting. I had to sing the song three times that night before they would let me off.[19]

It did not end there, of course. Ludlow had to sing it in every city in the South in which he appeared. By the time he reached Huntsville, Alabama, a community of less than 2000 inhabitants, he was so tired of the repeated encores that he decided to give a copy of the song to one of the newspapers so that people who liked it could sing it for themselves. Needless to say, they continued their requests, but at least from this account we know how some traditional southern singers might have learned the words, long before songsters ever reached them.

In the songsters, the Woodworth tune-title of "Miss Bailey" had been supplanted as a tune direction by the "Hunters of Kentucky" by about 1831, but the latter did not last long in the songsters as a tune direction—this, despite the fact that it is clear from twentieth-century evidence that the tune did last in folk tradition. There is a rendition of it, for example, from the Flanders Collection, sung by Lily Delorme of Cadyville, New York, in 1940, a singer who has one of the most extensive traditional repertories. Perhaps Mrs. Delorme descends from one of those prompters who helped Sol Smith with the words in 1825.

* * *

In each of the foregoing cases, the role of the stage in perpetuating the tune was important: a tune, which may have been in the oral tradition in a similar form prior to its performance in the theater, is popularized through appearance in a play. It is heard in many theaters in virtually the same version; it is taken up in print and circulated as parlor music for voice or instruments, while at the same time instrumentalists and singers in the oral tradition are also exposed to it, either from attendance at the theater or through hearing it in other venues.

At this point, however, the process becomes more mysterious, because some tunes are dropped while others maintain their presence in the oral repertory. The key to early

---

19. Noah Ludlow, *Dramatic Life as I Found It* (St. Louis: n.p., 1880), 112.

Example 9.4. Melodic profiles of some theater tunes that have lasted in tradition. "Vilikins and His Dinah," from Oliver Ditson, sheet music, n.d. (ca. 1846); "The Hunters of Kentucky," from *Amateur's Song Book* (Boston: Elias Howe, Jr.,1843); "The White Cockade," from *Howe's School for the Violin* (Boston: Elias Howe, Jr., 1843); "The Bay of Biscay O!," from C. Bradlee, Boston, sheet music, n.d.

popularity is probably the theatrical presentation, linked to the celebrity of the play or stage personality presenting it. But it seems that the key to longevity is also to be found in the tunes themselves—a more directly musical influence from the theater.

In ex. 9.4 we present four tunes that have remained in the oral tradition and either had their origins in, or at some point were strongly influenced by, theatrical traditions. The height of popularity for all of these tunes fell somewhere between the late 1780s and 1860 and was associated with theatrical presentation. The tunes are distinctive—their very recognizability is of course one of the key features of their popularity—but they do also have several general points of resemblance.

1. They all have clear-cut, directed melodic contours—moving up and down in straightforward ways by scale or triad, without hovering indecisively around one pitch or another.
2. Most of them utilize triadic structures—the exceptions being those with deliberate Celtic associations, which substitute a pentatonic structure. So, while "Hunters of Kentucky" uses a downward-moving triad as its opening motive, "Rose Tree" uses the pentatonic version.
3. They share the very clear-cut, though hardly unusual, AA'BA form or ABBA form of the typical broadside ballad, which has built-in repetition for memorability (modified in fiddle traditions by repeating each two-phrase strain).

The memorability of these tunes, then, is assured in multiple ways: their clear-cut outlines, their repetitive structures, based on easily reproduced melodic strategies, and, most important for this discussion, their association with the theater and the personal stamp that it brings. Their adoption into oral tradition, of course, brings changes, more in some cases, less in others. One could, in fact, posit three sorts of popularity for tunes in the nineteenth century. There are the tunes whose period of popularity lasts only a short while and then fades forever—possibly the nearest to our current meaning of a hit tune—an "ephemeral popularity." The second type is a tune introduced with varying degrees of initial popularity that is then stabilized in the repertory of nineteenth-century tunes and is still heard today, its melodic and often even textual identity essentially unchanged—achieving "long-term stable popularity." "Auld Lang Syne," with its ritual use at New Year's is a good example of this type. Popularized through use in a play in the early nineteenth century, it has become a traditional song, but has not been extensively reshaped.[20] The third type is a tune that starts out a hit, with all the makings of ephemeral popularity, and somehow makes its impact in such a way that it enters the process of oral tradition and undergoes transformations just as any folk tune would. This sort of "long-term processed popularity" is characteristic of theater tunes that have been taken up by the folk tradition, as has been seen in the case studies of "Rose Tree" and "Vilikins and his Dinah" in particular.

Several conclusions can be drawn from the foregoing case studies and others like them. First, that the use of tunes from oral traditions in the theater occurred on a regular basis in the eighteenth and nineteenth centuries. Second, folk music was constantly reinvigorated by accepting tunes from the theater, and some of these tunes have had very long lives in the folk repertory, sometimes in multiple forms. And third, that the already loose boundaries between instrumental and vocal music were continually crossed in the theater and in the music derived from it. A song such as "Rose Tree" became an instrumental tune, while an apparent fiddle tune like "Paddy Whack" was appropriated for a theater song text.

20. See Anne Dhu Shapiro [McLucas], "Sounds of Scotland in 19th-Century America," *American Music* 8, no. 1 (spring 1990): 75-77.

The evidence put forth in this paper should put to rest the notion that folk music of previous centuries was "pure" and uninfluenced by commercial traditions—in this case theater and printed editions of music associated with theater. One of the burdens that scholarship has placed on folk music is the very notion of purity of oral tradition, which tempts people to call it "timeless" and to treat it as if it has no history. On the contrary, as this study shows, many tunes have specific, traceable histories. An understanding of particular tune histories can lead us to a clearer concept of the historical development of folk music in much the same way that we understand the historical development of other musics.

APPENDIX 1

SUMMARY HISTORY OF TUNES USED IN *THE POOR SOLDIER*

This list is an expansion of a similar one by Roger Fiske included in appendix E, "Borrowings 1760-1800," in his book *English Theatre Music in the Eighteenth Century*, 2d ed. (New York: Oxford University Press), 611-12. The indicated titles of the airs are as given in the 1784 Dublin libretto of *Poor Soldier*, reprinted by Walter H. Rubsamen, ed., in *Irish Ballad Operas and Burlesques* (New York: Garland, 1974).

Sleep On, Sleep On, My Kathleen Dear
INDICATED TITLE: "Ulcian and Ha Oh!"
TRADITIONAL TITLE: "Fair Hills of Eire, O." Reputedly composed in the mid-eighteenth century, apparently by reworking an older song. This older song contains the refrain "Ulluchá dubh O," a corruption of which is undoubtedly the source of O'Keeffe's title. Thomas Moore used the melody for "Weep On, Weep On, Your Hour Is Passed." P. W. Joyce refers to this and some other uses of the air, but does not mention *Poor Soldier*, nor does Donal O'Sullivan. See Joyce, *Irish Music and Song: A Collection of Songs in the Irish Language* (Dublin: M. H. Gill and Son, 1901) and O'Sullivan, *Songs of the Irish: An Anthology of Irish Folk Music and Poetry with English Verse Translations* (New York: Crown, [1960]). Francis O'Neill prints variants of the melody as both "Sleep On . . ." (p. 18) and "Fair Hills . . ." (p. 64); see his *Music of Ireland: Eighteen Hundred and Fifty Melodies* (Chicago: Lyon and Healy, 1903).

Dear Kathleen
INDICATED TITLE: "Master Willy Blakeny."
TRADITIONAL TITLE: Scottish reel, "The Drummer," which appears in the first volume of James Aird's *A Selection of Scotch, English, Irish and Foreign Airs Adapted to the Fife, Violin, or German-flute* (Glasgow: James Aird, [1782]), and elsewhere. An Irish reel, "Good Morning Nightcap," printed by O'Neill, is a different melody. Untraced under the indicated title.

Since Love Is the Plan
INDICATED TITLE: none.
TRADITIONAL TITLE: A member of the widespread "Todlen Hame" tune family, which dates from the early eighteenth century. Roger Fiske (p. 611) identifies this variant as an Irish song, "The Irish Lover's Morning Walk," published ca. 1780, but does not specify the source. The most widely known use of this variant, however, is as the melody for Robert Burns's "O Whistle and I'll Come to You."

Out of My Sight
INDICATED TITLE: "Doots and Phiggeen."
TRADITIONAL TITLE: Francis O'Neill relates this to a melody called "Dennis Don't Be Threatening," printed by Bunting in 1796; see *Irish Folk Music: A Fascinating Hobby* (1910; reprint, Darby, Pa.: Norwood Edition, 1973), 180. O'Neill also says that "Dennis" is the progenitor of "The Dandy O," an air used by Thomas Moore for "The Young May Moon." Untraced under the indicated title.

Twins of Latona
INDICATED TITLE: none.
UNTRACED IN TRADITION, probably by Shield.

Meadows Look Cheerful

INDICATED TITLE: none.
UNTRACED IN TRADITION, probably by Shield.

How Happy the Soldier

INDICATED TITLE: "Little House Under the Hill."
TRADITIONAL TITLE: Both "How Happy . . ." and "Little House. . . ." O'Neill states that this jig (as "Little House") "was composed by the famous 'Piper' Jackson, who flourished about 1750" (*Irish Folk Music*, 103). The tune has some currency in the fife repertory.

The Wealthy Fool (a.k.a. "Friend and Pitcher")

INDICATED TITLE: none.
UNTRACED IN TRADITION. However, it sounds like a Scottish reel or strathspey and will perhaps turn up in some of the early Scottish publications.

Rose Tree

See Appendix 2.

Dermot's Welcome as the May

INDICATED TITLE: "Foodle, Foddle."
TRADITIONAL TITLE: Roger Fiske identifies it as an Irish song, but gives no title.
He also notes that "Moore later wrote for the tune 'Oh for the Swords of former time,' calling it 'Name Unknown'"; he probably got it from *The Poor Soldier* (p. 611).

Though Late I Was Plump

INDICATED TITLE: "There Was a School Mistress in Limerick."
TRADITIONAL TITLE: "Moll Roe" or "Moll Roe in the Morning." This title turns up as a tune indication for a much earlier ballad opera, *Jack the Gyant Queller*, by Henry Brooke, from 1749. Moore wrote for this air "One Bumper at Parting," by which name the tune is sometimes printed.

Farewell, Ye Groves

INDICATED TITLE: none.
TRADITIONAL TITLE: "Savourneen Deelish." The melody was used for the popular nineteenth-century song "The Exile of Erin." Moore later wrote for the tune "'Tis gone and for ever."

Spring with the Smiling Face

INDICATED TITLE: none.
UNTRACED IN TRADITION, probably by Shield.

Tho' Leixlip Is Proud

INDICATED TITLE: none.
TRADITIONAL TITLE: "Humors of Glen/Glynn"; probably Irish. Burns used this tune for "Their Groves of Sweet Myrtle."

Dear Sir, This Brown Jug

INDICATED TITLE: none.

TRADITIONAL TITLE: Both melody and lyrics predate *The Poor Soldier*. It appears as "Toby Reduc'd" in the second volume of *Clio and Euterpe: or, British Harmony* (London: Henry Roberts, 1762, reissued from 1759), 41.

You Know I'm Your Priest

INDICATED TITLE: none.

TRADITIONAL TITLE: Irish song,"Sing Ballinamona, Oro," which can be traced to at least the first half of the eighteenth century.

You the Point May Carry

INDICATED TITLE: "Pease Upon a Trencher."

TRADITIONAL TITLE: Same. Known first in the first volume of Aird [1782], 58. The melody appears in many fife tutors and collections, and it was used as a breakfast and dinner call in the military. Moore used this for "The Time I've Lost in Wooing."

Since Kathleen

INDICATED TITLE: "I'll Have a Wife of My Own."

UNTRACED IN TRADITION. The tune "I Hac a Wife o' My Ain" printed by Gow and others, is a different melody.

Finale

INDICATED TITLE: "Planxty Connor."

TRADITIONAL TITLE: Same (or "John O'Connor," "Mrs. O'Connor," etc.); by Irish harper Turlough O'Carolan.

APPENDIX 2
"THE ROSE TREE" AND FAMILY IN PRINT AND ON RECORD
(arranged chronologically)

We have seen all the variants noted in this list; they are presented in chronological order. Other early American printings of "Rose Tree" are cited in Oscar Sonneck, *A Bibliography of Early Secular American Music (18th Century)*, revised and enlarged by William Treat Upton (1945; reprint, New York: Da Capo, 1964), and Richard J. Wolfe, *Secular Music in America, 1801-1825, A Bibliography*, 3 vols. (New York: New York Public Library, 1964). "Rose Tree" also appears in numerous eighteenth century American manuscripts; see James J. Fuld and Mary Wallace Davidson, *18th Century American Secular Music Manuscripts: An Inventory*, MLA Index and Bibliography Series, 20 (Philadelphia: Music Library Association, 1980).

This does not include references to the large and diverse "Zip Coon"/"Turkey in the Straw" branch of the "Rose Tree" family. Alan Jabbour has discussed this group of fiddle tunes; see note 11 above.

We gratefully acknowledge the assistance of Ms. Ruth Nichols, Graduate Research Assistant at the Center for Popular Music in 1992-93, in compiling some of the references included in this Appendix.

Pre-Shield Variants

Scottish

James Oswald, *Caledonian Pocket Companion* (London: Printed for the author, [ca. 1760]), vol. 10, 17. "The Gimblet."

[James Aird], *A Selection of Scotch, English, Irish and Foreign Airs Adapted to the Fife, Violin, or German-Flute* (Glasgow: James Aird, [ca. 1782]), vol. 1, 42. "The Dainty Besom Maker."

W[illiam] McGibbon and J[ames] Oswald, *A Favourite Collection of Scots Tunes and Highland Airs, etc. for the Violin or German Flute with a Bass for the Violoncello or Harpsichord* (Glasgow: A. McGoun, [ca. 1795]), book 2, 124. "The Dainty Besom Maker." Though printed after Shield used the melody as "Rose Tree" in *The Poor Soldier*, this setting of the air is identical with that printed under this title in Aird, and probably derives from Aird rather than Shield.

Irish [post-Shield variants of a song thought to date from before 1775]

P[atrick] W[eston] Joyce, *Irish Music and Song: A Collection of Songs in the Irish Language* (Dublin: M. H. Gill and Son, 1901), 40. "Moreen O'Cullenan."

Capt. Francis O'Neill, comp. & ed., *O'Neill's Music of Ireland: Eighteen Hundred and Fifty Melodies* (Chicago: Lyon and Healy, 1903), 48. "Little Mary Cullinan."

"Rose Tree" Text and/or Tune, or other Usages Traceable to *The Poor Soldier*

Niel Gow, *A Second Collection of Strathspey Reels, Etc.. with a Bass for the Violoncello of Harpsichord, Dedicated (by Permission) to the Noblemen and Gentlemen of the Caledonian Hunt* (Edinburgh: Corri and Sutherland, [1788]), 29. "Old Lee Rigg or Rose Tree Strathspey."

[Daniel? Steele], comp., *A New and Complete Preceptor for the German Flute, Together with a Choice Collection of Songs, Marches, Duets, etc.*, [lst ed?] (Albany: Daniel Steele, [1810-12]), 18.

The English Musical Repository: A Choice Selection of Esteemed English Songs. Adapted for the Voice, Violin, and German Flute (Edinburgh: Oliver and Boyd, 1811), 127. "A Rose-Tree Full in Bearing" [sic].

Edward Riley, *Riley's Flute Melodies*, vol. 1 (New York: Riley, [1814-16]; reprint, New York: Da Capo, 1973), 9.

Thomas Moore and Sir John Stevenson, *A Selection of Irish Melodies* (Dublin: W. Power; London: J. Power, [ca. 1815]), vol. 5, 49. "I'd Mourn the Hopes that Leave Me."

Edinburgh Repository of Music, Containing the Most Select English, Scottish & Irish Airs, Reels, Strathspeys, etc. (Edinburgh: J. Sutherland, [1816?]), vol. 1, 25.

[Daniel? Steele], comp., *A New and Complete Preceptor for the Fife: Together with a Collection of Choice Marches, etc. etc.*, [2nd ed?] (Albany: Daniel Steele, [1817-23]), 15.

The New Musical and Vocal Cabinet, Comprising a Selection of the Most Favorite English, Scotch and Irish Melodies. Arranged for the Voice, Violin, Flute, etc. as Sung at the Theatres and Harmonic Meetings (London: Thomas Kelly, 1820), vol. 2, 25. "A Rose-Tree Full in Bearing" [sic], "Composed by Mr. Shield."

George Thomson, *The Select Melodies of Scotland, Interspersed with Those of Ireland and Wales, United to the Songs of Robert Burns, Sir Walter Scott, Bart., and Other Distinguished Poets* (London: Preston, [1823]), vol. 5, 5. "Killeavy." Identified as Irish. Setting by Beethoven; lyrics "written for this work" by William Smyth.

[Oliver? Steele], comp., *A New and Complete Preceptor for the German Flute: Together with a Collection of Airs, Marches, Hornpipes, Waltzes, etc.*, [3rd ed?] (Albany, N.Y.: Oliver Steele, [1828-31]), 38.

The Book of Songs: or, the Northern, Eastern, Western and Southern Vocalist (Watertown, N.Y.: Knowlton and Riggs, 1832), 137. Lyrics only.

Grigg's Southern and Western Songster: Being a Choice Collection of the Most Fashionable Songs. Many of Which Are Original (Philadelphia: J. Grigg, 1832), 95. Lyrics only. Also in 1835 edition.

[Oliver? Steele], comp., *A New and Complete Preceptor for the German Flute: Together with a Collection of Airs, Marches, Hornpipes, Waltzes, etc.*, [4th ed?] (Albany: Oliver Steele, [1832-33]), 12.

John Patterson, comp., *A New Preceptor for the German Flute: with a Collection of Airs, Duets, Marches, Waltzes, etc.*, 5th ed. (Albany: Oliver Steele, 1834), 11.

The Singer's Own Book: A Well-Selected Collection of the Most Popular Sentimental, Patriotic, Naval, and Comic Songs, 30th ed. (Philadelphia: Key and Biddle, 1835), 18. "I'd Mourn the Hopes that Leave Me. Air—The Rose Tree." Lyrics only.

The United States Songster (Cincinnati: U. P. James, [1836]), 136. Lyrics only.

"A Rose Tree in Full Bearing" (New York: E. Riley, [1836-42]). Sheet music.

[Ole Bull?]. *Ole Bull Violin Instruction Book: A Complete School for the Violin* (Boston: Keith's Music Publishing House, 1845), 35. "Rose Tree in Full Bearing."

Edward White L., *Boston Melodeon: A Collection of Secular Melodies, Consisting of Songs, Glees, Rounds, Catches, &c. Including Many of the Most Popular Pieces of the Day, Arranged and Harmonized for Four Voices* (Boston: Elias Howe, 1847), 6. "A Rose Tree in Full Bearing."

John Paterson, *A Preceptor for the Violin: With a Collection of Airs, Duets, Marches, Waltzes, etc.*, 10th ed. (Albany: Steele & Durrie, 1847), 10.

William Bradbury Ryan, *Ryan's Mammoth Collection: 1050 Reels and Jigs, Hornpipes, Clogs, Walk-Arounds, Essences, Strathspeys, Highland Flings and Contra Dances, with Figures, and How to Play Them* (Boston: Elias Howe, 1883), 253. "I'll Cloot My Johnny's Gery Breecks—Strathspey." Presumably this should be "grey" breeks. An unrelated tune titled "Johnnie's Grey Breeks" turns up occasionally in eighteenth century collections. Ryan's collection reprinted as *One Thousand Fiddle Tunes* (Chicago: M. M. Cole, 1940).

Kerr's First Collection of Merry Melodies for the Violin (Glasgow: James S. Kerr [ca. 1895?]), 21.

Kerr's Violin Instructor and Irish Folk-Song Album, Containing 158 Irish Airs (Glasgow: James S. Kerr, [ca. 1900?]), 23.

Kerr's Modem Dance Album for the Violin (Glasgow: James S. Kerr, [ca. 1900?]), 16.

Allan's Tit-bits for the Violin: 476 Popular Airs Specially Adapted for the Amateur Violinist (Glasgow: Mozart Allan, [ca. 1900?]), 32.

[Ed Harding], *Harding's All-round Collection of Jigs, Reels and Country Dances* (New York: Harding's Music House, 1905), 42.

Paul DeVille and Maurice Gould, comps., *Universal Album of 200 Jigs, Reels, Hornpipes, etc. for Piano* (New York: Carl Fischer, 1912), 47. "I'll Cloot My Johnny's Gery Breeks."

Peter Kennedy, *The Fiddler's Tune-Book* (New York: Hargail Music Press, 1951), 28.

Ralph Sweet, *The Fifer's Delight*, 5th ed. (Enfield, Conn.: Ralph Sweet, 1981), 58.

Randy Miller and Jack Perron, *New England Fiddler's Repertoire* (East Alstead, N.H.: Fiddlecase Books, 1983), [35], no. 67.

David Brody, *The Fiddler's Fakebook* (New York: Oak Publications, 1983), 235. "Rose Tree I." The second setting on the page, "Rose Tree II," is an unrelated tune.

Recordings

McConnell's Four Leaf Shamrocks, "Moore's Favorite" in *Medley of Polkas*. Recorded 25 October 1924, in New York City; master B 31121-1. 78 rpm release: Victor 19539. Irish-American; New York City.

Cameron Men, in medley with "Dashing White Sergeant" and "My Love She's But a Lassie Yet." Recorded ca. 1934, probably in Edinburgh; master Ml65. 78 rpm release: Beltona BL2217; LP release: *The Cameron Men: Classic Scots Fiddle Recordings from the Thirties*, Topic 12T321, Scotland.

David and Ginger Hildebrand, recorded and issued a CD in 1990 as *Over the Hills and Far Away, Being a Collection of Music from 18th-Century Annapolis*, H103, and Albany Records TROY042. Their source: "Abel Shattuck's Book," manuscript copybook in Library of Congress, ca. 1800. U.S.

Shape-Note Hymn(s)

Knoxville Harmony. 1838. Example reprinted in George Pullen Jackson, *Spiritual Folksongs of Early America* (1937; reprint, Gloucester, Mass.: Peter Smith, 1975), 118. Jackson also prints the melody and first stanza in *White Spirituals in the Southern Uplands*. (1933; reprint, New York: Dover, 1965), 166. See note below on the version of "My Grandmother" included on the same page.

Southern Harmony (1854; reprint, Murray, Ky.: Pro Musicamericana, 1966), 63. "Land of Pleasure." Same text as the *Knoxville Harmony* piece, but the melody shows considerable variation in detail, giving the impression of being a "good" traditional version.

Ibid., 131. "The Christian's Conflicts." Yet another variation of the melody.

"My Grandma's Advice"

"Grandma's Advice" (New York: Horace Waters, 1857). Sheet music. "Words and music by M." A. N. Johnson, "My Grandmother's Lesson" (Boston: Oliver Ditson, 1857). Sheet music.

Father Kemp's Old Folks Concert Music (Boston: Oliver Ditson, 1874), 87.

Heart Songs (Boston: Chapple, 1909), 302.

Albert Tolman and Mary O. Eddy, "Traditional Texts and Tunes." *Journal of American Folklore* 35 (October-December 1922): 401. Mentioned, and references given, but not printed. "Sung to Miss Eddy by Mr. Henry Maurer, Perrysville, O." Mr. Maurer's song is printed in Mary O. Eddy, *Ballads and Songs from Ohio* (New York: J. J. Augustin, 1939), 300. "Little Johnny Green," subtitled "Grandma's Song." Ohio.

John Harrington Cox, *Folk-Songs of the South* (1925; reprint, New York: Dover, 1967), 469. "Little Johnny Green." Lyrics only. West Virginia.

Ethel Park Richardson, comp., *American Mountain Songs*, ed. and arr. by Sigmund Spaeth (n.p.: Greenberg, 1927), 46; notes, 109. "My Grandmother."

Sigmund Spaeth, *Weep Some More, My Lady* (1927; reprint, New York: Da Capo, 1980), 160. "My Grandmother." Apparently taken from Richardson.

W. Roy MacKenzie, *Ballads and Sea Songs from Nova Scotia* (Cambridge, Mass.: Harvard University Press, 1928), 379. "Little Johnny Green." Lyrics only. Nova Scotia.

George Pullen Jackson, *White Spirituals in the Southern Uplands.* (1933; reprint, New York: Dover, 1965), 66. Prints an untitled version of "My Grandmother" recorded in 1931 from his mother, Ann Jane Jackson of Birmingham, Alabama. She learned it from the singing of "a hired girl in her mother's home in Monson, Maine, about 1859."

Earl J. Stout, ed., *Folklore from Iowa* (New York: American Folk-Lore Society, 1936), 21. "Little Johnnie Green." Lyrics only. Iowa.

Emelyn Elizabeth Gardner, *Folklore from the Schoharie Hills of New York* (1937; reprint, New York: Arno Press, 1977), 206. "Grandma'am's Advice." New York.

Dorothy Scarborough, *A Song Catcher in Southern Mountains: American Folk Songs of British Ancestry* (1937; reprint, New York: AMS Press, 1966), 375. Two lyric variants printed under the collective title "Die an Old Maid." North Carolina and New York City.

John Harrington Cox, *Traditional Ballads and Folk-Songs Mainly from West Virginia*, Publications of the American Folklore Society, Bibliographical and Special Series, 15 (American Folklore Society, 1964), 101. "Grandma." West Virginia/Pennsylvania, 1939.

Eloise Hubbard Linscott, *Folk Songs of Old New England* (1939; rev. ed., Hamden, Conn.: Archon Books, 1962), 243; notes, 334. "My Grandmother Lived on Yonder Little Green."

Emelyn Elizabeth Gardner and Geraldine Jencks Chickering, *Ballads and Songs of Southern Michigan* (1939; reprint, Hatboro, Pa.: Folklore Associates, 1967), 480. No version printed, but notation of a manuscript version (as "Little Johnny Green") in a manuscript compiled in 1882 and 1883. Michigan.

Ira Ford, comp & ed., *Traditional Music of America* (1940; reprint, with foreword by Judith McCulloh, Hatboro, Pa.: Folklore Associates, 1965), 316. "Grandma's Advice." Probably Missouri.

Vance Randolph, collector and editor, *Ozark Folksongs* (1946; revised ed., with an introduction by W. K. McNeil, 4 vols., Columbia: University of Missouri Press, 1980), vol. 1, 383. "Grandmaw's Advice." Arkansas and Missouri.

Arthur Kyle Davis, Jr., *Folk-Songs of Virginia: A Descriptive Index and Classification of Material Collected under the Auspices of the Virginia Folklore Society* (Durham, N.C.: Duke University Press, 1949), 176. "Grandma's Advice." Virginia.

Alton C. Morris, ed., *Folksongs of Florida* (1950; reprint, Gainesville: University of Florida Press, 1990), 363. Two lyric variants under collective title "Little Johnny Green"; no tunes. Florida.

Henry M. Belden and Arthur Palmer Hudson, eds., *Folk Ballads from North Carolina*, vol. 2 of *The Frank C. Brown Collection of North Carolina Folklore* (Durham, N.C.: Duke University Press, 1952), 467. "Grandma's Advice." They report four texts and one fragment, "but they are so closely alike that it seems sufficient to give one of them." Collected in North Carolina; one learned in South Carolina.

Lester A. Hubbard, ed., *Ballads and Songs from Utah* (Salt Lake City: University of Utah Press, 1961), 61. "Grandma Would Have Died an Old Maid." Utah.

Helen Creighton, *Maritime Folk Songs*, musical transcriptions by Kenneth Peacock (Toronto: Ryerson Press, 1962), 36. "Grandma's Advice." Nova Scotia.

Harry B. Peters, ed., *Folk Songs Out of Wisconsin* (Madison: State Historical Society of Wisconsin, 1977), 157. "My Grandmother Lived on Yonder Green." Wisconsin.

The Grandma Moses American Song-Book (New York: Harry N. Abrams, 1985), 138. "My Grandma's Advice."

Gale Huntington, editor, transcriber, and annotator, *Sam Henry's Songs of the People*, rev. Lani Herrmann (Athens: University of Georgia Press, 1990), 258. "Grandma's Advice." County Donegal, Ireland.

Recordings

"Uncle" Joe Shippee, "My Grandmother Lives on Yonder Green." In medley with "Oh Susanna" and "Johnny Get Your Hair Cut." Recorded ca. January 1926; master 106561-2. 78 rpm releases: Pathé 21164, Perfect 11237, Romeo 916. Fiddle, with unknown piano. Connecticut.

Miscellaneous Other Uses of Variants of "Rose Tree" tune

P[atrick] W[eston] Joyce, ed., *Old Irish Folk Music and Songs: A Collection of 842 Irish Airs and Songs Hitherto Unpublished* (1909; New York: Cooper Square Publishers, 1965), 257. "Captain MacGreal of Connemara." From the manuscript collection compiled by William Forde, a Cork musician, ca. 1840-50. Joyce notes that a "Ninety-eight song" was also written to this air, and that there is a 6/8 setting in the Forde collection titled "Johnny Gibbon's March."

Gale Huntington, editor, transcriber, and annotator, *Sam Henry's Songs of the People*, rev. Lani Herrmann (Athens: University of Georgia Press, 1990), 40: "The Cobbler." Collected ca. 1934. Ireland. First strain a variant of the first strain of "Rose Tree"; second strain unrelated.

Ibid., 56: "Mick Magee." Collected ca. 1938 from James McLaughlin, Newhill, Ballymoney, Ireland. Single strain tune; a variant of the first strain of "Rose Tree."

Recordings

Steeleye Span, air to "False Knight on the Road." Recorded 1970-72. LP releases: *Please to See the King*, Big Tree Records BTS 2004 (U.S.); *Almanack*, Charisma Perspective CS 12 (England). Martin Carthy, Ashley Hutchings, Maddy Prior, Tim Hart, and Peter Knight. Album notes give credit to William Whyte and Francis James Child for this song, but provide no explicit information regarding source. England; pop-folk band.

10

Go Tell Aunt Rhody She's Rousseau's Dream

Murl J. Sickbert, Jr.

"Go Tell Aunt Rhody" has been one of the United States' most beloved and often-sung folk songs during the last two hundred years. But in this century there is a periodic question or argument about its origin—is it truly American or was it dreamt by Rousseau? On page 58 of Alan Lomax's *Penguin Book of American Folk Songs* is the familiar folktune "The Old Grey Goose" (alias "Aunt Rhody"), followed by the comment:

> Based on a melodic formula, widespread in folksong, especially in children's songs, this tune is, by some, attributed to Jean-Jacques Rousseau, to whom it is said to have come in a dream. This nursery jingle became the universal lullaby of the white pioneers and has been found in every part of America as *Aunt Tabby, Aunt Sarah, Aunt Nancy,* etc.[1]

"Go Tell Aunt Rhody" became part of my childhood in 1950s Texas. I heard and learned it there when my family moved to San Antonio in 1951. In 1975, I took Bill Kearns's American music course, which required the completion of a folk-song project. "Aunt Rhody" as a tune seemed as good as any, but at the time I had no idea that I was about to embark on a multi-cultural, cross-chronological odyssey that was to prove not only fascinating, but life-long in the sense that the search and the finding has continued until now. It seems appropriate to contribute this updated version of the paper to a festschrift for Bill, since the paper touches on the two main areas of study that I've both learned from him and in which I have received major inspiration from him: American music and eighteenth-century music.

1. Alan Lomax, comp. and ed., *The Penguin Book of American Folk Songs* (Baltimore: Penguin, 1964), 58. There is also another folk tune known as "The Old (Ole) Gray (Grey) Goose," which has an entirely different melody and text.

Example 10.1. "Go Tell Aunt Rhody," as learned by the author as a child.

Go tell Aunt Rho - dy, go tell Aunt Rho - dy. Go tell Aunt Rho - dy the old gray goose is dead.

Burl Ives refers to "Aunt Rhody" as "a song that is completely American in origin,"[2] but seems to argue with himself in another earlier source: "the origin of this most popular of American ballads is not known. The melody was apparently used by Jean Jacques Rousseau in an opera in 1750 [*sic*], but it was also known in New England at an earlier date."[3]

Whether it is called Aunt Rhody, or some other Aunt, whether it is referred to as the Old Gray Goose (or if you happen to be English—Grey Goose), it is still the same old familiar tune (see ex. 10.1). It is Lomax's allusion to Jean-Jacques Rousseau and the "dream origin" that is particularly arresting. How can this melody, so well known as a quintessentially American folk song, be attributed to Rousseau? And further, what is the dream connection?

As early as 1903, the American editors of the then-popular anthology *The World's Best Music* had mentioned the Rousseau connection with the melody.[4] Richard Chase in his *American Folk Tales and Songs* alluded to the situation in 1956. He cited the song under the title "The Old Gray Goose Is Dead" and wrote:

> The melody is also known in [American] hymnals as "Greenville" (No. 187 in the Methodist hymnal) or "Rousseau's Dream," and in this use it has a second part. It appeared in an opera written by Jean Jacques Rousseau in 1750, and it is said that

---

2. Burl Ives, *The Burl Ives Song Book* (New York: Ballantine, 1953), 197-99.

3. Burl Ives, *Favorite Folk Ballads of Burl Ives*, vol. 2 (New York: Leeds, 1947), 6-7. Ives, in company with many others, has misquoted the date of Rousseau's *Le Devin du village* (1752-53). He does not make clear whether he means the "earlier date" is before 1947 or before 1750, but he casually implies without proof that the tune is at least of eighteenth-century American origin. If he is referring to Eloise Linscott's *Folk Songs of Old New England*, 207 (see below), he has obviously misread the reference. The "Good Shepherd" tune Linscott gives as a basis for the Aunt Rhody "variation" is probably also known as "Sinner's Call" and has been mistaken by others as synonymous to Rousseau's melody. The two tunes can be seen one after the other in George Pullen Jackson's *White Spirituals in the Southern Uplands* (1933; reprint, New York: Dover, 1965), 149-50. That these melodies are similar but by no means identical is plain from comparison. Jackson's idea that "Aunt Rhody" is merely a descendant of "Greenville" is explained on pp. 149 and 173 of *White Spirituals*. A curious text variant appears on p. 174, where "Tell Aunt Rhody the old goose's dead" is sung to the hymn tune "Come Thou Fount." Jackson connects this version with its own tune variant (p. 150), sung to texts already associated with "Greenville." A confused version of this tangled skein reappears in the redoubtable third edition of H. Wiley Hitchcock's *Music in the United States* (Englewood Cliffs, N.J.: Prentice Hall, 1988), 103-04. Hitchcock claims that the "Come Thou Fount of Ev'ry Blessing" tune was "resecularized to 'Tell Aunt Rhody'," a conclusion that cannot be supported if the melodies are carefully compared and—especially—sung.

4. Helen Kendrick Johnson, Reginald DeKoven, et al., *The World's Best Music: Famous Songs and Those Who Made Them*, vol. 2 (New York: University Society, 1903), 318. Sir George Grove had called attention to the connection of "Rousseau's Dream" even earlier, in 1878, but did not know about the rich and complex American connections.

Rousseau dreamed he went to Heaven and heard angels singing this melody as they stood around the throne of God.[5]

It is significant that the story of a divine dream is the connection between the tune used as a hymn and the tune as found in Rousseau's opera. It is this story and the probable origin of the melody with which the migratory odyssey of the tune begins.

Rousseau and *Le Devin du village*

In 1752, Rousseau composed *Le Devin du village,* a pastoral *opéra bouffe,* for the delectation of the French Court. Its official Paris representation on 1 March 1753 before the whole court proved a great success, and King Louis XV was reported to have gone about humming a favorite air, "J'ai perdu mon serviteur; j'ai perdu tout mon bonheur" in "the most off-key voice in his kingdom."[6] This was not, however, the melody we call "Aunt Rhody." That tune is found in a much later scene, as a gavotte in the pantomime no. 8 (divertissement or ballet). It is danced by "la villageoise," a shepherdess or country girl, to music without words, which perhaps made it attractive to inventors of song or hymn texts. Rousseau's melody is more ornate than the American folk version and has two additional parts or reprises, not one as Lomax gives it (see ex. 10.2).

There is no indication of a "dream origin" or even a somnambulistic connection in the work itself, nor is there an explanation of the title "The Dream of Rousseau," either in the popularity of *Le Devin* or its imitations. Rousseau's writings contain no hint of a dream origin for this melody or indeed any of the music for *Le Devin. Au contraire,* the circumstances are the exact opposite. Rousseau wrote the first of the music—if not the pantomime itself—so he tells us, in a fit of insomnia:

> My sleep having forsaken me in the night, I considered in what manner it would be possible to give in France an idea of this kind of drama [Italian opera buffa]. . . . In the morning, whilst I took my walk and drank the waters, I hastily threw together a few couplets, to which I adapted such airs as occurred to me at the moment. . . . In six days my drama, excepting a few couplets, was written. . . . The only thing now wanting was the *divertissement,* which was not composed until a long time afterwards.[7]

One possible explanation for the dream legend is that there has been an imperfect transmission of the circumstances of composition for an earlier opera by Rousseau, *Les*

---

5. Richard Chase, *American Folk Tales and Songs* (New York: New American Library, 1956), 176.

6. Jean-Jacques Rousseau, *Oeuvres complètes de J. J. Rousseau,* vol. 15: *Mémoires et correspondance: Les Confessions* (book 8, 1753) (Paris: P. Dupont, 1824), 170. The English translation is from *The Confessions of Jean Jacques Rousseau* (New York: Modern Library, 1945), 392. Jelyotte was the person reporting the King's enthusiastic but unmelodious rendering of Rousseau's tunes.

7. *Oeuvres complètes,* 160-61. "La nuit, ne dormant pas, j'allais rêver comment on pourrait faire pour donner en France l'idée d'un drame de ce genre; . . . Le matin, en me promenant et prenant les eaux, je fis quelques manières de vers très à la hâte, et j'y adaptai des chants qui me revinrent en les faisant . . . en six jours mon drame fut écrit, à quelques vers près. . . . Il n'y manquait que le divertissement, qui ne fut fait que longtemps après." The English translation is from *The Confessions of Jean-Jacques Rousseau Newly Translated into English,* vol. 2 (Philadelphia: J.B. Lippincott, [n.d.]), 31.

Example 10.2. Jean-Jacques Rousseau's *Le Devin du village* (1752), Pantomime. Transcribed from pages 64-65 of the 1753 edition published by Boivin.

Pantomime

Example 10.2, continued.

Muses galantes. Rousseau relates in the *Confessions* that he fell seriously ill in 1742, and that while in a feverish delirium ("dans le transport de ma fièvre") he formed the idea of composing an opera, and even "composed" (i.e., thought out) songs, duets, and choruses.[8] He continues by wishing it were possible to record the dreams of people ill with fever, so that their sometimes marvelous creations resulting from delirium could be preserved.[9] Whatever the cause of the "dream story," the tune from *Le Devin's* divertissement was known—at least in song adaptations and pianoforte variations popular in early nineteenth-century parlors—as "Le Songe du Rousseau," or in English as "Rousseau's Dream." The opera itself was certainly the model for imitative text and melodies of Madame Favart's own pastoral comedy of September 1753, *Les Amours de Bastien et Bastienne,* the libretto of which Mozart set as well in 1768.[10] Neither of these parodies contains the melody under discussion, although it is clear that the simplicity of their music follows Rousseau's example.

Two years before Mozart's charming imitation, in 1766, Charles Burney had adapted Rousseau's original work and performed it at Drury Lane. He had done this because his friends the Grenvilles had first heard *Le Devin* in Paris in 1753, had sent Burney a copy,

8. *Oeuvres complètes, Les Confessions* (book 7, 1742), 30.

9. Ibid. "O si l'on pouvait tenir registre des rêves d'un fiévreux, quelles grandes et sublimes choses on verrait sortir quelquefois de son délire!"

10. Charles-Simon Favart, *Théâtre de M. et Mme Favart* (1763; reprint, Genève: Slatkine Reprints, 1971), 5: [1]-47. Mozart's version (K. 50/46b) was written when he was twelve.

and had exhorted him to translate and adapt the piece. Burney immediately created *The Cunning-Man,* a singing (syllabic) translation of *Le Devin,*[11] but it was not until the great actor David Garrick became enthusiastic about the work that it was finally produced on 21 November 1766.[12] Burney wrote in a fragmentary memoir that Garrick's delight in the work was infectious:

> Now Burney, says he, if you who know French as well as Music, wd [*sic*] but help us to bring on the stage in England this piece, the Airs are so beautiful that I am sure it wd have great success.[13]

Two comments in the "Advertisement" from the published libretto of Burney's edition suggest that the music of Rousseau's original reached England in one form or another:

> . . . the Airs have been scrupulously preserved from change or mutilation; as the Translator always thought them so pleasing, and so much the music of nature, that the coincidence of the words with the music, would be their greatest recommendation: as they can hardly, indeed, fail to gratify the ear, when sung, however they may displease it, when read.[14]

But the second page of the Advertisement contains an italicized afterthought:

> Upon rehearsing the Music, it has been thought necessary to retrench the Second Act, for fear of satiety: for though the Airs and Dances, after the reconciliation of *Colin* and *Phoebe* [originally Colette], are by no means inferior to the rest; yet, as no other business remains to be done after that circumstance than mere festivity, the Editor, with some reluctance, submitted to the omission of such Airs as are printed with inverted commas: however, they will be all published, with the Music, in a few days.[15]

The *divertissement* in question was thus omitted "with some reluctance," but was presumably later published.[16] By 1790 Burney's English version of *Le Devin* had appeared in New York's City Tavern (on October 21 and 26). It was also presented on July 21 and 6 December 1794 in Charleston.[17] We have no way of knowing if the pantomime with

---

11. Charles Burney, *The Cunning-Man, a Musical Entertainment, in Two Acts, as It Is Performed at the Theater Royal in Drury-Lane. Originally Written and Composed by M. J. J. Rousseau* (London: T. Becket and P. A. de Hondt, 1766). Burney titled his version *The Cunning-Man* because in eighteenth-century England "cunning" had the connotation of "soothsayer" or "conjuror."

12. Roger Lonsdale, *Dr. Charles Burney* (Oxford: Clarendon, 1965), 70ff.

13. Charles Burney, *Memoirs of Dr. Charles Burney, 1726-1769,* edited from autograph fragments by Slava Klima, Garry Bowers, and Kerry S. Grant (Lincoln: University of Nebraska, 1988), 168.

14. Charles Burney, *The Cunning-Man,* advertisement.

15. Ibid. See, however, pp. 24-25 of this 1766 libretto, which shows that the Pantomime was omitted, even though the preceding "Pastoral Dance" was included. I have not been able to locate separate examples of the instrumental music for this English version.

16. Since the air "In my cottage obscure" was omitted (indicated by the inverted commas in the libretto) and there is no indication of the Pantomime following it, the melody was most likely not performed in Burney's original version. A later (1773) London edition of *The Cunning-Man* is cited in the *British Museum Catalog of Printed Music.*

17. O. G. Sonneck, *Early Opera in America* (1915; reprint, New York: B. Blom, 1963), 200-06.

the now-celebrated tune was included in these performances, but other evidence proves that "Rousseau's Dream" had arrived in the young United States no later than the early nineteenth century.

Rousseau's Dream Goes On: Parlor and Folk Music

Rousseau's popular melody continued to be published throughout the nineteenth century in three quite different forms: 1) as instrumental pieces; 2) as popular songs, both with sentimental parlor texts and with more folk-like texts that reflected American pathos and/or humor; and 3) as hymns with suitably religious texts. In fact, the melody has continued to exist in parallel form to our day in both the secular and sacred traditions, with many variants. These variants, which will be given later, are sometimes rhythmic, metrical, and/or melodic. The basic character and *Gestalt* of the melody is never lost, however, in spite of those who argue that "Aunt Rhody" is only a variant of a song not originating from "Rousseau's Dream."

It is revealing that detractors of the Rousseaunian origin of "Aunt Rhody" cannot agree on the real source of the tune. According to some it is the "Good Shepherd" hymn, or "Come Thou Fount of Ev'ry Blessing," or another folk song. Some insist, like Alan Lomax cited above, that the tune is simply based on a melodic formula common in folk song, and especially in children's songs. This scornful opinion of the antecedents of "Aunt Rhody" denies the long history of the tune and its connection to Rousseau. Late eighteenth-century and early nineteenth-century people familiar with the melody, which was widely known as "Rousseau's Dream," would not have mistaken it for any other.

The Secular Song and Its Variants: Melissa, Antoinette, et al.

Probably about 1788, the melody—which may or may not have been popularly called "Rousseau's Dream" at that point—had begun a new life as a parlor song. It appeared as "Sweet Melissa, Lovely Maiden" in a London publication by J. Dale.[18] The words, by one Charles James, are sentimental and are "adapted to the Piano Forte, Harp or Guitar." This was published with an appended "Variation on the same Air" for harp and guitar[19] (see fig. 10.1).

Sweet Melissa

Sweet Melissa, lovely maiden!
Would'st thou know what absence does,
Ask the flow'r so quickly fading
Why its tint no longer glows?
Soon the drooping Rose will sigh,
Beauty's gone and all things die.
Yet nor Rose, nor Skies distilling

---

18. *British Museum Catalogue of Printed Music Published between 1487-1800*, vol. 2 (Nendeln, Liechtenstein: Kraus, 1968), 552. The date cannot be given with precision, but on p. 125 of Charles Humphries's *Music Publishing in the British Isles* (London: Cassell, 1954), a publication date between 1786 and 1791 is indicated.

19. *British Museum Catalogue*, 437. The connection to "Rousseau's Dream" and the probable date of publication are given in this source and do not appear in the publication itself.

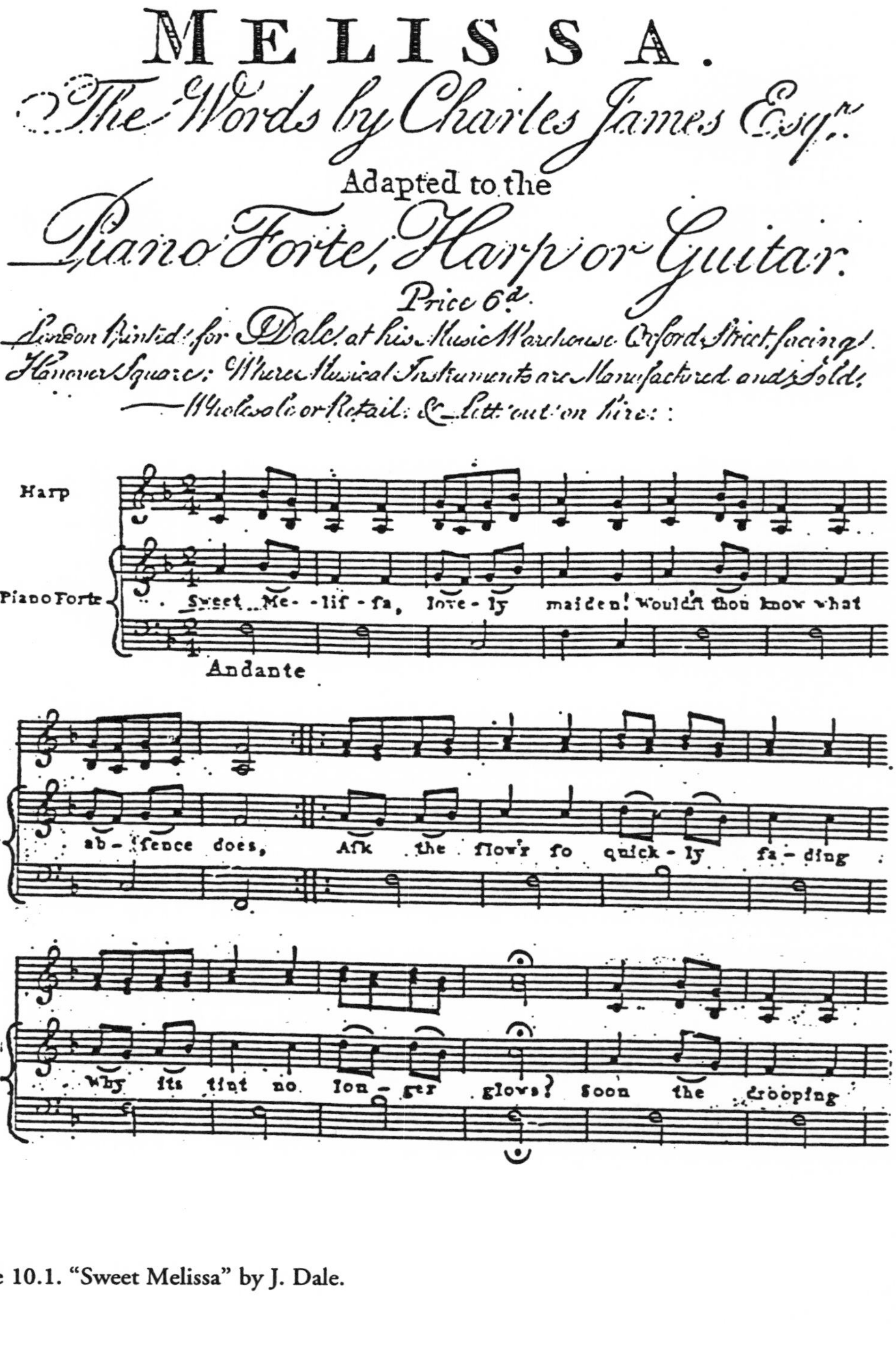

Figure 10.1. "Sweet Melissa" by J. Dale.

Rofe will figh, Beau-ty's gone and all things die.

Yet nor Rofe, nor Skies diftilling
Show'rs that weep their Charmer gone,
Feel her abfence half fo killing
As the Youth who pines alone
He the fecret anguifh feels,
Mourns, and ftill the caufe conceals.

Variation on the fame Air.

Guitar.

Figure 10.1, continued.

Show'rs that weep their Charmer gone,
Feel her absence half so killing
As the Youth who pines alone.
He the secret anguish feels,
Mourns, and still the cause conceals.

The earliest definitely dateable use of Rousseau's melody under its popular *sobriquet* "Rousseau's Dream" is found in a curious and—to our ears—somewhat risible composition of 1812, the *Variations on "Le songe de Rousseau"* by the great London pianoforte virtuoso John Cramer.[20] Its Beethovian introduction is followed by the comically simple and familiar tune and a series of ten variations giving an effect not unlike the later Dohnányi *Variations on a Nursery Tune* (see ex. 10.3).

A third version, "Hark! 'Tis the Breeze, from Moore's Sacred Songs, adapted to Rousseau's Dream by Sir J. Stevenson" was sold in 1825 by Dubois and Stodart in New York. "Hark 'Tis the Breeze," one of Thomas Moore's *Sacred Songs* (1816), was published and republished during the nineteenth century in volumes of this once extremely well-known poet's works. The use of melodies by composers popular in the early nineteenth century, such as Haydn, Mozart, and Beethoven, was suggested by the poet himself. This particular poem— religious in nature and perhaps providing a philosophical link with the hymn texts yet to be discussed—was to be sung to a melody by Rousseau, presumably "Rousseau's Dream." At least, this was the case in the already-cited adaptation of Moore's poem by John Stevenson.[21]

Hark 'Tis the Breeze (1825)

Hark! 'tis the breeze of twilight calling
Earth's weary children to repose;
While, round the couch of Nature falling,
Gently the night's soft curtains close.
Soon o'er a world, in sleep reclining,
Numberless stars, through yonder dark,
Shall look, like eyes of Cherubs shining
From out the veils that hid the Ark.

Guard us, oh Thou, who never sleepest,
Thou who, in silence throned above,
Throughout all time, unwearied, keepest
Thy watch of Glory, Pow'r, and Love.
Grant that, beneath thine eye, securely,
Our souls, awhile from life withdrawn,
May, in their darkness, stilly, purely,
Like "sealed fountains," rest till dawn.[22]

---

20. John Cramer, *Variations on "Le songe de Rousseau"* (London, 1812). A copy published by C.F. Peters in Leipzig [1818?] exists in the University of Colorado Music Library Special Collection.

21. Richard J. Wolfe, *Secular Music in America, 1801-1825: A Bibliography*, 3 vols. (New York: New York Public Library, 1964), no. 7664. Nos. 7663, 7665-70 represent several other instrumental versions. See also Wolfe, nos. 5277-80, and J. Bunker Clark, *The Dawning of American Keyboard Music* (Westport, Conn.: Greenwood, 1988), 133-34. I am indebted to Dr. Clark for pointing out the reference to William Blondell's variations mentioned there.

22. Thomas Moore, *Moore's Poetical Works*, vol. 4 (London: Longman, Orme, Brown, Green, & Longmans, 1841), 300.

Example 10.3. Introduction, theme, and beginning of variation 1 of J. B. Cramer's *Variations on "Le Songe de Rousseau"* (Rousseau's Dream).

Example 10.3, continued.

Rousseau's Dream

Example 10.3, continued.

Var. 1

A fourth popular song version, "Absence, the words adapted to the favourite air of Rousseau's Dream," was also available between 1820 and 1903 from publishers in the United States.[23] Otherwise known as "Days of Absence," it has a somewhat later text with a remarkably similar theme to "Sweet Melissa" and was anonymously written to the tune of "Rousseau's Dream" about 1820 (see ex. 10.4). This version was still being published at least as late as 1903.[24]

Cramer's piece is the only work of any pretension using Rousseau's tune, but there is another set of variations for piano four hands by T. Latour[25]—and possibly also an overture by him that supposedly contains "Rousseau's Dream." These examples all prove that the melody was known under this popular title on both sides of the Atlantic.

An additional texted version of Rousseau's Dream appears as a British lullaby or children's song of unknown date:

> Sleep, my baby, sleep like a lady,
> You shall have some milk when the cow comes home.[26]

---

23. Wolfe, nos. 7655-62. This version seems to have first appeared about 1820 by publishers in New York, Philadelphia, and Boston.

24. Johnson, DeKoven, et al., 318. The "Absence" text, with its Rousseaunian melody, a brief biography of Rousseau, and the connection of hymn and sentimental song alluded to above is seen here.

25. Wolfe, no. 7669.

26. George Grove, "Rousseau's Dream," *Grove's Dictionary of Music and Musicians* (London: Chappel, 1878). The basic article by Sir George was amended by W. H. Gratton Flood in the 2d ed. (1900) and retained in the 3rd (1927), 4th (1940) and 5th (1954) eds. (the lullaby appearing only in the latter). This article was one of the first (before and after the *World's Best Music*) to call attention to the connection of "Rousseau's Dream" and the Pantomime in *Le Devin du village*, but does not mention "Aunt Rhody" or the American hymn-tune development. It has been completely dropped from *New Grove*, nor in any form in the *New Grove Dictionary of American Music*.

Example 10.4. "Days of Absence" by Jean-Jacques Rousseau.[27]

Days of Absence

Not till that loved voice can greet me,
  Which so oft has charmed my ear,
Not till those sweet eyes can meet me,
  Telling that I still am dear:
Days of absence then will vanish,
  Joy will all my pangs repay;
Soon my bosom's idol banish
  Gloom, but felt when she's away.

All my love is turned to sadness,
  Absence pays the tender vow,
Hopes that filled the heart with gladness,
  Memory turns to anguish now;
Love may yet return to greet me,
  Hope may take the place of pain;
Antoinette with kisses meet me,
  Breathing love and peace again.

This is less a sentimental parlor song than a practical necessity (an English folksong?) for getting the children to sleep in the nursery. It does appear to be one British adaptation that may help to explain the myriads of folk variants that sprang up in the United States in the late eighteenth and nineteenth centuries. These were composed by ordinary people for use as lullabies, humorous songs to entertain and to relieve the drudgery of frontier life (play-party games),[27] and to while away long winter evenings or journeys to the West.

The American Folk Songs: Rhody, Nancy, et al.

The best-known of all the folk variants is our "Aunt Rhody," whose old gray goose dies in eternally untimely fashion, is mourned by her orphaned goslings (although their father survives in some versions), and thus prevents (or hastens?)[28] the manufacture of a highly useful feather bed.

---

27. The evidence for "Go Tell Aunt Rhody" having been a play-party game is slight, but consists of a novel and a new children's folk-song anthology: John M. Oskison, *Brothers Three* (New York: Macmillan, 1935), 47 ("Aunt Abbey"); and Katherine Krull, *Gonna Sing My Head Off! American Folksongs for Children* (New York: A. A. Knopf, 1992), 42.

28. Is it possible that we are so far removed in time from feather-bed manufacture that we have misconstrued the situation in "Aunt Rhody"? Perhaps there was a need to "tell Aunt Rhody" so the goose's feathers could immediately be plucked for use!

(1) Go (Run) tell Aunt Rhody (Nancy, Patsy, Tabbie, Dinah, etc.) [3x], the old gray
    (grey) goose is dead.
(2) The one she's been saving [3x], to make (her) a feather bed.
(3) She died (drowned) in the mill pond [3x], standing on her head.
(4) The goslings are crying (mourning) [3x], because their mother's dead.

This appears to be the basic version, one that is susceptible to endless variations and developments. The title—and/or the unfortunate Aunt—are also variously known as "The Old Gray (Grey) Goose," "Aunt Rhody" (Rody, Rhoda), "Rosie," "Nancy," "Nobbie," "Sally" (Sallie), "Tabbie," "Abbie," "Mandy," "Dinah," "Patsy," "Lucy," and "Martha." Some alternate or added verses are:

Saw, saw my leg off [3x], clear up to my knee.[29]
Tell her she died this morning [3x], With a pain across her head.[30]
She died last Friday [3x], with a pain all in her head.
She had one feather [3x], a-stickin' in her head.
Old gander's weepin' [3x], because his wife is dead.
She died last Friday [3x], it was a week ago.[31]
Monday she was buried [3x], Beneath the old oak tree.
She died with a pain [3x], in her left great toe.
The whole family's weeping [3x], because the mama's dead.

There is even an appeal to the (mock) sympathy of the audience:

Oh, ain't you sorry [3x], the old gray goose is dead?

Robert Winslow Gordon mentions variants of the goose's plight in which "she died happy," "she died swimming," or more picturesquely "she died a-kickin' her heels up o'er her head."[32] Linscott's *Folk Songs of Old New England* appears to provide a sex change for the fowl at the moment of mortality: "He died this morning [3x], Swimming across the pond."[33] One strange variant, "Aunt Tabbie," found in Gardner and Chickering's *Ballads and Songs of Southern Michigan,* is worth quoting in full:[34]

---

29. Mark Sullivan, *Our Times: The United States, 1900-1925,* vol. 2: *America Finding Herself* (New York: C. Scribner, 1927), 77 n.1. Several other texts (including "Lord, Dismiss Us with Thy Blessing") are mentioned in passing but not given in full in this source. Most of these are a sort of national doggerel naming the state capitals, the melody for which—very similar indeed to "Aunt Rhody"—is cited on p. 70.

30. William A. Owens, *Texas Folk Songs* (Austin: Texas Folklore Society, 1950), nos. 23, 262-63. See also the variants in Vance Randolph, *Ozark Folksongs,* 4 vols. (Columbia: University of Missouri Press, 1946-50, rev. 1980), 2:347-49 (no. 270).

31. *The Frank C. Brown Collection of North Carolina Folklore,* ed. Paul A. Brewster et al., vol. 1 (Durham: Duke University Press, 1952), 204-06. This and the next four verses cited are from this source. See also 3:177-78.

32. Robert Winslow Gordon, *Folk-Songs of America* (New York: National Service Bureau, 1938), vol. 13 (Nursery Songs), 85.

33. Eloise Linscott, *Folk Songs of Old New England* (Hamden, Conn.: Archon, 1962), 207.

34. Emelyn Elizabeth Gardner and Geraldine Jencks Chickering, *Ballads and Songs of Southern Michigan* (Ann Arbor: University of Michigan Press, 1939), 466 (no. 193). There is no explanation given of how the opening verse fits rhythmically with "Aunt Rhody" (here titled "Aunt Tabby").

(1) Old Mother Slipper-Slopper jumped out of bed, Ran to the window, said, "O John, the old gray goose is dead!

(2) Go tell Aunt Tabbie [3x], the old gray goose is dead.

(3) One she'd been saving [3x], to make a feather bed.

(4) Died in the garden [3x], for the want of bread.

The first verse can be understood only as a cross-fertilization from another folk song, "The Fox and the Goose," which Gardner and Chickering provide one page earlier than "Aunt Tabbie."[35] Because a goose also dies in this song, it is understandable that the confusion of verses occurred. In fact, the third verse of "The Fox and the Goose" is obviously the source for the Old Mother Slipper-Slopper verse:

(3) Old Mother Widdle Waddle jumped out of bed, And out of the window she popped her head, "John, John, John, the gray goose is dead, And the fox has come to the town O, town O, town O."[36]

Another textual variant is found in this same source:

(3) Died in the woodshed [3x], eating a crust of bread.[37]

Explanations for the goose's death are as various as the circumstances. In a variation ascribed both to Virginian country whites and to African-American sources, the goose is murdered: "Somebody killed it [3x], knocked it in the head"[38] or "She died with the slow fever [3x], out behind the shed."[39] An alternate explication in the same source allows for a different causal factor—dental, or is it accidental: "She died in the manger [3x], with toothache in her head."[40]

A further variant on the tune, with a completely novel text, comes from an unexpected source—the Pennsylvania Dutch. This version utilizes a double-verse variant

---

35. Ibid., 465 (no. 192). Curiously, the editors note that the song was written down in Greenville, Michigan. Is there some sort of an oblique relationship here, not only of text, but of place name and tune, since the hymn version was often known as "Greenville"? The difficulty with this idea is that there are numerous Greenvilles in the United States.

36. For a further variant of this connection, see "The Fox and the Goose" (no. 129) in *The Frank C. Brown Collection of North Carolina Folklore*, 3:178. Verse 4 is given as:

Old mother grey goose jumped out of bed
And out of the window she poked her head:
"Old man, old man, the grey goose is dead,
For I heard her holler 'Quing quath-e-o!'
For I heard her holler 'Quing quath-e-o!'"

Additional versions that follow retell the stories of Old Mother Hubbard, Old Mother Whittle, and Old Mother Widdle Waddle—all three with a black duck in place of the gray (grey) goose!

37. Gardner and Chickering, 466.

38. *Journal of American Folk-Lore* 26 (Lancaster, Pa.: American Folk-Lore Society, 1913): 130. This version is given in dialect. The note giving the tune "Ebeneezer" for "Aent Naency" is corrected on p. 373. See also Dorothy Scarborough, *On the Trail of Negro Folk-Songs* (Cambridge: Harvard University Press, 1925), 8, and Randolph, 2:347.

39. Randolph, 348.

40. Ibid.

Example 10.5. "Des bucklich Mennli," Pennsylvania Dutch folksong variant of "Go Tell Aunt Rhody."

1. Mar - jets wahn ich uff - schteh, Schau ich an di Wol - ke, Mud - der is di

Subb ge - kocht? Sin di Kieh ge - mol - ke? 2. Wann ich in mei kich - schtal Kumm

And five more verses

Fa mei Kie - che mol - ke, Schtet des buck - lich menn - li do Un fangt â zu schel - te

(double Dutch?) that retells the adventures of a little humpbacked house sprite, "Des bucklich Mennli"[41] (see ex.10.5).

These are only a few of many published sources, but other variants of "Aunt Rhody" are equally numerous and fascinating. Key choice, rhythm, and form of selected variants all show the influence of countless oral transmissions (see ex. 10.6). Whatever its true origin, nowadays it still continues to be sung from memory and in old and new arrangements just because it is part of the nostalgia and history of our musical past.[42] It is today still part of our folk heritage, found in many recordings by such artists as Pete Seeger, Burl Ives, Jean Ritchie, and others.[43] The melody, or references to it, can be found in several recent folksong sources, among them Randolph's *Ozark Folksongs*. Florence Brunnings's *Folk Song Index* of 1981 refers to several published settings and recordings of

41. George Korson, ed., *Pennsylvania Songs and Legends* (Baltimore: Johns Hopkins Press, 1949), 91-92. There are seven verses given here. Presumably the final, seventh verse is sung to the first eight bars of the melody as cited. For a somewhat different, perhaps more authentic, tune and verses, see Ruth L. Hausman, *Sing and Dance with the Pennsylvania Dutch* (New York: Edward B. Marks, 1953), 68-69.

42. Harry Robert Wilson, *Songs of the Hills and Plains* (Chicago: Hall & McCreary, 1943), 33 ("The Old Gray Goose"). This version has a verse not found elsewhere to my knowledge: "The barnyard is mourning, Barnyard is mourning [2x] A-waiting to be fed"; Burl Ives, *Favorite Folk Ballads of Burl Ives*, vol. 2 (New York: Leeds, 1949), 6; Hawley Ades, *Fred Waring Song Book* (Water Gap: Shawnee, 1962), 32 ("Go Tell Aunt Rhody"); Harry Taussig, *Folk Style Autoharp* (New York: Oak, 1967), 24; Ralph Alan Dale, *When I Met Robin* (New York: L.W. Singer, 1968), 19 ("Go Tell Aunt Rhody"). A variant verse of interest here is: "She died in the millpond [3x] From standing on her head."

43. Pete Seeger, *American Favorite Ballads* (Folkways FA 2321, [1958]), "Go Tell Aunt Rhody," Pete Seeger et al., *The Weavers Songbag* (Vanguard SRV-3001, [1967]), no. 4 "Aunt Rhodie"; Burl Ives, *Burl Ives Sings for Fun* (Decca DL-8248, [1956]), no. 4 "Aunt Rhody"; Jean Ritchie, *Folksongs For Children* (Bergenfield, N.J.: Prestige International, [1963]), "Lullabies"; John Avery Lomax, *The Ballad Hunter, Parts 9 & 10* (Washington: Library of Congress, Music Division, Recording Laboratory, [1958?]), "The Gray Goose." The Pennsylvania Dutch variant is recorded on George Britton, *Pennsylvania Dutch Folk Songs* (Folkways FA 2215, [1955]), no. 1 (not no. 3), "Des bucklich Mennli."

Example 10.6. Fifteen sources for variants of "Go Tell Aunt Rhody" listed in chronological order by date of collection or copyright.[a] (see footnote for ex. a, p. 144).

Example 10.6, continued.

a. Sources (key, of course, is immaterial):

1a-b. Cecil J. Sharp, *English Folk Songs From the Southern Appalachians*, vol. 2, "sung by Mrs. Laurel Jones" (1918), 345

2. Cecil J. Sharp, *Seventeen Nursery Songs From the Appalachian Mountains* (London: Novello, 1956), 3

3. Dorothy Scarborough, *On the Trail of Negro Folk-Songs* (Cambridge: Harvard University Press, 1925), 195-96

4a-b. Mark Sullivan. *Our Times: The United States, 1900-1925*, vol. 2: *America Finding Herself* (New York: Scribner's, 1927), 77, 70

5. Vance Randolph, *Ozark Folksongs*, vol. 2 (Columbia: University of Missouri Press, 1980), 347, "sung by Mrs. Frances Hall"

6. George Korson, *Pennsylvania Dutch Songs and Legends* (Baltimore: Johns Hopkins, University Press, 1949), 91-92, "sung by Mrs. Eva Roth"

7. Eloise Hubbard Linscott, *Folk Songs of Old New England* (Hamden, Conn.: Archon, 1962), 207, "recalled by Mrs. Jennie Hardy Linscott"

8. Harry Robert Wilson, *Songs of the Hills and Plains* (Chicago: Hall & McCreary, 1943), 33

9. John A. Lomax and Alan Lomax, *Best Loved American Folk Songs* [*Folk Song U.S.A.*] (New York: Grosset & Dunlap, 1947), 16-17

10. Burl Ives, *Favorite Folk Ballads of Burl Ives*, vol. 2 (New York: Leeds, 1949), 6-7

11. William A. Owens, *Texas Folk Songs* (Austin: Texas Folklore Society, 1950), 262-63

12. *The Frank C. Brown Collection of North Carolina Folklore*, vol. 5 (Durham: Duke University, 1962), 106-07 "sung by Miss Clara Hearne"

13. Hawley Ades, *Fred Waring Song Book* (Water Gap, Pa.: Shawnee Press, 1962), 32

14. Leslie Bell, *The Old Gray Goose*, ed. Hawley Ades (Water Gap, Pa.: Shawnee Press, 1981)

15. Peter Schickele, *Hollers, Hymns and Dirges* (Bryn Mawr, Pa.: Elkan-Vogel, 1989), 7

the melody.[44] A quite ingenious arrangement of "The Old Gray Goose" was published in 1981 by Leslie Bell and Hawley Ades.[45] There are several choral arrangements by George Lynn, Kirk Lewis Mechem, Keith Swanwick, and William Hall listed in the 1987 edition of *Secular Choral Music in Print*.[46] In 1989, Peter Schickele composed a haunting piano arrangement (see ex. 10.6, no. 15) , based, he says, on the classic Burl Ives rendition.[47] A new (1992) anthology of folksongs for children includes "Aunt Rhody."[48] And recently

---

44. Florence E. Brunnings, *Folk Song Index: A Comprehensive Guide to the Florence E. Brunnings Collection* (New York: Garland, 1981), 108-09. The list of variant titles here is impressive: "Go Tell Aunt Rhody," "Rhodie," "Rosie," "Abbie," "Tabbie," "Mandy," "Nancy," "The Old Gray Goose," "The Old Gray Goose Is Dead," "The Old Grey Goose," and "The Old Grey Goose Is Dead." Tune names listed are: "Greenville" and "Rousseau's Dream," "By Lo, My Baby," and "Watt's Cradle Song." These last two listings prove that the old lullaby given in *Grove* (1954) has been emulated by at least two later lullabies.

45. Bell, *The Old Gray Goose.*

46. *Secular Choral Music in Print*, 2d ed., vol. A (Philadelphia: Musicdata, 1987), 44, 305, 360, 645.

47. Peter Schickele, *Hollers, Hymns and Dirges* (Bryn Mawr, Pa.: Elkan-Vogel, 1989), 7.

48. Krull, 42. Two additional children's anthologies that feature "Aunt Rhody" are Aliki Brandenburg, *Go Tell Aunt Rhody* (New York: Macmillan, 1974) and Robert M. Quackenbush, *Go Tell Aunt Rhody, Starring the Old Gray Goose . . .* (Philadelphia: Lippincott, [1977]). There is also a lovely arrangement by Alec Wilder in *Lullabies and Night Songs* (New York: Harper & Row, 1965), 14-15.

(June 1992) there was a recorded performance of a (new?) American orchestral work with a dissonant quotation of "Go Tell Aunt Rhody" prominently stated in the French horns.[49]

The Hymn Version and Its Variants "Greenville," "Floods," and "Dismissals"

Paralleling the folksong development is the equally interesting history of hymn versions. Undoubtedly the tune was used over and over again for almost any text (sacred or secular) with the correct rhythm. Probably the earliest publication of any sacred text connected with the tune is found in John Rippon's *A Selection of Hymns*.[50] First published in London in 1787, the hymnal (without tunes) was meant for interdenominational use, but was apparently favored more by the fundamentalist, "low-church," lower-class religious sectors of eighteenth- and nineteenth-century Britain and the United States.[51] In some early American hymnals, Rousseau's melody is named "Rippon," alluding to this first published religious use, which by the 1820s had been reprinted many times in both countries.

Early hymn versions published originally in the United States are often found in the shape-note notation of so many early sacred song collections. Perhaps the first home-grown American version—a non-shape-note hymn—is in the Boston Handel and Haydn Society collection of 1825. Here it is named "Greenville" (see ex. 10.7).[52] The melody, ascribed to "Rosseau" (*sic*), is found on p. 209 together with the "Sicilian Hymn," here briefly titled "Sicily." The text (also known today as the "Sicilian Mariner's Hymn") is the John Fawcett "Dismissal Hymn," often set later to "Greenville" (i.e., "Rousseau's Dream") because the metrical lengths—eight and seven syllables—are the same. "Greenville" retains a semblance of its original Rousseaunian reprise form, so that the verse-lengths may be accommodated. The melody, as with virtually all the early hymn-books, is placed

---

49. From a program heard on the *Music in America* program (sponsored by the Lincoln automobile company) on radio station KVOD in Denver during the 7:00 p.m. hour, 6 June 1992. It has unfortunately proved impossible to retrieve or identify the piece.

50. John Rippon, *A Selection of Hymns From the Best Authors: Intended to Be an Appendix to Dr. Watt's Psalms and Hymns* (London: T. Wilkins, 1787), 259. It has so far proved impossible to track down the earliest edition of Rippon to contain "Greenville/Aunt Rhody," but it must have appeared before 1844, because the melody is ascribed to "Rippon" in *The Sacred Harp* of 1844. Rippon's *Selection of Hymns* appeared in numerous editions between 1787 and 1844 and after. There were at least eighteen London editions and eight American ones. The "First American Edition" was published in New York in 1792, and was followed by other editions originating in Boston, Philadelphia, Baltimore, and Elizabethtown (Pennsylvania?). The earliest appearance of the tune located so far is in the 4th ed. (1825) of *The Boston Handel and Haydn Society Collection of Church Music*. Interestingly, the tune does not appear in Rippon's *The Selection of Tunes in Miniature . . . Containing the Air and the Bass of All the Tunes in the Large Volume, Being Nearly 300 . . .* (London, 1806).

51. Even the American Presbyterians appear to have used the tune. A Canadian Presbyterian hymnal of 1897 also contains the melody. For further information on this source and three others, see below.

52. Lowell Mason, ed., *The Boston Handel and Haydn Society Collection of Church Music*, 4th ed. (Boston: Richardson and Lord, 1825), 233. This popular collection was reprinted over and over, running to at least eight editions (printings). In the 1835 edition of Mason's *Boston Academy's Collection of Church Music*, an odd coincidence is that the hymn-text immediately below "Greenville" (209), "Lord, Dismiss Us with Thy Blessing," has a nearly identical meter, has been associated with the tune for more than a century (see below), and is still the most commonly-found text today.

Example 10.7. "Greenville."

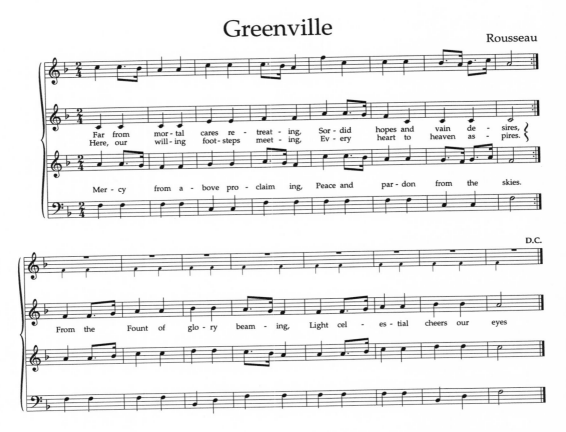

Greenville

Rousseau

Far from mor - tal cares re - treat - ing, Sor - did hopes and vain de - sires,
Here, our will - ing foot - steps meet - ing, Ev - ery heart to heaven as - pires.

Mer - cy from a - bove pro - claim ing, Peace and par - don from the skies.

D.C.

From the Fount of glo - ry beam - ing, Light cel - es - tial cheers our eyes

in the tenor and keeps also some of the original dotted-rhythms, just as Cramer's piano variations did. There is a change from Rousseau's 4/4 to 2/4, but the Cramer key of F remains in the Mason hymn. Mason probably intended his book for the use of the "cultured" middle and upper classes of his time. This meant that connections to Europe and Europeans were important and could explain the use of the French philosopher's tune.

"Sweet Affliction," which appears in *The Sacred Harp* of 1844 and many subsequent editions of shape-note hymnals, seems to be the first instance of the melody appearing in this type of hymnal for the common folk of the young United States, in this case the Primitive Baptists of the North- and Southeast (see ex. 10.8).[53] Here the source

53. See George Pullen Jackson, *Another Sheaf of White Spirituals* (Gainesville: University of Florida Press, 1952), 49. See also Jackson's *Down-East Spirituals and Others* (New York: J. J. Augustin, 1939), 241–42. Modern facsimile editions of *The Sacred Harp*—which exists in eight different revisions—are available: B. F. White and E. J. King, *The Sacred Harp*, 3rd ed. (1859; reprint, Nashville: Broadman Press, 1968), 145; *Original Sacred Harp, Denson Revision* (Kingsport, Tenn.: Kingsport Press, 1971), 145; the attribution in the last named is "John J. Rosseau [*sic*], 1752." Cf. with that of *The Boston Academy Collection*, 1835.

Example 10.8. "Sweet Affliction."

Sweet Affliction

attribution for the text only is "Rippon's Hymns, p. 541." The same hymn, with seven additional verses, appears in William Walker's *Southern Harmony and Musical Companion*, 1854 edition, although this hymnal appeared as early as 1835.[54]

The opening lines of some additional texts accompanying shape-note melodic versions associated with the tune found under the title "Importunity," as well as "Sweet Affliction," "Greenville," "Rousseau," or "Rippon" are: "Surely once thy garden flourish'd, ev'ry part look'd gay and green," "Far from mortal cares retreating," "Sordid hopes and vain desires," and "Savior, visit thy plantation, grant us, Lord, a gracious rain."[55] Two other early versions of the hymn are found in *Temple Melodies* (1851) and *The Shawm* (1853), the last named a joint effort of William B. Bradbury and George Root.[56] The three texts supplied in *Temple Melodies* are:

---

54. William Walker, *The Southern Harmony & Musical Companion: Containing a Choice Collection of Tunes, Psalms Odes, and Anthems, Selected from the Most Eminent Authors in the United States and Well Adapted to Christian Churches of Every Denomination, Singing Schools, and Private Societies* (1854; reprint, Lexington: University Press of Kentucky, 1987), 259.

55. Jackson, *White Spirituals*, 149. See also pp. 173-74 in which Jackson reiterates the commonly-held idea that the hymn antedates the "Aunt Rhody" song and brings up the Rousseau connection, but seems to indicate that the originator is J. B. Cramer. The correct date for Cramer's variations is 1814 (London, Chappell), not 1818. Also, it is curious that the "floods of tribulation," "rolling billows," and "gracious rain" all are connected with watery images. Perhaps this is why Aunt Rhody's goose died in the millpond.

56. William Batchelder Bradbury and George F. Root, *The Shawm: Library of Church Music, Embracing About One Thousand Pieces, Consisting of Psalm and Hymn Tunes* (New York: Mason, 1853), 201; Darius E. Jones, *Temple Melodies: A Collection of About Two Hundred Popular Tunes* (New York: Mason & Law, 1851), 137.

346.

(1) Jesus, I my cross have taken, All to leave and follow thee.
(2) Let the world despise and leave me; They have left my Savior, too.

347.

(1) Know, my soul! thy full salvation; Rise o'er sin, and fear and care.
(2) Haste thee on from grace to glory, Arm'd with faith, and wing'd with prayer.

348.

(1) Gently, Lord! Oh! gently lead us, Through this lonely vale of tears.
(2) In the hour of pain and anguish, In the hour when death draws near.

The Shawm utilizes the hymn text "Far From Mortal Cares." More tune variants and many additional texts appear in Henry Ward Beecher's *The Plymouth Collection* (1855-56) and Isaac B. Woodbury's *The New Lute of Zion* (1856).[57] Beecher's compilation is the earliest instance I have located that associates "Lord Dismiss Us with Thy Blessing" with Rousseau's melody, although as only one of seven alternate texts, including a Doxology. The "Dismissal Hymn" is much the more common text associated with Rousseau's gavotte-tune, especially as the nineteenth century closed. However, two further examples of hymns with still different texts are found in John C. Hollister's *Chants, Carols, and Tunes* (1871) and *The Christian Hymnal* (1871).[58] The dotted rhythm found in so many of the hymns is not commonly found in the folksongs. Ira Sankey's *Gospel Hymns* (1895) gives the tune in its F-major, dotted-rhythm form with the "Lord, Dismiss Us" text (ex. 10.9); the hymn "Come Thou Fount of Ev'ry Blessing" is found slightly earlier—surely conclusive proof that the compilers believed them to be two totally different hymns.[59]

Hymn versions of the melody—those given above are only a few from undoubted dozens—are found most often in Baptist, Methodist, Congregational, and other "low church" traditions in the United States in the late nineteenth and early twentieth centuries.[60] It is perhaps revealing that it is nearly always lacking in hymnals from the

---

57. Henry Ward Beecher, *The Plymouth Collection* (New York: Barnes, 1855), 16-17 (nos. 58-61); Isaac B. Woodbury, *The New Lute of Zion* (New York: Carlton and Porter, 1856), 190.

58. John C. Hollister, *Chants, Carols, and Tunes: A Supplement to The Sunday School Service and Tune Book* (New York: E.P. Dutton, [1871?]), 55; *The Christian Hymnal: A Choice Collection of Hymns and Tunes for Congregational and Social Worship* (Cincinnati: Chase & Hall, 1877), 323 (no. 840). It is interesting to note the inclusion of the hymn in a Sunday-School hymnal, acknowledging for the first time that this was considered suitable for children.

59. Ira D. Sankey et. al., *Gospel Hymns Nos. 1 to 6 Complete* (1895, reprint; New York: Da Capo, 1972), 494 (no. 732); "Come Thou Fount" is on p. 451 (no. 633). The certainty that no melodies are given more than once in the volume is clear: "all duplicate pieces have been omitted" (p. [2]), which is borne out by the alternate texts supplied for numbers of hymn tunes.

60. It is included in *The Methodist Hymnal* (Nashville: Methodist Book Concern, 1935), no. 187, with the text "Come, ye sinners, poor and needy, Weak and wounded, sick and sore; Jesus ready stands to save you, Full of pity, love and power: He is able, He is able, He is willing: doubt no more," with three additional verses. The same text is supplied to the melody in *The Mennonite Hymnary* (Berne, Ind.: Mennonite Book Concern, 1940), #459. In both hymnals the tune name is "Greenville," but can be found in the composer index under Rousseau's name. The Methodists reissued "Greenville" in *The Methodist Hymnal: Official Hymnal of the Methodist Church* (New York: Methodist Publishing House, 1939). In Charles Robinson's *The New Laudes Domini: A Selection of*

Example 10.9. "Lord, Dismiss Us."

John Fawcett, D. D.

Lord, Dismiss Us

J. J. Rousseau

Lord, dis - miss us with Thy bles - ing, Fill our hearts with joy and peace;

O, re - freash us, O re - fresh us, Trav - 'ling thro' this wil - der - ness.

Let us each, Thy love pos - sess - ing, Tri - umph in re - deem - ing grace;

"high church" traditions: Lutheran, Episcopalian, and Roman Catholic.[61] Among currently-used hymnbooks, the tune is found apparently only in the Mormon Hymnal.[62]

The Aunts Go Marching On

For now the voyage of Aunt Rhody and all the other aunts must come to a halt, but Rousseau's melody will—like a mighty army—go marching on. The tune appeared in print first in Rousseau's *Le Devin du village*,[63] became popular as "Rousseau's Dream" (when it was taken up by poets and composers of popular songs, parlor music, and

---

Spiritual Songs, Ancient and Modern (New York: Century, 1892), 93 (no. 227), the text is "Lord, dismiss us." Robinson's introduction alludes to earlier hymnals published in 1865, 1878, and 1884. These hymnals, like John Rippon's, appear to have been designed for inter-denominational use.

61. The melody may be found in one Lutheran hymnal: *The Hymnal and Order of Service Lectionary,* [4th] ed. (Rock Island, Ill.: Augustana Book Concern: 1930), 301 (no. 365). The text—a mission hymn—is: "Savior, sprinkle many nations, Fruitful let Thy sorrows be; By Thy pains and consolations Draw the Gentiles unto Thee. Of Thy cross the wondrous story, Be it to the nations told; Let them see Thee in Thy glory, And Thy mercy manifold." There are two additional verses.

62. *Hymns of the Church of Jesus Christ of Latter-Day Saints* (Salt Lake City: Church of Jesus Christ of Latter-Day Saints, 1985), "Lord, dismiss us with thy blessing" (no. 163). In this hymnal, as in the Methodist and Mennonite ones, "Greenville" is the tune name, but can be found in the composer index under Rousseau's name.

63. Thus strengthening the case for Rousseau's authorship. A journalist by the name of Élie Fréron did, however, charge Rousseau with plagiarizing the melodies of *Le Devin* from Italian musicians. See Maurice Cranston, *Jean-Jacques: The Early Life and Work of Jean-Jacques Rousseau, 1712-1754* (New York: Norton, 1982), 284. There is always the possibility that he merely borrowed it from a folk source of some sort—perhaps French or Swiss—and used the melody as local color in the pantomime danced by his "villageoise." Giving some strength to this caveat is the similarity of the phrase ending of "Greenville/Aunt Rhody" to the French *voyageur* song "Alouette." See for instance, Marius Barbeau's *Alouette: Nouveau Recueil de chansons populaires avec mélodies, choisies dans le répertoire du Musée National du Canada* (Montreal: Lumen, 1946), 11-14, perhaps betraying the French origin of the melodies. But one can hardly base an argument on the origin of so well-known and famous a folksong as "Aunt Rhody" on a theoretically earlier source, unless that source can be found. Indeed, Rousseau would probably fire off a post-mortem pamphlet in his own defense, if he were able. A more concrete and modern defense of the charge of plagiarism against Rousseau is in a French-Canadian version of the hymn "Greenville."

hymns), and has continued to flourish to the present time as the folksong "Aunt Rhody" et al., and as the hymn "Greenville."

Thus "Rhody" and her relatives have traveled from France to England then over to the shores and across the length and breadth of North America—especially to the United States—in the course of the 100 years from about 1760 to about 1860. We have observed its metamorphosis into part of our folk heritage during the succeeding century. During those travels (from Grenville to Greenville?) it became a sentimental song, a folksong, and a hymn. Its many verses ranging from the sublime to the hilarious have rung from genteel parlors to open-air revivals, to churches and cabins and covered wagons. If it did not begin as a truly American song, it has—like many of the people who sang it—become one by the process of naturalization. Most Americans I have talked to know "Rhody" well. This, if nothing else, proves that Aunt Rhody, whether in her folk or religious guise, has achieved immortality if not respectability. Nowadays she may not be anyone's dream, but she is a solid reality in our folk-musical heritage.

For the Canadian versions of "Greenville," see John Beckwith, ed., *Hymn Tunes*, The Canadian Musical Heritage, 5, (Ottawa: Canadian Musical Heritage Society, 1986). The four hymn versions appear as nos. 54a-d. The sources given are: (54a) Zebulon Estey, ed., *New Brunswick Church Harmony* (Saint John, 1835)—a remarkably early source!; (54b) G. W. Linton, ed., *The Union Chimes* (Toronto: [1868?]); (54c) L. E. Rivard, ed., *Chants évangéliques* (Montréal, 1862)—[the very interesting French-Canadian version; and (54d) *The Presbyterian Book of Praise* (Oxford and London, 1897 and later). This surely strongly suggests that Rousseau did not take the melody of his "Pantomime" from a French folksong, or such a source would have been noted.

11

Fanfares

for Six French Horns
for William Kearns

Karl Kroeger

12

The Piano Works of P. Antony Corri and Arthur Clifton, British-American Composer

J. Bunker Clark

One of the best musicians and composers to emigrate to the United States in the first quarter of the nineteenth century was Philip Antony Corri. The son of the Italian-born Domenico Corri, he was born in Edinburgh, probably in 1784.[1] Antony's sister was Sophia Giustina Corri, who married Jan Ladislav Dussek; his brothers Montague Philip Corri and Haydn Corri were also musicians.

Antony was established as a composer in London by about 1805 when a significant number of his piano works and songs began to be published, mainly by Chappell. His *L'anima di musica* (1810) is 121 pages long—the most extensive and thorough pianoforte tutor of its time, even in comparison with the better-known one by Clementi. It includes *Original System of Preluding*, also published separately.[2] He was one of the organizers of the London Philharmonic Society in 1813, and sang in its first concerts. Sometime afterwards, he disappeared from London's professional life, and emigrated to the United

---

1. Domenico (1746-1825) wrote, among other works, *The Singer's Preceptor* (1810), available in facsimile with his *A Select Collection of the Most Admired Songs, Duetts, etc.* in the series *Domenico Corri's Treatises on Singing*, vols. 1-4, ed. Richard Maunder (New York: Garland, 1993-95).

2. Chappell & Co., plate 101, pp. 81-113. The preface on p. 81 states: "The following pages are extracted from a work in four parts intitled L'anima di musica, in which the author has treated on every subject connected with pianoforte playing; these pages form the fourth part of that treatise."

States.[3] The apparent reason was marital difficulty with his wife, Elizabeth Augusta Corri, who was living with Lord Edward Hawke as his wife, calling herself Lady Hawke.[4] The first documented evidence of Anthony's presence in Baltimore is a reference to "Mr. Clifton, of this City" on a playbill for a 21 November 1817 performance of *The Feast of Apollo* at the Baltimore Theatre, in which he accompanied at the piano. Re-christened Arthur Clifton on 31 December 1817 at St. Paul's Episcopal Church, he married Alphonsa Elizabeth Ringgold the following day, New Year's Day 1818. It is not clear if Corri had obtained a divorce from his first wife; if he hadn't, then with this American marriage, he would have been commiting bigamy.

In 1818, Clifton became organist at the First Presbyterian Church; in 1823, he moved to the First Independent Church (Unitarian).[5] He also taught voice, and probably piano, and appeared in concerts as singer and pianist. He continued to compose songs

---

3. *History of the Philharmonic Society of London, 1813-1912* (London, 1912), 5, 8-9, mentions Corri as a founder and performer in 1813, and as performer as late as 11 June 1821 (p. 53) on a program that included "Mme Rosalie Corri." According to Lubov Keefer, *Baltimore's Music: The Haven of the American Composer* (Baltimore: J. H. Furst, 1962), 63-64 n. 9, however, Clifton was playing quartets in Philadelphia (*sic*) as early as 1813; he does not support his statement, however, with any documentation. Nathan Buckner (see next note) found evidence that Corri was still in London, as a director of the Professional Society, from November 1815 through April 1816. F. J. Metcalf, apparently the first scholar to connect Corri and Clifton, in "Philip Anthony Corri and Arthur Clifton," *The Choir and Musical Journal* 160 (April 1923): 75-76, reports that the Baltimore directory of 1814 includes an "Anthony Corri," who had a dry goods and grocery store—but whether this was our Corri is not determined. Clifton seems to have returned to England for a while in 1821, according to the Philharmonic Society program cited above. Perhaps this trip precipitated the following, printed in Boston's *The Euterpeiad*, 22 September 1822, p. 102:

A London paper contains the following advertisement—

ADVERTISEMENT—£100 Reward.

Whereas Philip Anthony Corri, Musical composer and Teacher, left this country about five years ago for New-York, and his present abode is desired to be known to the advertiser, but not for any hostile purpose. This is to give notice, whoever will, within six months from this date, furnish satisfactory information to Mr. Harmer, solicitor, Hatton Garden, of the present residence of the said Mr. Corri, so that an interview may be obtained with him shall be paid a reward of £100. N. B. It has been reported that the above named P. A. Corri after his arrival at New-York, proceeded to Philadelphia, thence to Baltimore, and there married a quaker lady: it has also been asserted that he is returned to England. The said P. A. Corri has a sharp Italian visage, sallow complexion, black curly hair, black eyes, and is bald on the crown of the head. He is forty years of age, 5 feet 8 inches high, and has a soft voice and gentlemanly manners.—London, June 17, 1822.

4. Nathan A. Buckner kindly shared a transcript concerning a court case, "Lord Hawke v. Corri, Calling Herself Lady Hawke," taken from *The Courier* (London), 18 May 1820. Since I wrote the present article, his dissertation was completed: "Philip Antony Corri/Arthur Clifton: His Life and Piano Works with a New Edition" (D.M.A., piano, University of Maryland, 1996), and Kallisti Music Press (Philadelphia) has issued (1997) his edition as *Philip Antony Corri: Complete Music for Solo Piano* and *Philip Antony Corri: Concerto da camera*.

5. A letter dated "Baltimore, 22 October 1818," from Arthur Clifton, organist of the First Presbyterian Church, and Thomas Carr, organist of the First Independent Church, assesses the newly installed organ: "We have tried and examined the Organ erected by Mr. Hall at the First Independent Church Baltimore and consider it without question the finest, richest and most complete Instrument in this City; and it is our opinion that a finer Organ could not have been built in Europe either for comprehension of variety or richness of effect. The execution of the whole interior and exterior reflects the highest credit on the skill and ingenuity of the Builder Mr.

and piano works that were published in Baltimore beginning in 1820. His opera *The Enterprise: or, Love and Pleasure*, with libretto by Col. W. H. Hamilton, was performed at the Baltimore Theater on 27 May and 14 June 1822. It was more ambitious than the usual English ballad opera or semi-opera, yet probably lacked the recitatives of Italian opera.[6] He published music from this opera in eighteen separate numbers in 1823.[7] Other publications are *An Original Collection of Psalm Tunes* (1819), *New Vocal Instructer* [*sic*] of 1820, and a newly-written, much smaller tutor, *New Piano Forte Preceptor* (1820),

---

Hall." A later letter, dated 29 March 1826, from Clifton to Cap[n] [Isaac] Phillipps, chairman of the Board of Trustees for the First Independent Church of Baltimore questions the conditions of his employment at the church:

> Allow me, through you as Chairman of the Board of Trustees for the first Independent Church, to make a request which I hope may not be consider'd by them as unjust, or occasion'd by dissatisfaction.
> It is now three years that I have had the honor to serve in your Church as Organist & to the best of my abilities, without ever having fail'd in punctuality. On the resignation of Mr. Carr I accepted the double duty of Organist and Leader at a very reduced salary, with the understanding that when the fiscal affairs of the Church were less embarrass'd, my salary would be more liberal.
> From a knowledge of the difficulties the Church labor'd under, I have never yet made any claim on the liberality of the Trustees, but now I hope it will not be deem'd premature, when I solicit their consideration that I am performing the duty of two, with the salary of one.
> If the Trustees are content with my efforts, and think me worthy of the situation I yet hold, may I hope that they will so evince their approval by encreasing [*sic*] my salary, thereby rendering it more commensurate with the duty I have to perform, and with that of my predecessor.

Alas, a letter of 7 January 1830 to the same Phillipps gives evidence that the situation had not improved:

> The short notice I had of any reduction being made in the already reduced Salary I received at your Church and the short conversation I had with you yesterday morning prevented me from properly contemplating the subject.
> I now beg leave, respectfully to state my reasons for objecting to the proposed reduction.
> I have held my situation of Organist and Conductor of the Choir at a rate by no means adequate to the double duty which in all other Churches is performed by two individuals. At St. Pauls—M[r] Meinicke & J. Cole for $400—at Christ Church by M[r] L. Smith (who is not a professor of music but a Bankers Clerk) and M[r] Dearley [Darley?] for $300—At M[r] Nevins Church by M[r] Smitt & M[r] Welsh for $300—and I believe at St. Peters by M[r] Sminke & another for $300—At the Cathedral at a great expence [*sic*]— Hence I have saved for the Church 50 or 100 dollars annually by assuming the double duty of organist and conductor or teacher of the Choir at a low rate; indeed at half what you formerly paid M[r] Carr—
> Under the circumstances, the Trustees will not take offence [*sic*] at my resigning a situation I cannot hold with satisfaction to myself, nor consequently, to my employers.
> If the funds of the Church are insufficient to defray the expense of the Choir, I regret, that in duty to my professional abilities, I cannot yield to my desire of acquiescing to their proposal—
> I would accept the situation of Organist alone at $200—but to lead, and teach the Choir is certainly worth a dollar a day.

My thanks to James R. Houston, organist of the First Unitarian Church, who in April 1983 sent copies and his transcriptions of these documents, which were rediscovered about two years before, along with documents associated with the foundation of the church in 1817.

6. See William D. Gettel, "Arthur Clifton's Enterprise," *Journal of the American Musicological Society* 2, no. 2 (spring 1949): 23-35.

7. Facsimile in Martha Furman Schleifer, ed., *American Opera and Music for the Stage: 18th and 19th Century*, in Three Centuries of American Music: A Collection of American Sacred and Secular Music, 5 (Boston: G. K. Hall, 1990).

revised as *Clifton's New and Improved Piano Forte Preceptor* in 1827.[8] He died in Baltimore on 10 February 1832. Compared to his contemporaries, the quality of his compositions is equal to those of other professionally-trained immigrants, such as the German-born Christopher Meineke (1782-1850) and the French-born Henri-Noel Gilles (1778-1834).

The purpose of this essay is to survey Corri-Clifton's piano works published on both sides of the Atlantic. (See the alphabetical list at the end for bibliographical details.[9]) Those that appeared in London in about 1805-18 can be put into the categories of sonata and divertimento, rondo, variations, and medley. First, the divertimentos, of which there are twenty-one. These are works in more than one movement, probably designated divertimento by the composer because few of the movements are in the form we now designate sonata-allegro, and the music is light in character. *Roses and Lillies* (1808) has three movements, all of which are in simple part forms. The Andantino in B-flat is in three-part form, with the second using the same material in the parallel minor. The second movement, Hornpipe, in the subdominant key, and the final Pastoral, in B-flat, are five-part rondos. By contrast, *L'Esperance* (1818) has only two movements. The Andantino calls for a finger slide; the Rondo includes many extensive scale passages or other passagework before the four returns of the main theme.

In the first movement of The Wilderness Sylph (1805?) Corri makes similar demands on the pianist, and specifically calls for the use of the pedal. The rondo scheme includes two related digressions in the minor mode—the second a variant of the first—and each return of the main theme is likewise different. A contrasting intermezzo precedes the final Marcia Promenada. A similar collection of movements is entitled La gioja (1814). The one-page introduction ends with a pianistically demanding cadenza (see ex. 12.1). The second movement, Andante con moto, and the third, "Waltz: Allegretto," are rondos. Divertimento alla Montanara (1813) exhibits yet another scheme. After a one-page introduction comes a march; the third movement (ex. 12.2) is the "Rondo a la Montanara."

Example 12.1. Corri, *La gioja*, mvt. 1, meas. 14-16.

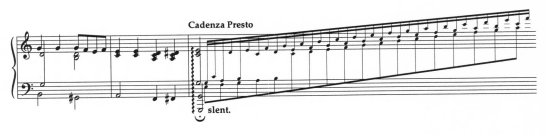

---

8. Posthumous 2nd ed. 1835, 3rd ed. 1839, 4th ed. 1843?; still included as for sale in the *Board of Music Trade Catalogue* (1870).

9. A complete list of his works, including his songs, is included in my Clifton article in *The New Grove Dictionary of American Music* (1986), partially based on an unpublished listing prepared by Geraldine Ostrove of the Library of Congress. I also furnished a more complete worklist in "Amerigrove Expanded: or, Worklists Prepared for, but There Was No Room for, *The New Grove Dictionary of American Music*," *Sonneck Society Newsletter* 12, no. 2 (summer 1986): 46-47.

Example 12.2. Corri, *Divertimento alla Montanara*, mvt. 1, meas. 1-8.

The Regatta (1812) is one of four divertimentos with a theme and variations movement. It is scored with accompaniment for a flute, but the composer supplies an *ossia* which enables a performance without the flute. A three-part Pastorale is succeeded by "La gondoletta—Venetian Air" with seven variations. *Helicon* (1811) begins with a three-part Larghetto movement, then follows with an air and four variations; the third and last movement is a rondo. The same plan without the introductory movement is followed in *La Selina*. *The Solitaire* (1811) begins with a set of five variations. Somewhat unusual is the second movement, entitled "Motetto," with the added NB: "The above Motetto may be omitted if considered too sombre." Not only is it somber, but the key is E-flat minor, a key not encountered very often at that time, especially in piano music intended for the amateur. It nevertheless serves as an introduction to the lively last movement, which I consider to be in sonata-allegro form. There are at least four identifiable themes and a closing theme (see ex. 12.3), and the telltale repeat mark at the close of the exposition. In the development a new theme in C major appears, and this key is retained in a recapitulation of themes 2, 3, and 4. Only after the restoration of the E-flat major key signature does the first theme return, and the movement finishes with the same closing material that had ended the exposition.

Example 12.3a. Corri, *The Solitaire*, mvt. 3, theme 1, meas. 1-8.

Example 12.3b. Corri, *The Solitaire*, mvt. 3, theme 2, meas. 32-39.

Example 12.3c. Corri, *The Solitaire*, mvt. 3, themes 3 and 4, meas. 48-63.

Example 12.3d. Corri, *The Solitaire*, mvt. 3, closing theme, meas. 72-80.

Sonata-allegro form is also discernible for the first movement of *Halcyon Days* (1816)—the movement-title of "Sonata" helps to identify it. I wonder if there might be some influence from Beethoven or, more likely, Corri's brother-in-law, Dussek, in the sudden change from G major to E major at the beginning of the development (see ex. 12.4). This is only a two-movement piece; the second is a rondo, for which the third digression is also a digression of key—from the tonic, C major, to the submediant, A-flat major.

Corri's divertimento *La galantina* (1816) is notable because it was also published across the English Channel: in Amsterdam, Berlin, Bonn, and Hamburg. I discern no musical reasons for this, since it is not especially better than his other divertimentos. A short introduction precedes an Andante con espressione. Its main theme twice alternates with digressive material in the parallel minor, yet the returns are not literal—in letters, ABAB! Instead of the final "A," Corio segues directly to the last movement, another rondo.

Corri wrote two sets of *Cottage Divertimentos* (ca. 1815), each set containing three. These six divertimentos are modest one-movement works, all in rondo form, and undemanding for the pianist. Three others are in a collection called *Three Divertisements* (1815), dedicated to three ladies—presumably sisters—Lady Augusta, Lady Laura, and Lady Arabella Vane, for whom these works are named. The slow introductions to "L'Augusta" and "L'Arabella" end with cadenzas which, if the dedicatees could play them,

Example 12.4. Corri, *Halcyon Days*, mvt. 1, meas. 56-63.

indicate they were very accomplished at the keyboard. The most interesting of these two-movement pieces is the Waltz, marked "scherzando," of "La Laura"—but only for its size, nearly seven pages in the original score, representing a full five-part rondo.

Only three works are specifically entitled sonata. *L'augurio felice* (1808) is, in its first movement, more tightly constructed than the few sonata-allegro movements within the divertimentos. The exposition has three fully-worked out themes, less so in the recapitulation, which is sixteen measures shorter (68 vs. 52 measures). The slow movement is labeled "Affettuoso con molto: Espressione e poco Adagio"; it establishes a serious mood in spite of its major key. The last, "Polonoise Allegretto," has the characteristic eighth-quarter rhythm associated with that dance. A rondo scheme is not very clear. The principal theme is succeeded by new material, a da capo to the original, then a new section marked "martiale," a varied return of the main theme, and finally an unadorned return.

La Eliza (1808) in its first movement has all the essential features of sonata-allegro form: in the exposition there are two themes, in tonic and dominant, as well as appropriate closing material, a development, and a complete recapitulation. There are many dynamic contrasts in the second movement, and Corri features some diminished-seventh and augmented-sixth chords. The last movement, "Waltz non troppo presto," is no simple dance, although the style is light. The main theme returns with a da capo marking after a long midsection, then again at the end of a new section marked "spiritoso."

In my opinion, Corri's best sonata is *La morte di Dussek: Elegiac Sonata for the piano forte with an accompaniment for a violin obligato and violoncello ad libitum: composed . . . in memory of that celebrated Musical Genius* (1816). Dussek died at Talleyrand's palace, in Paris, on 23 March 1812. His successor as music master to Talleyrand, Sigismond Neukomm, who was present when Dussek died, also wrote an *Elegie harmonique sur la mort de J. L. Dussek.* Dussek had left London in late 1799 or early 1800, partly because the firm of Domenico Corri & Dussek had gone bankrupt—Lorenzo da Ponte also lost money in the process—and partly because his marriage to Sophia, Antony's sister, had soured. Nevertheless, Antony's sonata is his most ambitious and serious in the form. I thought that he might have borrowed a theme of Dussek, especially for the middle movement, a theme and variations, but no theme from this sonata appears in the Dussek thematic catalog by Howard Allen Craw.[10] The first movement, in sonata-allegro form, is appropriately in F minor, "Allegro agitato e con Espressione" (see ex. 12.5a). The second key area, A-flat major, has at least two identifiable themes (exx. 12.5b and c), as well as

Example 12.5a. Corri, *La morte di Dussek*, mvt. 1, theme 1, meas. 1-8.

Example 12.5b. Corri, *La morte di Dussek*, mvt. 1, theme 2, meas. 31-38.

10. Howard Allen Craw, "A Biographical and Thematic Catalog of the Works of J. L. Dussek (1760-1812)" (Ph.D. diss., University of Southern California, 1964).

Example 12.5c. Corri, *La morte di Dussek,* mvt. 1, theme 3, meas. 65-72.

Example 12.6a. Corri, *La morte di Dussek,* mvt. 1. theme, meas. 1-16.

Example 12.6b. Corri, *La morte di Dussek,* mvt. 2, variation 2, meas. 1-16.

Example 12.6b, continued.

closing material. Most of the development is in F major until the retransition to the recapitulation.

The second movement is in theme and variation form (ex. 12.6a); the most effective variation probably is the second, in A-flat minor (ex. 12.6b).

Features of the finale are the syncopation of the first theme (ex. 12.7a), the utter simplicity of the second and third themes (Exx. 12.7b-c), and the effective modulation from A-flat major at the end of the exposition to the A major (B-double flat major) of the

Example 12.7a. Corri, *La morte di Dussek*, mvt. 3, theme 1, meas. 1-4.

Example 12.7b. Corri, *La morte di Dussek*, mvt. 3, meas. 29-40.

beginning of the development (ex. 12.7d). Whereas the violin part is a fully equal partner in the first movement, and in the exposition of this third movement, it is absent for much

Example 12.7c. Corri, *La morte di Dussek*, mvt. 3, theme 2, meas. 53-61.

Example 12.7d. Corri, *La morte di Dussek*, mvt. 3, transition from exposition to development, meas. 73-85.

of the development in this movement. A short coda brings the work to a quiet ("perdendoso") close.

The London publisher Chappell & Co. issued a series of twenty-four national melodies, of Ireland, Scotland, Wales, and England, arranged as rondos or as sets of variations by nine English composers during several years, up to 1813. Four, all rondos, are by Corri. They are based on the English tune by Dr. Arne, "Where the Bee Sucks" (no. 3 in the series), the Scotch tune "Green Grow the Rushes O!" (no. 9), the Welsh air "Nos Galen, or New Year's Night" (no. 17), and the Scotch melody "There's Nae Luck About the House" (no. 21). All have an introduction of one or two pages, usually with some motives from the forthcoming theme, and then the rondo itself. In each of the pieces, the theme reappears twice, interspersed with other material—not usually new themes but free elaboration presented with pianistic figuration often related to the national tune. One example is "Nos galen," the tune now associated with the Christmas carol "Deck the Halls with Boughs of Holly." The opening notes are from the theme; the rest is free. The descending five-note scale of the tune is naturally suited to elaboration, and there are a number of them in both digressions.

Several multi-movement works could have been called divertimento, but were not. *La Carolina: An Adagio and Rondo* (1808) is self-explanatory. I haven't yet been able to find a copy of *La Giorgiana, an Andante & Rondo* (1807) listed on the title-page of *La Carolina. Robin Adair* (1812) is a rondo-arrangement of the popular Irish tune. Both extant pieces have features previously seen in Corri's work.

The main movement of *La biondina pensosa* (1808) is an air in B-flat major with five variations. This air is also the basis of the introduction, labeled "Adagio patetico con anima," in G minor. The last movement, "Cantabile, con grand espresione: Amorosamento" is basically an arrangement of the first part of the first movement, but now in G major. The key scheme for the movements of *La biondina pensosa* is G minor, B-flat major, G major. There is a modulatory transition between the middle and last movements.

I am not sure of the proper category for *The Feast of Erin* (1808). Corri uses the term fantasy. Although there is some fantasy in his free material, I would opt for medley. After a one-page introduction, the first tune quoted is "Planxty Drury" (Carolan). The second movement, "Erin go Bragh," is in D major, which eventually gives way to a C-major section labeled "Maestoso" in march style. The third movement is based on a tune "The Summer Is Coming," while the last movement, "Planxty Kelly or Fly Not Yet," is arranged as a rondo. Of some interest are the keys of several returns of this tune. The main key is E-flat major; the first return is in B-flat, the third in G. The last return is once more in the tonic of E-flat.

Fantasia (1815-16) is designed for the expanded range of some pianos of the time; it is written, as noted on the title page, for piano "with or without the new Additional Keys." Whereas its normal range extends down to *C'* and up to *c''''*, alternate passages for the "Additional Keys," on separate staves, call for notes as high as *f''''*.[11] There are also

11. See Rosamond E. M. Harding, *The Piano-Forte*, 2nd ed. (Old Woking, Surrey: Gresham Books, 1978), 68; pl. 10, p. 80, has a photograph of a square piano (probably built during the 1810s, but definitely before 1823) by Goulding, D'Almaine, Potter and Co., with twelve "additional keys," *c#''* to *c''''*. I own a square piano by Goulding & D'Almaine, dating from 1823 or slightly later, in which the section of additional keys, obviously an alteration to the original design, provides the notes *a''* to the same *f''''* called for in Corri's piece.

alternate passages marked "The upper notes of these 16 bars may be played instead of octaves if too difficult" and "Adapted for a smaller hand." The *Fantasia* is an ambitious work, with fourteen pages of music. After the "Introduction ad libitum," in B-flat major and D minor, Corri introduces the D-major air "Of All the Girls"; it is arranged as a rondo with varied returns. The final section, eight pages long, is a demanding toccata in the tonic B-flat major, marked Presto and ¢, in which the prevailing motion is in eighth-note triplets. By the time of its publication, there must have been many piano students and amateurs of considerable skill in England.

Two London publications remain in this discussion. *The Casket* (1816) contains six simple waltzes, named for the jewels diamond, ruby, emerald, sapphire, topaz, and amethyst. Not so simple or straight-forward is *The Terpsichoread* (1808). I expected three dull country dances, as indicated on the title-page. Not so. "Lord Cathcart's Return" is a full-fledged five-part rondo, ABABA, with some material I can only describe as developmental, as in a sonata movement, before and after the second "B" (see ex. 12.8). "Knowle Park" is likewise a five-part rondo, while "The Labyrinth" is a set of seven variations in G major, plus a coda in E-flat major, in waltz style, that returns to the tonic.

Example 12.8. Corri, "Lord Cathcart's Return," from *The Terpsichoread*, meas. 123-57.

To sum up the importance of Corri's London piano works, I can only cite the variety of forms and movement-schemes in these publications, the demands on piano technique to the intended user, who were obviously talented amateurs, and the skilled manner in which Corri was able to put these pieces together.

In Baltimore, Corri, now Clifton, was not nearly as prolific in piano music.[12] Perhaps this was due to a heavier teaching load, and undoubtedly the composition and production of his opera *The Enterprise* had something to do with it. Yet early in his American career, in 1820, he published an assortment of his own music consisting of ten songs and five piano pieces. These are in the Library of Congress, and some of them escaped the eye of Richard J. Wolfe.[13] I speculated that he might have recycled some of his London music, and republished them under his new name, but he didn't. *Two Waltzes* (1820), dedicated to Miss Riggin, are real dance pieces, with no pianistic elaboration. Likewise, *Danse champêtre* (1820), "performed by The Miss' Durang &c. in Henri Quatre" is a straight accompaniment to movement on the stage. The same applies to *Caprice & Return Waltzes* and *Bugle & Star Waltzes*, both copyright the 1st of October 1823 by Clifton.

Clifton reflected his new nationality in a work published about 1821, *National Divertimento . . . in which are introduced Hail Columbia! with a new trio, and Yankee Doodle! with variations.* In the tradition of his London divertimentos, this is a compilation of movements. The "Hail Columbia" tune, with its new trio, are without elaboration, and the "Yankee Doodle" variations are not of the quality of his London pieces. I also find his *Medley Overture*, published about 1832-33, uninteresting, even though it was originally for full orchestra. The tunes are simply stitched together. Aside from the short overture, Clifton gives himself no opportunity for creativity even in the modulations or transitions between the twelve tunes.

Clifton wrote two occasional pieces, a genre not found in his London output. *Lafayette's Welcome to the U. States in 1824*, a march, was commissioned by the Baltimore committee that arranged the local activities connected with General Lafayette's visit there 7-11 October 1824.[14] It was copyrighted 17 August 1824, the day after Lafayette arrived in New York City. Except for several march movements in his London divertimentos, this

12. Clifton's piano works are also discussed in my book *The Dawning of American Keyboard Music* (Westport, Conn.: Greenwood, 1988).

13. Richard J. Wolfe, *Secular Music in America, 1801-1825: A Bibliography*, 3 vols. (New York Public Library, 1964).

14. For further details, see my article "American Musical Tributes of 1824-25 to Lafayette: A Report and Inventory," *Fontes artis musicae* 26, no. 1 (1979): 17-35.

must have been one of Clifton's first attempts at a real band march, subsequently arranged for publication as piano music. The other was *The Carrollton March*, "performed at the Ceremony of commencing the Baltimore & Ohio Rail-road, on the fourth of July 1828." At the time, Charles Carroll was the only surviving signer of the Declaration of Independence.

The remaining pieces to be surveyed are Clifton's theme and variations. The quality of these works is uneven. For example, the main problem of *The Mignonette Waltz* (1823) is the harmonic poverty of the theme itself—only tonic and dominant chords. The motives for the four variations are not particularly good, and once a pattern is set it continues for the whole variations without letup. Much the same applies to *The Bonny Boat* (1828-29).

Clifton's best two sets of variations were published in the 1820 collection mentioned earlier. The original melody of *Blue Eye'd Mary* was a song, perhaps by an otherwise-unidentified Robert Tuke, which was also arranged with variations by an amateur and by the Italian-American Stefano Cristiani.[15] Whereas the theme is buried in right-hand figuration and scales of 16th notes in Clifton's first variation, it appears intact—in three different tessituras—in variations 2, 3, and 4, with a variety of rhythmic accompaniments. Untypically for Clifton, the fifth variation is chordal, almost hymn-like, marked "con espress." The last variation and coda are based on three-note broken chords, with the theme represented by the high note of each chord. Although the workmanship is imaginative, clearly Clifton is restrained by the simple theme. Again, more variety of harmonic content would have helped. At least this one has the subdominant (IV) chord—as well as a III and VI.

After examining early American piano music for more than twenty years, I am still convinced that Clifton's *Original Air with Variations* (1820) is one of the finest of its time, certainly his best work written or published in the United States. Perhaps its success is due to the quality of the original theme (see ex. 12.9a). I've already mentioned that Clifton was a singer and voice teacher, and he composed many songs. His Italian background didn't hurt his gift of melody, at least in this one piece. The treatment in the five variations is also masterful. Rather than relying on various stock figurations to vary the tune, Clifton gives each variation an individual musical characteristic. Variation 1 (ex. 12.9b) is set in the low range, with certain notes of the original air appearing in the 16th-note rhythm shared by both hands. In variation 2 (ex. 12.9c), three strong chords are answered by 32nd-note fragments. As if to balance the low tessitura of the first variation, the third (ex. 12.9d) remains high on the keyboard, while scales and other right-hand figurations, in 16th-note sextuplets, cause variation 4 (ex. 12.9e) to be the high point of the set, in dynamics and virtuosity. In variation 5 (ex. 12.9f), marked "Finale," Clifton returns to his original theme, unornamented, over a murmuring sextuplet bass. A brief Coda ends the piece *pianissimo*.

---

15. Song: Wolfe 9418 (Tuke), Wolfe 893-905 (anonymous); variations: Wolfe 90 (amateur), Wolfe 2194 (Cristiani).

Example 12.9a. Clifton, *An Original Air with Variations*, theme, meas. 1-4.

Example 12.9b. Clifton, *An Original Air with Variations*, variation 1, meas. 1-4.

Example 12.9c. Clifton, *An Original Air with Variations*, variation 2, meas. 1-4.

Example 12.9d. Clifton, *An Original Air with Variations*, variation 3, meas. 1-4.

Example 12.9e. Clifton, *An Original Air with Variations*, variation 4, meas. 1-4.

Example 12.9f. Clifton, *An Original Air with Variations,* **variation 5, meas. 1-4.**

I hope this quick survey of the music by an almost-forgotten composer active in both England and the United States leaves the impression that there are some gems to be found in the piles of sheet music of the period. There are some questions I haven't been able to answer in this essay. First, why did London publishers come out with so many of Corri's pieces within a few years? Was it because he acquired a reputation for writing good music that was attractive to the talented amateur? Second, why did his production of the same kind of music fall off considerably in Baltimore? Was it due to a smaller musical market in America? Or was it because he was forced to reestablish his reputation under a new name, with only fifteen years until his death in 1832? It is clear that his music was popular in mid nineteenth-century America. There are many pieces by Clifton still listed in the *Board of Music Trade Catalogue* of 1870,[16] which indicates that some of it had a long life. For anyone looking for early nineteenth-century music to play on the piano, I can certainly recommend one composer: P. Antony Corri and Arthur Clifton.

---

16. Board of Music Trade of the United States of America, *Complete Catalogue of Sheet Music and Musical Work* (1870; reprint, New York: Da Capo, 1973).

APPENDIX (* = original copy in my possession)

P. Antony Corri, solo piano works published in London

L'augurio felice, sonata. Wilkinson & Compy., late Broderip & Wilkinson, 13 Hay Market, [1808];
reviewed in *The Monthly Magazine* (henceforth, MM), 8 August 1808.[17] Facsimile in *The
London Pianoforte School, 1766-1860*, ed. Nicholas Temperley (New York: Garland, 1985), vol.
7, pp. 249-62.

La biondina pensosa, air with introduction and finale. Rt. Birchall, No. 133 New Bond St., [1808].

La Carolina, an adagio and rondo. Rt. Birchall, 133 New Bond St., [1808]; reviewed in MM, 1
September 1808.

The Casket, containing six waltzes. Chappell & Co., 124 New Bond St., plate 334 [1816].

Divertimento alla Montanara. Chappell & Co., 124 New Bond St., plate 151 [1813]. Another edition,
Amsterdam: A. C. Steup.

L'Esperance, a divertimento. Chappell & Co., 50 New Bond St., plate 716 [1818].

La Eliza, sonata. L. Lavenue, 26 New Bond St., [1808]; reviewed in MM, 1 August 1809.

Fantasia. Chappell & Co., 124 New Bond St., plate 295 [1815-16].*

The Feast of Erin, fantasy . . . in which is introduced the original Irish airs of Planxty Drury, The
Summer is coming, Erin go Bragh, & Fly not yet. Rt. Birchall, 133 New Bond St., [1808].*

The Fugitive, sonata. Mitchell's Musical Library & Instrumental Warehouse, 159 Bond Street.
Unlocated.

La galantina, a divertimento. Chappell & Co., 124 New Bond St., plate 388 [1816]. Other editions,
Amsterdam: J. B. Nolting; Berlin: Paez; Bonn: Simrock; Hamburg: Böhme, Cranz.

La gioja, a divertisement. Chappell & Co., 124 New Bond St., plate 241 [1814].

La Giorgiana, an andante and rondo. Rt. Birchall, 133 New Bond St. Unlocated, but reviewed in MM,
1 May 1807.

Halcyon Days, a divertimento. Chappell & Co., 124 Bond St., plate 391 [1816].

Helicon, a divertimento. Chappell & Co., 124 New Bond St., plate 3 [1811].*

The Hey-Day, [2nd] divertisement. C. Mitchell. Unlocated; listed with "La Selina" [ca. 1810].

La morte di Dussek, elegiac sonata . . . with an accompaniment for a violin obligato, and violoncello ad
libitum: composed by P. Antony Corri in memory of that celebrated musical genius. Chappell
& Co., 124 New Bond St., plate 376 [1816].

National Melodies, consisting of the most admired airs of England, Ireland, Scotland & Wales,
arranged as rondos or with variations for the piano forte, and an introductory movement to each,
composed by the most eminent authors [including] Miss Cramer, P. A. Corri, Pauer, Graeff,
Griffin, Haigh, Latour, &c. Chappell & Co., 124 New Bond St. Index with no. 22 (plate 192)
dated 1 October 1813.

    No. 3. Where the Bee Sucks [Arne], arr. P. A. Corri, plate L75 [1812].

    No. 9. Green Grow the Rushes O! [Scotch], arr. P. A. Corri, plate 94 [1812].

    No. 17. Nos Galen, or New Years Night [Welsh], arr. P. A. Corri, plate 171 [1813].

    No. 21. There's Nae Luck About the House [Scotch], arr. P. A. Corri, plate 204 [1813].*

---

17. Information concerning these reviews kindly supplied by Nathan Buckner.

The Regatta, a divertisement . . . with an accompaniment for the flute, in which is introduced La
   Gondolette, a Venetian air with variations. Goulding, D'Almaine, Potter & Co., 20 Soho Square
   & 7 Westmorland Strt., Dublin, [1812].
Robin Adair, with an introductory movement, arranged . . . from the new edition as sung by Mr.
   Braham. For the author, by Chappell & Co., 124 New Bond St., plate 85 [1812]; reviewed in
   MM, 1 December 1812.*
Roses and Lillies, divertisement . . . consisting of an Andantino, Hornpipe & Pastoral. Rt. Birchall, 133
   New Bond St., [1808].*
La Selina, a third divertisement. C. Mitchell, 51 Southampton Row, Russell Square, plate (281), [ca.
   1810].
The Solitaire, a divertisement. For the author, by Chappell & Co., 124 New Bond St., plate 24 [1811].
   Later edition with new address, 50 New Bond St.
The Terpsichoread, three most admired country dances: Lord Cathcart's Return, Knowle Park, and The
   Labyrinth, arranged for the piano forte. Rt. Birchall, 133 New Bond St., [1808].
Three Cottage Divertimentos, books 1-2. Mitchell's Musical Library & Instrument Warehouse, 159
   New Bond Street, plate (290), [ca. 1815].
Three Divertisements. Chappell & Co., 124 New Bond St., plate 264 [1815].
The Wilderness Sylph, [1st] divertisement. C. Mitchell, 51 Southampton Row, Russell Square, [1805?].

P. Antony Corri, other works for piano and other instruments

Aglaia and Euphrosyne, serenade, piano & harp. Chappell & Co., 124 New Bond St., plate 62 [1812].
   Piano duet, plate 185 [1813].*
Concerto da camera . . . with accompaniments for two violins, flute, viola & violoncello. Chappell &
   Co., 124 New Bond St., plate 157 [1813].
La dolcezza, duet, harp and piano forte, with flute ad lib. Chappell & Co., 124 New Bond St., plate
   320 [1816].
Elysium, piano duet. Chappell & Co., 124 New Bond Street, [ca. 1815].
L'incanto, serenade, piano forte duet and harp, or piano solo with flute ad lib. Rt. Birchall, 133 New
   Bond St., [1808].

Arthur Clifton, solo piano works published in Baltimore (unless otherwise indicated)

Blue Eye'd Mary, with variations. For the author, 4 Gay St., [1820]. Wolfe 1912. Facsimile in J. Bunker
   Clark, ed., *American Keyboard Music through 1865*, Three Centuries of American Music, 3 (G.
   K. Hall, 1990), pp. 132-35.
The Bonnie Boat, with easy variations. J. Cole, plate 354, [1828?].
Bugle & Star Waltzes. Philadelphia: Geo. Willig, 171 Chesnut St.; copyright 1 October 1823 by the
   author. Wolfe 1913.
Caprice & Return Waltzes. Philadelphia: Geo. Willig, 171 Chesnut St.; copyright 1 October 1823 by
   the author. Wolfe 1914.
The Carrollton March, performed at the ceremony of commencing the Baltimore & Ohio Rail-road,
   on the fourth of July 1828. John Cole, plate 318, copyright 4 July 1828.

Danse champêtre, performed by The Miss' Durang &c. in Henri Quatre. T. Carr, 78 1/2 Baltimore St.; Philadelphia: for the author by G. E. Blake, [1820]. Wolfe 1915 variant.

LaFayette's Welcome to the U. States in 1824, a grand march and quick step. G. Willig for the author, copyright 1 August 1824. Wolfe 1929.

Medley Overture, in which the following favourite airs are introduced: Scots wha ha'e wi' Wallace bled, Oh! 'tis love, Lewis Gordon, Paddy O'Rafferty, Irish lilt, Cruskeen lawn, There's nae luck about the house, Tulloch Goram, Money in both pockets, The young May moon, Auld Robin Gray, and The Bonnie Highland laddie. Originally composed for a full orchestra, and arranged for the piano forte. John Cole & Son, plate 683, [1832-33?].

The Mignonette Waltz, with variations. Philadelphia: Geo. Willig, 171 Chesnut St. Copyright 1 October [1823?] by the author. Wolfe 1937.

Military Serenade . . . with an accompaniment for the flute. For the author by Carr, [1820-22].

National Divertimento . . . in which are introduced Hail Columbia! with a new trio, and Yankee Doodle! with variations. Philadelphia: G. E. Blake, 13 South 5th St., [ca. 1821]. Wolfe 1938.

An Original Air, with variations. T. Carr, 78 1/2 Baltimore St.; Philadelphia: for the author by G. E. Blake, 13 S. 5th St., [1820]. In Clark, ed., *Anthology of Early American Keyboard Music, 1787-1830*, Recent Researches in American Music, 2 (Madison: A-R Editions, 1977), no. 22.

Two Waltzes, composed & dedicated to Miss Riggin. Author, 4 S. Gay Street, [1820].

13

Music Research in Nineteenth-Century Theater: or, The Case of a Burlesquer, a Baker, and a Pantomime Maker

Deane L. Root

Nineteenth-century American musical theater remains almost entirely unexplored by musicologists. Common wisdom among scholars is that the source materials for the music remain obscure and—when they exist at all—are poorly documented; that the musical practices and styles of theater are therefore inscrutable, and any connections they may have had with more accessible opera or concert hall, band or popular music, or even with twentieth-century musical theater, are unclear at best. The resulting unfortunate misperception is that theater was not a significant or integral part of America's musical culture.

The purpose of this essay is to explore the research problems that confront music historians who deal with nineteenth-century musical theater in the United States. The title mimics those of burlesques and melodramas, but it is not whimsical. To illustrate central challenges and techniques for the discipline, I offer three examples of subjects who were prominent in mid-century American musical theater but who are absent from published music-research literature.

Musicology's Goals and Techniques

Musicology contributes as much to our understanding of human expression, intellect, and social interaction as it does to our ability to perform and appreciate music

An early version of this paper was presented at a special conference on Nineteenth-Century English-Language Musical Theater, hosted by the J. Pierpont Morgan Library in New York, 7-8 June 1985. I am grateful to Susan Porter for editorial suggestions, as well as her encouragement that the ideas merit a wider audience.

itself.[1] Its primary techniques are archival research, codicological study of music manuscripts as cultural artifacts, sketch studies of composers' manuscript score fragments and workbooks, iconography (the study of pictorial material), bibliography, studies of manuscript versions and printed editions of music, and the compilation of scholarly or performing editions, musical analysis, critical assessment of individual compositions and styles of music, biography, and contextual studies.[2] Among the goals of musicological endeavor are to rediscover lost works, reinterpret music for new audiences, explore the processes of artistic creation and performance as part of cultural history, and explicate the arts' wider cultural and societal contexts and importance.

Musicology contributes significantly to humanistic understanding of a wide variety of European and American musics, and its scholars—in the spirit of multiculturalism and the contextual models from other disciplines—have increasingly reached out in recent years to turn attention to ethnic musics, popular media such as film and jazz, and plebeian genres. Yet, while nineteenth-century music as a whole has been embraced by musicology's canon, American musical theater has remained outside it. Few textbooks and scholarly histories of Euro-American music mention musical theater; some treat it condescendingly, and what attention they do pay is typically devoted to Broadway operetta and musical comedy of the twentieth century.[3] Major encyclopedic reference works on music echo this treatment. Their entries for nineteenth-century American theater-composers, musicians, genres, and titles are sparse in comparison with European counterparts or American contemporaries in classical music. The few articles on theater composers are short and lack the discussion of significance or musical style that is *de rigueur* for contemporaries in other genres.

What are the reasons for the slight quantity and quality of musicological treatment of nineteenth-century American musical theater? Are there really only a few if any theater-composers, musicians, and works of merit? Is musical theater of such poor quality, so uninteresting, of such little value to society? Is the music so unsophisticated, so simple, that it cannot support extended probing musicological research?

---

1. The four most substantial discussions of the goals and philosophy of musicology as a discipline remain Claude V. Palisca, with Frank Lloyd Harrison and Mantle Hood, *Musicology* (Englewood Cliffs, N.J.: Prentice-Hall, 1963); the set of twelve articles inaugurating the *Journal of Musicology* 1, no. 1 (January 1982), collectively captioned "Musicology in the 1980s: Points of Arrival and Goals"; the proceedings of self-evaluative sessions at the 1981 conference of the American Musicological Society, edited by Claude V. Palisca and D. Kern Holoman as *Musicology in the 1980s: Methods, Goals, Opportunities* (New York: Da Capo, 1982); and the more idiosyncratic perspective of Joseph Kerman in *Contemplating Music: Challenges to Musicology* (Cambridge, Mass.: Harvard University Press, 1985).

2. For a discussion of musicological technique aimed at an audience outside the profession itself, see Denis Stevens, *Musicology: A Practical Guide* (New York: Schirmer, 1980). Kerman, in *Contemplating Music*, argues for greater emphasis on the "critical orientation" in musicology.

3. Edith Borroff's appraisal of the coverage of musical theater by music historians, "Origin of Species: Conflicting Views of American Musical Theater History," *American Music* 2 (winter 1984): 101-11, is a brief review of musicology's treatment of subgenres. She asserts that "most formal music historians have ignored or impugned [musical comedy], from ignorance or from prejudice against it as American. . . . The standard histories of western music have likewise ignored musical comedy."

The causes are many and complex, ranging from the philosophy of historiographical inquiry to the circumstances of archival preservation. Part of the answer lies in a musicological impulse to focus on (and contribute to) a pantheon of composers, great works, and worthy forms or genres of music identified and (largely) agreed to by generations of scholars.[4] But even those researchers with the will to turn scholarly attention toward musical theater have not yet created a base of reliable and detailed studies and editions, which would in turn support representative coverage of musical theater in textbooks and reference works. And this condition sends an unarticulated but clear message to students, teachers, theorists, lexicographers, and publishers: theater music is relatively unimportant, unworthy of critical inquiry, unrevealing for humanistic research, peripheral at best to liberal arts curricula, and an unsuitable and unproductive field for scholarship. The message is wrong, because it is borne of ignorance rather than insight.

This intellectual distancing stems in large part from the difficulty in accessing primary materials. Joseph Kerman recalls that when he started out to write his dissertation on music in Renaissance England, "in the 1940s and 1950s there was indeed a great deal of basic research that had not yet been undertaken. . . . [A]bsolutely central texts were still unavailable in those years."[5] That situation changed rapidly as musicologists devoted careers to locating, editing, and publishing editions of as many works and repertories as they could. Nineteenth-century American musical theater is in a similarly neglected position some fifty years later.

The most powerful and practical reason for the neglect lies not in the music itself, since the musical content and style of a representative sample of nineteenth-century American theater works have yet to be evaluated. The central problem is the utter remoteness of the work-texts themselves, the prohibitive difficulty musical scholars have encountered when they tried to find and gather the kinds of sources they are accustomed to using and for which they have refined their research techniques. Musicology holds that the autograph score and first edition of a musical composition are authoritative primary sources. But the manuscripts, printed scores, or parts that exist for other genres have been missing for the vast majority of these nineteenth-century theater works. They were either discarded, or were destroyed by fire or flood, or simply have not yet found their way into cataloged repositories, or were never created in the first place.

Musical-theater composers created works prescribed by extra-musical exigencies, freely borrowing from one another and from other repertories, interpolating new musical numbers and even entire sections into their shows during the performance run, and in other ways denying the "authority" version of a work that in other repertories musicology holds sacred. Except for the songs or dances that were printed and published as sheet music (and rarely did this exceed more than one or two pieces per show), a theater-composer's products were more functionally utilitarian and ephemeral, lacking meaning

---

4. An acknowledgment and reexamination of the "musicological canon" was the topic of a special session at the 1987 annual meeting of the American Musicological Society in New Orleans. The collection of essays edited by Katherine Bergeron and Philip V. Bohlman, *Disciplining Music: Musicology and Its Canons* (Chicago: University of Chicago Press, 1992), and ensuing reviews, have carried the discussion forward.

5. Kerman, 54.

outside their original context, and therefore unpreservable except as part of the work's score. The composer was often the conductor as well, leading the performances from the orchestra pit, in the perfect position to garnish and season the dishes served up according to the taste of the audience and management.

Furthermore, theater music was not adapted in sufficient quantity, as a repertory, for the concert venues that attracted earlier musicologists. By contrast, among of the first popular music that drew experienced music bibliographers and historians were the songs of Stephen Foster that were performed by Mme. Galli-Curci, Adelina Patti, Christine Nilsson, and other opera and recital stars of the late decades of the century, issued in arrangements performed by them and bearing their portraits, and recorded on early cylinders.[6]

A venerable form of musicological edition reflects this condition starkly. *Denkmäler*, monumental sets and anthologies representing the best, or most valued, or most influential works of a genre, era, or cultural region, have been compiled over the last century for a multiplicity of musics. Yet none has had a representative selection of nineteenth-century American music musical theater.[7] While a number of scripts of such works have been issued in twentieth-century anthologies (providing word-texts for literary studies), it was not until 1994 that the first series of editions of nineteenth-century American musical theater works was published, making a wide selection of titles—both the librettos and the music—accessible for the first time in the twentieth century.[8]

The original evidence for the theatrical elements of musical theater has survived better than the music. Most of the extant sources are non-musical, such as scripts (which may include lyrics and music cues), programs and handbills (which may list titles of musical selections), photographs, memoirs, third-person accounts, journal and newspaper articles (which may review the music and the performances), and business papers. These materials have generated most of the scholarly research and writing about musical theater. The information that musicologists can gather from these sources is largely non-musical,

---

6. Oscar Sonneck and Walter R. Whittelsey compiled the *Catalogue of First Editions of Stephen C. Foster (1826-1864)* (1915; reprint, New York: Da Capo, 1971). This was part of a series of bibliographies that Sonneck created in part to bring the Library of Congress music collections under control. He skirted nineteenth-century musical theater with some of them, in work extended by Richard Wolfe. See William Lichtenwanger, ed., *Oscar Sonneck and American Music* (Urbana: University of Illinois Press, 1983).

7. The American Musicological Society's series Music of the United States of America (1993-) has no plans to publish complete nineteenth-century musical-theater works, but no. 7 is devoted to songs by Edward Harrigan and David Braham, edited by Jon Finson. The major scholarly series containing editions of nineteenth-century American theater music are A-R Editions's Recent Researches in American Music, which includes William Shields's *The Poor Soldier* (1783, an English work widely performed in the United States), George F. Root's *The Haymakers* (1857), and Victor Pelissier's *Columbian Melodies* (1812, not a work for the theater, but music used in New York and Philadelphia theaters); G. K. Hall's Three Centuries of American Music, which has a single volume titled *American Opera and Music for the Stage* (1990), including piano-vocal scores of Alexander Reinagle's *The Volunteers*, Rayner Taylor's *The Ethiop*, Arthur Clifton's *The Enterprise*, and Reginald de Koven's *Robin Hood*; and Richard MacNutt's (and later Stainer & Bell's) *Music for London Entertainment, 1660-1800*, with several English works performed in America.

8. *Nineteenth-Century American Musical Theater*, 16 vols., ed. Deane L. Root (New York: Garland, 1994). See appendix for list of contents.

and therefore contextual. Music scholars who work productively in this field must extend and adapt the techniques traditional to musicology.

Rarely have musicologists collaborated with theater historians to seek a holistic view of the period. The major research conference devoted American musical theater, hosted jointly by the American Society for Theatre Research, the Sonneck Society for American Music, and the Theatre Library Association (at Greenvale, New York in 1981) presented nine panels, one of which (moderated by this author) was devoted to the nineteenth century.[9]

The prospect is brightening, but the unfortunate cycle bred by musicology's inattention to musical theater will be a long time shifting: sources remain relatively scarce, so musicologists continue to turn to other repertory; musical theater is under-represented in scholarly literature, so it is deemed less significant in our cultural history; it is undervalued as a product, so its source materials receive little attention, funds, or effort from the collectors and librarians engaged in locating and preserving cultural documents.[10]

The silver lining to this cloud is that the dominance of non-musical sources can cause musical studies of the theater to emphasize societal contexts and interrelationships between music and its surrounding arts and crafts to a far greater extent than in most other repertories of the century. Musicologists who choose to study musical theater will be rewarded if they are more imaginative in selecting the materials they use and in making them reveal their story about music.[11]

The Burlesquer

A case in point is John Brougham (1810-80), born in Ireland, active in England, and the leading author-actor-manager of topical burlesque on American stages for more than thirty years. He was the acknowledged master of music-infused parodies of literary classics and "multi-ethnic urban comedies,"[12] equally adept at critical social commentary and at puns and double entendres. Biographical information is moderately available: turn-of-the-

---

9. Glenn Loney, ed., *Musical Theatre in America: Papers and Proceedings of the Conference on the Musical Theatre in America* (Westport, Conn.: Greenwood, 1984).

10. A notable exception to this cycle is the American Music Research Center collection, built by Sister Mary Dominic Ray at Dominican College in San Raphael, California in the 1960s and 1970s around original editions and photocopies of eighteenth- and early nineteenth-century ballad operas. These became the core of the holdings of a new center of the same name, founded by William Kearns, director, and Karl Kroeger, librarian, at the University of Colorado at Boulder in 1991. See *American Music Research Center Journal* 1 (1991). Another useful cataloged repository, formerly a rental library with performance materials from the last third of the nineteenth century, is the Tams-Witmark Collection at the University of Wisconsin.

11. The benchmark for future work and a motherlode of information for the first two decades of the nineteenth century is Susan L. Porter's *With an Air Debonair: Musical Theatre in America, 1785-1815* (Washington: Smithsonian Institution Press, 1991). Making excellent use of the American Music Research Center's collection, and those of many other repositories, Dr. Porter's study is the first organic history (connecting the theater with its music) of early American musical theater, which is furthermore enlightened by an extensive understanding of the practical matters of staging and performing.

12. Pat M. Ryan, "The Hibernian Experience: John Brougham's Irish-American Plays," *Melus* 10, no. 2 (summer 1983): 33.

century books, contemporary newspaper articles, and an early dissertation.[13] The scant notice in the scholarly literature belies Brougham's presence in New York for most of the period between 1842 and 1879, where he wrote and performed in burlesques and melodramas, as well as for the "legitimate" drama at Wallack's, Park, Chambers Street, Winter Garden, Daly's, and other leading theaters, and even managed a theater in the 1850s and 1860s.

One of Brougham's romantic melodramas, *The Duke's Motto*, illustrates the difficulty of finding musical information on his stage works. This piece was first performed in London in January 1863, and in June the same year was brought to Niblo's Garden in New York.[14] The script has been published twice in the twentieth century,[15] but only one song identified with the show was published and survives in libraries: "Thou Art the Star," by the German theatrical composer Ferdinand Gumbert. The rest of the production's music was created by the theater conductor, Robert Stoepel (1821-87); Harvey B. Dodworth (1822-91), in the same capacity, contributed the music for a revival of the show.

Stoepel's name is preserved on scores, librettos, playbills, and programs, but no musicologist has researched his career or compositions.[16] The Dodworth family—Harvey and Allen, especially—were leaders in composing for and directing wind bands and in promoting social ballroom dance in mid-century New York, and historians of those genres have published research.[17] Harvey Dodworth also conducted at several theaters; his prominence in this capacity is attested to by the display of his name in advertisements for new productions. He even acted as publisher for some of his own works. But no further

---

13. Ryan notes that "just over a century after his death, he remains virtually unknown to the present generation of playgoers, readers, and even scholars." Brougham has an entry (with bibliography) in *The New Grove Dictionary of American Music*, written by William Brooks. Much of Brooks's information for that entry and for his article "*Pocahontas*: Her Life and Times" in the special musical-theater issue of *American Music* 2 (winter 1984): 19-48, was compiled while he was a fellow at the Smithsonian Institution. Irene Forsyth Comer's essay "Lotta Crabtree and John Brougham: Collaborating Pioneers in the Development of American Musical Comedy," in Loney, *Musical Theatre in America*, 99-110, based on her 1979 dissertation, describes a newly discovered Brougham burlesque of a Dickens novel; neither she nor any other author (besides Brooks) has yet discussed the music of Brougham's theatrical works. OCLC, the shared online catalog of American libraries, in July 1994 listed nine titles attributed to Brougham, mostly songs by other composers setting his words; one item, however, "Bob o Link Polka" (New York: Pond, 1865), is attributed to him as the composer. OCLC also listed twelve books or other items containing information about Brougham or his works.

14. Deane L. Root, *American Popular Stage Music, 1860-1880* (Ann Arbor: UMI Research Press, 1981), passim.

15. *The Duke's Motto: or, I Am Here!*, edited in Eugene Richard Page, *Metamora & Other Plays*, America's Lost Plays, 14 (Princeton: Princeton University Press, 1941), reprinted in Richard Penn Smith, *The Sentinels & Other Plays*, America's Lost Plays, 14 (Bloomington: Indiana University Press, 1965).

16. OCLC (July 1994) listed five titles by Stoepel: "Chant national hongrois" for piano (London: Jullien & Co., 185-?); *Hiawatha: An Indian Symphony* (New York: Hall, 1863), an 87-page opera vocal score (voice and piano) based on Longfellow's poem; "Chibiabo's Love Song" for tenor and piano (New York: Hall, 1863), from *Hiawatha*; "U.S. Army Calls: Military Quadrille" for piano (New York: Firth, Pond, 1862); and a libretto only for *The False Prophet*, a comic opera in three acts by J. Armoy Knox and Charles M. Snyder (New York: n.p., 1887).

facts have turned up about his contributions to *The Duke's Motto*, nor apparently has anyone researched his other musical contributions to the theater.[18]

One of Brougham's masterpieces was *Pocahontas* (1855), which was said to have been a favorite even with amateur troupes until late in the century.[19] The printed libretto, which contains no musical notation, attributes the score to James G. Maeder (1809-76).[20] There would have been an orchestral score from which the theater conductor directed, along with individual parts for the pit musicians, but these are lost. No selections were published, and no piano arrangements of the score or individual numbers survive. *Pocahontas* has not a single piece of music identified with it in catalogs of such major music repositories as the British Library, the New York Public Library, the Library of Congress, the Driscoll Collection at Newberry Library, or the Harding Collection at Oxford University.[21]

Partial explanation for the music's ephemerality lies in the burlesque genre itself. The music—like the script—was taken from (or at least suggestive of) other works, then adapted and rearranged to suit the allusions of the moment: the music was "dislocated and re-set" as Brougham's painfully osteographic pun acknowledged on the script. The originals, therefore, had precedence in the marketplace; publication of the parodies might have been resisted by owners (publishers) of the original copyrights; the topical references in the burlesque versions would have had meaning within the play, but might have been less comprehensible away from the script, outside the theater.

For many burlesques the music was not distinctive (according to critics), and therefore would not merit publication by itself. If the music did not achieve popularity or even familiarity with a wide audience, it could not stand on its own in the marketplace. Some music directors of shows changed selections frequently within a run, effectively preventing songs from becoming established with the public. Perhaps the strongest characteristic of burlesque was that the music so intimately served the satire, parody, and wit in texts whose topical references frequently changed; the lyrics were the chief interest, thus the music could be even more interchangeable. Whatever the rationale, the music from burlesques was published (and survives) in far smaller quantity than the playbills that advertised these shows, and represents a disproportionately small percentage of surviving theater music from the nineteenth century.

And yet music was an essential part of Brougham's stage works:

---

17. Rosetta O'Neill, "The Dodworth Family and Ballroom Dancing in New York," reprinted from *Dance Index* (1948) in *Chronicles of the American Dance*, ed. Paul Magriel (New York: Da Capo, 1978), 81-100; Frank J. Cipolla, "Dodworth" family in *The New Grove Dictionary of American Music*, includes bibliography. Cipolla, a band and wind-instrument historian, never mentions Harvey Dodworth's theatrical activities.

18. OCLC (July 1994) showed the following items by Harvey B. Dodworth: "Elizabeth Schottisch" (New York: H. B. Dodworth and Co., 1851, and later editions), "Fannie varsoviana" (New York: H. B. Dodworth, 1857), "The Philolexian March" (New York: H. B. Dodworth, 1854), and *The Rudimental Instructor for Valve Instruments* (New York: S. T. Gordon, 1876).

19. Brooks, 20.

20. *French's American Drama*, vol. 69 (New York: Samuel French, n.d.)

21. The only document listed on OCLC (July 1994) for *Pocahontas* is a promptbook for an unspecified production, with manuscript annotations.

[. . . m]usic occupies well over a third of *Pocahontas*; the songs in the show play a far more important role than in most contemporaneous burlesques. . . . Clearly Brougham and Maeder devised a score of remarkable ingenuity and wit, fully consistent with the densely-packed humor of the script.[22]

William Brooks speculates that publication of the *Pocahontas* score was impossible because so much of the music was taken from copyrighted material or at least parodied from copyrighted songs, but many variant versions and parodies of copyrighted songs survive in sheet-music collections.[23] Brougham and Maeder probably considered publication to be against their best interests financially: when show songs were published they were distributed as widely as possible, both to generate income through sales and to help advertise the authentic production and expose the counterfeit ones. By suppressing publication or even the circulation of manuscript copies, the authors could protect their property and reserve for themselves the right to perform authentic versions of their work, and thus hope to preserve their financial interest in box-office receipts. Forty years later, at the close of the century, the conditions that stifled publication of the *Pocahontas* score had shifted; by then a vastly expanded popular-music industry controlled much of what was offered on the stage, built strong distribution networks for sheet music, and employed new technology and mechanical media to enhance sales. But in the 1850s and 1860s, the authors carried the manuscript score and parts with them as they travelled from one production site to the next. Brougham confirmed, "[. . . t]here is no piano forte arrangement for the music of Pocahontas that I am aware of. I have myself merely the orchestral accompaniments."[24]

The fate of Brougham's papers is unknown; a fire or other disaster could have destroyed the unpublished works. Mrs. Maeder confirmed the loss of most of her husband's personal papers and performing library by fire or during his many moves around the country and across the Atlantic.[25]

What we know about Maeder's score is deduced through evidence in the printed script and through press comments. *Pocahontas* contained some forty musical pieces in its two acts. The script identifies only six tunes, well-known melodies (such as "Widow Machree," "Rosin the Bow," and "Old Dog Tray") that were parodied. Brooks notes that

---

22. Brooks, 32.

23. Copyright was undoubtedly less significant a disincentive to publish than the factors discussed earlier. Arrangements of well-known melodies, recomposed as fantasias for piano, or simply adapted for guitar accompaniment, were common in publishers' catalogs. Stephen Foster complained to his publisher, Firth, Pond & Co., in New York, and for a while received one or one and a half cents for every copy of other arrangers' versions of his music that Firth sold. But Foster never received payment for the arrangements of his melodies sold by other publishers.

24. Ibid. James Gaspard Maeder is represented on OCLC (July 1994) by a surprisingly long list of 30 entries (some of them duplicates) besides the *Pocahontas* promptbook, none identified, however, with that show. He arranged popular tunes for piano, wrote parlor ballads and piano pieces, created new songs for insertion into English-language productions of opera, and composed at least one "fairy opera," *The Peri: or, The Enchanted Fountain*, based on a tale by Washington Irving to a libretto by S. J. Burr (Albany: Weed, Parsons, 1850).

25. Ibid.

"extended pieces were constructed by splicing together fragments from many sources." The tune names in these collages were not specified; Brooks has sifted through thousands of tunes and lyrics from the period, matching patterns of words, meters, and references, to identify most of them.

> [. . . t]he musical allusions are as densely packed as are the literary and theatrical ones; and they range fully as widely, from grand opera through sentimental ballads and minstrelsy to folk songs. Moreover, the musical humor of *Pocahontas* closely parallels the linguistic humor; it entails the use of parody and allusion, stylistic juxtaposition, and even a kind of musical punning.[26]

Confounding any notion of a single authentic version, Brougham tinkered with the show to keep it contemporaneous. Moreover, he collaborated with different composers to add new tunes and rearrange old ones. He had no apparent loyalty to the tunes he and Maeder had borrowed. For *Pocahontas*, as for his other shows, Brougham asked the theater's pit-orchestra conductor—whoever that may have been at the time—to select and arrange music or to provide new specially composed pieces to suit the dramatic scheme. During his career he worked with New York's best composer-conductors, including Stoepel, Edward Everett Rice (1848-1924), whose own later *Evangeline* (1874) was the foremost American "operetta" of its decade, and Thomas Baker for *The Christian Martyrs* (1867), a "historical, religious, spectacular, zoological drama" produced at P. T. Barnum's museum.

The Baker

Thomas Baker was a composer, arranger, and conductor. Born in England (apparently), as early as the 1830s he was producing published songs and piano pieces in London, and in the 1840s he edited volumes of music for the piano. In the 1850s he produced piano arrangements of operas and—judging from library catalogs listing surviving music scores of the decade—was well established as a leading arranger of theater and dance music for the keyboard.[27] In 1854, after he had emigrated to the United States, his music—especially ballads for voice and piano—began appearing in American publishers' catalogs; he grew far less active as an arranger for publication, but far more as a theater arranger-composer-conductor. Anne Dhu McLucas has encountered Thomas Baker's name in her research of melodrama and pantomime:

---

26. Ibid., 34.

27. *The Catalogue of Printed Music in the British Library to 1980* (London: K.G. Saur, 1981-) reflects 70 British and 12 American imprints of songs, piano pieces, arrangements, reissue titles, piano tutors, and arrangements of other composers' works, published under Baker's name. Ironically, however, it contributes to the obscurity of the theater sources by omitting show titles from the sheet-music entries. The New York Public Library's *Dictionary Catalog of the Music Collection*, 2nd ed. (Boston: G. K. Hall, 1982) contains only six entries for Baker, of which two are duplicates of holdings in the British Library. OCLC (July 1994) had 24 items, mostly those reported in the earlier printed catalogues. The most remarkable of his songs is "The Song of the Contrabands, O Let My People Go, Words and Music Obtained Through the Rev. L. C. Lockwood, Chaplain of the Contrabands [escaped slaves] at Fortress Munroe, Arranged by Thomas Baker" (New York: Horace Waters, 1861), for four-part chorus and piano; the early date, just at the outbreak of the Civil War, makes this perhaps the first printed edition of the spiritual "Go Down Moses."

[Baker] led opera at Niblo's summertime promenade concerts at the Paradise Gardens, and was musical director for Laura Keene's and Wallack's theaters and for the productions of many others. He was apparently a competent and sought-after musician, working in collaboration with set designers and lighting specialists to achieve the melodramatic effects that were so beloved by audiences of the day.[28]

In 1861, the splashiest "grand burlesque spectacle" in New York was *The Seven Sisters*, staged by Laura Keene. The program attributes the music to Thomas Baker. His association with the biggest show of the year at the premier theater for extravaganza in New York marks him as a major musical figure in the city. In 1864 he wrote music for *Under the Palms*, a melodrama adapted from Alfred Lord Tennyson's poem "Enoch Arden."[29] And an advertisement in the *New York Times* for the premier of *The Black Crook* at Niblo's Garden in September 1866 proclaimed that this "Grand Magical Spectacular Drama" had "Especial New Music, composed by Thomas Baker, and produced under the baton of H. E. [sic] Dodworth." Baker was conductor at the Olympic Theatre at the time; the wording of the advertisement suggests that he was asked to provide the score for the new extravaganza because his reputation would help attract an audience, even though he was unavailable to lead the show from the orchestra pit. After the opening night, *The Black Crook* was subjected to frequent interpolations, deletions, and the addition of new scenes, making it difficult to ascertain just who provided which music. Later revivals (for which none of Baker's music was used, apparently) have added to the confusion.[30]

In sum, Thomas Baker was one of the most prominent theater composers and conductors in New York over three decades. He penned the melodies and wrote the orchestrations used in the pit, and led the musicians and singers in performance. Furthermore, his keyboard arrangements permitted stage music to enter the repertory of singers and pianists in the home. But the music he created for the American theater has

---

28. Anne Dhu Shapiro [McLucas], "Action Music in American Pantomimes and Melodrama, 1730-1913," *American Music* 2, no. 4 (winter 1984): 61. One of Baker's surviving piano pieces is "The Laura Keene Schottisch, as Performed at Laura Keene's Varieties" (New York: Firth, Pond, 1856), with a portrait and signature of Laura Keene on the cover.

29. McLucas discovered the set of manuscript orchestral parts for this work at Harvard University's Theatre Collection. The script, unfortunately, is incomplete, preventing reconstruction or study of the full work.

30. The hit song of the first production, "You Naughty, Naughty Men" by G. Bicknell, was an interpolation added several months into the run. David Ewen, in his *New Complete Book of the American Musical Theater* (New York: Holt, Rinehart and Winston, 1970), 45, names Giuseppe Operti as the composer of the original music, yet no music for *The Black Crook* written by Operti was published before the second revival (18 December 1871). Julian Mates, *America's Musical Stage: Two Hundred Years of Musical Theatre* (Westport, Conn.: Greenwood, 1985) and other historians have repeated this error. A search through all the music deposited at the Library of Congress identified with either *The Black Crook* or Operti has failed to turn up a single piece of his music for the show before 1871. Music for the show by Baker and several others began appearing in print in 1866; at least 12 pieces of sheet music bearing the name "Black Crook" had been published by 1871.

disappeared almost entirely; his biographical record has become a *tabula rasa*, an erased slate.[31]

The Pantomime Maker

Pantomime, an art relegated today mostly to circus and street mimes, was an integral part of theatrical genres in the nineteenth century. George L. Fox (1825-77) acted in melodrama, farce, burlesque, and especially pantomime during four decades. He dominated pantomime, defined the character of the white-face clown in America, and was acclaimed as a cultural icon by his contemporaries. His best-known production was *Humpty Dumpty* (1868), from which he spun off several shows loosely based on this nursery tale, including *Humpty Dumpty Up to Date*, *Humpty Dumpty Abroad*, *Humpty Dumpty in Every Clime*, *Humpty Dumpty at Home*, and *Humpty Dumpty, a Playful Paraphrase*. For the first and prototypical production, called a "spectacular ballet pantomime," Fox was author, producer, stage manager, and leading actor in the role of the Clown.[32]

Fox worked with an arranger, Anthony Reiff, Jr. (ca. 1830s-1916), to adapt well-known tunes and write the overture as well as (presumably) action music for *Humpty Dumpty*.[33] The show included ballet—Rita Sangalli of the original *Black Crook* corps was given top billing—and the program mentions a contra dance, a grand ballet in a subterranean grotto, a grand pas de deux in an enchanted garden, and a Polish national dance. There would also have been music to accompany the grand transformation scene.

Like *Pocahontas*, none of the seven productions of *Humpty Dumpty* survives even in part as printed music. Fox is both silent and invisible in the scholarly literature on

---

31. No standard reference tool gives even his life dates. There is no entry for Baker in any edition of *Grove's Dictionary*, including *The New Grove Dictionary of American Music*, nor in any other encyclopedic source. Like Brougham, he is missing from the major nineteenth-century musical biographical dictionary, F. O. Jones, ed., *A Handbook of American Music and Musicians* (1886; reprint, New York: Da Capo, 1971); from a mid-twentieth-century one, Charles Eugene Claghorn, *Biographical Dictionary of American Music* (West Nyack, N.Y.: Parker Publishing Co., 1973); and from the two most comprehensive lists of American musical figures, the *Bio-Bibliographical Index of Musicians in the United States of American Since Colonial Times*, ed. Leonard Ellinwood and Keyes Porter, 2nd ed. (1956; reprint, New York: Da Capo, 1971), and *Resources of American Music History: A Directory of Source Materials from Colonial Times to World War II*, ed. D. W. Krummel, Jean Geil, Doris J. Dyen, and Deane L. Root (Urbana: University of Illinois Press, 1981).

32. For a biography and discussion of Fox's stage techniques, see Laurence Senelick, *The Age and Stage of George L. Fox, 1825-1877* (Hanover, N.H.: University Press of New England, 1988). Senelick ignores the musical aspects of Fox's shows entirely; he never even mentions the composers, arrangers, or conductors, who would have to have collaborated with Fox to create suitable musical settings for his "silent" action.

33. See Root, *American Popular Stage Music*, passim; also Katherine Preston, *Opera on the Road: Travelling Opera Troupes in the United States, 1825-1860* (Urbana: University of Illinois Press, 1993). OCLC (July 1994) listed only three songs by Reiff—two of which were from Niblo's Garden concerts. It also identifies a collection of his papers discovered by Preston, at the Swem Library, College of William and Mary, containing a diary and memoir of tours in the 1850s.

American music history.[34] It will take tedious sifting through archival collections—and luck in turning up musical parts or scores—if we are ever to understand the musical techniques and substance of Fox's art.

Epilogue

Although the prognosis for musicological treatment of Brougham, Baker, Fox, their colleagues, and their works is guarded, it is essential that musicologists be encouraged to deal with the sources that do exist, and to identify previously unknown materials. The insights that the discipline can provide are valuable to theater studies.

It is a historiographic axiom that the attempt to write about a subject lying beyond living memory must be preceded and fostered by the systematic compilation of access tools. Moreover, the writing of excellent history depends on—and cannot precede—the ready availability of wide-ranging and detailed studies, so that the historian can become immersed in and experience as many of the factual interconnections of the topic as is possible.

The most fundamental need for musicologists dealing with musical theater of the nineteenth century is adequate bibliographical control of the musical resources. Bibliography is both a basic tool and a product of most musicological research. D. W. Krummel put it as a sensory dichotomy: "[. . . m]usic is essentially an aural experience of a temporary phenomenon, and hence impermanent[, while] bibliographical evidence of music . . . is mostly visual and must be capable of permanence and recall." Therefore, "[. . . t]he preservation, promotion, and specialized study of this evidence will—necessarily—remain the bed-rock of musical scholarship."[35]

Our access tools for nineteenth-century American musical theater—the central, inclusive lists of the library and archival materials that have been collected and made accessible to scholars—have very little representation of music from the theater-orchestra pit. Among all the scholarly literature, the chronicles and other reference books that aim at encyclopedic coverage constitute the largest body of information about nineteenth-

---

34. Scripts for some of Fox's pantomimes are in the New York Public Library. Other sources include published interviews in newspapers of the time. Studies prior to Senelick—none of them by music historians—include Walter H. Draper, "George L. Fox: Comedian in Pantomime and Travesty" (Ph.D. diss., University of Illinois, 1957); and Senelick's "George L. Fox and Bowery Pantomime," in *American Popular Entertainment*, ed. Myron Matlaw (Westport, Conn.: Greenwood, 1979), 97-109. Senelick in this article, p. 98, notes that Fox, "though heralded in his day" and "remembered for a generation afterwards as the funniest man of his time, has remained as mute in histories as he was in his pantos." Fox is bypassed by the *Grove* dictionaries and all the reference works listed above in n. 31. Fox and his family played important roles in one of the most influential works of American social and political history: Senelick's book details their relationship to George C. Howard (Fox's sister's husband), who—as Thomas Riis explains in the facsimile of *Uncle Tom's Cabin*, vol. 5 of Nineteenth-Century American Musical Theater (New York: Garland, 1994)—created the first important musical dramatization of Harriet Beecher Stowe's novel.

35. D. W. Krummel, "The Bibliographical Prognosis," *Journal of Musicology* 1 (January 1982): 33.

century American musical theater.[36] Their contents, however, as we might expect, are skewed away from the music, because the compilers' source materials were amusical. These books provide almost no information about the music itself; the prepossessions of the authors have steered the emphasis away from the music and toward the production record: performance dates, number of performances in the first run of the show, casts, names of composers and authors, song titles that made it to opening night and those that did not.

More frustrating—and more insidious for those students of musical theater who do not realize the difference—is that even the music that does remain obscures our understanding of the original sound from the pit. Nearly every extant piece of theatrical sheet music is arranged for solo voice and piano accompaniment or for piano solo; the original orchestrated scores and choruses seldom survive. Cues and any other means of coupling the music with action or dialogue in the script are rare in the printed editions. The sheet music merely shadows the original context of the score within the concomitant arts of choreography, staging, lighting, costume, and set, the very things that made the music an integral part of a multisensory medium.[37]

Musicologists can look to sister disciplines for guidance. Musical theater is more prominent and respected as a research area among literary historians. Indeed, the research press for musical theater is dominated by the traditions of literary and theater scholarship. Synopsis of plot, production history, biography, and (increasingly) contextual interpretations are the main objects of their core literature. Or musicologists can follow the example of their own colleagues. Less than a generation ago, Paul Henry Lang reminded his fellow musicologists that "Until recently, [operatic history] was neglected in the English language literature on music[;] more precisely, such literature was mostly the product of amateur enthusiasts."[38] Operatic history has now become an important topic at scholarly meetings and in the research literature.

Musicologists in the professional mainstream may dissent from this paper's view that a worthy subject awaits them in musical theater. An insistence on scores complete in themselves, and to music that is not subservient to action or dialogue, is firmly established (if not universally shared) in the discipline. James Haar, writing about pop music (but with implications for stage music as well), has claimed that close musicological study would be "anachronistic in concept as well as method, [when] applied to pieces that not only functioned but were intended as background music."[39] Ethnomusicologists and

---

36. Among the most prominent are Jack Burton's *The Blue Book of Broadway Musicals* (Watkins Glen, N. Y.: Century House, 1952); Gerald Bordman's *The American Musical Theatre: A Chronicle* (New York: Oxford University Press, 1978; 2nd ed., 1992), and his histories of individual genres beginning toward the end of the century; David Ewen, *Complete Book of the American Musical Theater* (New York: Holt, 1958), revised as *New Complete Book* (see n. 30); Stanley Green, *Encyclopaedia of the Musical Theatre* (New York: Dodd, Mead, 1976); and David Hummel, *The Collector's Guide to the American Musical Theatre* (Metuchen, N.J.: Scarecrow, 1984).

37. See Victor Fell Yellin's account of the challenges he faced in reconstructing a full score, in his introduction to *The Aethiop: or, The Child of the Desert*, Nineteenth-Century American Musical Theater, 2 (New York: Garland, 1994).

38. Paul Henry Lang, "Introduction," *Journal of Musicology* 1 (January 1982): 4.

39. James Haar, "Music History and Cultural History," *Journal of Musicology* 1 (January 1982): 5.

popular-music scholars would disagree. A growing number of musicologists are considering how musics operate in their performance venues and contexts, even if composed or performed as accompaniment to foreground arts or other activity.

Musicologists in the future will explicate the functions and values of American theatrical music as a social activity. As social historians, they will discover how composing, arranging, conducting, playing, singing, dancing, listening, publishing, collecting, and all other related activities worked in the lives of nineteenth-century practitioners. They will trace the rise of industries and social institutions built on these practices. They will explain how conductors and arrangers created music to accompany stage action, and why certain styles were chosen for public presentation. They will relate the composers' activities to those of the writers, musicians, performers, producers, publishers, and patrons. They will prepare *catalogues raisonnés* of composers' works. They will elucidate the procedure of creating pastiche scores of preexistent music, and account for the practice of an author working with several composers to create a unified work. And they will document the relationship of nineteenth-century theater with the popular-music repertories and industry, beginning with the practice of adapting familiar tunes with prior connotations, or using them asyntactically for specific references in a dramatic work. By explicating just these few questions about nineteenth-century musical theater, musicologists would immeasurably enrich the scholarly literatures in both music and theater studies.

In 1963, Claude Palisca wrote that "The musicologist is concerned with music that exists, whether as an oral tradition or a written tradition, and with everything that can shed light on its human context."[40] To the extent that the music of nineteenth-century American musical theater still exists in any way—even when only through circumstantial evidence in ephemeral documents—it is potentially of concern to musicologists who follow this tenet. Given musical theater's role as a principal means of entertaining and reflecting the society for which it was created, it is a crucial genre for illuminating music's artistic, cultural, and ultimately human context.

---

40. Palisca and Holoman, *Musicology*, 1.

APPENDIX

Contents of the series Nineteenth-Century American Musical Theater, edited by Deane L. Root
(New York: Garland, 1994)
Dates given are those of the version published, not necessarily
of the first (American) performance.

Volume

1   *British Opera in America*, edited by Susan L. Porter

    Children in the Wood (1795), music by Samuel Arnold (with substitutions and additions by
    Benjamin Carr and others), libretto by Thomas Morton; *Blue Beard* (1811), music attributed to
    Michael Kelly, libretto by George Coleman

2   *Early Melodrama in America*

    The Voice of Nature (1803), play by William Dunlap, incidental music by Victor Pelissier, edit-
    ed by Karl Kroeger; *The Aethiop* (1813), play by William Dimond, incidental music by Rayner
    Taylor, edited and orchestral restoration by Victor Fell Yellin

3   *Italian Opera in English*, edited by John Graziano

    Cinderella (1831), adapted by M. Rophino Lacy from Gioacchino Rossini, *La cenerentola*

4   *Later Melodrama in America*, edited by Anne Dhu McLucas

    Monte Cristo (ca. 1883), adapted by Charles Fechter from Alexandre Dumas, *The Count of
    Monte Cristo*

5   *Uncle Tom's Cabin* (1852), edited by Thomas Riis, play by George L. Aiken after Harriet
    Beecher Stowe's novel, music in part by George C. Howard

6   *The Collected Works of John Hill Hewitt*, edited by N. Lee Orr and Lynn Wood Bertrand

    Rip Van Winkle (1860), *The Artist's Wife* (1863), *The Vivandiere* (1879), *Taken In* (1879), *The
    Musical Enthusiast* (1872)

7   *The Collected Works of Alfred B. Sedgwick*, edited by Michael Meckna

    Dualities: *Leap Year* (1875), *My Walking Photograph* (1876), *The Spelling Match* (1875).
    Sketches: *The Big Banana* (1875), *The Charge of the Hash Brigade* (1876), *The Decree of Divorce*
    (1875), *A Gay Old Man Am I* (1875), *I Love Your Wife* (1875), *The Law Allows It* (1875), *Let
    Those Laugh Who Win* (1875), *A Mad Astronomer* (1875), *Molly Moriarty* (1876), *The Tail
    (Tale) of a Shark: or, the Wailing (Whaling) Experiences of Sally Simpkins* (1878), *There's Millions
    in It* (1875), *Tootle, Tootle, Too* (1875). Operettas: *Circumstances Alter Cases* (1876), *Estranged*
    (1876), *The Queerest Courtship* (n.d.), *A Single Married Man* (1883), *Sold Again and Got the
    Money* (1876), *The Twin Sisters* (1876). Burlesques: *Africanus Bluebeard* (1876), *Gambrinus,
    King of Lager Beer* (1876)

8   *Pasticcio and Temperance Plays in America*, edited by Dale Cockrell

    Il pesceballo (1862), by Francis James Child, English trans. by James Russell Lowell; *Ten Nights
    in a Bar-Room* (1890) by William W. Pratt, after Timothy Shay Arthur, *Ten Nights in a Bar-
    Room, and What I Saw There*

9   *African American Theater*, edited by Eileen Southern

    Out of Bondage (1876), by Joseph Bradford; *Peculiar Sam: or, The Underground Railroad* (1879),
    by Pauline Elizabeth Hopkins

10 *Irish American Theater,* edited by Katherine K. Preston
    The Mulligan Guard Ball (1879) and *Reilly and the 400* (1891), music by David Braham, script by Edward Harrigan

11 *Yiddish Theater in America,* edited by Mark Slobin
    David's Violin (1897) and *Shloyme Gorgl* (189-), by Joseph Lateiner

12 *Early Operetta in America,* edited by Charlotte R. Kaufmann
    The Doctor of Alcantara (1879), music by Julius Eichberg, libretto by Benjamin E. Woolf

13 *Early Burlesque in America,* edited by Richard Jackson
    Evangeline (1877), music by Edward Everett Rice, libretto by J. Cheever Goodwin

14 *Later Operetta, Part I,* edited by Paul E. Bierley
    El Capitan (1896), music by John Philip Sousa, libretto by Charles Klein

15 *Later Operetta, Part II,* edited by Orly Leah Krasner
    The Highwayman (1897), music by Reginald de Koven, libretto by Harry Bache Smith

16 *Grand Opera in America,* edited by Elise K. Kirk
    The Scarlet Letter (1896), music by Walter Damrosch, libretto by George Parsons Lathrop

14

A Childhood Recollection
"Lunch at the Putnam Camp"

To Bill Kearns, whose very spirit
opens the windows and doors to American music

Normand Lockwood

Lit - tle Pop - sie Wop - sie chick - a - bid - y chum,

He shall have his pie - sy wise - y and a sug - ar plum,

He shall yid - y pid - y in his

coach - y woach - y too

All a - round the park - y wark - y with his cock - a - doo - dle doo.

April 1991

15

The Yale Song Books, 1853-1978

Walter S. Collins

Among the numerous gaps in the serious study of our American musical heritage is the college song. For more than 300 years American college students have been writing and singing songs about their institutions, their activities, and their feelings. Few colleges lack a sentimental Alma Mater and a rousing football song or two, but there are thousands of other songs and verses in print through which young American students have expressed their creative and recreational enthusiasms. So far, however, very little research has been undertaken to increase our knowledge and understanding of this huge body of musical material.

The reasons for this neglect are, I suspect, several. In the first place, serious scholars no doubt believe that the musical and poetic value of the repertory is trivial, and it frequently is. But it is also true that the creators of the tradition were the more cultured and better educated members of their generations, young though they may have been, and they were probably more sophisticated musically than the general population. I would venture to state that the average quality of college music—at least before the 1930s—was higher than that of its contemporary popular music, which has been much better studied. Indeed, we are already discovering that a number of our more important composers contributed to the repertory when they were students. At Yale University alone, for example, Charles Ives, Cole Porter, and Douglas Moore wrote college songs that are interesting examples of their early efforts at composition (see appendix 3). Other composers must have been similarly active at other colleges, and there may even be unknown talented composers and poets who wrote *only* in this milieu; but until there are many additional investigations, we shall not know of them, nor shall we be properly able to evaluate the whole tradition.

Another reason for the paucity of research on the college song may be that the source materials for the music have become obscure and difficult to obtain. A generation or two ago old college song books were commonly available at low cost in second-hand book stalls. Now old books have become very difficult to find at any price, even in college towns themselves, and only a handful of new ones have been published since 1960. Furthermore, collections in college music libraries have usually limited themselves to the song books of their own institutions, if they have preserved even those. Comprehensive collections of published college songs from a variety of institutions hardly exist anywhere, even among the largest collections of Americana. The situation for unpublished songs is even worse.

The following bibliographic study of the twenty-three published editions of Yale University's song books is limited to uncovering, organizing, and describing the publishing history of the song books, leaving the more important matters of musical, literary, and even sociological study to another day. But it should provide an example of the kind of preliminary task that must be undertaken at all institutions with similar confusing series of song-book editions before the more substantive work can begin.

* * * * *

Isolated records of student singing and student songs at Yale go back to at least the early eighteenth century. For example, the 1860 edition of *Songs of Yale* gives the text of "Psalm LXV. From the version of Sternhold and Hopkins. Sung Sept. 12, 1718, at the Commencement . . . of Yale College." The 1953 edition prints a facsimile of the "earliest song written by Yale students (Daniel Tillotson, 1798 - David B. Wilcockson, 1798)," which is printed and dated 1 January 1796, though the "earliest known song" might have been more defensible statement. The opening verse of the song demonstrates how little students have changed in the last 200 years:

> Ye sons of Yale
> With visage pale,
> Come join the happy chorus;
> Vacation's near
> Our hearts to cheer,
> When girls & wine shall moor us.

Several other songs in manuscript from the same period also survive.

The Editions

During the 124 years from 1853 to 1978, twenty-three editions of Yale songs appeared in print. They were published as frequently as every two or three years at first, but as the decades went by the intervals between them became consistently longer and longer, until twenty-four years separated the last two. It is now over forty years since the last full edition in 1953, and there is no new edition in sight. For most of their history, the editions tend to fall into loose groups by editor and title. The following discussions will be based on these groups because the editions in each one have so much in common. (For full citations of the title pages, see appendix 1, and for a list of the first lines and dates of appearance of all the songs contained in the editions, see appendix 2.)

Songs of Yale, 1853, 1855, 1858, 1860:
The Root-Lombard-Porter Editions

The first four printed collections of Yale songs, edited by three students, fall naturally into a group with their common title *Songs of Yale.* They contain only texts without music, but they usually include the title of the tunes to which the texts should be sung, most of which appear to be well-known songs of the day rather than original student compositions. These editions categorize almost all of the songs in relation to certain annual student events and ceremonies. All four books incorporate interesting prefaces with histories of singing at Yale up to their time, explanations of the various ceremonies, and information on how the books were compiled.

"The Compilers" of the earliest published edition of Yale songs in 1853, Messrs. N. W. T. Root and J. K. Lombard of the class of 1854, present an informative preface. They say that they are "offering this little collection of College Poetry to the courtesy of the public," but that it cannot be complete. The reason given is that "almost every student has a loose collection of Songs which he has laid up from time to time," so the compilers can only "present all the old, popular 'stand bys.'" They also state their goal to be "illustrating customs at Yale, and of thus affording amusement to outsiders who may be curious in such matters. . . . We wish it understood that those we publish . . . were written by members of this College." The preface ends with "Explanations" of the various categories of texts such as "Boating," "Biennial Examination," the "Burial of Euclid," "The Football Game" (between the freshmen and the sophomores), and "Presentation Day."

The 1853 edition appropriately opens with "Gaudeamus igitur," the quintessential college song of all, that appears in every edition but one down to the last. The book contains forty-six song texts, the earliest having been written by a member of the class of 1841. The student authors are usually identified. It cites the name of the tune to which each song is to be sung but contains neither a table of contents nor an index.

The second edition (1855), evidently by Mr. Root acting alone, is similar to the first in most respects, except for the added statement that the demand for the first edition has been so strong that a new one is now needed. It contains forty-four songs, of which thirteen are new.

The third edition (1858) is the first of two produced under the direction of Edward C. Porter of the class of 1858. After only three years, he increased the contents of the book by about fifty per cent, including within the total of sixty-one songs a surprisingly large number of thirty-seven songs that had not been published before. The creative activity of the students at this time must have been enormous. For the first time an index of the titles appears, which arranges the songs under the usual categories of student activities.

Porter obviously had historical inclinations. His prefaces to this and especially to his edition of 1860 are the most interesting of any in the entire series for their discussions of the history of student music. The book also contains the first example of a dedication in an edition, in this case to "Francis Miles Finch, of the class of 1849, whose name is inseparably connected with the music of Yale." A sizable number of songs in the first four editions are attributed to Mr. Finch, but his other contributions are not revealed.

In 1860, two years after Mr. Porter was graduated, he produced the fourth and last edition of *Songs of Yale*. It contains by far the longest and most instructive preface in the entire history of Yale song books. After a brief courtesy statement about the perceived audiences for the collection, he describes how student singing began in the United States:

> The history of College music in this country,—by which I mean the singing of distinctively *Student Songs,* either original or otherwise,—extends, at farthest, over only a few years, and, so far as I can learn, Yale has been foremost among American Colleges in introducing not only some of the best songs of the German Students, but also a good degree of that enthusiastic song-spirit, which beautifies their University life. Yet it is not twenty years since Gaudeamus was first sung at Yale. The introduction of this song by the accomplished editor of the "Musical World," [Richard Storrs Willis][1] may be regarded as the commencement of College singing in this country.

Porter then inserted a short essay on the value of education that takes place outside the classroom, a brief publishing history of Yale songs, and the usual description of student ceremonies and occasions that are accompanied by music. In the edition itself, Porter increased the number of song texts to eighty and still found, after only two years since the previous edition, twenty-three new ones to add. He also included the earliest example of an index of first lines of songs.

Carmina Yalensia, 1867, 1873:
The Garretson Editions

The 1867 edition of *Carmina Yalensia* is especially noteworthy because it is the first Yale song book to publish the music of the songs along with the texts.[2] Editor Ferd. V. D. Garretson mentions Charles Elliot, who would later publish a number of song books of his own, as a music arranger, but unfortunately identifies few of the composers and still

---

1. Identified later in Porter's dedication of this edition as "Richard Storrs Willis, of the Class of 1841, who, by bringing 'Gaudeamus' to Yale, Awoke the spirit of College Music among the Students of America."

2. The first book of college songs with music was *College Song Book,* published in 1860 (Boston: Henry Tolman & Co.). The editor of that book, C. Wistar Stevens of the class of 1860 at Harvard, compliments Yale, Williams, and Dartmouth Colleges for their "vigorous efforts . . . to increase the number and quality of College songs." The book is not a Harvard song book, because Stevens includes more Yale than Harvard songs and nearly as many from Williams and Dartmouth. The tunes that Stevens publishes for Yale songs are very useful for identifying tunes that are only named in earlier Yale books. At least one, "A Song for Old Yale," uses a tune that is different from the one given in the later Yale song books with music.

includes a number of verses without music. The repertory of the 1867 edition begins the trend of declining emphasis on songs specifically tied to special events. In the manner of the German student songs of the era, most of the songs are arranged for male chorus with the melody appearing in the top voice. This volume was the largest so far published, with ninety-seven songs, fifty-six of which had not appeared before. For the first time, it includes indexes of both titles and first lines.

Garretson's second "enlarged" edition (1873) is a reprint of his first except for pages 46-77, in which seventeen new songs are inserted as part of the impressive total of 114, the second largest of the entire history of the song books. Since Charles Elliot had started his own editions by this time, Garretson called on J. O. Heald and S. T. Dutton to arrange the "popular new songs." He does not provide a preface but continues the two indexes. Among the innovations of this edition are the first arrangements attributed by name to Gustave Stoeckel[3]—many of which are still sung today—and the first mention of the Yale Glee Club, in the text of the song "A. B. C. D. E."

Songs of Yale, 1870, 1870[a], 1874, 1876, 1880.
The Elliot Editions

Charles S. Elliot, class of 1867, was the second most prolific producer in the history of Yale song books. In addition to contributing the arrangements to Garretson's two editions, he himself published five editions of Songs of Yale under his own name, though the second and fifth editions are really reprintings of the first and fourth respectively. Thus, only three of the five are actually new editions, and they do not contain as many new songs as one might expect. All in all, Elliot added only 22 new pieces to the repertory over a decade of five publications. All five are dedicated to his "Classmates of '67," even as late as 1880.

Elliot's first edition, which appeared between Garretson's two, contains fifty-five songs with tunes and nine with text only, making it the second edition to include music. Composers, arrangers, and authors are usually not identified. The edition is particularly noteworthy for the first examples of "Warbles," yodeling songs no doubt imported from Germany by Stoeckel though not identified with him, a genre that has been popular at Yale down to the present day. Also making their first appearance are several ethnic songs—in this edition humorous German songs, negro spirituals, and "coon songs"—a category of songs that grows and then shrinks throughout the history of college song books. There is no preface; an index of tunes appears at the end.

Elliot's second and third editions were hardly new. For the second edition he simply reprinted the first edition right through the index of songs that ended it; in the third, he tacked on five more songs, three new and two from pre-Elliot times. The added songs,

---

3. Gustave Stoeckel, who had arrived in New Haven from Germany in 1848, later became the prime musical force in the city and the College for a long generation. He assisted the earliest Yale Glee Clubs, though he never took on the title of "Director." He imported and translated many of the German student songs Porter so admired and founded the Yale Department of Music in 1890. In 1864, Stoeckel became the recipient of the first honorary degree in music ever bestowed by Yale College.

making a total of sixty-nine, are not even included in the reprinted index. As usual, he did not supply a preface or any other kind of introductory remarks for the edition.

Charles Elliot's name continues to appear on the title page as editor of the 1876 edition, but that page also states that the book has been "Revised and Enlarged by Elmer P. Howe, of the Yale Glee Club." Mr. Howe, president of the 1876 Glee Club, did not add much, however. The edition is still largely a reprint, providing only five completely new songs to the three added in the 1874 edition, plus a few more taken from Garretson's competing 1873 edition. There are nevertheless several noteworthy aspects to this edition. It is the first one of Elliot's editions to include indexes for both titles and first lines. It also contains the first preface of Elliot's volumes—written by Howe on 1 June 1876—which supplies a brief publishing history of Yale song books and repeats Edmund Porter's 1860 tribute to R. Storrs Willis, adding that Willis had introduced to Yale another long-time favorite song, "Integer vitae," as well as "Gaudeamus."

Secondly, the Yale Glee Club is discussed for the first time, more than just being named in the song "A. B. C. D. E." in Garretson's 1873 edition. The Glee Club celebrates 1861 as its founding year, and it is surprising that the song books of 1867 and 1870 fail to mention it. Now in 1876 Howe proudly identifies himself on the title page as "of the Yale Glee Club" and changes the final line of the song "A. B. C. D. E." to bring the date up to "1876."

Even more important is the role the Glee Club was evidently playing in changing the musical style of college songs, establishing a practice that has had a major impact on American music for male chorus ever since. In the song books before 1876, the melody usually appears, as in the German tradition, in the highest voice, the first tenor. A few songs in those books employ the curious transitional practice of giving the melody to the first tenor but pitching that voice below the second tenor in the arrangement. By 1876, however, the melody has clearly moved to the second tenor in the new songs, and the technique is discussed for the first time by Howe, who implies that the Glee Club was involved in that change. He says that "The Glee Clubs have added most of the better class of music, especially since 1871. . . . The melody of the new songs has been assigned to the second tenor, so that it may be sung as a solo and the other parts used as an accompaniment." Howe's five new songs all follow the new style, while those he borrows from the 1873 edition do not. Two of the new ones still are numbered among Yale's most loved songs: "Wake, Freshman, Wake," and "Our Strong Band Can Ne'er Be Broken," which later provided the melody for Cornell University's famous Alma Mater, "Far Above Cayuga's Waters."

The 1880 edition is largely identical to that of 1876, including even the 1876 date sung by the Glee Club in "A. B. C. D. E." mentioned above. The only apparent differences were the correction of errata in the index of 1876 and the move to Taintor Brothers Publishers in New York, which had published the Garretson editions of 1867 and 1873.

Yale Songs, 1882, 1885, 1888, 1889, 1889[a];

Yale Glees, 1893;

Yale Melodies, 1903;

Yale Song Book, 1906;

The Shepard Editions

Thomas G. Shepard became the first named "Musical Director" of the Yale Glee Club in 1873, but his name does not appear in a publication of Yale songs until nine years later. He was reputedly a likable, modest man who was content to let the students Garretson, Elliot, and Howe appear as the editors of the song books during that period. In the first of Shepard's four editions, he even lists the name of the student president of the 1883 Glee Club, Frank B. Kellogg, ahead of his own. The editions are all dedicated "to the Glee Club, Students, and Alumni of Yale College."

In the 1882 edition of *Yale Songs,* Kellogg and Shepard's volume of sixty-nine songs includes thirty-four new songs, the first major body of new repertory since Garretson's first edition of 1867. The change in the musical style discussed above is further chronicled in the Editors' Preface:

> In most cases, the melody is given to the Second Tenor, in conformity with the custom adopted by the students. The changes in the manner of singing many of the old songs, which have crept in during the past fifteen years, have been adopted, and each song now appears in the form in which it is at present used.

The editors add a note of "Especial Mention" just before the music: "When the pieces in this book are played, the upper score containing the First and Second Tenor parts should be played *an octave lower* than it is written." This statement is echoed in most of the succeeding editions over the next several decades. Also for the first time, Shepard supplies composers' names on a few of the songs, but he claims as his own only three compositions and a single arrangement. Most of the rest are German names not immediately recognizable today. Also noteworthy is a song with a whistled solo, the first such of a genre that would remain quite popular for the next several decades. The recent innovation of providing indexes for both titles and first lines of songs is continued.

Shepard and Kellogg's second edition of *Yale Songs* in 1885 (reprinted in 1888) is called "enlarged." Its first 103 pages are virtually identical to the complete 1882 edition—including the "Yale Glee club of 1883" mentioned in the song "A. B. C. D. E." From page 104 to the end, they add eight new songs and one from the Elliot editions, new to this series, for a total of seventy-eight.

As they had done before, Shepard and Kellogg in the 1889 edition simply reprinted an early edition and added new songs at the end. This edition is identical to the 1885 and 1888 editions through page 116, after which fifteen new songs are added, for a total of ninety-three in their cumulative system. Curiously, many of the songs added in this edition never became popular enough to appear in a later one. Most of them have texts and/or music provided by Shepard, a surprising number of which use the old-fashioned technique of placing the melody in the first tenor. Many of the rest are solos with simple choral accompaniment or a brief chorus section at the end. A second printing of this edition appeared in the same year with the only change, on the title page, identifying the publisher and the city of publication as "New York G. Schirmer" instead of the previous "New Haven, Conn. published by Shepard and Kellogg."

By the time of his 1893 edition, Shepard must have felt that the old cumulative editions of the 1880s had worn out their usefulness. For this edition he changed the title to *Yale Glees*, dropped Kellogg as co-editor, and provided thirty-three new songs for a total of only forty-three. Obviously, many of the old songs were disappearing, at least from the Glee Club repertory. He says in the preface that the songs were intended mainly for the Glee Club, and the old favorite "Integer vitae" appears in this edition with its melody in the second tenor for the first time. Most of the songs are by Shepard, again largely solos or choruses with the melody in the first tenor. For the first time some composers of the tunes, frequently students, are identified. Medleys combining a number of popular tunes first make their appearance as well. Whistled solos of considerable virtuosity have become more popular than the old yodels, and ethnic songs are less numerous than in most editions.

Shepard continued as director of the Glee Club until his death in 1905. In 1903 his last publication of Yale songs took on yet another new title, *Yale Melodies*, and he returned to his practice of citing the current president of the Yale Glee Club as his assistant editor. Shepard's muse continued unabated in this late part of his life. He added another thirty new songs from the decade since his last book, printing only seven that had appeared before. Many of the songs are of Shepard's composition, both choruses with melody (usually on top) and solos with choral accompaniment. Several new yodels by Shepard appear, but no whistling songs, the fashion (or student talents) having changed again. Student composers are identified, including "Chas. E. Ives, '98" with a sentimental song for solo voice and piano called the "Bells of Yale." Brian Hooker, '02, later a librettist for a number of Horatio Parker's works and a well-known lyricist on Broadway, provides several of the song texts. The percentage of black minstrel songs in this edition is higher than that in other volumes. Of greatest interest in student and alumni circles, perhaps, is the debut of the first true Yale football song, the famous "Boola, Boola," which is based on a minstrel song called "La Hoola Boola" by Bob Cole and Billy Johnson (1898).

Shepard's legacy lived on after him, his estate apparently having sold the copyrights for his publications to G. Schirmer Music Publishers of New York after his death. The 1906 volume, called *The Yale Song Book*, is the earliest one with a modern look to its printing style, perhaps because it is the first *designed* by a major music publisher. It is an anthology of eighty-seven of the 120 songs presented in Shepard's editions from 1882 to 1903. The only two songs that had not been published before were a humorous negro spiritual "The Old Ark" and a football song "The Undertaker Song," neither of which is given a composer, arranger, author, or source. Indeed, few of the other songs carry such identification, including even some of Shepard's compositions. The book does not contain a preface.

Yale Songs Illustrated, 1893:
The Barber Edition

This volume stands alone among all other editions of Yale songs. Donn Barber, who wrote the music for two of the songs in *Yale Glees* of 1893, was also an artist of some accomplishment. All of the twenty-two songs he reprints in this edition are from earlier Shepard editions, and each is accompanied by an illustration by Barber. The edition would be called a "coffee-table book" today. It is attractive to thumb through, but it cannot be used for singing since many of the songs contain the first page only (see fig. 15.1).

Figure 15.1. "Here's to Good Old Yale," from *Yale Songs Illustrated,* 1893 (Manuscripts and Archives, Yale University Library).

The New Yale Song Book, 1918:
The Goodale Edition

Frank Goodale, class of 1889, became musical director of the Yale Glee Club in 1906, after the death of Thomas Shepard, and remained in that post until 1921. The 1918 song book, coming twelve years after the previous one—the longest interval between editions up to that point—is his single published contribution to the tradition. His preface says that the songs in this edition "include not only those dear to former generations of Yale men, but also those sung on the campus during the last ten years, and many used by the Glee Club. Twenty-two of these songs have never before been published." A count reveals, however, that forty-three of the ninety-two songs in the edition had not appeared in any previous edition of Yale songs, so evidently twenty-one must have been borrowed from other published sources. Among the first appearances are such universally known songs as the "Whiffenpoof Song," "Aura Lee," "Shall I Wasting," and the football song "Bull-Dog."

The 1918 edition contains several elaborate whistling compositions by Goodale and the first songs to appear written by Cole Porter, class of 1913. Songs from other colleges are included for the first time, among them the Harvard and Princeton Alma Maters. The melody remains embedded in the second tenor most of the time, and medleys and spirituals are still popular.

Songs of Yale, 1934, 1953:
The Bartholomew Editions

In 1934, Marshall Bartholomew, director of the Yale Glee Club since 1921, published the first song book in sixteen years. The edition contains a record 119 songs, of which forty were new. Many of the latter are Bartholomew's own arrangements, not surprising since he became one of the most active arrangers for male chorus of his generation through his popular Yale Glee Club Series of octavos. His arrangements are still sung by male choruses throughout the world. The edition does not include a preface or dedication but does present pictures and brief biographies of his predecessors Stoeckel, Shepard, and Goodale.

In addition to the now customary indexes of titles and first lines, Bartholomew also offers a classified index to the songs for the first time since the earliest editions. The list reveals how the categories of the repertory had changed since the 1850s: "Songs of Yale," "Old Favorites," "Yodels" (but no whistling songs), "Humorous Songs," "Football Songs," "Songs for Special Occasions," "Songs of the South" (with subheadings of "Spirituals" and "Plantation Songs"), "Songs of the Sea" (revealing Bartholomew's personal interest in sea chanteys), and "Songs of Other Colleges."

Composers are identified when known. Two new songs of Cole Porter are included, and Douglas Moore, class of '15, makes his only appearance with a football song. In the newer choral songs, the melody is normally in the second tenor—including the premier appearances of songs in true barbershop style, which was a fairly young genre at the time. To avoid any misunderstanding, Bartholomew marks the location of the melody in each piece. "Integer vitae" is even published both ways with the statement "While Yale tradition has hallowed the version of 'Integer vitae' with the melody in the 2nd Tenor, the above form [with the melody in the first tenor] of this international students' song is the one generally used throughout Europe." Most, but not all, of the old-fashioned ethnic songs have disappeared.

As had Shepard and Goodale before him, Bartholomew published a swan-song edition of Yale songs just before leaving his position. It appeared in 1953—exactly a century after the first edition. The "250th Anniversary Edition" on the title page refers neither to editions of the book nor to the Yale Glee Club, but to Yale College itself, which was founded in 1701. He calls this the "sixteenth edition of Yale Songs," not explaining which of the previous twenty-one editions and printings he is omitting. The overall size of the edition is somewhat smaller than that of 1934, with 104 songs, of which twenty-eight are new. The yodels remain, but the whistling songs have never returned. Ethnic songs, other than spirituals, have nearly disappeared. Two new Cole Porter songs have been added, and Bartholomew's successor as director of the Yale Glee Club, Fenno Heath, contributed a composition and an arrangement.

The biggest change in the song categories Bartholomew indexes comes with the addition of what he called "Educated Barbershop," a term that never really caught on; it is now known widely as "a cappella vocal jazz." This group of songs recognizes the immense growth at Yale after World War II of the many small groups that sing unaccompanied arrangements of popular songs of the day. In the 1953 edition, however, only a few are actually post-war songs, most being arrangements of sentimental and amusing songs from before the war or from earlier editions of the song book. The vocal jazz style, in one sense, comes full circle historically in that the melody has usually returned to the top voice in the male arrangements after a long residence in the second tenor.

Among the small singing groups, the famed Whiffenpoofs, all male and all seniors, was the chief student group on campus from their founding in 1909 until World War II. Today there are as many as twenty student-run groups devoting vast amounts of time to the rehearsal and performance of currently popular songs. Since the arrival of female students at Yale in the 1960s, groups of mixed voices or all women's voices have enriched the musical environment.

Songs of Yale, 1978:
The Heath Edition

Upon Bartholomew's retirement in 1953, Fenno Heath became director of the Yale Glee Club. When Yale became co-ed and the Glee Club became a mixed chorus in the 1960s, over a century's accumulation of Yale songs arranged for men's voices was made largely obsolete. If old favorites were still to be sung by the Club as a whole, however, it was obvious that new arrangements needed to be made. Such arrangements by Heath and several students soon began to accumulate, and in 1978 Heath published ten old favorites in both the traditional male arrangements and in mixed-voice arrangements. He also added a medley for mixed voices of football songs from various colleges, including, of course, Yale. Heath retired in 1993 after forty years as director of the Glee Club, a longer tenure than that of any of his predecessors.

* * * * *

Heath's brief edition is the smallest and last in the long, long line of Yale song books. It may be that the lack of student interest in college songs as such will never again create sufficient demand for another edition. Or perhaps the intense student activity in arranging and singing the popular songs of their day—albeit not college songs specifically—will one day result in the publication of a different kind of edition. Such a book might be comprised of songs not written by students but arranged and sung by students at, rather than about, Yale. That, after all, has been one part of the tradition for almost 150 years.

Appendix 1: Title Pages of the Editions

SONGS OF YALE.
* * * * *
NEW HAVEN:
FOR SALE BY E. RICHARDSON,
NEW HAVEN HOTEL BLOCK.
1853.

SONGS OF YALE.
* * * * * *
NEW HAVEN:
PUBLISHED BY THOMAS H. PEASE.
PRINTED BY J. H. BENHAM.
1855.

SONGS OF YALE.
* * * * * *
NEW HAVEN:
PUBLISHED BY THOMAS H. PEASE.
PRINTED BY J. H. BENHAM.
1858.

THE
SONGS OF YALE.
* * * * * *
NEW HAVEN:
PUBLISHED BY THOMAS H. PEASE,
AT THE COLLEGE BOOKSTORE, CHAPEL STREET.
PRINTED BY J. H. BENHAM.
1860.

CARMINA YALENSIA.
A COMPLETE AND ACCURATE COLLECTION OF
YALE COLLEGE SONGS
WITH
PIANO ACCOMPANIMENT
COMPILED AND ARRANGED BY
FERD. V. D. GARRETSON.
NEW YORK:
Published by TAINTOR BROTHERS & Co., No. 229 Broadway.
[1867]

SONGS OF YALE:
A NEW COLLECTION OF COLLEGE SONGS.
EDITED BY
CHARLES S. ELLIOT, A. B.
NEW HAVEN, CONN.
CHARLES C. CHATFIELD & CO.
1870.

SONGS OF YALE
A NEW COLLECTION OF COLLEGE SONGS.
EDITED BY
CHARLES S. ELLIOT, A. M.
SECOND EDITION.
NEW HAVEN, CONN.
CHARLES C. CHATFIELD & CO.
1870.

CARMINA YALENSIA:
A COLLECTION OF
YALE COLLEGE SONGS
WITH
MUSIC AND PIANO-FORTE ACCOMPANIMENT.
COMPILED BY
FERD. V. D. GARRETSON.
ENLARGED EDITION,
WITH POPULAR NEW SONGS.
ARRANGED BY
J. O. HEALD AND S. T. DUTTON.
PUBLISHED BY
TAINTOR BROTHERS, 678 Broadway, NEW YORK.
[1873]

SONGS OF YALE:
A NEW COLLECTION OF COLLEGE SONGS,
EDITED BY
CHARLES S. ELLIOT, A. M.
THIRD EDITION.
NEW HAVEN, CONN.
CHARLES C. CHATFIELD & CO.
1874.

SONGS OF YALE:
A NEW COLLECTION OF COLLEGE SONGS.
EDITED BY
CHARLES S. ELLIOT, A. M.
REVISED AND ENLARGED BY
ELMER P. HOWE,
OF THE YALE GLEE CLUB.
FOURTH EDITION.
NEW HAVEN, CONN.
H. G. PHILLIPS.
1876.

SONGS OF YALE:
A NEW COLLECTION OF COLLEGE SONGS,
EDITED BY
CHARLES S. ELLIOT, A. M.
REVISED AND ENLARGED BY
ELMER P. HOWE,
OF THE YALE GLEE CLUB.
FIFTH EDITION.
1880.
PUBLISHED BY
TAINTOR BROTHERS, MERRILL & CO.
NEW YORK.

YALE SONGS.
A COLLECTION OF SONGS IN USE BY THE
GLEE CLUB AND STUDENTS OF YALE COLLEGE,
COMPLIED AND EDITED BY
FRANK B. KELLOGG,
President of the Yale Glee Club '83,
AND
THOMAS G. SHEPARD,
Musical Director of the Yale Glee Club since '73.
NEW HAVEN, CONN.:
PUBLISHED BY SHEPARD AND KELLOGG.
1882.

YALE SONGS.
A COLLECTION OF SONGS
IN USE BY THE
GLEE CLUB AND STUDENTS OF YALE COLLEGE.
COMPLIED AND EDITED BY
FRANCIS B. KELLOGG,
President of the Yale Glee Club of '83,
—AND—
THOMAS G. SHEPARD,
Musical Director of the Yale Glee Club since '73.
ENLARGED EDITION.
NEW HAVEN, CONN.
PUBLISHED BY SHEPARD AND KELLOGG.
1885.

YALE SONGS.
A COLLECTION OF SONGS
IN USE BY THE
GLEE CLUB AND STUDENTS OF YALE COLLEGE.
COMPLIED AND EDITED BY
FRANCIS B. KELLOGG,
President of the Yale Glee Club of '83,
—AND—
THOMAS G. SHEPARD,
Musical Director of the Yale Glee Club since '73.
ENLARGED EDITION.
NEW HAVEN, CONN.
PUBLISHED BY SHEPARD AND KELLOGG.
1888.

YALE SONGS.
A COLLECTION OF SONGS
IN USE BY THE
GLEE CLUB AND STUDENTS OF YALE COLLEGE.
COMPLIED AND EDITED BY
FRANCIS B. KELLOGG,
President of the Yale Glee Club of '83,
—AND—
THOMAS G. SHEPARD,
Musical Director of the Yale Glee Club since '73.
ENLARGED EDITION.
NEW HAVEN, CONN.
PUBLISHED BY SHEPARD AND KELLOGG.
1889.

YALE SONGS.
A COLLECTION OF SONGS
IN USE BY THE
GLEE CLUB AND STUDENTS OF YALE COLLEGE
COMPLIED AND EDITED BY
FRANCIS B. KELLOGG,
President of the Yale Glee Club of '83,
—AND—
THOMAS G. SHEPARD,
Musical Director of the Yale Glee Club since '73.
ENLARGED EDITION.
NEW YORK
G. SCHIRMER.
[1889]

YALE GLEES. A COLLEC-
TION OF THE SONGS
Recently prepared for and used
by the YALE UNIVERSITY GLEE
CLUB.
Compiled and Edited by THOMAS G.
SHEPARD, Musical Director of the
Club since '73.
PUBLISHED BY THOMAS G. SHEPARD, NEW HAVEN,
CONN., 1893.

Yale Songs Illustrated
FROM DRAWINGS BY
DONN BARBER—YALE, '93, S.
NEW HAVEN, CONN.   MDCCCXCIII

YALE MELODIES
A COLLECTION OF THE LATEST SONGS
USED BY THE
YALE UNIVERSITY GLEE CLUB
COMPOSED, COMPILED AND EDITED BY
THOMAS G. SHEPARD
MUSICAL DIRECTOR OF CLUB SINCE 1873
ASSISTED BY
JAMES W. REYNOLDS
PRESIDENT OF THE CLUB OF 1903
THOMAS G. SHEPARD, PUBLISHER, NEW HAVEN, CONN.
1903

THE
YALE
SONG BOOK
COMPILED FROM "YALE SONGS," YALE GLEES"
AND "YALE MELODIES"
NEW YORK
G. SCHIRMER
1906

THE NEW
YALE SONG-BOOK
A COLLECTION OF SONGS
IN USE BY
THE GLEE CLUB
AND STUDENTS OF YALE UNIVERSITY
COMPILED AND EDITED BY
G. FRANK GOODALE
MUSICAL DIRECTOR OF THE YALE GLEE CLUB
Price
Paper, $1.00, net; Cloth, $2.00, net
G. SCHIRMER
NEW YORK   •   BOSTON
[1918]

SONGS OF YALE
Compiled and Edited
By
MARSHALL BARTHOLOMEW, '07s
Director of the Yale Glee Club since 1921
G. SCHIRMER, Inc.—NEW YORK
[1934]

SONGS OF YALE
250th ANNIVERSARY EDITION
Compiled and Edited
By
MARSHALL BARTHOLOMEW
Director of the Yale Glee Club since 1921
G. SCHIRMER, Inc.—NEW YORK
[1953]

SONGS OF YALE
*In new settings for Mixed Chorus and in
Traditional Male Chorus Arrangements
A souvenir booklet prepared by Fenno Heath for
the annual Singing Dinner of the Yale Glee Club Associates
held at the University Club, New York City
on April 5, 1978.*

APPENDIX 2: ALPHABETICAL LISTING BY FIRST LINE OF THE
SONGS OF THE YALE SONG BOOKS

A.B.C.D.E.	1873, 1876, 1880, 1882, 1885, 1888, 1889
Ach, the moon, he climbs	1934, 1953
A glad four years together	1858, 1860
Ah me conditione	1870, 1870a, 1874, 1876, 1880
Ain't it a shame to steal on Sunday?	1934
Aj lucka, lucka siroka	1934, 1953
A lingering ray of the dying day	1860
Alma Mater! Alma Mater! Heaven's blessing	1853, 1855, 1858, 1860, 1867, 1870, 1870a, 1873, 1876, 1880
Alma Mater! Alma Mater! the moonlight	1858, 1860, 1867, 1873
Alma Mater! We ne'er shall forget thee	1867
Alumni Hall! Alumni Hall!	1867, 1873
A man and a maid went a-rowing	1893, 1906
A man who studied day and night	1903
Amo, Amas, I love the class	1853, 1855
And when the leaves turn red and fall	1918, 1934, 1953
An egg within a grocery	1934, 1953
Anni pleni gaudiis	1858, 1860, 1867, 1873
As a Freshman I couldn't decide	1893
As down the tide of time we're rowing	1858, 1860, 1867, 1873
As Freshmen first we came to Yale	1867, 1870, 1970a, 1873, 1874, 1876, 1882, 1885, 1888, 1889, 1906, 1918, 1934, 1953, 1978
As Freshmen first we come (alt. version)	1867
As I was walking down the street	1867, 1870, 1870a, 1873, 1874, 1876, 1880, 1889, 1893
A song for old Yale, for brave old Yale	1853, 1855, 1858, 1860, 1867, 1873, 1893, 1903, 1906, 1918, 1934, 1953
A song for the elms, the brave old elms	1858
A song of joy, let naught alloy	1893
As the blackbird in the spring	1918, 1934, 1953, 1978
As the New Haven train left Grand Central	1953
Audacia, this is the title	1853, 1855, 1858, 1860, 1867, 1873
Away down South in old Virginny	1893, 1906
Away, 'way back in the ages dark	1934, 1953
A welcome to thee, Yale	1860
B-a-ba, b-e-be	1867, 1870, 1870a, 1873, 1874, 1876, 1880, 1882, 1885, 1888, 1889, 1906
Baby needs a new pair of shoes	1918
Beneath these elms—whose sacred shade	1855
Beneath these sacred shades	1853, 1855, 1858, 1860
Biennials are a bore	1855, 1860, 1867
Bingo, bingo, that's the lingo	1934, 1953
Birds' love and birds' song	1893
Bowsman! push her from the shore!	1853, 1855, 1858, 1860
Bright college years, with pleasure rife	1882, 1885, 1888, 1889, 1906, 1918, 1934, 1953, 1978
Brothers all in unity, knit by love's	1858, 1860, 1867, 1870, 1870a, 1873, 1874, 1876, 1880
Brothers all in unity, mourning	1867, 1870, 1870a, 1873, 1874, 1876, 1880
Brothers! faithful, earnest-hearted!	1860
Brothers, for the last time gathered	1853, 1855, 1858, 1860
Brothers, now the time has come	1867, 1873
Buckwheat cakes! You flip 'em	1918
Burthened with fragrance	1858, 1860, 1867, 1873
By the flickering light of a fluid lamp	1855
Ca, ca, geschmauset! Lasst uns nicht	1858
Careless love, careless love	1953
Carolina, hoo-hoo	1903, 1918, 1934, 1953
Chew nane gin zhih	1934
Classmates, the day we keep	1858, 1860
Cocaine Bill and Morphine Sue	1934
Columbia, to glory arise	1953
Come all ye jolly Juniors	1855, 1860, 1867, 1873, 1885, 1888
Come, all you jolly fellows now	1918
Come along, Mary	1903
Come, brothers, and a song we'll sing	1893, 1906, 1918
Come brothers, let us puff away	1853
Come, classmates, gather round us	1855, 1867, 1873

Come, classmates, let us gather	1858, 1860
Come, join my humble ditty	1874, 1934
Come, join together, classmates	1860, 1867, 1873
Come, Juniors, join this jolly tune	1853, 1855
Come now, and listen to my tale of woe	1893, 1906, 1934
Come rally tonight	1873, 1874, 1876, 1880, 1882, 1885, 1888, 1889, 1906, 1918, 1934, 1953
Cosily placed in a big arm-chair	1893
Cradle's quiet, sing low	1903
Daniel in the lions' den	1889, 1906, 1918, 1934
Dar's someting rong a brewin' (see "There's something wrong a-brewing")	
Daylight is on the sea	1876, 1880, 1882, 1885, 1888, 1889
Dearest maid be shy	1885, 1888, 1889, 1906
Dere's animals an' animals	1953
Dere's an old camp-meetin'	1918, 1934
Dere was a moanin' lady	1918, 1953
Did you ever stop to think?	1918, 1934
Doctor Cook's in town	1918
Down on the Mississippi floating	1870, 1870a, 1873, 1874, 1876, 1880, 1882, 1885, 1888, 1889, 1906, 1918, 1934
Down over the hill	1953
Draw nigh, all Yale men who would dwell	1953
Drink to me only with thine eyes	1934, 1953, 1978
Drum-beats rolled o'er the silence	1934
Du bist wie eine Blume	1889
Ei! so wollen wir	1882, 1885, 1888, 1889
Erectis auribusque, a story we relate	1855
Eyes bright, hearts light	1885, 1888, 1889
Eyes of beauty	1867, 1873, 1882, 1885, 1888, 1889
Fairer than love of woman	1903, 1906, 1918, 1934, 1953
Fairer than love of woman (Medley)	1918
Fair Harvard, thy sons to thy jubilee	1918, 1934, 1953
Fair memories of college days	1934
Fair o'er the water the bright sun	1889, 1893a
Far away in the South	1903, 1906, 1918, 1934
Farewell, farewell, amid the shades	1858, 1860
Farewell, farewell, sweet echoes rise	1873
Farewell! farewell! the parting word	1858, 1860, 1867, 1873
Fast fading from our sight	1870, 1870a, 1874, 1876, 1880
Felis sedit by a hole	1867, 1870, 1870a, 1873, 1874, 1876, 1880
Fight, fight for Yale	1934, 1953
Finis nobis expetitus	1853, 1855, 1858
Floating away like the fountain's spray	1853, 1855, 1858, 1860, 1867, 1870, 1870a, 1873, 1874, 1876, 1880
For Yale, old Yale! come join the cheer	1903
Four revolutions of the sun	1867, 1873
Four years ago, a glorious crowd	1858, 1860
From our College hall we come	1893
Fundite nunc lacrymas	1853, 1855, 1858, 1860, 1867, 1873
Gather ye smiles from the ocean isles	1853, 1855, 1858, 1860, 1867, 1870, 1870a, 1873, 1874, 1876, 1880
Gaudeamus igitur	1853, 1855, 1858, 1860, 1867, 1870, 1870a, 1873, 1874, 1876, 1880, 1882, 1885, 1888, 1889, 1906, 1918, 1934, 1953
George Jones had a meetin' at his house	1953
Gin a body meet a body	1918
Go down, Ezekiel, to the valley	1934
Gone are the days when my heart	1918
Good night, ladies	1867, 1870, 1870a, 1873, 1874, 1876, 1880
Good night, poor Harvard	1934, 1953
Got my head wet in the midnight dew	1918, 1934
Graceful and easy	1918, 1934, 1953
Gray rocks by Heaven's own arches spanned	1853, 1855, 1858, 1860
Great-a-big nigger lyin' 'hind a log	1934
Greek Fixings (title) (in Greek)	1853
Ha! ha! it's over—Loudly we'll sing	1858
Hail to thee, queen of the silent night	1867, 1870, 1870a, 1873, 1874, 1876, 1880, 1882, 1885, 1888, 1889, 1903, 1906
Happy and gay are our hearts today	1853, 1855, 1858, 1860, 1867, 1873
Happy are we tonight, boys	1858, 1860

Hark! hark! now rumbles the bass	1882, 1885, 1888, 1889, 1906
Have you been to Antigone	1893
Have you ever been in Mobile Bay?	1934, 1953
Have you studied psychology?	1903
Here, about this pleasant spot	1860
Here's the team a-coming as of yore	1934
Here's to good old Yale, drink it down	1867, 1870, 1870a, 1873, 1874, 1876, 1880, 1882, 1885, 1888, 1889, 1893, 1893a, 1906, 1918, 1934, 1953
Here's to Yale, to old Yale	1853, 1855
Here to-day with with joy unmingled	1867, 1873
Hidden half by silken hangings	1893
Honored in song and story	1867, 1873
How can I bear to leave thee?	1882, 1885, 1888, 1889, 1906, 1918, 1934
How sweet it is when twilight falls	1889
How very glad we'd be to sing	1882, 1885, 1888, 1889, 1906
Humpty Dumpty sat on a wall	1882, 1885, 1888, 1889
Hurrah! we're free forever	1860
I am a Sunday-school scholar	1889, 1906
I am going far away	1885, 1888, 1889, 1906
I arise from dreams of thee	1885, 1888, 1889, 1906, 1918, 1934, 1953
I came an emerald Freshman	1855, 1860, 1867, 1870, 1870a, 1873, 1874, 1876, 1880
I got a mule, her name is Sal	1934, 1953
I got shoes, you got shoes	1934, 1953
I had a dream the other night	1853, 1858, 1860
I hear them angels callin' loud	1934, 1953
I just can't afford York Street clothing	1953
I know not whence it cometh	1873, 1876, 1880, 1882, 1885, 1888, 1889
I'm a member very noted	1953
I met her in gay Newport	1893
I'm going far away	1882
I'm going to tell you about myself	1893, 1903
I'm Pierre de Bonton de Paris	1885, 1888, 1889, 1906, 1918, 1934
Im Wald und auf der Haide	1885, 1888, 1889, 1906
In Amsterdam there lives a maid	1934, 1953
In Brooklyn city there once did dwell	1885, 1888, 1889, 1906, 1934
I never saw a purple cow	1918, 1934
In good old colony times	1889
In heaven, in heaven the rapturous song	1867, 1873
In my boyhood's happy hour	1918, 1934
In our little boat we glide	1893
Integer vitae	1858, 1860, 1867, 1870, 1870a, 1873, 1874, 1876, 1880, 1882, 1885, 1888, 1889, 1893, 1906, 1918, 1934, 1953
In the class of 1778	1953
In the garden of Eden old Adam sat	1903
I once proposed unto a lovely maid	1893, 1906
I took my charming Dolly	1889, 1893a, 1906, 1918
It's a way we have at old Yale	1867, 1870, 1870a, 1873, 1874, 1876, 1880
It was a lover and his lass	1918
It was a most particular, peculiar old	1903, 1918, 1934, 1953
I've a jolly sixpence	1870, 1870a, 1874, 1876, 1880
I've been looking through the dictionary	1953
I've lost my poodle	1903, 1906
I went to the river	1882, 1885, 1888, 1889, 1906
I will sing you a song	1903
I wish I was in Boston city	1867, 1870, 1870a, 1873, 1874, 1876, 1880
I wish I was in the land ob cotton	1934, 1953
I wish I were a granger	1893
I wish I were a rhinossoriacus	1934
Jack and Jill went up the hill	1870, 1870a, 1873, 1874, 1876, 1880
Jes' wait a little while till I tell ye	1906
John Brown had a little injun	1867, 1870, 1870a, 1873, 1874, 1876, 1880
Jollity (no text; whistle & piano)	1918
Joshua fit the battle of Jericho	1953
Jovial the song we raise, boys	1858, 1860, 1867, 1873
Junior, Junior, fussing Junior	1903
Juniors, hail the present hour!	1853
Just wait a little while	1882, 1885, 1888, 1889
Kind friends, your pity pray bestow	1870, 1870a, 1874, 1876, 1880, 1885, 1888, 1889, 1906

Lady, let the rolling drums	1882, 1885, 1888, 1889
Lamb of God, behold us meeting	1867, 1873
Landlord, fill the flowing bowl	1867, 1870, 1870a, 1873, 1874, 1876, 1880, 1893, 1906, 1918, 1834, 1953
Lauriger Horatius	1858, 1860, 1867, 1870, 1870a, 1873, 1874, 1876, 1880, 1882, 1885, 1888, 1889, 1906, 1918
Lauriger Horatius ("Il Puritani")	1870, 1870a, 1874, 1876, 1880, 1882, 1885, 1888, 1889, 1906
Let bards in strains of triumph sing	1858, 1860, 1867, 1873
Let every good fellow now fill up	1858, 1860, 1867, 1870, 1870a, 1873, 1874, 1876, 1880
Let others sing the wedding ring	1853
Let us now in youth rejoice	1858, 1860, 1867, 1870, 1870a, 1873, 1874, 1876, 1880
Lightly afloat swims our gallant boat	1853, 1855, 1858, 1860
Light of leading, Elihu	1918
Linonia, the wreaths of glory	1853, 1855, 1858, 1860, 1867, 1870, 1870a, 1873, 1874, 1876, 1880
Little Lamb, little Lamb	1953
Little Tommy Tucker	1918
Lonely round the portals of the college	1858, 1860
Look ahead, look astarn	1934, 1953
Love, the brook lisps all day long	1903
Lux, Lux, Lux, Lux et Veritas	1953
Mantling shade, hill and glade	1882, 1885, 1888, 1889, 1893a, 1906
Many times ere now we've parted	1853, 1855
March, march on down the field	1918, 1934, 1953
Mary had a little lamb	1867, 1870, 1870a, 1873, 1874, 1876, 1880, 1885, 1888, 1889, 1903, 1906, 1918, 1934
Mavourneen, Mavourneen	1934, 1953
Me gettee married	1882, 1885, 1888, 1889
Mildred, Maud, and Mabel	1953
Mingle we here, old brothers dear	1858, 1860, 1867, 1873
Miss Annabelle Birby lived way out	1934, 1953
Mother of men, grown strong in giving	1918, 1934, 1953
My Aunt Dinah was a good old sinner	1918, 1934
My Bonnie lies over the ocean	1882, 1885, 1888, 1889, 1906
My comrades, when I'm no more drinking	1885, 1888, 1889, 1906, 1918, 1934, 1953
My Evaline, say you'll be mine	1918, 1834, 1953
My husband's a saucy foretopman	1934, 1953
My name it is O'Hoolihan	1882, 1885, 1888, 1889, 1906
My sweet, my sweet	1918, 1934, 1953
Ned Horton comes to college	1860
Night's dusky mantle shrouds	1893
Not a long time to come	1903, 1906
Now I'm in an awful condition	1918, 1934
Now the first on my charm	1953
Now through the midnight	1882, 1885, 1888, 1889, 1918, 1934, 1953
Now, when Willie was still	1953
Nut-brown maiden	1876, 1880, 1882, 1885, 1888, 1889, 1893a, 1906
O blithe and gay are summer hours	1858, 1860
O domus praestans	1860, 1867, 1873
O'er the lake ripples break	1893, 1893a
Of all the starry hosts above	1893, 1906
Off we go to take a ride	1918
Oft in our future course	1867, 1870, 1870a, 1873, 1874, 1876, 1880
Oh! a hero's life I'll sing	1870, 1870a, 1874, 1876, 1880
Oh! carry him off! Old Euclid's dead	1853, 1855
Oh Delta Kappa Epsilon	1885, 1888, 1889
Oh! de ol' ark's a-moverin'	1934, 1953
Oh de red coon brushin'	1934
Oh! does the Freshman smoke	1867, 1870, 1870a, 1873, 1874, 1876, 1880
Oh, Eleazar Wheelock was a very pious man	1934, 1953
Oh! I am a jolly Switzer boy	1873, 1876, 1880, 1882, 1885, 1888, 1889, 1903, 1906, 1934, 1953
Oh, Lord Jeffery Amherst	1934, 1953
Oh! Love, must I linger	1873
Oh! Mary had a little lamb	1873, 1876, 1880, 1882, 1906
Oh, more work for the undertaker	1906, 1918, 1934
Oh, my name is Solomon Levi	1918, 1934
Oh! papa is out breaking rocks	1893, 1906, 1934, 1953
Oh, rose, climb up to her window	1934, 1953
Oh! sad the light must fall tonight	1858, 1860, 1867, 1873

Oh say, can you see	1934, 1953
Oh! stern the power that brings the hour	1860, 1867, 1873
Oh, the anchor is weighed	1934, 1953
Oh the bright stars do shine	1934
Oh! the bull-dog on the bank	1873, 1874, 1876, 1880, 1882, 1885, 1888, 1889, 1906, 1918, 1934
Oh! the home we loved	1867, 1870, 1870a, 1873, 1874, 1876, 1880, 1882, 1885, 1888, 1889
Oh! 'tis joy to me	1882, 1885, 1888, 1889
Oh! we are happy sons of Yale	1853, 1855
Oh! when you hear the roll	1873, 1874, 1876, 1880, 1882, 1885, 1888, 1889, 1906, 1934, 1853
Oh where, oh where has my little dog gone	1870, 1870a, 1873, 1874, 1876, 1880, 1882, 1885, 1888, 1889, 1906, 1934, 1953
Oh, Yale was begun back in Sev'nteen-one	1953
Old Aunt Jemima, won't you hand down	1903, 1918, 1934
Old dog Tray, ever faithful	1873, 1876, 1880
Old Euclid is departed now	1858, 1860, 1867, 1873
Old man Horace, sprigged with bay	1867, 1870, 1870a, 1873, 1874, 1876, 1880
Old Noah, he did build an ark	1870, 1870a, 1874, 1876, 1880
Old Tom Wilson a-lyin' in the bed	1953
Old Yale holds many honors	1858, 1860, 1867, 1873
O light as the foam-crest	1858, 1860
Once again, once again, hither brothers	1860
Once more again we come	1853, 1855
Once more united here	1860, 1867, 1873
Once on a time there was a man	1867, 1870, 1870a, 1873, 1874, 1876, 1880, 1882, 1885, 1888, 1889
Once we hear our sires relate	1853
One gentle, balmy afternoon in May	1889
One poor unfortunate Sophomore wight	1853, 1855
One, two, three, four	1918, 1934
On, gallant company	1882, 1885, 1888, 1889, 1906
On Springfield mountain	1867, 1870, 1870a, 1874, 1876, 1880
On the swaying limb of a rubber tree	1903
Onward we go, smashing the foe	1934, 1953
O! sad and sweet the thoughts	1860, 1867, 1873
O the bright stars do shine	1903, 1918
Our strong band can ne'er be broken	1876, 1880, 1882, 1885, 1888, 1889, 1906, 1918, 1934, 1953, 1978
Our tranquil day's last glimmering ray	1867, 1873
Over all the lonely way	1889, 1893a
Over the banister leans a face	1885, 1888, 1889, 1893a, 1906
O! Yale's a jovial college	1858, 1860
Pass gently, ye moments	1853
Peter Piper picked a peck	1918
Poet of the laurel wreath	1858, 1860, 1867, 1870, 1870a, 1873, 1876, 1880
Proud rides our bonny bark	1853, 1855, 1858, 1868
Put your clumsy pitcher where the stream	1853, 1855, 1858, 1860
Ring out, sweet chime	1903
Rise, ye gallant sons of Yale!	1853, 1855
Roll, Jordan, roll!	1934, 1953
Romanza (no text; humming and whistle)	1893
Round all the room the holly hung	1893
Sans souci polka (no text; humming and whistle)	1893
Sa, sa, geschmauset!	1860
Saw my leg off	1867, 1870, 1870a, 1873, 1874, 1876, 1880
Shall I, wasting in despair	1918, 1934, 1953, 1978
She brought him in his breakfast	1953
She hath no gems of luster bright	1889, 1893a, 1906, 1918, 1934, 1953,
She's the pride of my heart	1934
Should auld acquaintance be forgot, and never	1860, 1867, 1870, 1870a, 1873, 1874, 1876, 1880
Should auld acquaintance be forgot, and thoughts	1867, 1873
Should fortune prove unkind	1893, 1893a, 1906, 1918, 1934
Should these old times be e'er forgot	1853, 1855, 1858, 1860, 1867, 1873
Shout high the anthem	1867, 1870, 1870a, 1873, 1874, 1876, 1880
Show me the Scotchman	1889, 1906, 1918, 1934, 1953
Sing a song for Yale	1953
Sing, oh sing Yalensians!	1860
Sister Mary wore three lengths of chain	1953
Sleep, my love, and peace attend thee	1918

APPENDIX 3: SONGS BY WELL KNOWN COMPOSERS

Charles Ives, class of 1898
    "The Bells of Yale"   *Yale Melodies* (1903, 88)

Cole Porter, class of 1913
    "A Football King"   *The New Yale Song Book,* (1918, 164)

    "Annabelle (Antoinette) Birby"   *Songs of Yale* (1934, 106)
                                              Songs of Yale (1953, 73)

    "Bingo, That's the Lingo"   *Songs of Yale* (1934, 128)
                                              Songs of Yale (1953, 205)

    "Bull-Dog"   *The New Yale Song Book* (1918, 169)
                                                  Songs of Yale (1934, 129)
                                                  Songs of Yale (1953, 202)

    "The Elizabethan Club"   *Songs of Yale* (1953, 77)

    "The Crew Song"   *Songs of Yale* (1953, 82)

    "The Motor Car"   *The New Yale Song Book* (1918, 120)

Douglas Moore, class of 1915
    "Good Night, Poor Harvard"   *Songs of Yale* (1934, 132)
                                              Songs of Yale (1953, 210)

16

Hermann Lawrence Schreiner, Music Merchant and Tunesmith in the Nineteenth-Century South

Nancy R. Ping-Robbins

Historians and music scholars have given considerable attention to early musical activities in the northeastern area of the country. The paths of tradesmen, preachers, and Yankee entrepreneurs have been traced as they went about the business of making music, money, or converts. Scholars are now examining the popular music of the twentieth-century south as blues, ragtime, and jazz have won the hearts of the world, but only a few studies have appeared on the musical life of the Deep South before the twentieth century, particularly before the Civil War.[1]

Life in the antebellum Deep South, dependent on a slave-based agricultural economy, differed from that in the Northern states because the settlers of the south had

---

1. The situation is improving rapidly. There are a number of dissertations now on several of the towns and cities of the South, including Savannah, Norfolk, Columbus (Georgia), Charleston, Knoxville, and Nashville; my "Music in Antebellum Wilmington and the Lower Cape Fear of North Carolina" (Ph.D. diss., University of Colorado, 1979) is one that attempts to cover all aspects of musical life in that chosen town during the antebellum period only. Excerpts of material that relates to the considerable African American population there was published in Nancy R. Ping, "Black Musical Activities In Antebellum Wilmington, North Carolina," *Black Perspective in Music* 8, no. 2 (fall 1980): 139-60. Several studies of music or musicians in New Orleans have been published recently, including Warren Carl Fields's "Theodore La Hache and Music in New Orleans, 1846-1869," *American Music* 8 (fall 1990): 326-50. A more comprehensive, wide-ranging study is Wiley L. Housewright's *A History of Music and Dance in Florida, 1565-1865* (Tuscaloosa: University of Alabama Press, 1991). A study of mine that addresses the activities of a number of music teacher/composers in the Southeast was published in *Report of Proceedings: Ph.D. in Music Symposium (April 5-7, 1985)*, College of Music, University of Colorado at Boulder, 1988, 51-61.

not come to the colonies out of religious conviction. They emigrated to find and accumulate wealth through acquiring land and slaves; good living for the privileged was assumed to be a natural by-product. The movers and shakers in the wealthy port cities of the Old South were well-educated, well-read, erudite individuals who cultivated the art of conversation and patronized the arts by hiring music tutors for their children and accomplished musicians for their private parties.[2] But for all citizens, life in the United States during the course of the nineteenth century saw profound changes. The south's slave-based economy necessarily collapsed as a result of the Civil War, leading to tremendous hardship for all (except, perhaps, those who profited from the events of the 1860s).

By mid-century the huge influx of immigrants from Europe had a growing effect on the cultural life of the country. Many ordinary German musicians had emigrated during the formation of the German republic; some, such as the Damrosch family, settled in urban areas of the Northeast. Others pressed on, going west, or south—as did Hermann L. Schreiner, the subject of this essay. These German "professors" and concert artists sometimes struggled to gain recognition and influence outside the most cultivated urban areas. In the 1870s, when Hans von Bülow toured the United States as a pianist, his formal, rather difficult concerts led to audience reaction that was often negative or minimally positive at best. The cultural soil of middle America in the nineteenth century was hard-packed and unyielding for his sort of serious music. Theodore Thomas's success with programming more difficult repertory with his orchestras during the last third of the nineteenth century might have been quite different if not for the musical training that many German music teachers imparted across the country.[3] Scott Joplin clearly indicated that his successes were the result of training by his German music professor in Texas.[4] As this essay demonstrates, the career of Schreiner documents his role and influence in training young people in several communities throughout the south. The influence of these music teachers and musicians lasted well into the twentieth century; it served as the foundation upon which substantial accomplishments in the musical arts in the United States were built.

Hermann Lawrence Schreiner was a typical "professor" of music. Although he was quite young when he left Germany, his influence on the residents of his new homeland was to be of great and lasting significance. Schreiner's activities in Wilmington, North Carolina, his first permanent residence in this country, demonstrate how deeply the

---

2. A certain Herr von Robinson was apparently hired to provide music for a party at the Bellamy Mansion in Wilmington in 1851, but could not because he was "recalled to the Opera Hosue in Paris." Furthermore, a certain "Baron O." of Zurich, Switzerland, sent out invitations to a splendid ball to be held in Smithville, south of Wilmington, also in 1851. "Multiple orchestras were hidden out of sight as the guests toured the grounds and mansion"—Ping, "Music in Antebellum Wilmington," 147-48.

3. An interesting new perspective on how musical tastes were raised at the turn of the century can be seen in Linda L. Tyler's "'Commerce and Poetry Hand in Hand': Music in American Department Stores, 1880-1930," *Journal of the American Musicological Society* 45 (spring 1992): 75-120.

4. See Theodore Albrecht, "Julius Weiss: Scott Joplin's First Piano Teacher," *College Music Symposium* 19, no. 2 (fall 1979): 89-105, for an account of Joplin's formal music study with Herr Weiss, his resultant interest in European "classics," and his gratitude as shown through the gifts of money he later gave to Weiss.

influence of a teacher can affect a community or family through the years. During the 1850s, Schreiner taught the three girls of the Harriss family; one of them, Laura Harriss, became a serious amateur musician. She collected the scores of nineteenth-century operas that she heard in professional performances, probably singing some passages herself at home, and she also collected hundreds of pieces of sheet music. Her musical archive, now known as the Howell Collection at the Randall Library of the University of North Carolina at Wilmington, contains close to 800 items, including many of Schreiner's published pieces. Harriss's musical abilities served as a model to her family. Her granddaughter and namesake, Laura Howell Norden Schorr, who often noted the influence of her grandmother, pursued a career in music. After completing a master's degree in music composition, Schorr performed in the North Carolina Symphony Orchestra, wrote a column about music in a Charlotte-area newspaper, and was known as a teacher, composer, and civic arts leader.

Schreiner came to the United States in 1849 to seek his fortune through teaching, composing, publishing, and selling music. In these respects, he is representative of many musicians who immigrated to the United States during the nineteenth century. In other respects, Schreiner was not the typical musical immigrant in the southern towns and cities to which his career took him. He was a leader who spoke out on cultural issues and took action to achieve his goals. His essays on music and music education, along with letters to newspaper editors and critiques of concerts, were published in Wilmington newspapers and later in Macon, Georgia. Over the next two decades, he continued his leadership in other ways as a member of the musical community of Savannah, Georgia. In all the communities in which he lived any length of time, he became known for his popular marches and other compositions, written for brass bands, friends, and students. Some of his pieces attracted much wider recognition. He became even better known when he and his family founded a publishing company in 1862. His penchant for speaking his mind apparently got him into sticky situations more than once during his search for a community in which to settle, and he had personal problems that may have contributed to his troubles in the music business in the 1870s and 1880s. But Schreiner was not a person who shrank from difficulties.

Chronology

Schreiner was born in 1832 in Hildburghausen, Thuringia; he was educated at the Gymnasium in his hometown, and later attended Realschule at Meiningen. Because of his talent for music, he became a piano student of Laugert and organ student of Boenhardt, eventually graduating from Leipzig Conservatory. Armed with letters of introduction, on his arrival in the United States, Schreiner first approached Charles L. Grobe in Wilmington, Delaware, for help in finding a job. A little more than a year later, he decided to take advantage of "an excellent offer to go south" to Wilmington, North Carolina.[5]

Upon his arrival, Schreiner immediately advertised for music students, took a church organist position, and within a few months was associated with a brass band. Although

---

5. Obituary, *Savannah Morning News* (hereafter *SMN*), 7 September 1891.

Schreiner was unaccompanied when he first arrived in North Carolina, by 1853 his family had joined him: his father, John C. Schreiner, 44 years old; his mother, Caroline Schreiner, just two years younger than her husband; and his brother, Sigmund A. Schreiner, who was about nine years younger than Hermann.[6] These family members joined with Hermann in opening a music store.

After six years in Wilmington, the family headed west to Knoxville, Tennessee, where Hermann again advertised for music students, but one year later (1857) they moved to Macon, Georgia. There Hermann once more advertised for music students, formed the Macon Amateur Brass Band, gave concerts, took another church organist job, and—with his family—opened another store. In 1862, Schreiner took the radical step of establishing a publishing business in Macon; his company became the major, if not the only, music publisher in the south after the fall of New Orleans. In 1863, the family bought out the Zogbaum Co. of Savannah, expanding the family business to include stores in Savannah and Augusta as well as in Macon. Hermann moved to Savannah in 1863 and remained there for the rest of his life, although he made annual trips to the Northeast and, later, to Germany. In addition to his business and community music activities, he again served as a church organist.

The young man who came to the United States in 1849, composing new works as he moved from town to town and dedicating them to various young lady students, finally found himself a wife in Savannah. The *Savannah Morning News* (31 December 1869) carried the announcement that "Miss Carrie Gemenden and H. L. Schreiner, both of this city, were married by the Rev. E. M. Gilbert at the bride's residence (Augusta, Macon, and Charleston please copy)."[7] One of Schreiner's compositions about this time was "The Honeymoon Polka," advertised in the J. L. Peters catalog of 1871.

After bearing two children, his young wife died in 1874. Schreiner then entered into a legal controversy with his father-in-law over custody of his two children and possession of the estate (probably a dowry). In 1875, Schreiner abducted the children, taking them as far as Baltimore before being arrested for kidnapping. He was released shortly and allowed to take the children, George (later of Gera) and Cassie (later Mrs. Katchen Statefeld of Leipzig) to Germany to live with their relatives.[8] Fifteen years later, in 1889, Schreiner remarried, this time to Ingeborg Lofgren. But two years later, he died in Germany after contracting pneumonia en route across the Atlantic.[9]

Church Organist and Teacher

Hermann Schreiner apparently considered securing a church organist position central to his career as a musician; it seemed to be his first goal upon arriving at a new community. He played at First Presbyterian Church in Wilmington and Macon, and at

---

6. 1860 United States Census, Bibb County, Georgia.

7. Newspaper editors in those days would often publicly give permission to neighboring editors to publish items in their own local papers. Apparently editors in major towns regularly read other regional editions.

8. *SMN*, 5 and 7 June 1875.

9. *SMN*, 7 September 1891.

Christ Church in Savannah. Even when he went to Savannah to open a new branch of his family's music business, he took a position as church organist.

Schreiner's second goal was to attract music students. By examining his advertisements, one can learn a great deal about his earliest days in Wilmington, N.C. When he first arrived in 1851, he announced a "School for Instruction of Music, PIANO, and SINGING."[10] Within two weeks he increased his offerings to include tuning and repair of pianos, and instruction in "Piano, Organ, Violin, Flute, etc."[11] On 8 October 1852, Schreiner added a note to his usual fall advertisement offering music lessons in the *Wilmington Daily Journal:*

> He much prefers to instruct his pupils at their private dwellings; as he knows from experience that it is the most beneficial course of instruction.

We learn that not enough students materialized in the first two weeks from his notices for piano and voice students, for he expanded his advertisement to include anything and everything ("etc."). His comments on teaching in the home imply that business overhead is considerably lower when one teaches in the student's home. Clearly it was not easy to make a living as a music teacher in Wilmington.

In 1856, when the family moved briefly to Knoxville, the young man added guitar to his teaching list.[12] This versatility was expanded even more in his Macon announcements in July 1869: he advertised a "Conservatoire Musicale" with "instruction in piano, guitar, harp, melodeon, organ, sacred and secular vocal music, and thorough bass."[13] The wider range of lessons offered in Knoxville and Macon perhaps can also be attributed to the presence of his father and brother, both music teachers.[14] Hermann was also associated with the Home Institute in Macon as "Professor of Music," at the same time continuing as a private instructor.[15]

Performer

Evidence of Hermann Schreiner's involvement as a performing artist is scarce. In Wilmington his students gave a concert in 1853, but the first concert in this country known to have involved Schreiner himself took place in Macon on Friday, 14 May 1858. The event was announced as a "Grand Concert by Messrs. Hermann Lawrence and Sigmund A. Schreiner's musical classes assisted by the Presbyterian Choir and German Singing Society, in all from 40 to 50 performers at Ralston's Hall." The editor of the *State*

---

10. *Wilmington Daily Journal,* 24 October 1851.

11. Ibid., 7 November 1851.

12. Emma Katharine Crews, "A History of Music in Knoxville, Tennessee, 1791-1910" (Ph.D. diss., Florida State University, 1961), 87.

13. *Macon Daily Telegraph* (hereafter *MDT*), 14 July 1860.

14. Macon City Directory, 101. His father, John C. Schreiner, advertised for students when he arrived in Wilmington in 1853, offering lessons in "piano, flute, guitar, violin, violoncello, and all other string and brass instruments" (*Wilmington Tri-Weekly Commercial,* 27 May 1853).

15. *MDT,* 13 September 1860.

Press put in a good word for the new additions to the Macon musical and German community, pronouncing the concert a "brilliant affair."[16]

The custom of giving end-of-the-year concerts to present one's students to their parents and the community was well established by Schreiner's time. His entire music class assisted the Macon Philharmonic Society in a "Grand Vocal and Instrumental Concert" on 7 June 1860. Schreiner was to conduct, according to advance publicity in the June 8 issue of the *Macon Daily Telegraph*. The editor had more to say about this event in two issues following the concert. On June 8 he noted that "the singing of some of the ladies would have done honor to the great vocalist Piccolomini." On June 9 he was more specific:

> We cannot refrain from making mention of the singing of Miss Kate P., whose execution of that beautiful and difficult piece of music, "Tama Siccomo gli Angeli" was equal in our opinion to anything we have ever heard. . . . The concert was under the direction of Prof. Schreiner, who is a thorough master of his profession.

In 1861 Schreiner was involved with a series of fund-raising concerts for the Confederate Soldiers' war relief. The first one may have been on Friday night, May 24, according to a small announcement in the editorial column:

> Soldier's Concert
>
> The Concert Friday night was very successful. The audience was large and enthusiastic. The new National song with the music by Schreiner awakened a tempest of enthusiasm.[17]

This new National Song was very likely "Cheer, Boys, Cheer" or "God Defendeth the Right," both of which appeared later in the year on another program.[18]

Probably as a result of his leadership role at the May concert, Schreiner was elected chairman of the German adopted citizens group in Macon during the summer.[19] This precipitated a series of fund-raising concerts, most of which raised about $100 each. The "German Artillery" gave a vocal and instrumental concert on October 16; the *Macon Daily Telegraph* published the program that same day. Hermann Schreiner is listed as a solo pianist in his own compositions, "Home Sweet Home Fantasie" and "Battle Manassas, a Descriptive Fantasia" (*sic*). He also performed Wallace's "Star of Love" piano solo, and the German Singing Society performed an operatic chorus. Otherwise, the concert consisted of popular and novelty numbers. In the review two days later, half the space was devoted to comments on Schreiner's "Battle Manassas," including a complete listing of all the parts of the work: "Soldier's march in camp, Cannons booming, Trumpets call the alarm, Yankee Doodle advancing, Dixie answering, Yankee Doodle and Dixie fighting (both airs played together, Yankee Doodle with the left and Dixie with the right hand), Yankee Doodle running, Dixie victorious! Sweeping the Field." This concert

---

16. *Georgia State Press,* 13 and 20 May 1858.

17. *MDT,* 27 May 1861.

18. Ibid., 17 September 1861.

19. Ibid., 29 July 1861.

netted $93 for the southern war cause, according to Schreiner's letter to the newspaper a few days later.[20]

After Schreiner moved to Savannah in 1863, he continued to perform, both as soloist and with groups. On 1 January 1868 the *Savannah Daily News Herald* reported that the Savannah Quartette Club had performed the previous day at Masonic Hall, with Prof. H. L. Schreiner at the piano. The same group performed at the Theatre on October 16 of that year for the benefit of the Metropolitan Steam Fire Engine Company. One additional notice appeared in the *Savannah Morning News* some years later: in 1874, a benefit was held for a Mr. and Mrs. Wallace, with the assistance of Mr. H. L. Schreiner and others of the musical profession of Savannah.[21]

Founder and Leader of Brass Bands

An important goal for Schreiner, as he moved to each of the larger towns in which he lived, was to form, or to be associated with, a brass band. By December 1851, shortly after his arrival in Wilmington, the Amateur Brass Band was formed and new instruments ordered.[22] No hard evidence has been found that Schreiner, in fact, was the founder of the Amateur Brass Band, but circumstantial evidence suggests that he was a catalyst for its founding. The instruments were ordered shortly after the Schreiners opened their music store (the only music store at the time) and the amount spent happened to be exactly the same as the amount required for another Amateur Brass Band founded in Macon after the Schreiners moved there.

Most bands in Wilmington and other towns marched with specific military groups for regular parades and other activities. For several years, the Amateur Brass Band was associated with the German Volunteers, but in 1856 the first indication of a rift between some members of the group and Schreiner appeared in an account of the Moore's Creek Victory celebration:

> The Wilmington Light Infantry and the Pioneer Cadets, preceded by the Amateur Brass band; and the German volunteers, preceded by *Schreiner's* Band, marched on board the *Brothers* in fine military style.[23]

This was the first known mention of a band called "Schreiner's," and it was possibly the last, as Schreiner and his family departed for Knoxville shortly thereafter.

By 24 September 1860, Schreiner was again involved with a brass band, this time in Macon. The new Macon Amateur Brass Band was to be established with the same investment in new instruments ($300) as the Wilmington Amateur Brass band required nine years earlier. Although a group of citizens put up the money, the Schreiners provided the instruments through their music store.[24] There is reason to believe that this group eventually took the name "Macon Cornet Band." Schreiner was involved as conductor of

20. Ibid., 26 October 1861.

21. *SMN,* 30 September 1874.

22. *Wilmington Daily Journal,* 30 December 1851.

23. *Wilmington Daily Herald,* 28 February 1856.

24. *MDT,* 23 November, 2 June, 24 September, and 23 November 1860.

the Macon Cornet Band for fund-raising concerts during the early war years, according to announcements in the local newspaper.[25]

Composer

Schreiner apparently composed only those pieces that he needed as a teacher, that might make a splash in the commercial market, or that might serve as a patriotic contribution in his community. His compositions and arrangements were performed frequently on numerous programs, including the Tableaux Vivants, one of which was presented on 20 September 1861 in Macon. For this event, another "Soldier's Benefit," each half of the presentation was opened with a song "adapted" by Schreiner: first, "Cheer, Boys, Cheer!" and, after intermission, "God Defendeth the Right."[26] Schreiner's total known output is about fifty-six works, including a few arrangements of other composers's melodies.[27]

During Schreiner's stay at Wilmington, he appears to have written at least thirteen pieces, most of them dedicated to young ladies. Some publications name ladies who must have been his students, only a few years younger than he. His later pieces, written during and after the Civil War, are more attentive to military, political, or judicial community leaders. A few pieces relate to local or regional geography of cities: the "Ocmulgee Schottisch," named for the Ocmulgee River outside Macon, and the "Vineville Quickstep," recognizing the small town of Vineville in the vicinity of Macon. In the 1870s, he wrote the "Cassie Waltzes," undoubtedly for his small daughter Katchen, whose American nickname was Cassie.

That Schreiner continued to compose some new works throughout his life is attested to by an announcement from the *Savannah Morning News* of 17 May 1881:

> We acknowledge the receipt from Mr. H. L. Schreiner the author, of a copy of the new march dedicated to Palestine Commandery No. 7. Every gallant knight should have a copy of it.

But as the years wore on, Schreiner seems to have composed less and less, if we can judge by the works advertised in the newspapers or by publishers' lists on the backs of other sheet music of the time.

Although most of his works are in the popular styles of the time—waltzes, polkas, schottisches, songs, marches, and even a mazurka—he did compose more substantial pieces. Most of these latter compositions were mentioned in passing as parts of concert programs, probably were not published, and now, apparently, are lost. Among his dances, two of the polkas are described as "Polka Brilliante: The Stars and Bars Polka" and "The Forest Leaf Polka," composed in Macon in 1861 and 1862, respectively. Other rather difficult, elaborate works include "The Louise Grand Waltz" (Wilmington, 1853), and

---

25. Ibid., 28 June 1861.

26. Ibid., 19 September 1861.

27. There is a partial listing of Schreiner's compositions in Ping, "Music in Antebellum Wilmington," appendix E (pp. 584-86), with a list of scores in the Howell Collection (p. 587) and photocopies of a few complete piano and vocal scores (pp. 588-615).

"Schottisch di Bravura," op. 14 (Wilmington, 1854). "Cotton Planter's Convention Schottisch" attracted considerable press coverage since it won a gold medal presented by the Cotton Planters' Association. This composition was "composed and dedicated to the members of the Cotton Planters' Association, with a faithful likeness of the Hon. Howell Cobb, President of the Cotton Planters' Convention. This piece, being a copyright, can only be had by the Publishers, John C. Schreiner and Sons, Cotton Avenue."[28]

"Nobody Hurt" was another favorite that the Schreiners advertised frequently.[29] The title was a headline used often in the newspapers during the early part of the war, not only in reports of battles but also to head commercial department store advertisements and other such consumer-oriented material. The Schreiners' main retail rival, J. W. Burke, also carried some of Schreiner's compositions for sale. "Secession Polka" was advertised by J. W. Burke in 1861 as "New Music for April."[30]

Many of Schreiner's composition were aimed at the brass band market. A number of his surviving works are clearly piano versions of band pieces. One can almost hear the baritone solos in the trios or the cornet duets in the second strains. These arrangements were made available to the public through the Schreiner music stores in Wilmington, Macon, and Savannah. One of Hermann's earliest extant pieces in the Howell Collection , "The Cornelia Waltz," is dedicated to a young lady in Maine and was published for piano solo in 1852. The Howell copy contains pencilled bow markings, indicating a performance with violin, perhaps for an indoor party or dance. The work also was performed by the Amateur Brass Band of Wilmington and resembles many of the favorite German "bierstube" band pieces. Schreiner's harmonic vocabulary here is only mildly interesting: a brief diminished-seventh chord for color, otherwise mostly tonic and dominant chords.

"General Lee's Grand March" is a good example of Schreiner's way of writing simple material that still is musically effective. Although the date of publication (and composition) is unknown, the title page tells us that it was written after Schreiner moved to Savannah (post-1863). There are only two thematic ideas in the brief march, the first altered slightly in the march proper for a second strain, the second theme introduced in the trio as a cornet solo.

"Stonewall Jackson's Grand March" is much grander, with repetitive eighth-note triplets in the accompaniment, a strongly delineated second-strain theme, and a new idea in the trio. Notations printed in the score of this work indicate beyond the shadow of a doubt that the work was created for brass band performance, even though it was published for piano. The second strain has a brief, recurring trumpet "fanfare," while the trio melody is marked "baritone solo," with cornet and horns coming in later.

Schreiner wrote few original songs, although publishers' lists show his name on several. Most were merely adaptations of others' compositions (he used Henry Russell's "Old Arm Chair" as the music for "The Soldier's Grave," words by Ottolengui). He blatantly claimed authorship of other publications, such as "Do They Think of Me at

---

28. *MDT*, 1 January 1861.

29. Ibid., 8 July 1861.

30. Ibid., 12 April 1861.

Home" (published by Jos. P. Shaw of Rochester), which was actually composed by Charles Glover. Still another approach Schreiner took in order to be able to offer some vocal music in his personal publishing catalog was to list the composer of the "melody" with himself as "arranger." This was the case with Stephen Foster's "Come Where My Love Lies Dreaming." Schreiner's "arrangement" merely uses Foster's four-part harmonization as accompaniment, with the exception of the second phrase where he breaks the chords into eighth-note arpeggios. Several individuals claim authorship to a tune known as "God Will Defend the Right." Schreiner's publication, with himself listed as composer, is titled "God Defendeth the Right."

John Hill Hewitt (1801-90) was a longtime close friend and a partner with the Schreiners in a branch of their publishing firm in Augusta, Georgia. Hewitt also collaborated with Schreiner on a number of pieces. "When Upon the Field of Glory" was their southern response to the Yankee "When This Cruel War Is Over" (known in the south as "Weeping, Sad, and Lonely," by Charles Carroll Sawyer).

Schreiner's goals as a composer were probably never realized—he had no nationwide hit on the scale of some of John Hill Hewitt's, Henry Russell's, or Stephen Foster's works—although his "Clarendon's Grand March" did sell sixteen hundred copies in its first month.[31]

Self-appointed Music Critic

On 24 June 1854, Schreiner's one-thousand-word essay "Music" was published by the *Tri-Weekly Commercial* of Wilmington. In this article he admonishes both parents and teachers concerning the best approach to helping children become musicians. He warns that changing teachers too frequently is not in the child's best interest, since each teacher follows a different mode of teaching. He observes that musical education in "this country" is considered "an accomplishment of the fairer sex." Schreiner notes that efforts to establish music classes and lessons for young boys (and gentlemen) in Wilmington were the result of his observation of their ignorance of such accomplishments, as well as a response to requests by parents of boys in Wilmington after the boys were banned from Schreiner's pupils' concerts because of their unrulyness.[32]

He also expresses his opinion on the "trashy music put up in cheap form as sheet music, used so much now a days for instruction"; it is an attitude typical of nineteenth-century German immigrant musicians, and one that carried over into the twentieth century. The two songs he mentions as typical "trashy music" heard in Wilmington homes are "Jim Cracked Corn, I Don't Care" and "Old Bob Ridley, He, Ha, Ho," favorite minstrel show tunes of the Virginia Minstrels and Kunkel's Nightingale Troupe, respectively.[33] Schreiner's outspoken language is evident in this article when he criticizes the results of instruction generally found "now a days":

> But I say, your daughter's music education is ruined, and she will only be, if she take
> lessons till she is grown, nothing beyond a poor bungler. Parents, it will be your

31. Ping, "Music in Antebellum Wilmington," 105.

32. Ibid., 97-98.

33. The first is the tune also known as "Blue Tail Fly," 1846; the second, "Old Bob Ridley," 1853.

duty, as well as advantage, not to throw your hard earnings so easily away, but save it for your old age, that it may do you some good, at least more than it does your children.

Young Schreiner then proceeds to discuss how music is divided into two parts—tones and rhythms. He continues with an admonition to the teachers of music, parents, and "scholars" regarding their respective duties. He ends with the realistic prediction that

> this course of instruction, as systematical as it is, will very often not suit both scholar and parents, as they expected to do great things in a short time. And while the scholar is imperceptibly getting over the most difficult part, the beginning, her teacher is changed for one who in their opinion can do much better.

Four years later, in Macon, Schreiner again voiced his opinions for the general reading public, his first public statement since arriving in Macon from Knoxville the previous year. On this occasion, his essay to the *State Press* (again titled "Music" and at least a thousand words in length) was in response to an earlier article criticizing a local religious groups' opposition to theater and music. Evidently Schreiner felt that the issue needed more forceful and knowledgeable arguments than those presented by another writer (identified only as "Garrick"). He did not shrink from involving himself in controversy. The lengthy account is almost an aesthetic event in itself. He begins slowly, gradually building momentum with increasingly strong, emotional language, and climaxing with a poem of considerable drama and eloquence. Throughout the body of the essay, he stresses the historical role of music in the ancient world as well as in the Middle Ages and the Renaissance. His emotional pitch builds in fervor as he describes the effects of singing martial songs in revolutionary France and the United States. His final blow is to compare the non-music lover with "scoundrel foxes or glutton swine."[34]

Hermann Schreiner's essays and letters to editors are often informative and reveal considerable musical knowledge. These and other types of communication seem to suggest the self-assurance that was typical of some of the German musicians who arrived in the United States in the nineteenth century with superior training and skills. He missed few opportunities to set others straight on the path to higher cultural levels, whether it be the teaching of community children, appreciation of touring artists, selling the best sheet music arrangements or pianos, or elevating public knowledge and opinions.

Music Retailer and Publisher

The entire Schreiner family—mother, father, and two sons—banded together shortly after all had arrived in Wilmington in 1853 to open a retail outlet—Schreiner's Music Store—selling pianos, all kinds of music, and instruments for brass and string bands. Hermann, who advertised that he had arranged all the music for the Amateur Brass Band, offered to arrange music for six-, eight-, twelve-, or fifteen-member bands.

---

34. *Georgia State Press,* 4 March 1858.

He also noted in one advertisement that he could get any published piece of music within three days.[35]

When the Schreiner family moved to Macon in 1857, they again opened a music store, at Cotton Avenue and Second Street, this time under the name "J. C. Schreiner and Sons."[36] From time to time during his years in Macon, Hermann and his father, John C., used their music store advertisements as a forum to discourse on musical taste, particularly in competition with their business rival, J. W. Burke, also a music retailer. One such advertisement appeared on 22 December 1861, in the *Macon Daily Telegraph*. Headlined "NEW MUSIC," with a list of some recent publications, including "God defendeth the Right," the proprietors ended with the following statement:

> Our monthly bulletin of new MUSIC may be small, but contains only such pieces as we have tried, and there-fore recommend. A great deal of TRASH is published which we do not offer.

Burke, Schreiner's main competition in Macon, responded to some of Schreiner's advertisements with his own polemic. One was published in the *Daily Telegraph* on 17 February 1862, although it had been submitted three days earlier:

> We offer for sale a lot of new Music just received from the publishers in New Orleans. It is not necessary for us to prate (as some dealers do) continually about our taste in selecting Music, and that we don't sell TRASH—and that ours is the genuine and all such PATENT MEDICINE claptrap. The character of our music is too well established for this.

Immediately above the Burke advertisement there appeared a response from the Schreiners, posted the day after Burke's (February 15):

> The Music public will be surprised to hear that we are accused of prating, by some other Dealers, when we inform them of the FACT. These very dealers, had on hand a lot of spurious copies of "My Maryland," and had to apply to us for the genuine copy to supply their customers.

On February 18, the Schreiners published yet another rebuttal to Burke's comments on "other dealers":

MY MARYLAND

> Provaci! Procavi! Are the contents of the last article of "some other dealers." WE accept the "amende honorable," although we were somewhat surprised that they should have forgotten their "holy calling" and adopted the worldly maxim: "Running down their neighbors' goods to praise their own ware." In this they have been signally foiled, and we have established, first, that there are spurious copies and they had them. Second, that we had such large orders as to be able to spare them a single copy only. SIC TRANS.[37]

---

35. *Wilmington Daily Journal*, 15 October 1852.

36. 1860 Macon City Directory, 92.

37. *MDT*, 18 February 1862.

The Schreiners' music store in Macon claimed to be one of the earliest businesses to offer monthly installment terms on purchases of pianos,[38] although their store offered much more than just music and musical instruments by this time. One advertisement in 1860 mentions watches, clocks, jewelry, silverware, fancy goods, optical instruments, six different makes of pianos, a variety of music instruments, and much sheet music. Schreiner also served as agent for the Presbyterian Depository, selling its *Psalms and Hymn Books.*[39]

In 1860, Schreiner's advertisement claimed that he had travelled six weeks in the northeast selecting new inventory; two weeks of that time was devoted solely to selecting 20,000 pieces of sheet music![40] Among the sheet music advertised for sale were two of his own compositions, "The Secession Quickstep" and "Noli me tangere."[41] Shortly after the first announcement offering "The Secession Quickstep," another advertisement proclaimed that 200 copies of the piece had been sold in two weeks, causing him to order a second printing.[42]

A major advertising war was carried out in the Macon newspapers from 1861 to 1862 as the blockade began to squeeze out normal sources of supply. Burke and Schreiner's stores both published lengthy lists of sheet music for sale and editorialized in their advertisements on the merits or demerits of their rival's goods. When New Orleans fell to the Union during the summer of 1862, the newspaper advertisements ceased. By fall, the readers knew why: since no sheet music could be obtained from New Orleans, Schreiner had gone across Union lines to the north and brought back from Cincinnati his own font of musical type to set up a publishing firm. This was the beginning of several years of successful business for the Schreiner family. Not only were they able to print Hermann's original compositions, but they were able to publish other composers's music also, the most notable being John Hill Hewitt, who contracted to John C. Schreiner and Sons in October 1863 exclusive rights for his compositions and shortly thereafter set up shop as the Augusta branch of that house.[43] After the war Hewitt returned to Savannah where he wrote music for the Schreiners and edited a musical journal for them.[44]

"Schreiner and Sons" was the "only regular music publisher in the south after the fall of New Orleans" doing an "immense business," and "selling their publications from

---

38. Ibid., 17 October 1860.

39. Ibid., 27 February 1861.

40. Ibid., 25 September 1860.

41. Ibid., 28 December 1860.

42. Ibid., 28 February 1861.

43. Richard Harwell, *Confederate Music* (Chapel Hill: University of North Carolina Press, 1950), 36.

44. *SMN,* 9 October 1890. The writer does not specify exactly when Hewitt returned to Savannah. It could only have been briefly, considering Hewitt's presence in Virginia and Baltimore in subsequent years. His involvement in the journal could only have been through the mail from an out-of-state residency. The journal may have been the *Southern Musical Journal* (nos. 1-11 issued in Savannah between October 1871 and December 1882). There may also have been some connection between the Schreiners and/or Hewitt and the *Southern Musical Journal and Educational Eclectic,* published in Macon in 1883 (vol. 1, nos. 1-10, January-October 1883). Note that the later journal begins a month after the last known issue of the *Southern Musical Journal* (December 1882).

Richmond to Mobile, [with] sales averaging several hundred dollars a day." In spite of these claims, by 1890 the firm's inventory still had "a quantity of this old confederate music."[45] Schreiner's publishing company faded away after the war, perhaps because of the depressed southern economy and the circumstances of his customers. Patriotic fervor couldn't win customers after the war was lost, with food and basic necessities so scarce.

During and immediately after the Civil War, Schreiner and Sons continued to operate retail establishments in Macon, Savannah, and Augusta. But by 1872, John C. Schreiner and Sons were no longer listed in the Macon City Directory; John C. had passed away in 1870 and the Macon store evidently was closed. In Savannah, the business continued under Hermann's management in their store at St. Julian and Congress Streets opposite the Pulaski House.[46] In order to survive after the war, however, the dedicated musician was induced to provide a broader range of financial endeavors. In 1869-70, one advertisement referred to his business as a "book store"; another indicated that he sold adding machines.[47] He also leased studio space in his store to other musicians for giving music lessons and tuning pianos.[48] By 1872 he was advertising parlor organs, and in 1874, Bibles and testaments.[49]

Schreiner's business continued to operate despite the economic problems of the early 1870s. He was the sole agent in town for Steinway, Weber, Gables, and Southern Gem pianos;[50] he received awards at the regional fair in Thomasville.[51] By 1876, however, he also served as ticket agent for a subscription concert series, and stocked toys and Christmas goods.[52] In 1882, he was selling excursion tickets to summer resorts for Central Railroad of Georgia.[53]

In the early 1870s, a mysterious series of events took place that no doubt contributed to his shift in fortune. On 13 December 1873 the *Savannah Morning News* reported the following:

> Yesterday morning Sheriff John T. Ronan sold at auction the contents and stock of the Book and Music Store of H. L. Schreiner, levied upon by virtue of a fi fa in the favor of George Ch. Gemenden. The entire stock was knocked down to Mr. Joseph Lippmann for $6500 who bid it in for Mr. Gemenden.

This Mr. Gemenden was almost certainly the father of Schreiner's first wife, Carrie Gemenden. The underlying reasons for the financial liquidation of Schreiner's business

45. *SMN*, 9 October 1890. There were isolated publications elsewhere in the south, but Schreiner's was the only firm to publish significant numbers of pieces.

46. According to the 1867 Savannah City Directory.

47. *SMN*, 14 May 1870; 10 February 1869.

48. Ibid., 6 January 1870.

49. Ibid., 1 January 1872; 6 May 1874.

50. Ibid., 8 October 1873.

51. Ibid., 10 November 1873.

52. Ibid., 23 April 1876. He had been appointed ticket agent for the railroad as early as 1876 (*SMN*, 5 January 1876).

53. Ibid., 1 June 1882.

assets are unknown at this time. Perhaps the loss of the Macon branch after his father's death created too great a financial strain on the remaining branches; perhaps Schreiner himself was not really a very shrewd businessman and lost too much after the death of his father; or perhaps Mr. Gemenden was trying to regain control of financial assets associated with his daughter's dowry, since she died very shortly thereafter and may have already been gravely ill. Whatever the reason, the loss of his music stock could explain why Schreiner's business interests began to branch out into other areas.

Conclusion

Schreiner was prominent in the community, though not always as successful as he might have wished. But his music store became a landmark in Savannah. As late as 1890, the *Savannah Morning News* published a letter sent from General Beauregard to Schreiner in which he said:

> I remember well my visits to your music store in Savannah . . . and my enjoyment in listening to your artistic music.[54]

Schreiner maintained high standards in both his teaching and performing. He was trained in the European tradition, which included knowledge of Latin, but he was also a practical man and wanted to make a living. He composed music that he knew would have a market. He did not give up his feeling for his homeland or his standards in music when he arrived in this country at the height of the minstrel show craze. He took it upon himself to inform the communities in which he lived about the art of music—the teaching of it and of its importance to each human being. His sometimes dogmatic attitude and insistence on artistic superiority perhaps contributed to his difficulties with some of the communities in which he lived, particularly those without a strong German community. But he was highly regarded and well-known. Schreiner served in many capacities to further music in nineteenth-century America. He founded and developed brass bands in Wilmington, Macon, and Savannah, and arranged and composed numerous works for these groups. He was a spokesman for the musical arts, in part as a result of his classical training in Germany, but more from his own inner convictions. Other German immigrants in his communities—and there were numerous others—did not speak out as he did. He was also influential through his publishing and composing activities during a critical time in the south. Schreiner's musical and entrepreneurial careers are representative of the many nineteenth-century composer/teachers in hundreds of communities throughout the country who, during their lifetimes, directly shaped the public's perception of music and who indirectly influenced later generations to appreciate the art of music.

---

54. Ibid., 28 February 1890.

17

"Unknown," No. 13
in *They Said . . .* , from
The Art of Belly Canto

Gordon Myers
1 December 1984

Those of you who think you know ev-ry-thing are ve-ry an-noy-ing to those of us who do.

18

Chadwick and Parker of New England: Composers, Allies, and Friends

Nicholas E. Tawa

American composers of art music were rare figures in the cultural landscape for many years. During the first half of the nineteenth century, American society did not usually encourage their creative propensities, and musical training of a thorough nature was difficult to obtain in this country. The comparative lack of urban centers, the difficulty of transportation, and the poor means of communication further limited the audience for whom these composers could write, and only a few professional performing groups existed to give a hearing to those works that were created. Even fewer were the financial rewards offered creative people. It was, therefore, of some importance for composers of art music to form friendships with each other if only to strengthen their common goals.

After the Civil War, matters improved. Americans began to be more receptive to art music. Immigration from Europe, and from Germany in particular, produced a steadier supply of well-trained musicians. As cities grew, a larger population added to the potential audience. The accumulation of wealth also allowed new patrons to funnel surplus money into the arts. National and international transportation became easier with the advent of railroads and steamships. The telegraph and an improved postal service facilitated communication. Those Americans who desired a thorough education could now more easily obtain it abroad or, eventually, at home. Nevertheless, America continued to provide a less hospitable locale than Europe for composers of art music. Teaching, which often consumed a large part of their time, was their chief means of income. Performers continued to prefer European compositions to American ones. Hardly any publishers were willing to publish—or capable of issuing—musical works other than piano pieces, songs, and anthems. It was, therefore, still important for composers to form support networks in order to provide each other with essential comfort and assistance.

For American music to become more viable, composers in the United States needed to participate in cross-fertilization—to stimulate them, to broaden their outlook, and to encourage greater productivity. They also needed companions who understood their problems, would keep up their morale, and would give them a sense of common purpose. Keeping this in mind, it is instructive to identify and examine the close relationship between two of America's master-composers, George Chadwick (1854-1931) and Horatio Parker (1863-1919). Indeed, it is impossible to understand Parker's creative life without taking into account his connection with his older colleague. Chadwick was first Parker's teacher, then his warm friend. As will be shown, theirs was an all-embracing friendship not frequently found between composers at any time. And this friendship was of importance during the late nineteenth century, as composers of American art music were attempting to get more than a toehold in a new somewhat unreceptive cultural environment. The sincere alliance and cooperative affiliation of these two artists went a long way toward keeping their creative energy alive during the many moments of disparagement and disheartenment that were the lot of the American composer.[1]

Each man gave a needed strength to the other in a period when many music societies and theater managers failed to program American art music, when the public preferred popular music or tried-and-true European compositions, and when federal, state, and local governments took no interest in, and refused any financial aid to, cultural activities. One recalls Chadwick's bitter remarks: "The composers of America (some of them were once referred to by an evening newspaper as 'local and suburban composers') have reason to be grateful that they have not been put into a class by themselves as freaks and curiosities." On the other hand, it was still vexing that they were expected to feel grateful when an organization like the Boston Symphony Orchestra allowed "the despised American composer(s)" to be heard "side by side with their contemporaries of European birth."[2]

Chadwick, after some preliminary musical education at the newly-founded New England Conservatory, had gone to Germany to study theory and composition under Salomon Jadassohn (1831-1902) and Josef Rheinberger (1839-1901), respectively. He first met Parker in 1881 and was his mentor in theory and composition at the New England Conservatory during that, and the following, year. He found that his student, only nine years his junior, had already acquired a noticeable fluency in harmony, modulation, and melody. Moreover, Chadwick thought he detected some individuality in Parker's adolescent works. He also discovered that Parker had an independent frame of mind. Parker frequently contested Chadwick's strictures concerning form, counterpoint,

---

1. For a more detailed examination of the reception of nineteenth-century American composers, see Nicholas E. Tawa, *The Coming of Age in American Art Music* (Westport, Conn.: Greenwood, 1991), ch. 1 and 2.

2. *New England Conservatory Magazine-Review* 5 (1914): 67.

and fugue, but, in the end, diligently performed the tasks assigned him: "His lessons usually ended with his swallowing his medicine, but with many a wry grimace."[3] It was Chadwick who first perceived his student's genuine gift for composition and convinced Parker's parents to send him to Munich to finish his schooling under Rheinberger.[4] Significantly, Parker always insisted that Chadwick was his principal influence and that Rheinberger only developed "the seeds sown by his American teachers which contained most of the germs of art truth."[5]

In 1893, an interviewer noted: "Were it to do over again the largest mistake he would correct would be that of confining his musical education to Germany. France he holds to have the atmosphere most conducive to composition. Equally conservative and bound to correct usage, there is about the musical environment of France an expansive enthusiasm and a romantic tincture, more like that of out country."[6] Parker certainly was aware of Chadwick's travels to Giverny, France while a student, with a group of young American painters under the guidance of Frank Duveneck, and, over the years, he surely noticed Chadwick's gradual leaning toward a French style as he grew older.[7] It was the stiffness and unimaginative methodology of German education, not the solid command of techniques it conveyed, that both men questioned. Chadwick claimed, and Parker confirmed: "I believe in a sound contrapuntal education, then as much harmonic breadth as possible. I believe in form, but not formality."[8]

The following incident, recounted in Charles Ives's *Memos,* suggests that Chadwick never forgot the privilege that he could presume as Parker's mentor. In March 1898, Chadwick traveled to New Haven to hear a performance of his *Melpomene Overture.* By this time, Parker was a member of the faculty at Yale University and was also the conductor of the New Haven Symphony Orchestra. While in town, apparently after a luncheon that included the enjoyment of several steins of beer, a mellow Chadwick wandered into Parker's class in Strict Composition. Ives, who was a student of Parker, describes the occasion in a marginal note that appears on a copy, by George Price, of Ives's song "Ich grolle nicht":

> Geo. W. Chadwick came into class this afternoon (on [his] way back from Heiblein's),[9] sat down behind me and Puss—Lord! [what a] beer breath! When Chadwick came in, Parker [was] objecting to the too many keys in the middle [of *Summerfields*]—Geo. W. C. grinned at it and [at] H. W. P. Of this song, Prof.

3. George Whitefield Chadwick, *Horatio Parker* (New Haven, Conn.: Yale University Press, 1921), 7-8.

4. Isabel Parker Semler, in collaboration with Pierson Underwood, *Horatio Parker* (New York: Putnam's Sons, 1942), 44; see also William K. Kearns, *Horatio Parker, 1863-1919: His Life, Music, and Ideas* (Metuchen, N.J.: Scarecrow, 1990), 7.

5. Kearns, 50.

6. *Musical Courier* 26, no. 14 (5 April 1893): 20.

7. Victor Fell Yellin, *Chadwick, Yankee Composer* (Washington: Smithsonian Institution Press, 1990), 35-36.

8. Louis C. Elson, *The History of American Music,* revised to 1925 by Arthur Elson (New York: Macmillan, 1925), 172.

9. Ives misspells the restaurant's name, which is "Heublein's."

Horat[io] P[arker] said it [was] nearer to the G[rolle] of Schumann than the *Summerfields* was near to Brahms.

But Chadwick said the *Summerfields* was the best. C. said "The melodic line has a natural continuity—it flows—and stops when [rounded out]—as only good songs do. And [it's] different from Brahms, as in the piano part and the harmony it takes a more difficult and almost opposite [approach] to Brahms, for the active tranquillity of the outdoor beauty of nature is harder to express than just quietude. In its way [it's] almost as good as Brahms." He winked at H. W. P. and said "That's as good a song as you could write."

Ives adds a further comment in the *Memos*: "[This was] written on the sides of the ms. of this and [of] the *Summerfields* sketch copy after I got back . . . as at that time (1897-8) Chadwick was the big celebrated man of American music."[10]

In addition to being Parker's mentor, Chadwick quickly proved himself to be a sincere and warm comrade. Both men have remarked on the rapport that developed between them. Nothing was allowed to affect the closeness of their relationship. One notes that after both men married, their families spent a great deal of time together, especially during the summer, despite indications that their wives did not get along with each other.[11] Each man came willingly to the other's aid in personal matters, small and great. As an example of a small matter, Chadwick wrote to Parker in March 1889: "Parker, if you've got any of that B & H 20 line music paper I wish you would lend me ten sheets." As for a greater one, in the summer of 1902, Parker's daughter, Lottie, had a riding accident and broke her pelvis. Her anxious father wrote to Chadwick: "The problem now is to make the weeks of lying on her back as short and pleasant as may be. Please write to her cheerfully and ask Ida [Mrs. Chadwick] to do so, too, and Mrs. Preston. I am not in the right mood to give you much news."[12] Other letters show the younger man genuinely distressed over his friend's painful and crippling attacks of gout, an affliction that the older Chadwick could never quite shake off.

Their similar backgrounds and professional pursuits made them sympathetic to each other. Both were of Puritan descent and Massachusetts born. Both were organists, church music directors, educators, and choral and orchestral conductors. Both held strong opinions about the music world that they communicated to each other. Parker, for instance, wrote to Chadwick from Europe on 19 April 1902:

You have perhaps heard that Cambridge has offered me the degree of Mus. Doc. Whiting's[13] idea is that it resembles wearing a crown on top of a plug hat. I have always respected and shared your prejudice against musical as well as other doctors, but there are Doctors and Universities and Cambridge has been conferring the degree for so many hundreds of year that they can probably do it by now so that it

---

10. John Kirkpatrick, ed., *Charles E. Ives: Memos* (New York: Norton, 1972), 183-84.

11. Yellin, 49.

12. Semler, 87, 143.

13. The New England composer Arthur Whiting (1861-1936) was a friend and colleague of both Chadwick and Parker.

will stick. At any rate, I shall be in very good company and lucky if I don't turn out the worst of the lot.[14]

Their correspondence shows them sharing the same feelings and ideals. Furthermore, whatever inner characteristics they revealed to each other had much to do with their New England background—the transcendental idealism of Ralph Waldo Emerson, Amos Bronson Alcott, and Henry Thoreau; the strong New England sense of duty that drove them to demand the best of themselves in their music and their conduct; and the continuous yearning to express something beyond the inanities of everyday living. They wished to contribute to America's slender body of artistic musical works. Their carefully crafted compositions, they hoped, would move the public not only by the force of their individual melodies, attractive rhythms, and climactic passages, but also by more exceptional attributes—those of high-wrought moral feeling and tragic or comic vision. These were attributes to be found in the classical plays of Aeschylus, Aristophanes, and Shakespeare, and in the music of Bach and Beethoven. There was a great deal that was classical and oftentimes distinguished about both men's realization of musical structure.[15]

Whether Chadwick and Parker achieved what they had set out to do was a matter they preferred to leave to time and the public. They did not possess the arrogance that would have allowed them to proclaim every work they wrote as a masterpiece. Yet they were also human and sometimes apt to be carried away by enthusiasm. If one occasionally erred in the direction of a unilateral declaration of his composition's extraordinary musical worth, the other as often as not pricked his inflated ego. On the other hand, each was quite ready to give praise to the other's music if he felt an accolade was warranted. For example, Chadwick became truly overwhelmed when he heard "Jam sol recedit" from Parker's oratorio *The Legend of Saint Christopher* (1898), appreciating its technical mastery and profound expressiveness. When his old friend described it as "an unsurpassed masterpiece," Parker was spurred on to further creativity.[16]

Parker once asserted hesitatingly: "A composer is at times a partly unconscious instrument who records beauties thrust upon him, flowing through him from heaven and earth. He does not always know what he writes, however perfect it may be. . . . But the high aim and simple integrity of great composers are no accidents. Such men have made themselves perfect instruments by their life and work and thought." Then he proudly added: "However much we owe to men from other countries . . . the progress made has been our own progress, and we have made it."[17]

Concerning nationalism and originality, both men agreed that one should not cultivate originality for its own sake without taking into account the musical content and how it should be received by a specific audience. Those approaches to creativity struck both men as artificial. They preferred to let whatever was American and individual about their music come about as a natural unforced manifestation of their New England backgrounds, and their constant endeavors at artistic creation. As noted by Chadwick,

---

14. Semler, 141.

15. See Tawa, 108-23, 157-69. These observations are echoed in Kearns and Yellin.

16. Kearns, 124.

17. Horatio Parker, "Our Taste in Music," *Yale Review* 7 (1918): 787-88.

Parker once observed: "Music, in a broad sense[,] is cosmopolitan and universal; more or less nonsense is talked about a national school of music. The Californians are inheritors of the musical arts of the ages, just as we in New England are."[18] Arlo Bates, who was an intimate of both men, surely had them in mind when he wrote of a fictional band of Boston's artists in his novel *The Pagans*:

> Whatever their faults and extravagances, whatever their errors and intolerance, they were sincere, self sacrificing and ardent beyond the men who made up the world about them; a group of eager lovers of truth and art who had been drawn together by mutual aims and enthusiasms. Their fierceness had been in defense of honesty and sincerity, their disinterestedness was attested by the fact that any one of them might have made his peace with Philistia and been rewarded for his complaisance had he so chosen. Doubtless they had their faults and foibles, yet their comradeship, in its essential purport had been true and noble.[19]

This camaraderie certainly influenced the type of work the younger Parker chose to write. Following Chadwick's early ventures into symphonic works—the *Rip Van Winkle Overture* (1879) and a Symphony in C major (1882)—Parker did likewise, with his *Venetian Overture* (1884) and the Symphony in C minor (1885). Chadwick's cantata *The Viking's Last Voyage* (1881) stimulated Parker to write *The Norseman's Raid* (1881), and the opera *Judith* (1901), based on the Biblical tale of a heroic woman who leads the Hebrews in their struggle against domination, is echoed in Parker's opera *Mona* (1903), whose protagonist is a woman warrior who inspires the British in their revolt against Roman rule. Kearns, in his study of Parker, also discusses several other Chadwick compositions that serve as models for similar ones of Parker. Kearns notes that even as late as 1918, just months before his death, Parker completed *The Dream of Mary*, which drew on Chadwick's *Noel* (1907-08) for its story and musical structures. Moreover, Kearns points out that Parker's chamber works reflect those by Chadwick and Foote[20] in such matters as the frequency of canonic passages and the treatment of significant themes in contrapuntal combination.[21]

In his posthumously-published autobiography, Foote speaks of meeting with Chadwick, Parker, and the composer-pianist Arthur Whiting at the St. Botolph Club in Boston during the 1880s for after-dinner conversations about music in general and their compositions in particular; he comments that the discussions were very candid and criticisms outspoken. In an earlier article, Foote notes that these meetings were among his most "cherished remembrances." He also recounts how the friends offered to the others their compositions in manuscript; there was usually some criticism, which was apt to be

---

18. "Impressions of California Music," an interview with Chadwick in *New England Conservatory Magazine-Review* 6 (1915): 39.

19. Arlo Bates, *The Pagans* (Boston: Ticknor, 1888), 262.

20. Arthur Foote (1853-1937) studied music with John Knowles Paine at Harvard University, and is considered one of the important composers of the second New England school.

21. Kearns, 9-10, 210-11, 140-41.

"caustic" but "always helpful. The talk was honest and frank to a degree, and one was certainly up against the unadorned truth. I learned a lot from it."[22]

These exchanges among Chadwick, Parker, Foote, and others about creative problems and solutions were constant. They met in their homes, at clubs, and in restaurants. It was as if they wished to establish and sustain a set of principles through which their artistic exertions would seem to make sense and have merit. They debated the nature of beauty; evolved criteria that would distinguish those works, among the pieces they produced, that most embodied high craft; and aspired to achieve a lofty aestheticism. They conceived for themselves the artistic obligation of laboring to achieve something artistically meaningful for the sake of earnest music lovers, their country's civilization, and their own personal vision. They submitted newly completed compositions to each other for evaluation, in part to learn if they measured up to the gauges for determining excellence and in part to help decide if any particular work marked an advance on the road toward finer quality and expression.

Chadwick also remembered these meetings, saying he and his friends liked to come together after concerts, when they

> gathered about the same table in convivial intercourse, whetting each other's wits with thrust and parry—rejoicing in each other's successes, and working for them too, but ever ready with the cooling compress of gentle humor or sarcasm if perchance a head showed an undue tendency to enlarge. And in that invigorating atmosphere of mutual respect and honest criticism, they worked with joy and enthusiasm, knowing that if only their work was good enough it would be pretty sure of a hearing sooner or later.[23]

After sojourning in New York for a while, Parker moved back to Boston in 1883 in order to assume the position of organist and choirmaster at Trinity Church. He was extremely happy to live again near his family and musical companions, writes an acquaintance: "Here he found his old friends, Chadwick, Foote and Whiting, and spent many happily contentious hours in their company. . . . He once described the criticism . . . that these young men made of one another's music as 'characterized by candor rather than courtesy.'"[24] In his memorial to Parker, Chadwick also commented on the move: "In 1883, Parker was called to Boston to assume the position of organist and choirmaster at Trinity Church. The close proximity of his old home [in Auburndale], the congenial companionship of his old friends, the active musical life of Boston, his growing reputation, all stimulated him to further effort."[25]

Chadwick, it should be said, was always a willing and understanding supporter, not only of Parker but of other younger composers. When, in 1900, an incensed Arthur Farwell realized that, in the musical circles of the United States, European composers were

---

22. Arthur Foote, *An Autobiography* (1946; reprint, New York: Da Capo, 1979), 55; "A Bostonian Remembers," *Musical Quarterly* 23 (1937): 41.

23. G. W. Chadwick, "American Composers," in W. L. Hubbard, ed., *History of American Music,* vol. 8 of *The American History and Encyclopedia of Music* (Toledo: Irving Squire, 1908), 13.

24. Semler, 83.

25. Chadwick, *Horatio Parker,* 14.

invariably put ahead of American ones, he says he found a responsive listener in Chadwick: "I went to Chadwick with my troubles, and found him sympathetic." Chadwick teased with "but what are you going to do about it?" Farwell's reply, "I am going to fight," won Chadwick's warmest commendation.[26]

Chadwick also tried to aid the younger composers. In 1916 he assisted in founding the Boston Composers' Club, whose meetings were modeled on those earlier informal meetings with Parker, Foote, and Whiting. He intended that the club serve its members by helping to increase general interest in American works, to propagandize for performances of their works, and by allowing members to give each other mutual assistance. Fifteen composers immediately joined, among them Charles Martin Loeffler, Henry Gilbert, Frederick Converse, and Edward Burlingame Hill.[27]

Chadwick's advocacy of mutual assistance is clearly demonstrated by the many actions he and Parker took on behalf of each other's music. In 1886, Parker received a letter from Chadwick saying that he had been working on Franz Kneisel, leader of the Kneisel Quartet, to schedule a performance of Parker's string quartet. When the performance was postponed, Chadwick wrote: "Kneisel gave me for an excuse for not playing your Quartet that so many people wanted to hear the Brahms Sextette that he was obliged to put it on the programme to the exclusion of the great American work!" But Kneisel promised to program it later. In the same letter, Chadwick advised Parker to change the title of his orchestral Allegro in B-flat to *Venetian Overture,* "which is not only a good tune but a good name also (which is rather to be chosen than great riches)."[28] Parker complied. At another time, Chadwick wrote: "I would like to do 'King Trojan' but I am afraid of the M.S.S. parts which our girls and boys [of the New England Conservatory] are not used to. However, if you can send me the orch. to try, I should like to make the experiment."[29]

As director of the Worcester and Springfield Music Festivals in Massachusetts, and as conductor of the instrumental and vocal ensembles of the New England Conservatory, Chadwick had it in his power to advance performances of his and Parker's compositions. For example, after Parker completed his cantata *The Kobolds,* for chorus and orchestra, to a text by Arlo Bates, Chadwick conducted it at the May 1891 Springfield Festival. Chadwick's most significant service to Parker, however, came during the first four months of 1912 when he, with Loeffler, Walter Damrosch, and Alfred Hertz, served as judges for an American opera composition competition, sponsored by the Metropolitan Opera Company. Although the operatic works were submitted anonymously, their authors' identities did not remain unknown. The prize and eventual performances at the Metropolitan went to Parker's *Mona,* which was deemed superior to operas proferred by Arthur Nevin and Charles Wakefield Cadman, among others. Some New York journalists, however, detected collusion in the award.[30]

---

26. Arthur Farwell, "Pioneering for American Music," *Modern Music* 12 (1935): 118.

27. Ibid.; *New England Conservatory Magazine-Review* 6 (1916): 120-21.

28. Semler, 84.

29. Ibid., 88.

As head of the music department at Yale University and conductor of the New Haven Symphony Orchestra, Parker was able to reciprocate. We have already noted Chadwick's trip to New Haven for a performance of his *Melpomene Overture*. Parker was also able to arrange performances at the summer festival in Norfolk, Connecticut, since he was a good friend of Carl Stoeckel. Stoeckel was director of the Litchfield County Choral Society; he conducted the chorus in their annual summer concerts, but he also imported soloists and an orchestra that was comprised of members of the New York Philharmonic. Not surprisingly, choral and instrumental works of Chadwick and Parker were heard at, and sometimes even commissioned for, these performances. Among these were Parker's *Collegiate Overture* for orchestra, and *King Gorm the Grim* and *The Dream of Mary* for voices and orchestra, as well as Chadwick's *Aphrodite, Tam O'Shanter,* and *Anniversary Overtures* for orchestra, and *Noel* and *Land of Our Hearts* for voices and orchestra. These works were well received by their audiences, who heard nothing "academic," nor anything that suggested dogged compliance with conventional rules, in the music.

A constant criticism of American composers during this period was that, unlike their European counterparts, they were not really composers, but educators. The European composer was viewed idyllically as a solitary creator who was not tied down to a mundane profession. It was, of course, a false view that was answered by Arthur Farwell, who noted that in the United States, professors of music were composers, whereas in Europe they were theorists and historians. He saw nothing stultifying in the composer as academic. Rather, he commented, the role of composer-teacher was a valuable one, because students took pride in their teacher and felt a desire to emulate him.[31] Both Parker and Chadwick, of course, were associated with institutions of higher learning. Chadwick began teaching at the New England Conservatory in 1880 and became the conservatory's director in 1897. Parker went to Yale in 1894 and was appointed dean in 1904. Without question, they discussed educational ideas and problems, and what they hoped to achieve at their respective schools. Both had illustrious careers as teachers of the next generation of composers. In addition to Parker, Chadwick's students include Edward Burlingame Hill, Daniel Gregory Mason, Henry Hadley, Frederick Shepard Converse, Arthur Farwell, Arthur Shepard, and William Grant Still. Parker, in turn, was the teacher of Charles Ives, Quincy Porter, Douglas Moore, and Roger Sessions.

Chadwick and Parker thought alike on what constituted proper musical instruction. They felt strongly that it should be oriented toward actual music making, not just to theory and history. The older Chadwick set the example for his friend. He was aware of the limitations that Harvard had placed on Paine, allowing him to teach only history and theory, and banning all applied music instruction, thus keeping future musicians and composers from the necessary practical experience they needed to flourish. In contrast, at the Conservatory, Chadwick started an opera workshop, organized a student symphony orchestra, offered courses in orchestration and composition, and allowed his students to hear readings, by the school's performing ensembles, of their fledging works. Allan Langley says of his teacher, Chadwick, that he "admired nothing without force, form, and

---

30. Kearns, 61-62.

31. Ibid., 264.

solid backbone. He had small respect for 'youth-neurosis,' the self-indulgence that gloats over a minor discovery, all the futility of passing preoccupations to composition. . . . He kept us level-headed by honest criticism."[32] Chadwick's instructional book *Harmony* was first published in 1897, and was quickly adopted as the standard text by schools throughout the country, including Yale.

In like manner, when Parker went to New Haven and Yale University, he set about strengthening the choral society there, building the symphony orchestra, and conducting both. Moreover, the performing groups became "indispensable" laboratories for the students in the music department, since they "furnished the necessary experience for composers, conductors, singers, and players who were studying in the school."[33] The university's administration strongly supported the orchestra, after Parker succeeded in making them see it "as a proper adjunct to" the academic music courses. At least one concert each season was devoted to orchestral compositions by students at Yale. The public grew so delighted with the concert series furnished by Parker that it encouraged the building of Woolsey Hall, a concert hall that seats more than 2,000 people.[34]

Colleagues, students, and friends were shocked when Parker died in 1919, after a period of sickness and intense mental anguish over those who had suffered and perished during the first World War. He had just completed *A. D., 1919*, a cantata for soprano, chorus, and orchestra, to a text by his colleague, Brian Hooker, that pictured this anguish effectively. A bereft Chadwick then composed a moving *Elegy*, "in memoriam Horatio Parker."

For the next ten years or so, until his death in 1931, Chadwick felt a growing loneliness. He increasingly felt the loss of colleagues, such as Parker, with whom he had been able to freely discuss whatever was on his mind, and of other close friends who could cheer him in those instances—now increasing in number—when he needed someone to stand by him.

Boston's hegemony as the center of America's art-music came to an end during these years, as New York City took over the leadership, becoming the focus for native musical creativity. Many younger composers, with different musical values than those of Chadwick and Parker, were coming into prominence. Beginning in the 1920s, Nadia Boulanger, in France, replaced Chadwick as the principal mentor to America's musical youth. Aaron Copland and Roger Sessions pioneered different pathways for musical composition in the United States. With the onset of artistic modernity, it became the fashion to belittle Chadwick and Parker for the way they had conducted their lives and for the music they had written. It is only at the close of the century that we have begun to respect their sincerity and artistic integrity, appreciate their talent, and reappraise their benefactions to musical literature.[35]

---

32. Allan Lincoln Langley, "Chadwick and the New England Conservatory of Music," *Musical Quarterly* 21 (1935): 52.

33. Chadwick, *Horatio Parker*, 14.

34. Elson, 178.

35. See Tawa, 191-201.

It is refreshing to look back a century to the friendship of these two men. It was fortunate that professional rivalry was absent from their makeup, for it would have made impossible the strength each was able to give the other. Neither man tried to hobnob with famous or trendy people nor tried to exalt himself at the expense of others. They enjoyed a satisfying companionship with musical colleagues, benefitted by the closeness of their relationship and never tried to pass off pretentious or inferior pieces as works of art. Indeed, the criticisms heard at their informal get-togethers would immediately have smacked down anything that lacked solidity. In their conversations, in letters to each other, and in everything they accomplished, they reveal themselves as adhering to unambiguous values and beliefs, which permitted them to communicate with musical precision.[36]

Yet they did not have the encouragement afforded the twentieth-century composer, or of an American musical tradition to which they could respond, or alter, or discard. Because of this, we must admire them all the more. What they accomplished was fresh for their time. In the United States, they represented the thoroughly trained and truly competent composer, whose very well-written music merited the admiration given it by music lovers of their time. The music of Chadwick and Parker also warrants the esteem of latter-day Americans, who can look back to this earlier era and appreciate what these composers were attempting and the problems that confronted them.

---

36. Informative in this regard are books like Foote's *An Autobiography,* Semler's *Horatio Parker,* and Chadwick's *Horatio Parker.*

19

Early Bands in an Idaho Railroad Town: Pocatello, 1887-1930

Mary DuPree

When twenty-two year old Iowan William Worel stepped off the train in the small settlement of Pocatello, Idaho Territory, in 1886, he was travelling as a cornetist with a theater orchestra. While in Pocatello, he was persuaded by a group of local citizens that he should settle there and establish a band and an orchestra. Worel continued on the road with the theater troupe for that season, but returned to Pocatello, where he became the best-known band master in the town's early history.[1] The development and location of settlements like Pocatello and other Idaho towns was determined by the railroad; often it was only by railroad that there was convenient transportation from town to town. In the case of Pocatello, the railroad created the town, was its major industry, and the reason for its ethnically diverse population.

The settlement of Idaho by European and American immigrants had begun in the 1860s with mining communities in the central and southwestern mountains. Agriculture on both dry and irrigated land in southern and north-central Idaho and the wealth of timber in the north drew more and more settlers in the 1870s and 1880s. By 1884, the Union Pacific had established the Oregon Short Line through Idaho to link Wyoming and Oregon from east to west, and Utah and Montana from south to north. The town of Pocatello was at the junction of these lines, with the mountains of southeastern Idaho to its south and east and with the great Snake River plain to its north and west. By 1887,

---

1. Letter from Worel's daughters Oda, Cecil, and Maude to Evelyn McLeod [1977], in Ruth Barrus, "Music of the Upper Snake River Valley," archives, Ricks College, Rexburg, Idaho.

the population of the "Gate City" was around 200,[2] but it was to grow rapidly over the next thirteen years: in 1900 the U.S. census recorded Pocatello's population as just over 4,000.

The young and booming town of Pocatello of course had to have a band—to furnish music for parades, dancing, and concerts, and to establish for all to see and hear that Pocatello was a town of importance. Bands had been formed in Idaho as soon as there were communities of any size; there were short-lived, small town bands in the mining communities of Idaho City, Silver City, and Placerville in the 1860s, and over the next two decades bands became common in the largest as well as the smallest communities. As in the eastern part of the nation, the bands were all-male,[3] and evolved from all-brass to mixed brass and woodwind ensembles towards the end of the century. The enthusiasm for bands in this thinly populated and somewhat unruly territory is captured in this 1883 news item in the *Blackfoot Register* about an incident which took place twenty five miles west of Pocatello:

> An excursion [train] from Salt Lake City to Caldwell [Idaho] passed through here Thursday night. A brass band accompanied them, when they arrived at American Falls, a lot of cowboys, not having the fear of the law before them, stopped the train and with drawn revolvers, compelled the band to play for their amusement, after they were satisfied they allowed the train to proceed.[4]

By 1887, Pocatello had its own band,[5] which played for the town's July fourth ceremonies, was the beneficiary of a fund-raising dance in the dining room of the Union Pacific Hotel, performed for the county fair in Blackfoot, and serenaded the visiting superintendent of the Union Pacific Railroad. The band was evidently fairly good: it was considered at least the equal of the Ogden (Utah) band that "condescended to favor us with two or three tunes as they passed through Pocatello" on their way to Boise on the train that year,[6] and was chosen over other regional bands to play at the county fair in Blackfoot for a fee of $75. In 1888, the *Register* noted that the band played in Shoshone (100 miles northwest of Pocatello) and Soda Springs, as well as regularly serenading on the street in Pocatello.

2. H. Leigh Gittins, *Pocatello Portrait* (Moscow: University of Idaho Press, 1983), 37.

3. At this time there were occasionally all-women bands, especially in the midwest and on the west coast, but it was much rarer for women to be included in predominantly male bands. The exceptional mixed bands, including those documented in Kansas, may have been shaped by the lack of a full complement of male performers in very small communities. In Idaho, however, very small towns either had very small, all-male bands, or drew on men from a wider geographical area to have a sufficient membership. See Margaret and Robert Hazen, *The Music Men* (Washington: Smithsonian Institution Press, 1987), and Kim Stockton, "The Golden Age of the Band in Western Washington and Oregon: Mens' and Womens' Bands 1890-1930" (M.A. thesis, University of Idaho, 1988) on women in bands.

4. *Blackfoot Register*, 29 December 1883, 2.

5. We are entirely dependent on local newspapers for information about the very early bands; the 1887 citations from Blackfoot's *Idaho News* seem to indicate the Pocatello band was already well established by then. There is a gap between 1889 and 1893 not covered by extant Blackfoot or Pocatello papers.

6. "Pocatello Items," *Idaho News*, 9 July 1887, 1.

With its burgeoning population, Pocatello was home to several bands, and several band leaders, by 1900. Casual nomenclature for the bands that served Pocatello in the early days make it difficult to distinguish among them: there was the Gate City Band, the Philharmonic Band, the O. S. L. Band (Oregon Short Line, sometimes called the Shop Employees Band) as well as Worel's Band, which may have been another name for one of the other bands. Around 1895, the two most frequently mentioned briefly merged to become the Gate City O. S. L. Band. The members of this group were mostly railroad employees—coach gang leader, car repairer, coach cleaner, engineer, and leader Worel himself was a drill pressman for the O. S. L.—but there was also a shoemaker and a blacksmith.[7] Five of these men are also in the first photograph we can definitely identify as a Pocatello band (fig. 19.1). Dated 1893, it shows a large group of twenty-six men and boys in dressy mufti. The instrumentation is essentially a "silver" ensemble—a brass band of valved, "bell-up" instruments ranging from E-flat cornet down to E-flat bass, trombones, and percussion—plus four clarinets.

The period 1894 to 1907 is one of the two richest in Pocatello's band history. It is clear that the bands stood at the center of an active cultural life at this time. There were also four resident social orchestras,[8] a Chautauqua, and various artists and groups coming to the Opera House, including the Hungarian violinist Eduard Reményi, the Boston Lyric Opera Company, and a troupe presenting *Uncle Tom's Cabin*. Weekly band concerts and serenades entertained the community most summers during these years, at various locations since the city does not appear to have provided a bandstand. This program of the Gate City Silver Band was given at the Railroad Park:[9]

> March, King Cotton . . . . Sousa
> Overture, La Grand . . . . Ripley
> Phenomenal Polka (for cornet) . . . . Hartman
> Mr. A. W. Reed
> Andante and Waltz, Bonito . . . . Gorton
> Song and Dance, Schottische . . . . Goble
> Serenade, Angel Dreams . . . . Ripley
> March, Honeymoon . . . . Sousa
> Newport, Love's Delight . . . . Ripley
> Quadrille, Riverdale . . . . Ripley
> Hustling Galop . . . . Goble

The bands performed for Decoration Day[10] ceremonies, Labor Day parades (which were much more important in this union town than in other parts of Idaho), for baseball

---

7. Photo with annotations on back owned by William Worel, "Gate City OSL band" on bass drum. Bannock County Historical Society. Employee bands were common in the U. S. at this time, but were quite rare in Idaho, where there were very few companies large enough to sponsor a band.

8. All of the orchestras were conducted by men who were also town band directors, and three of the four orchestras were linked with town bands.

9. "In the Social Swirl," *Pocatello Tribune*, 18 July 1896, 7.

10. Now Memorial Day.

Figure 19.1. City Gate Band, 1893.

games and dances, and they greeted visiting dignitaries at the railroad station. When President Theodore Roosevelt made a brief stop in May 1903, both the Woodmen of the World Band and the Indian Band from the school at the Ft. Hall reservation, just north of Pocatello, played.[11]

Fourth of July parades and dances always featured bands. It was common in this, as in other areas of Idaho, for communities within one region to alternate as hosts for a consolidated celebration for the surrounding towns, so bands from Pocatello, Blackfoot, Soda Springs, and Idaho Falls would appear in either their hometown or the neighboring town, depending on who was hosting the "Big Fourth of July Celebration." And on occasion a band from outside the region, such as the Royal Italian Band from Salt Lake City, would be brought to town for holiday parades.

Shortly after the turn of the century, there was a gradual reduction in the number of Pocatello bands. It is not clear whether this is due to the consolidation of existing bands, or to an actual decline in band activity (see fig. 19.2). The city of Pocatello was thriving economically at this time, and the Oregon Short Line was expanding its operations, but in 1901 the Gate City Band, and in 1903 the O. S. L. Band, ceased activities. At the same time, bands sponsored by two fraternal organizations—the Woodmen of the World and the Eagles—assumed the status of town bands. Both included members from earlier bands; the W. O. W. band was led by William Worel.

It is clear that a major problem for the early bands was a lack of financial support from the city or an organization like the Commercial Club (Chamber of Commerce), which helped support bands in some other Idaho communities. The *Pocatello Tribune* addressed this lack of support after the new W. O. W. Band treated Pocatello's citizens to an "masterly" concert in 1902. Now, said the *Tribune* writer, it was the town's duty to encourage them.

> Boise City has bought for their band no less than three sets of instruments, at a cost of no less than $1,200 a set, saying nothing of the music and the uniforms. Hailey within the year has organized a band and given it a set of very fine instruments. Blackfoot has also encouraged their band in a like manner. Likewise Soda Springs. And the Pocatello band boys buy their own instruments; the W. O. W. furnish the uniforms and the band hall.[12]

Just three years earlier, the *Tribune* reported that Worel asked that his band (not the W. O. W. Band) be paid $115 for two days worth of playing in Pocatello for the celebration of the return of the troops after the Spanish-American War. The organizers responded by bringing in bands from two nearby towns, Blackfoot and Menan, who played for free, and Worel was publicly chastised in the paper for asking to be paid. A band member responded in the paper that the city not only did not support the band financially in any way, but had not even granted a request that the band be allowed to

11. "Chief of the Nation," *Pocatello Tribune*, 28 May 1903, 1 and 4. The Fort Hall reservation was just north of Pocatello. Bands were often formed in reservation and mission schools in the nineteenth century, predating by decades public school bands. Music instruction at federal expense is encouraged in the Federal Indian School Course of Study, *Annual Report of the Commissioner of Indian Affairs* (Washington: Government Printing Office, 1890), 156-60.

12. "The Band Was Out," *Pocatello Tribune*, 29 May 1902, 1.

Figure 19.2. Gate City O. S. L. Band, William Worel, director, ca. 1895.

practice in the city hall.[13] While the towns listed in the newspaper article above did provide municipal support for their bands around the turn of the century, most, like Pocatello, did not. When fraternal organizations like the Eagles and the W. O. W. emerged at this same time, it seems logical that they would assume the sponsorship of existing bands, or form new ones from the pool of band musicians in the community. As in the case of Pocatello, this sponsorship provided the fraternal organization with visible status, and provided bands with fancy uniforms (apparently for the first time) and a regular place to rehearse.

The decades from about 1887 to 1907 can be described as the first period of Pocatello's town band history. It was characterized by numerous bands—sometimes as many as three—that provided the city's music at a time, a wide range of activities both within Pocatello and around southeastern Idaho, and a lack of formal community funding. After 1907, there appears from newspaper reports to have been only one band— the newly-revived Gate City Band—active in Pocatello. In 1915, a Pocatello concert band appeared to compete with the Gate City Band; the director of the second group, W. A. Samms, issued a plea that the bands "try to settle our differences" and "get together as one band." He echoes an earlier theme when he pleads that "there is little enough encouragement for the membership of one band to maintain rehearsals and be in position to fill engagements, and still less reason for the existence of two bands within the city."[14]

This second period (1907-18) represents the numerical peak for Idaho's town bands. Polk's *Idaho State Gazetteer* for 1914 lists about ninety-five town bands, while by 1916 there are about seventy bands listed. World War I brought an end to many of these bands as the members went off to Europe, and often the bands did not reorganize after the war. The Gate City Band, however, continued to be active during the war, and by 1918 its hegemony was ended with the formation of a new Municipal Band. During the third period (1918-30), a social issue surfaced that must have festered in the community for many years, but was not acknowledged in any public forum I have been able to uncover.

Pocatello was different from almost all other Idaho towns, due to its cosmopolitan population. By the turn of the century there were distinct Greek, Italian, Irish, French, Chinese, Japanese, and African-American enclaves within the town, drawn by jobs on the railroad and in the railroad shops. A major part of the story of Pocatello's town bands is, in fact, the exclusion of members of these communities from the early bands, followed by the success of one of these groups in establishing its own musical presence in Pocatello.

That southern Europeans and minorities were excluded from the early bands is apparent from the northern European names and faces of the members of the bands in the 1890s and from personal reminiscences of old-time Pocatello residents.[15] A first wave of Italians came to Pocatello in the early 1890s, yet Tony Cuoio and other older members

---

13. "The Band Question, *Pocotello Tribune*, 4 October 1899, 1.

14. "Bandsmen Invited to Fraternize," *Semi-Weekly Pocatello Tribune*, 21 July 1915, 3.

15. One possible exception may have been a regimental band that appears to date from the Spanish American War. A photograph of this band by Benedicta Wrensted shows as many as five or six men who appear to be southern European within the group of twenty-two. It is not certain, however, that this is a Pocatello band. (Photo in the collection of the Bannock County Historical Society.)

of the Italian community remember that Italians, and also Greeks, were excluded from the bands, as they were from other aspects of the city's "white" cultural life. Cuoio recounts, for example, that at the old Auditorium downtown, there were three levels of seating, the highest called "'Nigger Heaven,' where the foreign people—Greeks and Italians—would sit with the negroes. Because of our dark skin we were classified as niggers."[16] While there is no photographic or written evidence from the first two decades of the twentieth century that would confirm the continued exclusion of southern Europeans after the turn of the century, none of the people I interviewed for this project thought that Italians or Greeks participated in the town bands of this period. They were positive that African-Americans, Chinese, and Japanese did not.[17]

Events in 1918 and 1919 helped set the stage for the second major period of Pocatello bands. The 1918 July fourth parade contained divisions representing the Japanese, Italian, Greek, and Chinese communities. A "municipal band" played for the parade and gave a concert that evening.[18] The Gate City Band had played for another celebration about six weeks earlier: a commemoration of the third anniversary of Italy's entry into the war. This event, which was organized by the Cristoforo Colombo Society, was evidently attended by more than just the Italian community.[19]

In 1919, the July 4th festivities combined with a massive welcome for the returning troops. The *Tribune* noted that the Gate City Band gave both a late morning concert and an evening concert, and that there were two parades: in the morning a military parade, led by the Municipal Band and an evening parade led by the Gate City Band. The morning parade included the sections representing the various nationalities as in the previous year, as well as new English, French, and Indian divisions.[20]

Two important changes are reflected in the reports of the Municipal Band that summer. One is that the band was "holding regular practice in the Commercial Club hall, and is giving a series of concerts under the city ordinance making provision for musical entertainment." This is the first indication that a Pocatello band had formal city recognition and support.[21] Practice sessions at Commercial Club Hall is further evidence

---

16. Tony Cuoio, interview, November 1990, Pocatello. I am grateful for Kenneth Harten, a long time member of the Pocatello Municipal Band, for sharing this interview, and also the Eugene Lombardi interview, with me. Kenny had been working on history of the "modern" Pocatello band at the time I began this project, and was very generous in helping me make contact with former band members.

17. This ethnic exclusivity was shared with bands throughout the country. While one might expect that there was a lessening of social barriers on the "frontier," the makeup of Idaho town bands indicates that, concerning barriers of ethnicity and gender (see n. 3, above), this was not the case.

18. "July 4th Pageant a Fine Event," *Semi-Weekly Pocatello Tribune*, 2 June 1918, 2.

19. "All Joined in a Fine Pageant," *Pocatello Tribune*, 24 May 1918, 1.

20. "Pocatello Greets Lads. . .," *Pocatello Tribune*, 3 July 1919, 2.

21. Small Idaho cities such as Lewiston and Twin Falls had also initiated municipal support for their bands in the past decade. Margaret and Robert Hazen (p. 197) point out that this "institutionalization" of town band funding—whether by a city council decision or a state-wide initiative such as the band laws of Kansas and Iowa, passed around 1920—was widespread around the country and signaled "both a decline in the public's enthusiasm for bands and the demise of the time-honored tradition of self-support. While the latter was certainly true, evidence from Pocatello and elsewhere in Idaho suggests that the "decline in enthusiasm" was later in coming to Idaho.

of its "official" status. The second important change is seen in the list of members, which includes three or four Italian names: Joe Masero, Jos. Coia, Henry Coia, and (perhaps) J. H. Verran.[22]

Perhaps it was Italy's status as ally to the United States in the war against the "terrible Hun" that began to turn the tide against the segregation of the Italian community in Pocatello in the late 1910s. The citywide celebration organized by the Cristoforo Colombo Society in 1918, mentioned above, may be indicative of this, and the recognition of Pocatello's multi-ethnic character in its July 4th parades may also represent a liberalization of racial attitudes at this time.

During the summer of 1919, the *Tribune* regularly listed the upcoming weekly programs of the Municipal Band, which performed at various sites around the city. This program was given on the court house grounds Sunday, August 30:[23]

> March, "The Girl of Eagle Ranch" . . . . English
> "Sand Dunes," Oriental . . . . Gay
> "Johnny's in Town" . . . . Meyer and Alman
> "Zuleika," Turkish Love Song .Wheeler
> Waltz, "In Old Wisconsin" . . . . Carlton
> "How 'Ya Gonna Keep 'Em Down on the Farm?" . . . . Donaldson
> Serenade, "Eventide," clarinette and baritone . . . . King
> March, "Clarinda" . . . . Galuska
> Dedicated to George W. Landers,
> Clarinda, Iowa Military Band
> "STAR SPANGLED BANNER"

By 1918, not only had the Italians begun to be a presence in the "white" town bands, but they had formed a band of their own. In the winter of 1919 or 1920 the Italian band played for the funeral of John Caccia. Tony Cuoio and Carmine Zaccardi both remember this funeral because it was so cold that the instruments's valves froze, as did the players' fingers, and the procession had to stop to warm up in homes on the way from the Catholic Church to the cemetery.[24] Cuoio, Zaccardi, and others recount that in its early days the Italian band played most frequently for Italian funerals, intoning dirges on the way to the cemetery.

The leader of the early Italian Band was Dan Landucci, a retired Italian bandmaster who came to Pocatello around 1916. Landucci supported himself primarily by giving music lessons. His teaching included the use of solfège, "teaching by hand" (possibly a reference to the Guidonian hand), and intensive drill in reading notation. Parents were usually present for lessons, and Landucci enforced extremely strict discipline at band

---

22. "Street Dance Tuesday Night. . . ," *Pocatello Tribune*, 28 July 1919, 5.

23. "Band Concert Sunday Night," *Pocatello Tribune*, 30 August 1919, 5. This band had an instrumentation of flute, two clarinets, baritone sax, five cornets, four altos, one tenor, three trombones, baritone, two basses, and two drums.

24. Tony Cuoio and Carmine Zaccardi, interviews, November 1990, Pocatello.

practice.[25] Cuoio indicates that although the students in Landucci's Band could not afford uniforms, they were much better musicians than those in the other bands who generally played by ear. Most of the band members were beginners, but a few had played in Italian army bands during World War I.[26]

The photo taken around 1919 (see fig. 19.3) shows twenty-nine members, ranging in age from about eight to twenty-five, clustered around Landucci. Their mode of dress ranges from formal to overalls under dark jackets, and the collection of instruments is similarly varied: in addition to one bass and two snare drums, there are nine clarinets (an unusually large number, even for Italian bands), and brass instruments including a helicon bass, a tenor saxhorn, and a type of Italian alto horn called "genis" by interviewees.[27] While most of Landucci's band were Italians, there were a few non-Italians: Eugene Lombardi identified a Lopez, a Stavros, and a Hudson in this picture, and said there was also "an Indian," Phil Lavata, who sometimes played in the Landucci band.

The Landucci Band was probably active only from about 1918 to 1922. According to Zaccardi (who, in fig. 19.3, is third from the left in the bottom row), this band was, at least for a while, the only band in town.[28] It is probably the Landucci Band which is noted in the *Tribune* as having played for numerous community events in the summer of 1922. It was at the head of the Italian contingent at the Decoration Day and Labor Day parades, gave a "delightful" concert on the court house grounds on at least one occasion,[29] and was invited to play in Soda Springs, sixty miles away.[30] Nevertheless this Italian band was obviously considered second in status to the National Guard's 116th Cavalry Band, which led major civic parades in 1921 (the first year it is mentioned) and 1922, and was referred to as "the band" in the newspaper.

The cavalry band was dissolved due to the demobilization of the Idaho National Guard in August 1922, and it seems that at least one group—the American Legion—felt it would be inappropriate for the Italian Band to become the municipal band (as railroad, Woodmen's, Eagles, and cavalry bands had in the past). The *Tribune* reported on August

25. Kenneth Harten, "Early Bands in Pocatello" (typescript, n.d.), got this information from a conversation with Tony Cuoio, which was not recorded. Emma Scogna Rocci's study *Italian Wind Bands: A Surviving Tradition in the Milltowns of Pennsylvania* (New York: Garland, 1990), 140-42, indicates that strict discipline, the intensive study of solfège, and the participation by parents were also characteristic of similar bands in the east.

26. Eugene Lombardi, interview, 7 July 1989, Pocatello.

27. Lombardi indicated that the upright bass in this photograph was left by "an earlier Italian band" that was in Pocatello in 1910. I have found no other evidence of this earlier band.

28 Carmine Zaccardi, interview 23 October 1990, Pocatello. The *Pocatello Tribune* also records the brief life of a Pocatello Bannocks Band in 1920; it may have been associated with a baseball team of the same name. From 1921 to 1924 there was also a Boy Scout band, which was then sponsored by the Demolays until 1927. This boy's band marched occasionally in civic parades. Payette, Idaho also had a Boy Scout band and a Girl Scout band at this time. These bands marched and performed extensively, and served as training ensembles for the adult Payette County band. Pocatello's first high school band was organized in 1923.

29. "Town Talk: Gave Band Concert," *Pocatello Tribune*, 31 May 1922, 12.

30. Zaccardi interview.

31. "Organizations Cooperate with Local Post . . .," 6.

Figure 19.3. Italian Band, Dan Landucci, director, ca. 1919.

30 that a committee had been formed by the American Legion to work with William Worel (now a florist) to form a band "that will be a credit to the city."[31] The American Legion did, in fact, have a band the next year, but it lasted only one season.

For the following three seasons, the two bands supplying Pocatello's music were the Italian Band and the resurrected Oregon Short Line Band. It is not clear why the O. S. L. Band was restored after an almost twenty-year hiatus. It appeared in 1923 about the time of a Pioneer Days celebration largely sponsored by the O. S. L.:[32] perhaps O. S. L. management felt such a celebration, and the reorganization of a company band, would restore company loyalty after a 1922 strike.[33] This bitter strike was the cause of a number of Italians, probably including Dan Landucci, leaving Pocatello in 1922.

The Italian Band, expanded with a new generation of children, including three girls, was directed briefly by Paul Pasta ("old man Pasta") and then by his son, cornetist James (Jimmy) Pasta, who were newcomers to Pocatello. It rehearsed at the newly-constructed hall of the Cristoforo Colombo Society (Columbus Hall). Significantly, by 1925 the Italian Band was being referred to as the "Pocatello band" or the "Municipal band." It led the Decoration Day parade that year, gave weekly concerts at various locations around the city, and its formal photograph appeared in the *Tribune* (fig. 19.4).[34] According to the *Tribune*, attendance at its concerts was "upwards of 1,000."[35] By September a bandstand had been erected at the "Pocatello bowl" on the bench west of downtown, and a new road made the last few band concerts of the year "easily accessible by motor."[36]

This band's status was further reinforced when, early in 1927, the Idaho legislature passed its version of the Iowa Band Law, authorizing municipalities to levy taxes for the support of community bands.[37] Within two months of the passage of the Band Law, Pocatello had acted on the overwhelmingly positive vote for its band levy and authorized the expenditure of $2,000 for its municipal band. Shortly afterwards, the Chamber of Commerce band commission voted to formalize the city's relationship with James Pasta and his band. The newspaper report indicates the decision did not come automatically:

> The band commission has been meeting several times a week since its appointment to consider ways and means of organizing a municipal band for which Pocatellans voted a tax levy at the last city election. Several local musicians were discussed as

32. "Stage All Set for Big Show," *Pocatello Tribune*, 7 August 1923, 1 and 7.

33 It is not clear to what extent the O. S. L. supported its band financially. It did provide the uniforms. None of the informants I have interviewed played in this O. S. L. band, so I have been unable to find out if the band members were paid for rehearsal and performance time, and for trips with the band. It was not an uncommon practice for this to happen; during this same period the Denver Rio Grande Western Railroad paid its employees their regular hourly wage when they were out on "band business." Jim Baker interview, Twin Falls Public Library Oral History no. 4, Twin Falls, Idaho.

34. "Band Concert This Evening," 25 July 1926, 4.

35. "Pocatello Band Concert Draws Many Listeners," *Pocatello Tribune*, 26 July 1926, 13.

36. "Pocatellans Hear Concert at Bowl," *Pocatello Tribune*, 27 September 1926, 5.

37. See n. 21.

Figure 19.4. Pocatello Municipal Band, James Pasta, director, 1925.

possible directors but a decision in favor of Mr. Pasta was made out of consideration for the services he has rendered without charge in the past.[38]

The allotted $2,000 was paid to James Pasta between June and November of 1927, and similarly the next year.

The band held city-wide auditions, and the band's membership roster, published along with the announcement of the band's first concert, showed an increasing inclusion of non-Italian musicians.[39] In 1927 and 1928, Pasta's band gave weekly concerts from mid-June through September. The Sunday evening concerts, usually consisting of about ten pieces, often included cornet solos and arrangements by Pasta. Waltzes, marches, sentimental songs, and opera and operetta transcriptions were the rule; the paper reported that attendance was excellent and the audience enthusiastic. This 15 July 1928 lawn concert is typical:[40]

> March. The Agitator . . . . McFall
> Selections from Opera "La Maritana" . . . . Wallace
> Songs from the Old Folks . . . . arr. by Lake
> (Request)
> Oro e Lavoro, Valse di Concert . . . . arr. by Pasta
> Overture "Frolic of the Fairies" . . . . Biggs
> My Blue Heaven, foxtrot . . . . Donaldson
> (Request)
> Waltz "Ramona" . . . . Wayne
> Trombone novelty "A Slippery Success" . . . . Chenette
> March "Sheik Parker Triumphal" . . . . Chenette
> Star Spangled Banner

We now come to the final stage of Pocatello's early community band history. In the late 1920s, the Municipal Band and the O. S. L. Band coexisted, and even shared some membership. While it was the Municipal Band (still predominantly Italian) that gave regular concerts, the Pocatello O. S. L. Band was taking on a new role (fig. 19.5). In 1927 it travelled to Provo, Utah, and in the following two years to Boise for the all-system Union Pacific Railroad athletic meet.

During these years railroad employees came from Omaha, Los Angeles, Portland, and points in between to compete in swimming, trapshooting, track and field, fire fighting, beauty, and band contests. Thirty-one members of the band were part of a group of 200 Pocatello O. S. L. shop employees who took the train to Boise for the competition, which took place on 26 and 27 August 1928.[41] The Salt Lake City and Pocatello bands competed for the O. S. L. unit championship, playing a required piece—Franz von Suppé's *Poet and Peasant* overture—and two optional pieces. Pocatello also competed in the system-wide class A contest with Portland, Denver, Los Angeles, and Salt Lake bands,

38. "Municipal Band for Pocatello Planned," *Pocatello Tribune*, 5 June 1927, 5.

39. "First Concert of Summer Season Tonight at Park," *Pocatello Tribune*, 19 June 1927, 12.

40. "Tenth Concert of Series Sunday at High School," *Pocatello Tribune*, 11 July 1928, 5.

41. "Rail Employees Move on Boise for Big Event," *Pocatello Tribune*, 26 August 1928, 9.

Figure 19.5. O.S.L. Band, James Pasta, director, 1929.

playing another required von Suppé piece, the *Light Cavalry* overture, and two optional pieces.[42]

The following year, again in Boise, the Class A contest number was Antonio Carlos Gomez's *El Guarany* overture, and Pocatello's optional number was the "Grand Selection from Maritana" by William Vincent Wallace. Three of the bands also provided original marches dedicated to individual officials of the Union Pacific system: Pocatello's contribution was the "Overland Limited" march by James Pasta, dedicated to W. M. Jeffers, vice president of operations, the Portland band offered the "Portland Limited" march "by the band's cornetist," and Los Angeles presented the "Gold Coast Limited" march (composer unknown). While reports of prize winners are rather confused in the newspapers, it appears that the Pocatello O. S. L. Band did itself proud: its score in the class A competition was 90.2, compared with Los Angeles's 97.1, Portland's 79.6, and Denver's 78.6.[43] The purpose of these games, including the band contests, was made clear by a Union Pacific executive: such meets had "an excellent effect on the morale of the employees of the entire system, producing a finer esprit de corps than could be achieved any other way."[44]

Pasta's contribution of a new march for the Union Pacific competition was natural, since by late spring of 1929 he was the conductor of the O. S. L. Band as well as the Municipal Band. And despite the fact that the paper continued to refer to two different bands, they had virtually the same personnel. Trumpet player Kenneth Harten remembers slipping in to watch the rehearsals of the band that summer; it practiced in one of the O. S. L. shops, on a metal platform that functioned as a second floor where it was as "hot as blazes."[45] The forty-member unified band reduced its summer schedule to one concert every two weeks because of the expense involved in having such a large ensemble,[46] but with continued financial support from the city, and continued enthusiastic audiences at its concerts, it concluded the decade stronger than ever.

It seems appropriate to mark the end of Pocatello's early band history in 1930. After years of competing bands, bickering between groups, and lack of community support, Pocatello finally had one well-supported town band. It also seemed to have reached a degree of reconciliation between its "white" and Italian communities. In 1930, James Pasta left Pocatello for parts unknown, but after a transitional year a reconstituted Pocatello Municipal Band was formed under Guy Gates, member of a large Italian family which had contributed three members to Pocatello's earlier Italian bands. Sixty-five years later, this band still gives concerts throughout the summer at the Ross Park bandstand.

---

42. Competing for the Class B prize were Laramie (Wyoming), Albina (Oregon), and Ogden (Utah).

43. "Class A Trophy in Band Contest Won by Los Angeles Musicians," *Idaho Statesman,* 4 September 1929, 6.

44. "W. M. Jeffers of Omaha among Visiting Officials," *Idaho Statesman,* 26 August 1928, 1.

45. Harten, 3.

46. "Concert by Municipal Band Greatly Enjoyed," *Pocatello Tribune,* 9 July 1929, 10.

20

Arthur P. Schmidt:
The Publisher and His American Composers

Wilma Reid Cipolla

"Pioneer Publisher of American Music." This facile, albeit accurate phrase, commonly used to describe the nineteenth-century Boston publisher Arthur P. Schmidt, deserves much closer scrutiny. Schmidt has been hailed as the first American publisher to issue symphonic and chamber music scores by native American composers, and as the primary supporter of the Boston Group—Amy Beach, George W. Chadwick, Arthur Foote, Horatio Parker, John Knowles Paine, and Edward MacDowell. Although he is justly famous for publishing full orchestral scores, in actuality large works constituted a very small portion of Schmidt's total output. Nor was his catalog focused exclusively on the "Boston Six." Schmidt also supported a large body of minor American composers, who came not only from Boston, Schmidt's adopted home, but from many other parts of the United States as well.

Who are these composers? What proportion of Schmidt's catalog was devoted to Americans? How many major American works did he issue, and which composers did he feature in his various catalogs? Answers to these questions, to the extent that they may be determined, lie in his business correspondence and advertising pieces, rich resources that form the basis for this exploration into Schmidt's relations with his composers.[1]

---

1. The Arthur P. Schmidt Company Archives in the Music Division at the Library of Congress is a large repository that documents the firm's activities in Boston, Leipzig, and New York. It consists of the original manuscripts from which the music was printed, correspondence, and business records, including plate books, publication books, stock books, and cash books. The Library of Congress has recently processed the Schmidt Archives and has produced a finding aid which lists all the composers represented in the Archives.

Beginnings

The A. P. Schmidt Company was established 2 October 1876 in Boston, at 40 Winter Street, heart of the city's commercial district. Its founder, Arthur P. Schmidt (1846-1921), emigrated to Boston from his native Altona, Germany in 1866, and began his publishing career working for G. D. Russell & Co. After ten years with Russell, Schmidt opened his own business as a retailer and importer of foreign music, including the popular Litolff Edition. The first Schmidt catalog, copyright 1876,[2] bears the heading:

> New and Elegant Editions of Celebrated Classical
> and Popular Compositions, As Used in the Conservatories of
> all Countries.
> Unrivalled for Correctness, Beauty and Cheapness.
> Imported and For Sale By Arthur P. Schmidt.
> Agent for the Catalogues of Ashdown & Parry, Henry
> Litolff, and P. Jurgenson.

This initial foray into the publishing world advertised about fifty titles, all of them by European composers, consisting primarily of piano studies and sonatas by Bach, Beethoven, Haydn, Mozart, and Schumann, as well as orchestral scores for the nine Beethoven symphonies.

Five months later, on 26 March 1877, Schmidt issued his first copyright, A. P. S. 1,[3] a sacred choral work for mixed voices, "Deus misereatur," by the Boston organist and teacher S. B. Whitney (1842-1914).[4] The next two plate numbers were assigned to a piano piece by Widor and a choral arrangement of a Saint-Saëns work by Charles H. Morse (1853-1927), a student of John Knowles Paine and founder of the Northwestern Conservatory of Music in Minneapolis. A. P. S. 4, issued on 18 August 1877, was a book of organ preludes and postludes by George E. Whiting (1840-1923), head of the organ department at the New England Conservatory of Music.

Another four years passed before Schmidt published any works by composers who are today recognized as major American figures. On 11 January 1881 Schmidt issued two choruses for men's voices by George W. Chadwick, "Margarita" and "Reiterlied" (A. P. S. 164 and 165 respectively), and in February another Chadwick work, "The Viking's Last

---

Schmidt's voluminous business correspondence is preserved in indexed letter-press copybooks, reference to which is cited by using the initials "APS" followed by the name and years of the specific copybook and page(s) on which the letter may be found. Foreign letter copybooks are denoted by the abbreviation "FL," general letters as "GL." There are also innumerable boxes of letters to Schmidt from various individuals, which are cited by the abbreviation "PC" (personal correspondence) and the writer's name.

2. This is the only catalog located to date that bears the 40 Winter Street address. Most of the catalogs cited in this essay are from the Schmidt Archives at the Library of Congress; they are bound into a scrapbook that is kept with the business records.

3. These numbers are the plate numbers that Schmidt assigned in sequence.

4. The Library of Congress has a copy of the first edition of "Deus misereatur."

Voyage," for solo voice and male chorus, appeared. In November a Chadwick song, "The Miller's Daughter," was issued, and in December Schmidt's first work by John Knowles Paine, "The Realm of Fancy," op. 36, a cantata for solo voices and mixed chorus, was published. In 1882 Schmidt issued three songs by Horatio Parker, several piano pieces and choral works by Chadwick, and another cantata by Paine, the vocal score for *Phoebus Arise*, op. 37.[5] Two more years elapsed before Schmidt offered two songs by Arthur Foote ("Go, Lovely Rose" and "When Icicles Hang by the Wall"); then in February 1885 Amy Beach's first song, "With Violets," op. 1, no. 1, appeared.

Catalogs and Composers

If Schmidt did not initiate his publishing activity with works by the so-called Boston Group, which composers did he publish in the years between 1877 and 1881? His first 160 plate numbers, mostly piano and vocal pieces, were largely devoted to works by contemporary European composers; just slightly more than one-third featured works by Americans. These included the Boston organists Henshaw Dana (1846-83) and Henry M. Dunham (1853-1929), longtime organ teacher at the New England Conservatory of Music; George W. Marston (1840-1901), organist and teacher in Portland, Maine; singers Vincenzo Cirillo (fl. 1882), who was probably from Boston, and W. H. Fessenden (fl. 1887) of New York City; as well as James H. Wilson (1843-?), a prolific composer of art songs from Newport, Rhode Island. The list of piano composers included Edward Baxter Perry (1855-1924), a traveling lecture-recitalist, and Oscar Weil (1840-1921), teacher and critic from San Francisco. Mixed in with new works were pieces by Bach, Saint-Saëns, Tchaikovsky, etc., arranged by Americans—Foote, Morse, Whitney—who had also written original compositions for Schmidt.

In 1881 Schmidt issued his first major catalog, *The Teacher's Guide: A Catalog of Music*, a seventy-nine page listing of over 500 piano and organ pieces, songs, and choral works. Heavily slanted toward European composers, with many adaptations, opera arrangements, and English ballads, it contained titles by fourteen American composers. The second edition of the catalog, issued in 1885, boasted an eighteen-page appendix,[6] in which three cantatas by Paine, opp. 36-38, were listed. A group of musicians active in Boston made their first appearance: the tenor Charles R. Adams (1834-1900); teacher/composer O. B. Brown (fl. 1886); New England Conservatory professors Charles Dennée (1863-1946) and James H. Howe (1856-?), later head of the music department at DePauw University; the popular pianist and teacher Stephen Emery (1841-91); historian and critic Louis C. Elson (1848-1920); and pianists Clayton Johns (1857-1932) and John Orth (1850-1932). Three well-known women were represented: song-composer Helen Hood (1863-1949), Scottish-born pianist Helen Hopekirk (1856-1945), and soprano Clara Kathleen Rogers (1844-1931). Both Hopekirk and Rogers also taught at the New England Conservatory.

---

5. The orchestral score for this cantata did not appear in a Schmidt catalog until 1900.

6. The 1881 catalog was issued from Schmidt's second business address, 146 Tremont Street. The second edition bears his third address, 13 & 15 West Street, where he was located from 1884 to 1892.

In 1882 Schmidt issued a catalog of music for strings, the eighty-four page *Catalogue of Instrumental-Music Carefully Selected for the Use of Teachers, Students and Amateurs*. However, the chamber music was exclusively European and the orchestral works were collections of overtures and dances for small orchestra.

Schmidt's next major catalog, a sixty-one page supplement to *The Teacher's Guide*, appeared in 1888. Like the 1881 catalog, the contents were mostly piano pieces and songs by European composers. But in the intervening years Schmidt had accepted manuscripts from quite a few more stateside composers (approximately one-quarter of the songs were American); he also commissioned arrangements of pieces by European composers.[7] Boston composers included the critic and teacher William F. Apthorp (1848-1938) and organist/conductors E. Cutter, Jr. (fl. 1899), Frank Lynes (1858-1913), J. C. D. Parker (1828-1916), and Arthur W. Thayer (1838-89). Other Easterners were the Pittsburgh conductor Frederic Archer (1838-1901), Philadelphia organist and choirmaster W. W. Gilchrist (1846-1916), and G. D. Wilson (1833-97), a composer from Nyack, New York. Four women made a brief appearance (few of their works were included in subsequent catalogs): Mrs. C. F. Chickering (dates unknown), wife of the piano maker Charles Frank Chickering; Mary Bradford Crowninshield (dates unknown) and Hattie P. Sawyer (dates unknown), both composers of church music and songs; and pianist Mary Knight Wood (1857-1944), who lived for many years in Florence, Italy. The 1888 catalog contained considerably more part-songs than the 1881 edition, along with three cantatas, two by Paine and Horatio Parker's *King Trojan*. Other than piano and organ works, no instrumental music was listed.

In 1889 Schmidt issued another substantial catalog. This sixty-three page *Catalogue of Music Published by Arthur P. Schmidt* omitted the standard phrase "Publisher and Dealer in Foreign and American Music," which was invariably used on title pages of earlier catalogs. Works by Edward MacDowell appeared for the first time, along with pieces by the New York composer-pianist Henry Holden Huss (1862-1953); Boston composer Margaret Ruthven Lang (1867-1972), daughter of the well-known teacher and conductor B. J. Lang; and Arthur Weld (1862-1914), the New York conductor. Other new American names included B. C. Blodgett (1838-1925), a Boston organist who later taught at Smith College and Stanford University; W. L. Blumenschein (1849-1916), a choral conductor in Dayton, Ohio; Bruno Oscar Klein (1858-1911), New York organist and pianist; and F. A. Porter (1859-?), professor of piano at the New England Conservatory.

The 1889 catalog also is the first to list chamber and orchestral works by American composers: the Foote Piano Trio, op. 5, the Chadwick Piano Quintet in E-flat, and full scores for Chadwick's Symphony no. 2 in B-flat and Paine's Symphony no. 2 in A, *Spring*. This would seem to refute the oft-quoted statement that the first symphonic score by an

---

7. Publication of European works edited by American composers was a device to gain copyright protection in the U.S. Although many titles in the 1881 catalog were probably arrangements, Schmidt did not identify the editors by name until the 1888 catalog. Composers frequently listed in that catalog as having "revised and fingered" piano music included O. B. Brown, Arthur Foote, Junius W. Hill, George W. Marston, John Orth, Ernst Perabo, and Oscar Weil. Translations of vocal music from the original German or Italian into English were done by Allen A. Brown, John Sullivan Dwight, Louis C. Elson, and Caroline Hazard.

American composer was issued by Schmidt in 1880.[8] That publication, John Knowles Paine's *Im Frühling*: Symphonie no. 2 in A für grosses Orchester, op. 34, was not solely a Schmidt venture, but was jointly issued by Schmidt and August Cranz of Hamburg under a Cranz plate number, [C.] 5450.[9] The "first [true] orchestral score by an American published by an American house"[10]—Chadwick's Symphony no. 2 in B-flat major, op. 21 (A. P. S. & Co. 1559) —did not appear until 1888. Four years earlier Schmidt had published parts to Arthur Foote's Quartett in G moll, op. 4, which was very possibly the first chamber music piece by an American to be issued by an American publishing house.

Schmidt also issued "novelty lists" to publicize each season's new titles. One such, the *List of Musical Novelties, Season of 1892-93*, highlighted three major new works by Foote: the Piano Quartet, op. 23, and orchestral scores for the Symphonic Prologue *Francesca da Rimini*, op. 24, and the Serenade for Strings, op. 25, along with vocal scores for cantatas by Beach, Chadwick, Foote, Lynes, Marston, and Whiting. Arthur Bird's Third Little Suite, op. 32, was cited as "in press." Score and parts for the Bird work were subsequently advertised in the twenty-eight page *Supplement to Graded Catalogue of Music* (ca. 1895), along with Chadwick's Symphony no. 3 in F major and MacDowell's *Im Oktober*, op. 42a (1893).[11]

It was probably about this time, but certainly before 1892, that Schmidt issued his first brochure devoted to the music of a single individual—a four-page list of the vocal and instrumental compositions of Stephen Emery, complete with portrait and brief biography. During the next ten years he published similar pamphlets for Beach, Chadwick, Foote, and MacDowell.[12] He also did one for Californian John W. Metcalf (1856-

8. The statement "In 1880 John K. Paine's Spring Symphony was issued, being the first orchestral score published for an American composer" first appeared in "Publisher Arthur P. Schmidt: Quarter-Centennial Anniversary," *Musical Courier* 43 (2 October 1901): 34. A version of the statement appeared in Arthur Foote's tribute on the occasion of Schmidt's death in *Musical America* 34, no. 3 (14 May 1921): 55. Foote's article was cited in Christine Ayars, *Contributions to the Art of Music in America by the Music Industries of Boston, 1640-1936* (New York: H. W. Wilson, 1937), 39, and repeated by Foote in his biographical essay on Schmidt in the *Dictionary of American Biography* (New York: Scribner's, 1964), vol. 8, 440. See also William Arms Fisher, *One Hundred and Fifty Years of Music Publishing in the U. S., 1783-1933* (Boston: Ditson, 1933), 119, and the entries for Schmidt in *New Grove Dictionary of American Music* (1986) and *Music Printing and Publishing*, ed. D. W. Krummel and Stanley Sadie (New York: Norton, 1990).

9. Joint publication with a German firm was a fairly common occurrence in Schmidt's early years as a publisher. For instance, five of Foote's first publications were jointly issued by Schmidt with German publishers: opp. 1 and 3 (both 1882) with Cranz; op. 5 (1884) with B. Schott's Söhne; and opp. 4 (1885), 6 (1885/86) and 9 (1886) with Henry Litolff's Verlag. Opp. 1, 3, and 5 bore plate numbers from the German house; the others had A. P. S. numbers.

10. Victor Fell Yellin, *Chadwick: Yankee Composer* (Washington: Smithsonian Institution Press, 1990), 96.

11. MacDowell's First Suite, op. 42, as published in 1891, comprised only four movements. In 1893 *Im Oktober* was issued as a "supplement" under opus number 42a. In the complete five-movement suite, it was inserted after the second movement and became the new third movement.

12. None of these catalogs have publication dates. Approximate time frames were calculated from the publisher's address on the flyers and the latest works listed.

1926), author of "Absent," Schmidt's all-time best seller.[13] Other special catalogs were *Favorite Songs by American Composers* (ca. 1896) and *Woman's Work in Music* (ca. 1901), which listed pieces by forty-five and seventeen American composers, respectively.

Despite all this activity, large works represented only a small portion of Schmidt's total output, and European composers were still in the majority. For instance, of the forty-two composers whose pieces were advertised in the piano section of his *Graded List of Musical Novelties, 1898-99*, only nine were American. Understandably, because of language considerations, more than half of the songs were by Americans. The same proportion of American to European names is found in Schmidt's most extensive novelty list, a fifty-page publication which appeared in 1903-04.[14]

Schmidt's interest in American composers appears to have become more focused after 1899, when he purchased the P. L. Jung catalog from Kurt Moebius. Moebius, manager of the New York office of Breitkopf und Härtel, issued only two catalogs in his short career as a publisher under the pseudonym P. L. Jung. Both of the Jung catalogs were devoted largely to American composers, the most significant being MacDowell.[15] Moebius had become acquainted with MacDowell through the Breitkopf connection, since a number of MacDowell's compositions were published by the German firm.[16] After the Jung acquisition, Schmidt became MacDowell's major publisher and dedicated considerable effort to promoting MacDowell's music.[17]

In addition to MacDowell, about half of the composers published by Jung were carried over to the Schmidt catalog. Henry Hadley (1871-1937), who appeared in the first Jung catalog, became one of Schmidt's principal composers; George Templeton Strong (1856-1948)[18] was also prominently represented. Others who came to occupy a significant place include New York organists John Hyatt Brewer (1856-1931), P. A. Schnecker (1850-1903), and Gerrit Smith (1859-1912), as well as Jules Jordan (1850-1927), a singer and composer of Providence, Rhode Island.

American Composers in Leipzig

In 1889 Schmidt established an office in Leipzig, a commission agency under the auspices of Friedrich Kistner, a firm that handled a number of foreign publishers. From

13. Other than a reference to his death in the Metcalf correspondence in the Schmidt Archives, the only biographical information to be found was in *The Musician* 40 (April 1925): 40.

14. *Graded List of Musical Novelties: Season 1903-04.*

15. Moebius's 1896 catalog, *Jung's Publications: A List of Music Composed Chiefly by Americans*, contained works by thirty composers, all but two of whom were Americans. The 1898 catalog, bearing the same title as the 1896 one, included a large number of arrangements by MacDowell, and works by forty other composers, about one-quarter of them Europeans.

16. For more background on the Jung connection and information on the relation between Schmidt and MacDowell, see Margery Morgan Lowens, "The New York Years of Edward MacDowell" (Ph.D. diss., University of Michigan, 1971).

17. MacDowell compositions carried a higher than normal royalty (15% rather than the customary 10%), because Schmidt had to pay Moebius a 5% royalty on all MacDowell works sold. This arrangement continued until 1926.

18. In the Schmidt catalogs he is listed as Templeton Strong.

the German branch Schmidt issued publications that were different from those of the Boston office. To distinguish between the two series, he gave his new series S. plate numbers instead of A.P.S. numbers. The first 122 publications from Leipzig were primarily piano and chamber music works by European composers, many of them edited, however, by American composers.[19] The first "pure" American work—MacDowell's Suite für grosses Orchester, op. 42, published in score, with parts and a piano duet version (S. 123-125)—appeared in 1891. The next American work to be issued from Leipzig, in 1892, was Arthur Bird's Dritte Kleine Suite für grosses Orchester, op. 32, again in full score, with parts and a piano duet version, bearing plate numbers S. 199-201. A third large American work, published in score and parts in 1897, was Beach's *Gaelic* Symphony (S. 436).[20]

Within a short time Schmidt accumulated a sizable Leipzig catalog. In November 1890, only a year after opening the office, he brought out his first publications list, *Verzeichniss des Musikalien-Verlags von Arthur P. Schmidt in Leipzig.* Fourteen pages long, it enumerated some fifty works in ten categories by twenty-six composers, ten of whom were Americans. In addition to six new works by MacDowell, Schmidt introduced to the German market two more of his most famous composers—Chadwick and Foote—along with a surprising number of less familiar musicians—the English-born Boston Symphony Orchestra violinist Charles N. Allen (1837-1903), along with Dennée, Huss, Klein, Marston, J. C. D. Parker, and Whitney. Besides the usual piano pieces and songs, there were three American chamber works: Chadwick's Piano Quintet, Foote's Violin Sonata, op. 20, and Whitney's Piano Trio, op. 30.

Four years later, in 1894, Schmidt issued a sixteen-page *Nachtrag* to the 1890 catalog. Like the 1888 *Supplement* to his 1881 *Teacher's Guide*, the contents of the *Nachtrag* were substantially new and considerably expanded; spread over eighteen categories, there were pieces by forty-eight composers, twenty of them Americans. Additions to the list of now familiar figures were Beach, Bird, Hood, Lang, Paine, Rogers, and Strong; joining the less well-known names were Brewer, Dunham, Lynes, and Whiting, along with New England Conservatory teacher Benjamin Cutter (1857-1910) and German-American piano teacher Arnoldo Sartorio (1853-1936). Chamber music works included a piano trio by Cutter (op. 24) and a violin sonata by Rogers (op. 25). An important new category was the orchestral section, which listed scores and parts for Bird's Third Little Suite, op. 32; Chadwick's dramatic overture *Melpomene*; Foote's Serenade, op. 25, and Symphonic Prologue *Francesca da Rimini*, op. 24; and MacDowell's First Suite, op. 42.

Some fifteen years later, about 1908, the piano catalog alone was forty-five pages long, representing a significant increase in production for the Leipzig trade.[21] However, of the 111 different composers included, only sixteen were Americans. To the names who

---

19. For example, O. B. Brown, Charles Dennée, Philip Hale, Edward MacDowell, and George Templeton Strong.

20. Although Schmidt's Leipzig publications appeared first in Germany, many of them were also listed in his Boston catalog, as was the case with these works.

21. I am indebted to John May, of May and May, Ltd., antiquarian booksellers of Tisbury, England, for the loan of this item, *Verzeichnis Ausgewählter Klavier-Musik.*

appeared in the 1890 and 1894 catalogs—Beach, Chadwick, Dennée, Foote, Klein, Lynes, MacDowell, Sartorio, and Strong—Schmidt added Porter and three Europeans who were now part of American musical life but enjoyed big reputations in Europe as well: operetta composer Rudolf Friml (1879-1972), pianist/conductor Rudolph Ganz (1877-1972), and pianist Leopold Godowsky (1870-1938). Other new composers were Northwestern University teacher G. A. Grant-Schaefer (1872-1939), New York piano teacher Otto Hackh (1852-1917), and Lizette E. Orth (d. 1913), wife of John Orth, who had been represented in Schmidt's first major catalog. Two American piano concertos were advertised, but only in two-piano form: Beach's Concerto in C-sharp minor, op. 45, and the Ganz *Konzertstück*, op. 4.

Why did Schmidt establish this Leipzig office? Statements in the correspondence suggest that his initial purpose was to obtain manuscripts from European composers for the American market.[22] But at the same time, he saw himself as an advocate for the American composer. In the following letter Schmidt encouraged Franz Schaeffer, his commission agent in Leipzig,[23] to accept Foote's Twenty Preludes for the Piano, op. 52, for the German catalog:

> The prejudice against works by American composers will surely be overcome in time, as has already been the case with the works of MacDowell. It is always well to have a specialty; and I think that bye-and-bye, if properly introduced, some of the works of my American composers would also become a profitable investment for the Leipzig house.[24]

Further correspondence with Schaeffer describes Schmidt's efforts to gain international recognition for his American composers through advertisements in *Die Musik* and *Signale für die musikalischen Welt*.[25] Schmidt felt that performances of works abroad were also important, as demonstrated by this letter:

> Can't you in some way get a performance of MacDowell's Suite for me, somewhere on the Continent? I should be perfectly willing to give the material required for this purpose. It is really of very great importance to me to have a performance of this work procured by our Leipzig house.[26]

---

22. In a letter dated 17 April 1907, Schmidt states "the obtaining of suitable manuscripts from European composers, is after all, the most important part of the duties of the Leipzig house." APS to Henry Austin, *FL 1907-1908*, 44.

23. Schaeffer, a "Mitarbeiter" (i.e., collaborator) of Kistner, devoted himself mainly to commission accounts. In addition to Schmidt, he handled similar accounts for the Russian music publisher M. P. Belaiev, the Danish firm of Wilhelm Hansen, and most of the important foreign publishers. For this information I am indebted to Dr. Imogen Fellinger of the Staatliches Institut für Musikforschung, Preussicher Kulturbesitz, Berlin (letter to the author, 26 April 1985).

24. APS to Franz Schaeffer, 28 October 1903, *FL 1903-1905*, 114.

25. "I think, that after all, I would very much like to have a full page advertisement of MacDowell's compositions as published by us, in *Die Musik*. I would like a page facing either one of the pages of reading matter or perhaps one facing a page of the music which is inserted in this magazine. . . . In the *Signale* I would also devote some of the space for which we are contracted, for the advertisement of MacDowell's works." APS to Franz Schaeffer, 28 October 1903, *FL 1903-1905*, 114.

26. APS to Franz Schaeffer, 28 October 1903, *FL 1903-1905*, 113.

In 1907 Schmidt apparently decided that the commission arrangement through Kistner was not producing the results he wished, so he began making plans to establish his own office in Leipzig. In November he sent his trusted employee Henry Austin[27] to Europe for eight months, during which time Austin effected a change in employees and a move to different quarters.[28] Shortly after Austin's return to Boston in June 1908, Schmidt wrote the following to Max Kutschmann, manager of the new Leipzig branch:

> I would like to request you to realize that you have associated yourself with an American firm which has built up its success by fostering the productions of American composers. . . . By merely publishing works by German composers, whose works can also be had by every other German publisher, we should not likely be able to meet with any great success. The aim of every firm must be to secure something which is a specialty in its particular line. Since we have taken hold of pushing MacDowell, as he ought to have been pushed several years ago, we have succeeded in introducing his compositions even in Germany.[29]

Schmidt and His Composers

Correspondence in the Schmidt Archives portrays Arthur P. Schmidt as a person of strong principles and astute business sense. His interest in promoting American composers was balanced with an overriding concern for what would sell, a position that he regularly communicated to his composers, as seen in this thumbnail portrait by the Boston composer Mabel Daniels (1878-1971):

> Schmidt has the kindest of hearts but how he loved to bluster. He always began by bewailing the fact that certain of my choral pieces had practically no sale, the difficulties of a publisher making both ends meet, the high price of paper, etc. — but as he invariably ended by accepting anything I brought, I listened patiently.[30]

Schmidt conveys his stance on this issue particularly well in a letter to Henry Hadley:

> I think I have sufficiently proved that I am not the publisher who is working only for immediate results. There must be some equivalent, however, to me from whatever I may publish. If I publish more serious things, I am also entitled to the publication of lighter works for which other publishers can send enormous checks, . . . these would also enable me . . . to publish works for which little or no remuneration can be anticipated. . . . I also have been proud of publishing whatever I considered best, but I cannot continue to merely publish this class without receiving from the respective composers at the same time the encouragement of being offered

---

27. Henry Richter Austin (1882-1961), a London-born organist, was employed by Novello and Bote & Bock before emigrating to Boston in 1906 to work for Schmidt.

28. Schmidt's Leipzig address from 1889 to 1907 was Rabenstein Platz 5, the same address as Kistner. The 1908 move was to 16 Lindenstrasse, the same building where B. Schott's Söhne was located. Schott bought Schmidt's Leipzig catalog in 1910.

29. APS to Max Kutschmann, 9 December 1908, *FL 1908-1909*, 155.

30. Mabel Daniels, "Memoirs," Daniels papers, Folder 51, 11:4, Schlesinger Library, Radcliffe College. I am indebted to Adrienne Fried Block for this quotation.

also that which, while they may consider it to be of less value, from a musical point of view, is, on the other hand, of remunerative value to me as a publisher.[31]

Schmidt did not hesitate to point out to his composers that his commercial expertise would benefit them as well as him, as in this letter to John W. Metcalf, his best-selling song writer:

> I think that, in the end, you will find it to your advantage also, if you would leave the matter of laying out the manuscripts and fixing the retail price, to me. I like to make money, also; for that very reason consider it detrimental if retail prices are put too high. To put your little song on seven pages, would be absolutely impossible. You, yourself, would consider the spacing ridiculous if I followed your advice in that direction. The best I can do is to spread the song on four pages. I can put the poem in front of this, and make the song 50 [cents]. From a business man's point of view, I should prefer to leave the words out and to make the retail price 40 [cents].[32]

As the firm's primary, and, for a long time the sole, editor,[33] Schmidt was very careful in selecting works for publication. It is evident from his letters that he went over each piece, no matter how slight, with a fine-toothed comb. For titles with potential, he was likely to suggest changes that would make them more marketable, ranging from minor details, such as tempo and expression markings, to basic compositional concept. The following series of instructions to Metcalf illuminate this aspect of the publisher's craft:

> Of the three piano pieces I like "Remembrance" and "Repose" which I think might sell quite well. They should be phrased and fingered carefully; and aside from this, I should advise, in order to increase their practicability, to take out some of the technical difficulties, especially large stretches for the left hand, where this can be done without marring the beauty of the composition.[34]

> Yours of the 3rd together with manuscript of Easter Anthem received. While it is a very good composition, attractive in many ways, it does not strike me as being sacred in its conception. Could not the accompaniment, which is more adapted for the pianoforte, be changed to suit the organ a little better? I think that some of the solo work in the first part should be harmonized for the chorus, which at present only comes at the end.[35]

> The song "At Nightfall" [second only in popularity to "Absent"] I like very much, in one way. On the other hand, do you not think, yourself, that instead of repeating the same phrase again and again, the words, increasing in passionate sentiment in

---

31. APS to Henry Hadley, 27 October 1899, *GL 1899-1901*, 81.

32. APS to John W. Metcalf, 30 December 1901, *GL 1901-04*, 48.

33. Schmidt retained tight editorial control over his publishing until 1912, when he turned over this responsibility to Henry Austin, one of the three partners who took over the business in 1916. Reference found in a letter of APS to Rudolf Friml, 5 March 1912, *GL 1911-14*, 379.

34. APS to John W. Metcalf, 4 April 1902, *GL 1901-04*, 176.

35. APS to John W. Metcalf, 10 January 1903, *GL 1901-04*, 465.

the second verse from sentence to sentence, should also have a different setting in the music, increasing the climax unto the end?[36]

Schmidt was meticulous in the mechanical details of publishing as well, a fact well appreciated by his most discerning composers. Amy Beach described his catalogs as "very handsome in their appearance and [they] show an amount of high-class publishing which does great credit to you and to America as well."[37] Regarding her own works, she wrote "how delighted I am with the appearance of ["Summer Dreams"]. In every respect it meets my wishes most fully, and I am sure that no one could fail to appreciate the daintiness of coloring and printing."[38] Normally quite formal in her communications to Schmidt, she was unusually effusive in this card: "Dr. Beach and I are simply overjoyed at the appearance of the new compositions [unspecified]! The title pages are most beautiful each in its own way, and strikingly attractive. . . . That red is superb!"[39]

Although Schmidt was a determined and constant letter-writer (there are twenty-four bound copybooks in the Schmidt Archives at the Library of Congress), he repeatedly stressed that he would much rather meet with the composer in person to discuss matters. To Charles Dennée, he wrote:

> I am sorry that you were not able to talk the matter of these manuscripts over with me. . . . Things issued in a hurry are not always as satisfactory as I wish to have them; and for that reason I want to have the publishing done under my own personal supervision, desiring at the same time the advice of the composer on many little points which may come up in connection with the same. Past experience has again and again shown me that this is the best method, bringing the most satisfactory results to all parties.[40]

In delicate dealings with composers he was respectful and polite, even self-effacing, as in this letter to Henry Clough-Leighter (1874-1956), long-time editor for E. C. Schirmer, which accompanied the return of an unacceptable manuscript:

> I do not feel that I would be able to make a pecuniary success for you, out of this work. As you have received from me, comparatively little on the numbers published heretofore, I would not like to entirely lose your confidence in my ability as a publisher. It also is for your interest that the work should meet with success. While my judgment may be entirely at fault, I do not feel that I should be able to secure much of a remuneration from the same for you. I should be pleased to explain my opinion more fully if you desire, at our next interview.[41]

36. APS to John W. Metcalf, 12 June 1903, *GL 1901-04*, 647.
37. Amy Beach to APS, 28 November 1900, *PC*, Beach.
38. Amy Beach to APS, 16 August 1901, *PC*, Beach.
39. Amy Beach to APS, 12 October 1903, *PC*, Beach.
40. APS to Charles Dennée, 11 August 1898, *GL 1897-99*, 880.
41. APS to Henry Clough-Leighter, 27 November 1905, *GL 1904-06*, 668.

However, if Schmidt went out of his way to promote a composer, he expected to be recognized for what he had done. MacDowell's insistence on perfection was particularly annoying, judging from this letter to Schmidt's Leipzig agent:

> I also felt sorry in regard to the errors in the MacDowell advertisement. Still, it is not a matter of very grave importance after all. I think that the composer, instead of merely finding fault, should have expressed some gratification over the fact that we spent the money for a whole page advertisement of his compositions.[42]

When protecting his business interests, Schmidt expressed his views quite forcefully, especially if he felt that a composer was being unreasonable. In 1901, after Henry Hadley had won the Paderewski Prize for his Symphony no. 2, *The Four Seasons*, Schmidt agreed to publish the score of the symphony, offering to renew Hadley's contract and asking for first choice of all new compositions for the next five years. But since the financial results from the previous contract had not been all that had been hoped for, Hadley asked for a three-year contract instead.[43] Schmidt's pride was ruffled, since he was not "in the habit of dickering in matters of this kind . . . [having] made my proposition after carefully thinking it over," and saying that the poor financial results were "surely not my fault. I have not made any complaint on account of the money which I have invested; neither do I do so now."[44]

A series of letters ensued, in which Hadley made new demands. Schmidt displayed a rather hot temper, refusing to agree to any concessions and threatening twice to call off the negotiations. On the other hand, he did not want to sever his friendly relationship with Hadley, writing: "while . . . we might not be able to continue to do business with each other, we surely wish to remain friends, and therefore avoid all disagreements."[45] It was Hadley, though, who finally made the conciliatory gesture. After saying that he considered Schmidt's "offer covering the annual publication of my scores, . . . an open-hearted and liberal one," he let Schmidt know that he was surprised that "two little requests of mine . . . should have evoked the feeling shown in your letter and completely changed your attitude," a reaction that was not "in accordance with usual liberal views." Hadley's desire to get the symphony published led him to conclude "So let us have done with all talk about throwing up the sponge and quitting the ring. As for smashing contracts etc. God forbid say I. Amen say you. Let us . . . proceed to business as originally agreed upon and be good friends as ever."[46]

Within a few days Schmidt had reconsidered his decision on publishing Hadley's *Prize Symphony*, which appeared in full score the next year. Although Schmidt published no more large works by Hadley, they remained good friends, and when Hadley moved

---

42. APS to Franz Schaeffer, 3 February 1904, *FL 1903-05*, 187.

43. Henry Hadley to APS, 20 November 1901, *PC*, Hadley.

44. APS to Henry Hadley, 21 November 1901, *GL 1901-04*, 4.

45. APS to Henry Hadley, 25 November 1901, *GL 1901-04*, 7.

46. Henry Hadley to APS, 26 November 1901, *PC*, Hadley.

into new quarters in New York in 1903, Schmidt presented him with a chandelier for his studio.[47]

Conclusion

Arthur P. Schmidt's career as a publisher of large symphonic works by American composers reached its high point in the first decade of the twentieth century. Sometime between 1904 and 1908 he put out a sixteen-page *Trade List of Music Books* of several hundred titles, among them scores and parts for twelve works for orchestra.[48] Then in 1908 he brought out his last three large works—Paine's *Oedipus Tyrannus* for tenor voice, male chorus, and orchestra, op. 35,[49] MacDowell's symphonic poem *Lamia*, op. 29, and the Violin Concerto in G, op. 22, by the Polish *émigré* pianist Sigismond Stojowski (1869-1946)—while making plans to issue Beach's Piano Quintet, op. 67, the next year. Recognizing the rewards and risks of publishing three big works at once, he wrote to Austin, who was still in Leipzig: "Is not this glory enough for one year? Incidentally, enough expense?"[50]

Considering the financial depression in the United States at the time,[51] it is to Schmidt's credit that he was willing to make the necessary investment of resources to publish expensive new works. Again, writing to Austin, he said: "While there is hardly any expectation of profit in the publication of [*Lamia*]," with fifty-eight pages of manuscript, "I am very glad indeed that we can add it to our catalogue."[52] Monetary support for publication of *Oedipus Tyrannus* came from Paine's widow, who advanced Schmidt the sum of $450 for engraving of the orchestral score and autographing of parts. Schmidt considered this piece "quite an advertisement for us. . . . I shall turn over to Mrs. Paine all monies received from the sale of copies of Oedipus, until the cost of producing the same has been received."[53]

It is obvious that Schmidt regarded these works as especially significant, for he exhibited more than his usual concern for the quality of the finished product. Regarding the MacDowell and Paine works, he asked Austin:

47. Henry Hadley to APS, 26 October 1903, *PC*, Hadley.

48. Three exceptions to the almost purely American focus in Schmidt's orchestral catalog were the Serenade for Wind Instruments, op. 104, by the German pedagogue/composer Salomon Jadassohn (1831-1902), the Barcarolle for Piano and Strings, op. 60, by the Danish composer Ludwig Schytte (1848-1909), and two of the *Four Shakespearean Overtures*—"Romeo and Juliet" and "Macbeth"—by the renowned German composer Joachim Raff (1822-82), edited by MacDowell.

49. Paine's incidental music for the play *Oedipus Tyrannus* was originally published in vocal score in 1881; a revised version followed in 1895. The full orchestral score was not published until 1908.

50. APS to Henry Austin, 26 February 1908, *FL 1907-08*, 365.

51. Schmidt took a lighter than usual tone in this letter of 28 January 1908 to Henry Austin in Leipzig: "Yours . . . from Berlin, received this morning; also card from Mr. [Ludwig] Schytte [one of Schmidt's most prolific European composers]. The latter throws a very nice light on the differences in conditions; you two drinking Champagne in one of the most fashionable resorts in Berlin, while we, in our financial depression, have to be satisfied with the good old Adam's ale." *FL 1907-08*, 318.

52. APS to Henry Austin, 6 March 1908, *FL 1907-08*, 377.

53. APS to [Max Kutschmann], 6 October 1908, *FL 1908-1909*, 45-46.

... to make quite sure that the proofs will be read very carefully. I do not know whether Röder's usual proof-reader could be properly trusted with reading these works. . . . Will you be good enough to look out for this, as works of this character, of which second editions are rare, should be as correct as they possibly can be. I should, for that reason, be quite willing to pay someone for extra proofreading. Will you also request Röder's to have the score of the MacDowell "Lamia" treated very carefully; i. e. , keeping the same as clean as possible.[54]

After Schmidt's retirement from the business in 1916, publication of new orchestral and chamber music works ceased. However, the firm's traditional interest in choral music was continued by Schmidt's successors, all former employees.[55] The post-1920 *A Complete Catalogue of Octavo Music* advertised orchestral parts for seventeen large cantatas, all but three of which were by American composers. In addition to two cantatas by Beach, three by Chadwick, and one by Hadley, there were works by Brewer, Jordan, and Whiting. New names in this category included William Berwald (1864-?), head of the theory department at Syracuse University, Chicago organist Rossetter G. Cole (1866-1952), J. Lamont Galbraith (dates unknown), and German-American choral conductor Reinhold L. Herman (1849-ca. 1920).

Perhaps the best single source for answering the questions posed at the beginning of this essay is a seven-volume set of Schmidt catalogs issued in 1914, which contains the names of some 1000 individual composers.[56] A count reveals that only one-quarter of them can be identified as Americans; the remaining three-quarters of the names appear to be European. The American composers most frequently represented in these catalogs include five of the "Boston Six"—Beach, Chadwick, Foote, MacDowell, and Paine—and a rather curious mixture of major and minor names—Boston singer Eben H. Bailey,[57] Boston singer and organist Elias Blum (1881-?), Brewer, Hadley, Lang, Lynes, Metcalf, Schnecker, Boston organist Charles P. Scott (1868-1926), and San Francisco organist H. J. Stewart (1856-1932).

Although the bulk of Schmidt's publications were in small forms—for piano, voice, and chorus—it was the large American works for orchestra for which he is most remembered:

---

54. APS to Henry Austin, 16 March 1908, *FL 1907-08*, 391. C. G. Röder, of Leipzig, was one of Schmidt's primary engravers and printers.

55. Henry Austin, Harry Crosby (d. 1945), and Florence Emery (d. 1946) bought the firm in 1916, renaming it The Arthur P. Schmidt Co. They remained owners until 1959, when the catalog was sold to Summy-Birchard. It was at this time that the company records and musical manuscripts were given to the Library of Congress by David K. Sengstack, then president of Summy-Birchard.

56. This seven-volume set bears the cover title "Illustrated Catalogues," the individual titles being: Piano Music, Vocal Music, Anthems and Part Songs-Mixed Voices, Anthems and Part Songs-Womens Voices, Anthems and Part Songs-Mens Voices, Music for the Violin and Other String Instruments, Organ Music. However, since Schmidt dropped titles from his catalogs over the years, these volumes do not represent a complete listing of all composers published by Schmidt.

57. The only biographical reference that was found for Bailey was a death notice for his wife, Emma H., also a singer, that appeared in *Musical America* 44, no. 5 (20 November 1926): 31.

Beach:	Symphony in E minor (*Gaelic*), op. 32
Bird:	Third Little Suite, op. 32
Chadwick:	Symphony no. 2 in B-flat
	Symphony no. 3 in F
	Dramatic Overture, *Melpomene*
Foote:	Symphonic Prologue, *Francesca da Rimini*, op. 24
	Serenade for String Orchestra, op. 25
	Suite in D minor for Orchestra, op. 36
Hadley:	Symphony no. 2 in F minor, *The Four Seasons*, op. 30
MacDowell:	First Suite for Orchestra, op. 42
	Symphonic Poem, *Lamia*, op. 29
Paine:	Symphony no. 2 in A (*Spring*)
	Oedipus Tyrannus, op. 35
Stojowski:	Violin Concerto in G, op. 22

These are the titles—the likes of which rarely, if ever, appear in the catalogs of other American music publishers of the day—that brought Schmidt fame as the "pioneer publisher of American music."

21

Abigail Stone

Randall Shinn

The story begins in an American town in 1908. Elias Stone is a puritanical minister whose daughter Abigail has an extraordinary voice. A visiting soprano discovers Abby's voice and offers to help her begin an operatic career. Elias vehemently opposes this. Later Elias catches Abigail at a dance, and after a public argument she leaves homes to study with her mentor. She becomes a successful opera singer. After twenty years of silence, Elias asks her to visit. This meeting becomes a bitter clash, and Elias has a stroke. When Abigail visits him again, Elias no longer remembers her existence. Surrounding this tragic core are comic and romantic subplots.

The libretto and the music for the work use diverse elements. The libretto includes quotes from the Bible, Walt Whitman's *Leaves of Grass*, nursery rhymes, hymns, and patriotic songs. The characters span a gamut of classes, from banker to janitor. The music contains quotes from church hymns, nursery tunes, and patriotic songs, and the style encompasses popular music and classical music.

If he were real, Elias would no doubt be appalled by this work. From his puritanical viewpoint anything that is not useful, productive, sacred, or morally uplifting is frivolous and worthless. He would say that frivolous pastimes distract us from serious, meaningful pursuits, are potentially sinful. For the sake of our morals, Elias would want concerts to be pious, sober affairs that feed our souls properly spiritual music—music elevated above the commonplace.

His puritanical viewpoint requires all worthwhile activities to have a serious, moral purpose. I find this viewpoint repressive and unjustifiable. Who says life is serious? As Joseph Campbell said, "not one shred of evidence exists that life is serious." Who says pleasurable, sensuous experience is worthless? When Alexander Baumgarten introduced the term "aesthetics" he sought to establish a science of sensuous knowledge, whose aim was beauty, as opposed to logic, whose aim was truth. For many people, experiencing beauty is crucial to the meaning of life.

My opera is too worldly to please Elias, tied as it is to ideals of sensuous beauty and theatrical entertainment. Many traditions of the theater make room for both eloquence and vulgarity, for both the lofty and the commonplace (some examples are Shakespeare, *commedia dell'arte*, Mozart, and Monteverdi). This opera follows that tradition, and ragtime rhythms have just as much place as impassioned arias. Abigail likes to dance, and dancing requires music whose attractions are openly physical. Physicality ("the world's body" in John Crowe Ransom's phrase) is what Elias most fears and despises, in himself and in the world.

As composer and librettist I use whatever material I need to tell the story. The aim is to be effective in the theater. Portions of the tale are sad, and there I wear a sad mask and write sad music. Other parts are comic, and there I wear a smiling mask. In one sense Elias need not worry, I will speak his part as "truthfully" as any other. On the other hand he is right, all this theatrical make-believe is aimed at earthly beauty and secular entertainment. These aims may be dear to me, but they stand in opposition to his puritanical morality.

Abigail Stone

ACT I

Scene One

An American city in 1908. The interior of a church.
Reverend Elias Stone and the church choir are onstage.

Randall Shinn

22

Community Theater, *Caliban by the Yellow Sands,* and Arthur Farwell

John Graziano

It was "a cloudless, almost flawless night"[1] in late May 1916 when, at 8:45 o'clock, a chorus of bugles announced to more than ten thousand people at the Stadium of the College of the City of New York (later known as Lewisohn Stadium) the start of the rescheduled first performance of *Caliban by the Yellow Sands.*

Caliban was one of a series of community masques and pageants conceived by Percy MacKaye (1875-1956);[2] its chief aim was to bring poetry and drama to large community participant groups, while uniting drama, art, and music into a unified artistic production. The playwright explained that he chose to write in this genre because "the masque is a poem primarily intended to be heard rather than to be read . . . . Poetry appeals essentially to the ear, and is an art of the spoken word . . . A masque is a poem that can be visualized and acted." MacKaye described his masques as a counter-balance to the trends of theatrical productions at the turn of the century:

> [With] the stage tending more toward visualization, and poetry tending more and
> more toward the spoken word, where shall we look for the co-ordinating

---

1. *New York Times,* 25 May 1916. The planned premiere, scheduled for the previous evening, was postponed due to rain (*New York Times,* 24 May 1916, 11).

2. For additional details on Percy MacKaye, the MacKaye family, and their contributions to American arts and letters, see Jane P. Franck, "*Caliban* at Lewisohn Stadium, 1916," in *Shakespeare Encomium,* ed. Anne Paolucci, City College Papers, 1 (New York: City College, 1964), 154-68. I am most grateful to Barbara Dunlap, archivist at the Morris Raphael Cohen Library of the City College, for her assistance in providing me with the library's materials on *Caliban.*

development? I think we shall find it in the community masque. The community masque draws out of the un-labored and untrammeled resources of our national life its inspiration and its theme. It requires our young poets to get closely in touch with our national life, with our history and with contemporary-parer attitudes and ideals.[3]

To achieve a masque of distinction, MacKaye assembled a team of prominent artists to work with him. These included Arthur Farwell, then director of the New York Music School Settlement and an active force in the encouragement of community participation in musical events,[4] who was commissioned to write and assemble the musical numbers; the famous Austrian-born architect, interior decorator, and theatrical designer (best remembered today for his *Ziegfeld Follies* productions) Josef Urban (1872-1933), who devised the spectacular lighting effects and the stage set for the "Outer Structure"; and Robert Edmond Jones (1887-1954), hailed on Broadway in 1915 for his revolutionary fluid stage sets and brilliant costumes, who designed the sets for the "Inner Scenes" and costumes.[5] MacKaye's original plan for *Caliban* called for 2400 performers; some 1500, including about thirty professional actors, a chorus of 500, and an orchestra of eighty actually participated during the presentation.

Caliban was the result of two years of planning. It was intended to serve as the culmination of a great national Shakespearean celebration; in the Greater New York community, the celebration would involve all constituents of the population.[6] The masque was structured to serve two goals: the commemoration of the three-hundredth anniversary of William Shakespeare's death, and the furtherance of an aesthetic concept that MacKaye envisioned as "part of a movement which shall bring poetry to the service of the entire community, which shall make poetry democratic, in the best sense of the word, and that the result of this movement will be to create conditions likely to produce out of the soil of America a great renascence of the drama."[7]

MacKaye hoped that the community masque would allow poetry to reach a larger audience. He told Joyce Kilmer that in St. Louis, where one of his earlier masques had been given in 1914, after the masque had been produced,

---

3. *New York Times*, 14 May 1916, 13-14, Sunday Magazine interview with poet Joyce Kilmer.

4. In the appendix to the published edition of the masque, MacKaye notes that Farwell "has devoted probably more attention than any other American composer to this community type of musical art" (p. 157). See also a discussion of Farwell's interest in community music and pageantry in Evelyn Davis Culbertson, *He Heard America Singing: Arthur Farwell, Composer and Crusading Music Educator* (Metuchen, N.J.: Scarecrow, 1992), 165-84.

5. For additional information on the contributions of Urban and Jones to *Caliban,* see Franck.

6. The program for *Caliban* lists seven pages of "Supplementary Celebrations." These included neighborhood pageants (*As You Like It* in Flushing), sermons (Temple Israel of Harlem), public and private school presentations (scenes from *Merchant of Venice,* performed by students at Public School 75, Brooklyn), lectures ("Shakespeare's Relation to Modern Thought and Art" at the American Museum of Natural History), and various other miscellaneous groups and presentations.

7. *New York Times*, 14 May 1916, interview with Joyce Kilmer.

8. Ibid.

nearly every high school boy and girl in the town was writing masques. . . . I read my . . . masque before assemblies of ministers, in negro high schools, before clubs of advertising men, at I.W.W. meetings—before men of all conditions of life and shades of opinion. It afforded them a sort of spiritual and intellectual meeting place; it gave them a common interest. Surely that is a democratic function.[8]

The four principal characters of *Caliban*—Prospero, Ariel, Miranda, and Caliban—are drawn from *The Tempest*; Setebos, who is Caliban's father, is also a protagonist, represented in this production by a forty-foot puppet. The dramaturgical structure of the masque is quite complex. It is constructed from an alternation of "Outer" and "Inner" structures. The "Outer Structure" consists of the three stages on which the participants perform original text by MacKaye. In the "Inner Structure" sections, MacKaye quotes text from various Shakespeare plays. Chart 22.1 reproduces the diagram of the "Inner Structure" given by MacKaye in the appendix of the published text.

The Prologue sets the action for the theme of the masque: "the slow education of mankind through the influences of co-operative art, that is, of the theatre in its full social scope."[9] Each of the three acts includes excerpts from Shakespeare's plays,[10] while the three interludes feature the community participants in historical pantomimes. In the Epilogue, all the participants join: "Amid the assembled thousands, who kneel down with him, Caliban kneels on the earth. There, with all the others, he raises his arms toward Shakespeare with a great gesture of aspiration, while the invisible choirs burst into song."[11]

Although it is beyond the scope of this essay to discuss the complex plot of *Caliban* in detail, MacKaye's description of the "First Action" from Interlude II[12] can serve as a demonstration of his attempt to introduce meaningful historical concepts as well as well-known historical figures into a larger theatrical context:

FIRST ACTION: GERMANIC
COMMUNITY ACTORS [150]
Comprise
Participants [150]
Individuals [2]

Forerunner [Einschreier]	Out-crier [Ausschreier]
Pantomime Actors [6]	*Musicians* [10]
Doctor Faustus	Ten Pipers
An Apprentice	*Symbolic Group* [22]
Lucifer	Doctors [8]
Two Devils	Priests [4]

---

9. Program for *Caliban*, 17.

10. The Inner Scenes in act 1 are taken from *Antony and Cleopatra, Troilus and Cressida*, and *Julius Caesar*; in act 2 from *Hamlet, Romeo and Juliet, Merchant of Venice*, and *Winter's Tale*; in act 3 from *As You Like It, Merry Wives of Windsor*, and *King Henry the Fifth*. A few lines from several plays are used in other parts of the masque. The Inner Scenes represent visions in Prospero's mind and are always seen on the Cloudy Curtain stage.

11. Program, 24.

12. Appendix, *Caliban by the Yellow Sands*, 184-87.

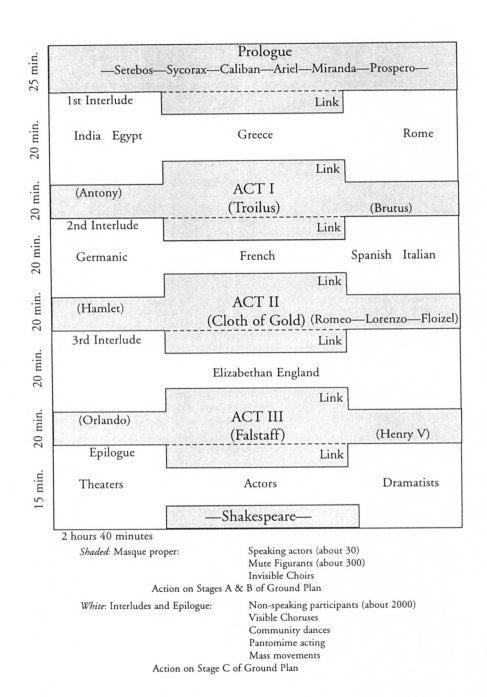

25 min.	Prologue —Setebos—Sycorax—Caliban—Ariel—Miranda—Prospero—		
20 min.	1st Interlude	Link	
	India Egypt	Greece	Rome
20 min.	(Antony)	Link ACT I (Troilus)	(Brutus)
20 min.	2nd Interlude	Link	
	Germanic	French	Spanish Italian
20 min.	(Hamlet)	Link ACT II (Cloth of Gold)	(Romeo—Lorenzo—Floizel)
20 min.	3rd Interlude	Link	
		Elizabethan England	
20 min.	(Orlando)	Link ACT III (Falstaff)	(Henry V)
15 min.	Epilogue	Link	
	Theaters	Actors	Dramatists
		—Shakespeare—	

2 hours 40 minutes

Shaded: Masque proper: Speaking actors (about 30)
Mute Figurants (about 300)
Invisible Choirs
Action on Stages A & B of Ground Plan

White: Interludes and Epilogue: Non-speaking participants (about 2000)
Visible Choruses
Community dances
Pantomime acting
Mass movements
Action on Stage C of Ground Plan

Chart 22.1. Community Masque, "Caliban," Inner Structure.

Helena

Artists [9]
Melancholia [1]

Citizens of Nüremberg [110]
Men and Women [110]
Apprentices [40]

THEME

On a street of Nüremberg, in their Shrovetide festival, a band of Apprentices enact, on a wheeled stage, a pantomime scene from an early version of "Doctor Faustus." Time: Sixteenth century.

ACTION

At Prospero's final words in Act I, the playing of pipes is heard at the right Interlude Gates, where enter a band of Apprentices, accompanying a wheeled street-stage, drawn by donkeys with bells and set with a three-fold scene of Earth, Heaven, and Hell. Some of the Apprentices are masked, some disguised as fools. They enter, singing an old German folk song, and march to the centre of the ground-circle (between the altar and the south entrance), where the stage pauses. Before them has hastened a forerunner (Einschreier), blowing a horn and shouting: "Schauspieler! Doctor Faustus!"

Along with them, Pipers accompany their singing. Behind them follow folk of Nüremberg, gaping peasants and merry-making young people.

From the left gate, meanwhile [in obscure light], enters a graver group, clad symbolically as Doctors of Learning, Priests, and Artists, accompanying another wheeled vehicle, the stage of which is wholly curtained from view.

These stop at some distance from the former group, and look on from a place of shadow.

And now, where the first stage has paused in a place of brighter glow, the Actors appear and begin their pantomime.

Doctor Faustus appears on the Middle Stage, Earth. There, amid his astronomical instruments, he greets the gaping crowd and points a telescope toward the place of Heaven. Suddenly a comet flashes above the stage. An Apprentice inquires the reason. Doctor Faustus explains it by revealing its two fathers—the Sun and the Moon, which now appear shining simultaneously in Heaven.

At this sorcery, Lucifer comes from Hell, signifies to Faustus that his hour has come, and that he must follow him. Faustus begs a last wish, which Lucifer reluctantly grants. He begs to see once more his beloved Helena of Troy.

Then in Heaven appears Helena, who comes to Faustus on Earth and embraces him. But now Lucifer—summoning two tailed devils with pitchforks—bids them drag Faustus from the arms of Helena, who flees back to Heaven, disappearing there, as Faustus is prodded and haled to the up-bursting flames of Hell, amid the exultant laughter of Lucifer.

At this finale, the stage and its audience moves off through the left gate, while the graver Symbolic Group—crossing right at deep shadow—pauses at the centre.

There, for a moment, the curtains of their pageant stage are drawn, revealing—in mystic light—a dim-glowing tableau of Albrecht Durer's Melancholia.

As this pales into darkness, the Group with its curtained stage moves vaguely off, and vanishes through the right gate of the Interlude.

In an article published before the premiere, Arthur Farwell described his varied contributions to *Caliban*:

> Music had to be written for the action of the masque proper, for the inner-stage scenes and for the interludes. . . . The music I have written . . . consists of every conceivable form. Most of the actors' words have to be spoken to the accompaniment of orchestral music. Then there is choral singing, purely orchestral compositions, songs, and mere cries or entrance fanfares. In the case of the music for the interludes this is used merely to accompany the pantomime for the massed crowds before the Greek stage.[13]

Farwell (as well as MacKaye) strongly emphasized in his public statements that Caliban was not conceived as an Elizabethan masque; Farwell also pointedly noted that his music was not intended to be "archaeologically correct," and that he had "striven to write modern music for this modern theme."[14]

In the program Farwell cites the characteristic musical themes that represent the chief characters. Prospero and Setebos are mirror images of the same idea. Prospero's theme, a trumpet call that descends an octave and returns, is in harmony with the higher spheres, but in dissonance with the lower (see ex. 22.1a); Setebos's theme is the opposite, in harmony with the lower, in dissonance with the upper (see ex. 22.1b). Both motives are bitonal; Prospero's pits the C-major call against a B-major "lower sphere," but Setebos's pits the same call, now inverted, against a C-sharp minor "higher sphere," respelled in Farwell's example as D-flat, E (natural), A-flat. The mirror image extends to the rhythm of the two spheres, which is also exchanged, from ♩♩ to . Although the programme examples show both calls in C major, in the actual music (ex. 22.1c), they appear at the tritone, making the tonal contrast even greater. Caliban's theme (ex. 22.2) "is uncouth, boisterous and passionate," while Miranda's (ex. 22.3) has a "flowing and graceful character."[15] Farwell also gives incipits for three choral pieces that are prominent in the masque, and mentions two large numbers, both of which include "Setebos" choruses.

Example 22.1. Prospero's motive (a); Setebos's motive (b).

---

13. *New York Tribune*, 14 May 1916.

14. Ibid.

15. The brief excerpts given by Farwell are all that survives of these orchestral numbers. The orchestration chosen by Farwell for *Caliban* in these outdoor performances consists of six trombones, eight trumpets, six tubas, eight horns, with augmented woodwinds including six clarinets, and strings (*Musical America*, 3 June 1916, 4). Three songs were arranged from the choruses by Farwell in 1917; they are orchestrated for conventional orchestra and are the only orchestrations of *Caliban* that appear to survive.

Example 22.1c. Excerpt from "War."

Of the music written for *Caliban*, only the choral parts published by G. Schirmer in 1916 appear to be extant. Orchestral pieces, as well as some introductory sections to choral numbers, such as the Prelude to Ariel's Choirs (no. 2), were not published; the full score of the original production has disappeared.[16]

The surviving music for *Caliban* suggests that the forty-four year old Farwell was synthesizing various harmonic influences. In "Come unto These Yellow Sands," and other

Example 22.2. Caliban's theme.

Example 22.3. Miranda's theme.

16. See Brice Farwell, *A Guide to the Music of Arthur Farwell and to the Microfilm Collection of His Work* (Briarcliff Manor, N.Y.: Estate of Arthur Farwell, 1972).

Example 22.4. Opening of "Come unto These Yellow Sands."

pieces that fall into Prospero's or Ariel's sphere, one notes MacDowell-inspired chromatic harmonies and voice-leading (see ex. 22.4).

The music associated with Setebos, on the other hand, is clearly influenced by Debussy and Scriabin (see ex. 22.5). In these numbers, Farwell seems particularly drawn to altered seventh chords (meas. 13-16), parallelisms (meas. 1 and 2, etc.), and chords built on fourths (meas. 1 and 7). There is often a resolution to an implied dominant-seventh chord, but the expected tonic chord does not often follow (see meas. 4 and 10).

Example 22.5. Excerpt from "Roman Orgy and Vision of the Cross."

While every extant number retains a key signature, and is nominally tonal in design, the music given in ex. 22.5, which is in G minor, demonstrates Farwell's migration from traditional harmonic progressions.

Another number that illustrates Farwell's harmonic style and his compositional technique is the chorus "Spirits of Ariel and Setebos in Conflict" from the Prologue. It is labeled "Canonic Chorus-Mixed Voices" (see ex. 22.6). An orchestral introduction using Caliban's theme gives little indication of a tonic goal. At meas. 11, D appears as a pedal, indicating a dominant function. But in meas. 17, the addition of the flatted fifth disguises that chord's role as a D-major dominant-seventh. The canon begins in meas. 18, harmonized by a G-major chord. The progression that follows, however, is anything but traditional. After the opening chord, Farwell goes, at two measure intervals, to F-major, C-major, and B-minor chords. At meas. 28, the third phrase begins once again on a G-major chord. At the end of the fourth phrase, there is a tenuous cadence on G major (meas. 36-37), but it quickly disappears in favor of E minor (meas. 38-39). The number concludes with an E-minor chord, which is not, however, achieved through an expected cadential progression (meas. 40-42).

The two-voice canon itself is also of interest. Rhythmically, Farwell maintains a strict repetition of pattern. Intervallically, however, he has composed a tonal, rather than real, canon. He starts the first phrase at the interval of a major second (meas. 18, 20), but at the second phrase (meas. 22, 24) the interval of imitation is reduced to a minor second, only to return to the major second at the end of the phrase (meas. 27, 29). The third phrase starts at a perfect fourth (meas. 28, 30), but switches to a minor third (meas. 30, 32). The final phrase starts once again at a perfect fourth, but through the use of a chromatic alteration in the men's part at measures 36 and 38, the canon again closes at a minor third. These intervallic changes do not appear to be mandated by localized tonal considerations; rather, they seem to have been introduced by Farwell to give the canon an overall tonal ambiguity. To judge from this number and the other surviving choruses, it is evident that the choral parts are effectively written, and one can imagine that the 500 amateur singers (of whom only 350 could perform in each performance) sang their numbers enthusiastically.

At various points in *Caliban,* Farwell briefly uses a whole-tone scale, a constructed eight-tone scale, and other alternate melodic structures. He also includes an Omaha Indian melody, as "recorded by Alice Fletcher," to serve as a substitute for an Egyptian Priest's chant in the first interlude, as well as the Gregorian chant "Vexilla regis prodeunt."

Farwell's music for *Caliban,* with its altered chords, parallel harmonies, and unclear tonal areas, is indeed the modern music (in turn-of-the-century American eclectic style) that the composer had striven to write. But within its modern style, there are enough references to earlier styles of Romantic music that audiences could respond to it positively.

* * *

The spectacle of the masque was an important part of MacKaye, Urban, and Jones's plan. The music, however, was from the start intended to be "invisible." The chorus and orchestra, led by Louis Koemmenich,[17] were never seen by the audience. They performed in a box-like structure that was built above the Inner Stage. The sound was projected from

---

17. Koemmenich (1866-1922), who was director of the Oratorio Society of New York, led the large chorus, including many members of his chorus, as well as the orchestra, which was recruited largely from the Metropolitan Opera.

Example 22.6. "Spirits of Ariel and Setebos in Conflict."

Example 6, continued.

the box and, according to the reviews, could be heard even when the music was very quiet, throughout the stadium, which for many in the audience was almost two city blocks (about 400 feet) away.[18] In fact, several reviewers pointedly noted that although much of the dialogue was unintelligible, the music was always audible. One reviewer went so far as to suggest that audiences should see *Caliban* twice, once during the day with the script in hand, and once in the evening to see the spectacle.[19]

Most of the reviews lauded MacKaye's concept; many reported on Farwell's music in generally positive terms:

> The music itself was of a breadth and dignity fitting to the spirit of the performance. . . . In general the music provided a subdued background which heightens the significance of the scenes as they proceed. . . . [The musical numbers] are perhaps not strikingly individual in themselves, but their total is such as to make the musical setting a distinct merit of the whole production.[20]

> It would not be the truth to say [Farwell] has written a score distinguished by invention, imagination and procedure, but he has written one that at a single hearing seemed serviceable above most such pageant pieces . . . if he seldom impresses the detached ear, he is always appropriate to the moment in the masque, . . . [and] steadily fulfills the chief necessity, usually overlooked, of an accompaniment to such a pageant.[21]

> Mr. Farwell's music was of invaluable assistance. It is not great music, of course, in any sense of the word. But it is appropriate and dignified. The effect . . . was to lend mystery and impressiveness to the spectacle. At times it was extremely beautiful and even in its most commonplace moments it was expressive.[22]

The most extended review appeared in *Musical America*, where Herbert Peyser discussed Farwell's music in detail:

> The music . . . was singularly excellent in that it accomplished its composer's purposes and proved itself worthy of all esteem on the basis of its intrinsic qualities. Mr. Farwell understands the essentials, the potencies and limitations of community masque music as no other musician in America to-day. . . . He has here surpassed his earlier experiments not only in general felicity of result, but in boldness of dimension. . . . It is modern without subtle complexities and almost unfailingly direct. . . . Modern effects of powerful dissonance Mr. Farwell utilizes to enforce an

---

18. A reviewer noted the "the designer of the stage and auditorium [Josef Urban] evidently possesses a fine working knowledge of the elusive science of acoustics, for the ease with which the music was heard over the huge space was quite remarkable. While the actors had to use full voice to make themselves heard, the orchestra and the chorus suffered no such handicap. They were able to indulge in soft effects which carried perfectly, and their power of expression was thus considerably heightened." *New York Times*, 25 May 1916, 12.

19. *Musical Advance*, 2 June 1916.

20. *New York Times*, 25 May 1916.

21. *New York Evening Transcript*, 27 May 1916, part 3.

22. Louis Sherwin, *New York Globe*, 25 May 1916.

obvious or symbolic dramatic situation—as in the chorus of conflicting spirits of *Prospero* and *Setebos*—the opposing spiritual principles—an interesting canon [see ex. 22.6], though the unwary hearer may miss the contrapuntal effect in the open air. . . . Most of the music has been orchestrated in such fashion that it carries readily in the open.[23]

The influential music critic Henry E. Krehbiel, however, writing in the *New York Tribune* almost two weeks before the premiere of *Caliban*, called into question many of Farwell's and MacKaye's aesthetic assumptions. After suggesting that MacKaye was attempting to write a play more ambitious than Goethe's *Faust*, which would "exploit pretty much everything in the world of dramatic art and its accessories from the earliest historical times down to to-day, and to enlist for the eye, ear and mind a great many things which belong wholly to the sphere of learned speculation," Krehbiel sarcastically continues "It is so tremendous a mouthful that it will never be masticated, still less digested, by either authors, performers, readers, or hearers."

Following a brief description of the basic philosophical thrust of MacKaye's masque, Krehbiel moved on to a consideration of Farwell's contribution. Since the masque had not yet been heard, Krehbiel probably used a copy of the piano-vocal score as the basis for his article. He noted that the music associated with the third interlude (the Elizabethan England pantomime) would be appropriate to the period, and was not subject to "the anachronism which runs riot everywhere else."[24] Krehbiel was particularly annoyed that Farwell had composed new music for some of Shakespeare's lyrics rather than use works by earlier composers: "Mr. Farwell might have found settings much more beautiful than his own in the works of composers who wrote when Shakespeare might still have been a living memory." After complaining that Farwell misunderstood the intent of Shakespeare's lyric to "Come unto These Yellow Sands," Krehbiel cites Farwell's settings of "As the Bee Sucks" and "Under the Greenwood Tree"; of the latter song he says: "There is a setting of this exquisite song as old as 1687, but Mr. Farwell preferred to make one of his own for two-part men's chorus. We forbear to institute a comparison." Krehbiel's negative assessment of the war music (exx. 22.1c, 4, and 5 above) as "dynamic and intervallic rudeness," is diametrically opposite from Peyser's laudatory analysis; generally, he dismisses Farwell's effort entirely.

The basis for Krehbiel's criticisms of Farwell seems to have been connected to his perception that since *Caliban* was designed to teach its lesson by historical methods, it was incumbent upon its creators to reproduce, wherever possible, the music that was appropriate to the historical period of the scene. He apparently refused to accept Farwell's (and MacKaye's) statements that *Caliban* was not an Elizabethan masque but a modern one.

---

23. *Musical America*, 3 June 1916, 3-4. Peyser notes that Farwell was assisted in the orchestrations by the composers W. H. Humiston, Israel Amter, Deems Taylor, and Chester Ide.

24. This music is not included in the piano-vocal score. The *Tribune*, however, had featured an article in which Cecil Sharp, who is listed as arranger of Interlude III, discussed the contributions of the New York Center of the English Folk Dance Society (14 May 1916).

In spite of Krehbiel's objections, *Caliban* was a great success. Isadora Duncan happened to be in New York on her way to South America; she was so interested that she volunteered to interpolate several of her dances at every performance.[25] Audiences filled Lewisohn Stadium for each performance. The final performance was to have occurred on May 29, but the demand for tickets was so great that the run was extended through June 6. Excursion trains brought spectators from as far as Boston and various points in New Jersey.[26] Although President Wilson was invited to attend the opening performance, he was not able to be present. He did, however, send a note to MacKaye that was printed in the *Times*. Buoyed by their success, MacKaye and Farwell collaborated the following year on *The Christmas Tree*, and Farwell continued to write other community music pieces during the next decade.

In the early years of this century, American creative artists finally began to feel that they had shaken the yoke of European culture. They envisioned works that would demonstrate the uniqueness of American thought. Percy MacKaye and others worked to bring culture to the masses, to make the arts, in his words, more "democratic." *Caliban by the Yellow Sands* was intended as the work that would generate a national interest in community theater. While MacKaye's earlier masques had been successful, their subjects were not of international importance. The celebration of the tercentenary of Shakespeare's death, however, was an event that would generate great interest, even on the part of the masses. And what better way was there to educate them than by a community theater presentation that integrated drama, music, dance, and pageantry in the masque?

> It was a real—not a typical—New York audience that saw the first performance of the Masque last night. . . . People from the shops and factories, many of them, arrived as early as 6:30, bringing their suppers with them. From that time on limousines, taxicabs, trolleys, Fifth Avenue buses and the subway kept a steady stream of patrons coming.[27]

In contrast to Krehbiel's impressions, an editorial in the *New York Tribune*, "Is New York a Community?," offered a positive assessment:

> Whatever the effect for the future, the present demonstration of a real and existing community spirit is altogether noteworthy. . . . The success of "Caliban" is unmistakable. . . . All the arts speak in the stadium, and all with a vigor and freshness to be proud of.[28]

---

25. *New York Herald*, 24 May 1916. Duncan is not mentioned in any reviews I have seen.

26. *New York Sun*, 29 May 1916.

27. *New York Times*, 25 May 1916.

28. *New York Tribune*, 26 May 1916.

While *Caliban* was not the financial success its backers had projected,[29] and while its text may not always have been audible and the concept of community masque may not have led to MacKaye's hoped-for "renascence of the drama," it succeeded in bringing together in performance many diverse groups of the city, and, as such, might be considered one of the first major multicultural events of this century.[30]

29. An article in the September 1916 *New York Review* noted that, in spite of receipts of $150,000, there was an unexpected $25,000 deficit. The hoped-for profit that was to be turned over to City College for a permanent Shakespeare memorial statue was not available, and additionally, the masque organizers were sued by the College for over $6,000 to repair the sod in the stadium. True to form, the deficit was blamed on the expense of the orchestra, which cost $12,000.

30. Among the many groups participating in the masque were the Neighborhood Players of the Henry Street Settlement, the Pan-Hellenic Union in America, the German University League, the Alliance Française, the MacDowell Club with the Washington Square Players, the Band of the Hebrew Orphan Asylum, the New York Center of the English Folk Dance Society, and various area colleges, including Vassar College, Lehigh University, and Rutgers University.

23

The *Musical Quarterly* and American Music

Karl Kroeger

The *Musical Quarterly* has long been considered one of the musical world's most respected journals. Its reappearance after a hiatus of two years (1987-88) is a cause for rejoicing, for, although journals devoted to serious discussions of musical topics are now fairly common, we can still ill-afford to lose one with the long tradition, high reputation, and broad appeal that has characterized the *Musical Quarterly* over the years.

Founded in 1915 by Rudolf Schirmer, president of the music publishing firm G. Schirmer, Inc., the *Musical Quarterly* was intended as a "contribution to music in America."[1] With the selection of Oscar Sonneck, then Chief of the Music Division of the

---

1. Oscar G. Sonneck, "After Ten Years," *Musical Quarterly* 10, no. 4 (October 1924): 459. Sonneck offered the following account of the origin of the *Musical Quarterly*:

In "a survey of music in America" read before the Schola Cantorum of New York, in 1913, I casually averred that so far every attempt to produce and permanently maintain a musical magazine of the highest type, such as flourish in Europe, had failed in America. Several years later I heard that this remark had challenged the attention of the late Rudolph E. Schirmer. At any rate, early in 1914 Mr. Schirmer visited me at the Library of Congress. In the course of conversation, and tactfully avoiding any reference to that remark, Mr. Schirmer declared the time ripe for the realization of his ambition and that of his brother Gustave, whose premature death had occurred in 1907, to publish as an integral part of the labors of the house of Schirmer a musical magazine. Evidently neither Gustave nor Rudolph Schirmer, . . . both of whom, as highly cultured men of affairs, saw in the profession of music publishers something higher than a merely money-making activity, desired for this particular purpose a "house organ." Indeed, Mr. Rudolph Schirmer left no doubt that he thought of this particular magazine much more as a contribution to music in America, in memory of his brother, than as a commercial enterprise.

Library of Congress and one of America's most perceptive musical scholars, as the journal's first editor, Schirmer demonstrated that he wanted to produce a journal of the highest standards, not just a house organ to hawk the wares of his publishing firm. Through two world wars and the Great Depression, the financial and philosophical commitment of G. Schirmer, to the *Musical Quarterly* was unswerving. Only in 1985, when G. Schirmer itself stood in great financial difficulty, did this support falter, and the *Quarterly* was taken over by the publisher Macmillan. Never a money-maker, the *Quarterly* must have been a drain on the resources of its new sponsor, and in 1986 the decision was made to discontinue the journal. In 1989, it reappeared, now published by Oxford University Press.

This break in the *Quarterly*'s continuity offers a convenient juncture at which to look back over its publishing history and assess some of its contributions to music. Seventy-two years of uninterrupted service to musical scholarship is an enviable record that few journals, domestic or foreign, can match. This essay will focus on the *Quarterly*'s commitment to publishing articles concerned with American music.[2] The founding editor, Oscar Sonneck, was the first music historian to recognize the need for and value of systematic historical studies in American music. His pioneering work in bibliography, musical sources, and historiography is still today a foundation stone of serious research in early American music. One might expect, then, that the *Musical Quarterly* would at least welcome if not emphasize articles on American musical topics. But before focusing on the specific theme of this essay, a brief look at the publication history of the *Quarterly* will provide a context for the discussion.

Sonneck edited the journal from 1915 until his death in 1928. He was succeeded by Carl Engel, a frequent contributor to the *Quarterly*, who had also followed Sonneck as Chief of the Music Division of the Library of Congress. While Engel did not share Sonneck's intense concern for early American music, he was a cultured man and an eloquent writer, whose broad interests encompassed many musical areas.[3] Engel's tenure as the *Quarterly*'s editor lasted from 1929 until his death in 1944. He was followed briefly by Gustave Reese, who had been associate editor and business manager during the later years of Engel's editorship. Reese, who taught at New York University and also served G. Schirmer as publications director at the time, edited the *Quarterly* for only one year. He was followed by Paul Henry Lang, whose twenty-eight and a half years as editor of the journal (1945-73) is not only the longest duration for a single editor, but also the last extended period of editorial continuity the *Quarterly* has seen. Neither Reese nor Lang were particularly interested in American music, but as music historians as well as editors, they were concerned with quality research in any musical area and largely continued the traditions established by Sonneck and Engel.

2. By American music is meant the music of, musicians in, and musical topics concerned with the United States. An "Americana Index to *The Musical Quarterly*, 1915-1957," by Hazel Gertrude Kinscella, was published in *Journal of Research in Music Education* 6, no. 2 (fall 1958): 5-144.

3. A sampling of Engel's musical interests in found in his collection of essays *Discords Mingled* (New York: Alfred A. Knopf, 1931). Among fifteen articles in this book, only one—on jazz—deals with American music. The rest are commentaries on European historical subjects and aesthetics.

The next thirteen years saw a succession of four editors of the journal. Lang was followed by Christopher Hatch (1974-77),[4] who was succeeded by Joan Peyser (1977-84). Paul Wittke came on as "acting editor" for three issues in 1984,[5] before the editorial reins of the journal were taken over by Eric Salzman. Salzman introduced himself to his readership as "neither a musicologist nor a theorist," but "a composer (of music theater primarily) and a writer (of words for music as well as words about music)."[6] Salzman was editor for two years before the journal's collapse in 1986, and returned to edit the revived *Quarterly* in 1989.

* * *

In a prospectus sent out in October 1914, Sonneck outlined the editorial objectives of the *Quarterly*:

> The appeal of the magazine will be to cultured music lovers and musicians who take an interest in more or less scholarly discussions of problems that affect the past, present and future of the art of music. It is not to be a magazine devoted to the technical or professional interests of the music teacher, virtuoso and musical antiquarian.[7]

In an editorial foreword in the first issue of the *Quarterly*, Sonneck elaborated further on the journal's objectives.

> Publisher and Editor are agreed not to throttle THE MUSICAL QUARTERLY at birth with a "program." Whatever they propose under this head, has received publicity through the Prospectus.
> And the "policy" of the magazine? That may best be defined by this subtle alteration of a good old doctrine: Audietur et altera pars.[8]
> It follows that the Editor does not commit himself either in this or in subsequent numbers to the opinions expressed by contributors. THE MUSICAL QUARTERLY will be their forum, not his.
> If contributors view the world of music from an angle opposed to his own, so much the better.[9]

As Sonneck conceived the magazine, its purpose was to publish good, thoughtful articles on a wide range of musical subjects. These subjects were to be in no way limited, but no special attention was to be given to any particular one. According to Sonneck, the

---

4. Hatch had been associate editor of the *Quarterly* since October 1969.

5. Wittke had been assistant editor of the *Quarterly* in 1968-69 and returned as associate editor in 1978.

6. Eric Salzman, "Editorial," *Musical Quarterly* 71, no. 1 (1985): i.

7. Sonneck, "After Ten Years," 460. The prospectus, a complete copy of which was not available for study, contained the statement that the *Quarterly* would present "serious and thoughtful reading matter, but not too heavy, or too erudite, or too brilliantly put." The editor of *Musical Courier* 59, no. 18 (4 November 1914): 23, in reviewing the prospectus, although wishing the new journal well, could not resist the following jab: "Then follows a list of contemplated contributors all of whom doubtless will be glad to hear that they are not too brilliant."

8. "Let the other side also be heard" is the translation of the Latin phrase.

9. Sonneck, "After Ten Years," 460.

10. Gustave Reese, "A Postscript," *Musical Quarterly* 30, no. 3 (July 1944): 368.

Quarterly was "not [to] include news items, editorial paragraphs, reports of concerts, etc., nor a review department."[10] Over the years, most of these items were, in fact, included. In 1923 Carl Engel began writing a "Views and Reviews" section, which presented capsule reviews of recent publications. Although formal book reviews did not begin until 1944, a "Quarterly Book List" started in 1930. A regular editorial section began in 1945, soon after Paul Henry Lang assumed the editorship. "The Current Chronicle," a section devoted to reviews and discussions of important concert performances, began in 1939 written by the critic Paul Rosenfeld. But Rosenfeld's column lasted for only two years. "The Current Chronicle" resumed in 1948, with various contributors reporting on concert activity; it ended in 1976. Finally, in 1952, the *Quarterly* began printing advertisements for music-related publications near the end of each issue.

As these regular sections were added to the *Quarterly*, naturally the number of articles that could be published in each issue diminished.[11] During Sonneck's editorship, when little else was admitted to the journal, the *Quarterly* averaged ten to twelve articles per issue. During Engel's time, as features were added, the number dropped to eight or nine. During Lang's editorship, when editorials, book reviews, and "The Current Chronicle" were regular sections, the number dropped even further—sometimes as low as four or five. It has remained generally at five or six articles per issue, with few exceptions, until the present day.

From the beginning, the *Quarterly* attracted some of the finest writers of the day on musical topics. During Sonneck's editorship, such well-known historians and writers as Lionel de la Laurencie and Michel Brenet[12] from France; Edward Dent, J. A. Fuller-Maitland, and W. H. Hadow from England; and Olin Downes, Waldo Selden Pratt, and Daniel Gregory Mason from America contributed to the *Quarterly*'s pages. Later contributors also comprise a sizeable "who's who" in musicology during the twentieth century. They represent a breadth of disciplines and subjects, from ancient and Byzantine music to modern compositional techniques, as well as ethnomusicology and popular music. Although many of the features that Sonneck said the *Quarterly* would not include were later incorporated into the journal, one area in which it has remained faithful to his vision has been the diversity of its topics. Throughout its history, the *Quarterly* has had no program, emphasized no cause, supported no particular group or viewpoint, but has published a wide range of scholarly research whose only common link is its diversity.

During the seventy-two years from 1915 until the break in 1986, the *Quarterly* published 2,202 articles, not including reviews, editorials, "The Current Chronicle," and other special sections (see table 23.1). Among these were 316 devoted to some aspect of American music (see table 23.2), which is just under 15 per cent of the total. One can see from this figure that, although the *Quarterly* regularly published articles on American topics, it was not a special advocate for American music. Naturally, the three editors who

---

11. The *Quarterly* has always maintained an issue size of between 144 and 160 pages.

12. Michel Brenet is the pseudonym for Marie Bobillier, whose distinguished contributions to French musical history range from Ockeghem to Berlioz.

edited the *Quarterly* the longest—Sonneck, Engel, and Lang—published the bulk of the articles, both general and American. But when American topics are viewed in terms of percentage of total articles published by an editor, the results are surprising: according to this criterion, the editor who did the most for American music was Gustave Reese.[13] Fully a third of the thirty-six articles published under his editorship was American, while the editor who seems to have done the least is the one with the greatest reputation as an American scholar—Oscar Sonneck—with less than ten per cent.

Table 23.1
Number of Articles Published and Percentage of Total

Sonneck	Engel	Reese	Lang	Hatch	Peyser	Wittke	Salzman	Total
605	550	36	678	81	184	17	51	2202
27.4	25	1.6	30.8	3.7	8.4	0.8	2.3	100

Table 23.2
American Articles Published and Percentage of Total

Sonneck	Engel	Reese	Lang	Hatch	Peyser	Wittke	Salzman	Total
59	108	12	83	9	29	3	13	316
9.7	19.6	33.3	12.1	11.1	15.8	17.6	25.5	100

Sonneck's lack of emphasis on American subjects was certainly not due to lack of interest. While editor of the *Quarterly*, Sonneck himself published at least eleven articles on American topics and his book *Early Opera in America*.[14] He seems to have preferred publishing his American articles in other journals, such as *Musical Courier, Musical America*, and *Papers and Proceedings of the Music Teachers National Association*. We may account for Sonneck's gingerly approach to American subjects in two ways. First, he was concerned with establishing a solid reputation for the *Quarterly* among his European colleagues. He had modeled the journal on similar European periodicals, such as *Die Musik* and *Revista musicale italiana*.[15] He could best accomplish his purpose by sticking closely to the standard musicological research topics of that day: the great men and significant events in musical history. An overemphasis on American topics could have been viewed as chauvinistic by Europeans, who, according to Sonneck, "think very little of music in America."[16] Second, there were relatively few writers of stature doing

13. This, of course, does not really present an accurate picture of the situation. Because Reese was editor of the *Quarterly* for only one year, and since the articles he published were probably already in the editorial pipeline, we don't get a clear indication of his commitment to American music. Engel seems to have done the most among long-term editors in this area, with almost twenty per cent of the articles he published being on an American topic.

14. Significantly, only one of these articles was printed in the *Quarterly* until after Sonneck's death in 1928: "The American Composer and the American Music Publisher," first printed in the *Papers and Proceedings of the M.T.N.A.*, and reprinted in vol. 9 of the *Quarterly*, 1922. Sonneck contributed ten articles to the *Quarterly* during his editorship, but these, except for his memorial tribute to Rudolph Schirmer and his decennial review of the *Quarterly*'s accomplishments, dealt with European music. See Irving Lowens's bibliography of Sonneck's writings in *Oscar Sonneck and American Music*, ed. William Lichtenwanger (Urbana: University of Illinois Press, 1983), 247-55.

15. Sonneck, in "After Ten Years" (p. 462), wrote: "Ten years is not a very long span in the life of magazines. THE MUSICAL QUARTERLY is still young compared with such magazines as the 'Revista Musicale Italiana' and 'Die Musik' from which it originally drew much of its editorial inspiration."

significant research in American music. Sonneck published those who were available—Frances Densmore on American Indian music, Natalie Curtis Burlin on African-American music, John Tasker Howard, William Treat Upton, and Daniel Gregory Mason on contemporary topics. Yet, without a steady supply of quality articles, even with the best will in the world, Sonneck could do no more than he did. However, of the fifty-six issues of the *Quarterly* edited by Sonneck, only sixteen lacked an article on some American topic; often there were two or three per issue—which at the time usually contained ten to twelve articles.

During his almost sixteen years as the *Quarterly*'s editor, Carl Engel published the most articles on American topics—108, approximately 20 per cent of the total he edited. Engel also published the first issue of the journal devoted entirely to Americana—volume 18, no. 1 (January 1932)—which contained twelve articles on American music and musicians (see fig. 23.1). Five of these deal with twentieth-century music, five with the nineteenth century, and two with eighteenth-century topics. The issue must have been planned for some time, for the distinguished roster of authors and the balance among the subject areas suggest a deliberate effort to focus broadly on American music.[17] Engel edited sixty-two issues of the *Quarterly*; only thirteen do not include an article dealing with some aspect of American music.

Gustave Reese's brief term as the *Quarterly*'s editor, from July 1944 through April 1945, resulted in only four issues and thirty-six articles, twelve of which were American. Reese's editorship was obviously a stop-gap measure following Engel's unexpected death and was too short to leave much of an imprint upon the *Quarterly*. Given the normal delays in periodical publishing, the American articles that Reese published had probably been accepted by Engel.

Paul Henry Lang began his long tenure as the *Quarterly*'s editor, following much the same attitude toward American musical topics as Engel and Sonneck had shown. During the first five or six years, one or two American studies appeared in most issues, but beginning in the early 1950s it was not uncommon for three or four issues to pass without an American topic.[18] This practice continued through the 1960s until Lang's retirement in 1973. Of the 114 issues of the *Quarterly* edited by Lang, forty-eight are without articles on an American subject.

---

16. Oscar Sonneck, "European Fallacies and American Music," *Music* 19, no. 3 (January 1901): 220; reprint in *Oscar Sonneck and American Music*, 10.

17. Some articles may have been commissioned especially for this issue. For example, it seems unlikely that writers like W. J. Henderson, a well-known music critic, Randall Thompson and Arthur Farwell, distinguished American composers, and Marian MacDowell, widow of Edward MacDowell and director of the MacDowell Colony, would have written their articles without a specific request from Engel. The balance of the articles and their chronological progression, from contemporary topics back through the nineteenth century, ending with two eighteenth-century studies, bespeak of editorial planning and supervision.

18. During this time important articles on American music began to appear in the *Journal of Research in Music Education* and occasionally in the *Journal of the American Musicological Society*. With other forums open to them, serious researchers in American topics were no longer limited largely to the *Quarterly* as they had been.

JANUARY, 1932   VOL. XVIII, No. 1

THE MUSICAL QUARTERLY

Founded in 1915 by Rudolph E. Schirmer, under the Editorship of O. G. Sonneck

PUBLISHED IN JANUARY, APRIL, JULY, AND OCTOBER

Entered as second-class matter December 31, 1914, at the Post-Office at New York, N. Y.,
under the Act of March 3, 1879

THREE DOLLARS A YEAR   SEVENTY-FIVE CENTS A COPY

G. SCHIRMER (Inc.) NEW YORK

3 East 43rd Street

Figure 23.1. First all-American music issue.

Although he edited only fourteen issues of the *Quarterly* during his three and a half year editorship, Christopher Hatch seems to have followed closely in Lang's footsteps: six of these issues failed to include an American article.

Joan Peyser had hardly gotten her feet wet as the *Quarterly*'s new editor when she received an anonymous letter signed only "Concerned American Musicologists." The author or authors of the letter

> expressed regret over "one issue containing exclusively articles on twentieth music and another on American music. . . ." The writers claimed that "more than anything else what made MQ a great journal was its inclusion of substantial articles on music of the Middle Ages, renaissance and baroque."[19]

This letter is a strange one, for, although there had indeed been a recent issue dealing with the problems of contemporary music,[20] none dealing exclusively with American music had been published since Engel's American issue in 1932. One would have to go back more than twenty years to find an issue that included more than two American articles.[21] In a "Prefatory Note," Peyser lectured both the letter-writers and the musicological community that "musicologists in the past may have been blinded to the merits of their own time and country by the length and richness of the European heritage."[22] Noting that "an occasional issue on a single subject heralds no striking departure of attitude toward musicology as a major discipline," Peyser introduced the contents of a second issue devoted entirely to American subjects with

> hopes of seducing some of those very scholars who have concentrated on the music of other times and places into looking at their own garden. It is not Versailles: no straight paths or manicured flower beds. But it contains music of stature, vitality, and grace. Most particularly it contains music theater and jazz—a unique contribution to world culture—and one that is, in any lexicon, loveable.[23]

The issue contained ten articles; most deal with contemporary issues in American music, but several concerned with its earlier history. Studies of popular music, theater music, and jazz are also included, giving this issue an unusually well-rounded contents. Peyser's commitment to American music, however, seems more verbal than actual. Of the twenty-seven issues she edited, eleven contained nothing American, and most others offered only one or two studies.

Peyser left the *Quarterly* after completing the first number of volume 70. Her place was taken for the remaining three issues in that volume by Paul Wittke, who had been an editorial assistant at the journal, and whose function was to hold the line until a new

---

19. Joan Peyser, "Prefatory Note," *Musical Quarterly* 65, no. 2 (April 1979): 145.

20. Volume 64, no. 2 (April 1978) included seven articles and a commentary section, all dealing with twentieth-century composers.

21. The last issue of the *Quarterly* to contain more than two articles on American topics was vol. 42, no. 4 (October 1956).

22. Peyser, ibid.

23. Ibid.

editor was brought on board. In each of the three issues he edited, Wittke included one American article.

Eric Salzman began his editorship of the *Quarterly* with an editorial outlining his view of the journal's place in the contemporary musical world. Unlike the early years when the *Quarterly* was almost alone in publishing serious, scholarly studies of music in English, Salzman noted that "other journals—impressive and scholarly publications— have sprung up to absorb and disseminate the special fruits of difficult labors."[24] He defined the *Quarterly's* role as giving greater emphasis to contemporary music, American music, non-Western music, vernacular music, issues of music in society, relationships between music and language, and between music and the other arts. Salzman viewed this as "only an affirmation and enlargement of the *Quarterly's* historic mission viewed and reviewed from the perspective of the latter part of the twentieth century."[25]

Although he edited only eight issues of the journal before the break, Salzman followed through on his plan by publishing thirteen American articles on a variety of twentieth-century topics, including several on popular music and musical theater. Two of these issues, however, contained nothing American. Salzman retained the editorship through volume 75 (1991), with Paul Wittke again temporarily taking over the reins for volume 76 (1992). A new editor, Leon Botstein, appeared with the first issue of volume 77 (1993) and seems intent on continuing Salzman's emphases mentioned above.

The American subjects that have been included in the *Quarterly* are as varied as one might expect in a journal devoted to diversity (see table 23.3). Yet a few emphases and trends may be discerned. One of the major continuing emphases of the *Quarterly* has been articles on contemporary American composers — composers who were alive and productive at the time the writings about them were published. Sixty-five of the 316 American articles, about one-fifth of the total, fall into this category. It is the only topic that runs through the whole roster of editors, with Lang and Engel leading the field. While some of the featured composers were published by G. Schirmer, this was not a ploy to advertise in-house composers. Many non-Schirmer composers were covered as well, and those published by Schirmer were among the leading creative artists of the day. Twentieth-century American composers who were not alive at the time the writings about them were published represent another important subject block, with twenty-six articles. This category is the only one that actually increases in activity following the Lang editorship, with several important articles on Ives and Varèse leading the way.

During the early years, much concern was given to an assessment of contemporary musical life in America. Sonneck published a number of essays on music education, musical attitudes, and aesthetics. These articles seemed to have a two-fold purpose: to record current concerns and interests in American musical life, and to explain American attitudes to both the domestic and foreign readership of the *Quarterly*. Although Engel published a few articles of this kind, with later editors they disappear almost entirely.

Another topic emphasized early on but that later fell by the editorial wayside was ethnic musics. Sonneck and Engel published a number of articles dealing with American

---

24. Eric Salzman, "Editorial," *Musical Quarterly* 71, no. 1 (1985): ii.

25. Ibid.

Indian music, African-American music, and music of various ethnic groups. While Lang published half-a-dozen articles on American Indian music, subsequent editors issued nothing at all in the area of ethnomusicology.[26]

Table 23.3
American Subjects

	Son	Eng	Rees	Lang	Hat	Pey	Wit	Sal	Total
Composers (123 articles)									
General articles	5	4	0	2	0	0	0	0	11
Contemporary	5	16	1	30	1	5	2	5	65
18th century	0	4	0	2	1	1	0	0	8
19th century	2	7	0	3	1	0	0	0	13
20th century, not contemporary	1	4	0	4	4	7	1	5	26
Other musicians (39 articles)									
Musicologists	1	7	3	1	0	1	0	0	13
Critics	0	2	0	0	0	0	0	0	2
Performers	0	7	3	2	0	0	0	0	11
Writers	2	1	0	4	0	1	0	0	8
Others	1	1	1	0	0	2	0	0	5
17th and 18th centuries (27 articles)									
Sacred music	0	3	0	3	0	0	0	0	6
Secular music	1	2	0	2	1	1	0	0	7
Musicians	1	2	0	2	0	0	0	0	5
Musical life	0	2	0	4	0	3	0	0	9
19th century (28 articles)									
Sacred music	0	4	0	2	0	0	0	0	6
Secular music	1	2	0	4	0	0	0	0	7
Musicians	1	4	0	1	0	0	0	0	6
Musical life	0	1	0	4	1	3	0	0	9
20th century (43 articles)									
Aesthetics	5	1	1	0	0	0	0	1	8
Music in colleges	4	0	0	0	0	0	0	0	4
Music in performance	1	3	1	1	0	1	0	0	7
Musical places	3	5	0	0	0	0	0	0	8
Recorded music	0	3	0	1	0	0	0	0	4
Technical studies	0	1	0	1	0	0	0	0	2
War and music	2	0	1	0	0	0	0	0	3
Miscellaneous studies	4	1	1	1	0	0	0	0	7
Ethnomusicology (38 articles)									
General studies	1	1	0	0	0	0	0	0	2
AmerIndian music	6	5	0	6	0	0	0	0	17
African-American music	2	6	0	0	0	0	0	0	8
European ethnics	4	5	0	2	0	0	0	0	11
Music education (3 articles)	3	0	0	0	0	0	0	0	3
Popular music (15 articles)									
General studies	1	0	0	0	0	3	0	0	4
Jazz	1	2	0	2	0	1	0	2	8
National songs	1	2	0	0	0	0	0	0	3
Totals	59	108	12	83	9	29	3	13	316

---

26. This may have been influenced by the publication, beginning in 1957, of the journal *Ethnomusicology*, which seems to have drawn away many of the articles which earlier the *Quarterly* would probably have published.

A third topic of interest to the earlier editors that later ones have thus far bypassed often begins with the title "The American Composer and . . ." These general articles attempted to acquaint the readership with the problems, interests, and relationships of America's musical creators. They were apparently dropped in favor of specific studies of particular composers, although these often did not cover the same ground as the general ones.

Finally, a fourth area of interest that was pursued only by the early editors of the *Quarterly* deals with music in various American locales. It was apparently important to Sonneck and Engel that places and activities like the MacDowell Colony and the Bethlehem Bach Festival be known to the general readership. Later editors seemingly did not share this interest, perhaps because "The Current Chronicle" now covered important musical events.

While earlier editors occasionally admitted an article on jazz—usually of the "what is it and should we take it seriously" type—later editors not only gave space to jazz but to other types of popular music as well. Although the numbers are too small to really suggest a trend, they certainly show a change in attitude. The later authors no longer question the value of popular musics or try to convince the reader of the topic's worth—that is taken for granted. Instead, they offered serious studies of technique, style, and aesthetics that bring these subjects into the mainstream of scholarly investigation.

From its inception, articles on contemporary American music and musical life have appeared in the *Quarterly* more frequently than those on the eighteenth and nineteenth centuries. This emphasis was probably due more to the interests of the writers than to the editors. Contemporary America, particularly in the earlier years of the *Quarterly*, seemed to offer a more fertile field for tilling than the barren plains of the eighteenth century or the rocky pastures of the nineteenth. Composers such as Henry F. Gilbert, George W. Chadwick, John Alden Carpenter, and Howard Hanson, whose music was new and whose stature seemed significant, apparently presented more attractive subjects than earlier composers, who were largely unknown and whose music was unplayed. America was entering a period of vigorous growth, and current and future prospects were optimistic. Thoughtful articles on music in contemporary life and education and present-day attitudes toward musical experiences probably seemed more relevant than studies of bygone days and long past attitudes. Yet the *Quarterly* never ignored earlier American music, and some important studies by such writers as John Tasker Howard, Virginia Larkin Redway, Mauer Mauer, and Hans Nathan, to name only four, were also published. These articles are spread evenly throughout much of the life of the *Quarterly*.

How then may the *Quarterly*'s attitude toward American music be summarized? It may fairly be said that American music was treated as equitably as any other musical topic. It was not emphasized, but it was certainly not denigrated. When editors received well-written articles of significance concerned with American music, they were published along side those dealing with the great men and important events of European music. Except for the two issues, nearly fifty years apart, dealing solely with American music, the topic was treated as any other subject of interest to the readership. By placing American research on an equal footing with that dealing with Bach, Beethoven, the

Renaissance, or music at Versailles, the *Quarterly's* editors were saying, in effect, that American musical topics were just as important in their own way as European subjects. This is a refreshing attitude, and quite in keeping with Sonneck's philosophy of *audietur et altera pars* — let the other side also be heard.

Although scholars of American music now have a number of outlets for their research studies, the *Musical Quarterly*, with its broad-based readership, will probably continue to be important. As pointed out earlier, this diversity of interests has always been one of the journal's strengths. Eric Salzman, in outlining the *Quarterly's* mission as he saw it, specifically mentioned American music as one of its emphases. This was reaffirmed by its current editor, Leon Botstein, who in his inaugural essay listed "American Musics" as being a primary concern. It will be interesting to follow the future developments of the journal as it seeks to find a solid and useful place for itself in today's plethora of special interests.

24

Musical Emissary in America: Nadia Boulanger, Normand Lockwood, and American Musical Pedagogy

Kay Norton

Good music was standard fare in the early life of Normand Lockwood (b. 1906). His mother was an accomplished violinist, his father chaired the violin department and conducted the symphony orchestra at the University of Michigan, and his uncle was a concert pianist with an international reputation. Young Lockwood received piano lessons at an early age, played timpani in his father's orchestra as an adolescent, audited harmony classes at the University of Michigan in his teens, and spent the academic year 1924-25 studying composition with Ottorino Respighi in Rome. Among all the musical influences in his cosmopolitan life, however, Lockwood gives credit to only one teacher—Nadia Boulanger (1887-1979). Only after his studies with her did he embark upon a career as a productive composer, an activity that he has sustained from 1928 until the present day.

The affiliation between Lockwood and Boulanger comprises several elements. The preparations that brought each of them to their first meeting in 1925 are an initial consideration, and their formal interactions as teacher and student from 1925 to 1928 represent another. Following a fellowship at the American Academy in Rome from 1929 to 1932, Lockwood began a third stage by incorporating some of her teaching principles into his own teaching style. His varied and highly successful teaching career led him to faculty positions at Oberlin College, Union Theological Seminary, Columbia University, Westminster Choir College, Yale University, Queens College, Trinity University, the University of Oregon, the University of Hawaii, and the University of Denver. Another dimension of the Boulanger-Lockwood story is represented by their differences, seen in his departures from her pedagogical style. Finally, their more equitable standing as peers in later life is reflected in correspondence and reminiscences.

Lockwood was joined on the path from Paris to the American academic world by other Boulanger students of the 1920s such as Melville Smith, Walter Piston, and Louise Talma. Virgil Thomson's later observation, that Nadia Boulanger's pupils were "teaching in our every conservatory and college, carrying on her traditions of high skill, expressive freedom and no nonsense,"[1] is supported by Boulanger's estimation that she taught over 600 American students between 1921 and her final years.[2] As one of the most successful of those pupils, Normand Lockwood has combined the potency of Boulanger's methods with an unpretentious Yankee ingenuity to make a lasting contribution to American musical pedagogy.

Preparations

The chemistry that produces a superior mentor-student relationship is as elusive as it is desirable. In the case of Nadia Boulanger and Normand Lockwood, similar family backgrounds may have prepared the way for the affinity between Boulanger and the gifted but musically unschooled American. As it had been in the Boulanger home, music education was an accepted and sustaining part of the Lockwood family life. Both were the offspring of a well-known professor of music at a nationally famous university and, not surprisingly, both had discovered music at an early age. Boulanger, however, had been trained during her youth to conform to the rigors of discipline, imposed by her overbearing mother, the Russian-born Raïssa Myschetsky Shuvalov Boulanger. Nadia's home study with her father Ernest Boulanger began at age seven, and organ lessons with Louis Vierne followed a year later. At the age of nine, she audited her first class at the Paris Conservatoire, where Ernest was a professor of voice. The twelve years that followed were brilliantly successful: she received a first prize in solfège in 1898, a second prize in harmony in 1900, a first prize in harmony and second prize in organ in 1903, and an unprecedented three first prizes in organ, accompaniment, and fugue in 1904. To cap these honors, she won the Conservatoire's Second Grand Prix de Rome for her cantata *La Sirène*.[3] Beginning with performing, composing, and writing criticism, and eventually concentrating on teaching after 1918, Nadia Boulanger pursued her career with the same unyielding singleness of purpose from adolescence until the last months of her life.

Although Lockwood's career tenacity is comparable to that of his mentor, his early achievements are less remarkable. He was fascinated by the many manifestations of music, but his innate shyness made performing unbearable. The gap between his early compositional impulses and his ability to express them was equally frustrating. Prior to his first formal compositional study at age eighteen, he had written a few simple songs,

---

1. Virgil Thomson, "'Greatest Music Teacher'—at 75," *New York Times Magazine*, 4 February 1962, 35.

2. Bruno Monsaingeon, *Mademoiselle: Conversations with Nadia Boulanger*, trans. Robyn Marsack (Manchester, England: Carcanet Press, 1985), 57. This was first published as *Mademoiselle: Entretiens avec Nadia Boulanger* (Paris: Editions Van de Velde, 1981).

3. Teresa Walters, "Nadia Boulanger, Musician and Teacher: Her Life, Concepts, and Influences" (D.M.A. diss., Peabody Conservatory of Music, Peabody Institute of Johns Hopkins University, 1981), 7.

piano arrangements of familiar tunes, several original pieces for piano, and informal counterpoint exercises completed as a part of his early piano lessons. Some of these works showed promise, but most were undistinguished. Small wonder that Lockwood's arrival in the salon of an active master composer such as Respighi would have proven less than productive. As Lockwood admits, "It was ridiculous—I wasn't ready. He wasn't the kind of teacher who could [help] an inexperienced novice. He was probably very good, though, I'm sure of it."[4] Lockwood left Rome in 1925, still lacking the fundamental tutoring he needed at the time. That need would finally be addressed later in the same year in the studio of Nadia Boulanger.

Interactions

For many American composers in the 1920s, the Parisian artistic milieu exuded an almost irresistible appeal. There, for the first time, Lockwood and others heard Krenek's *Johnny spielt auf,* Honegger's *Le Roi David*, Schoenberg's *Pierrot lunaire*, Debussy's *Pelléas et Mélisande*, Musorgsky's *Boris Godonov*, Hindemith's *Das Marienleben*, and works by Ravel, Milhaud, Florent Schmitt, and Roy Harris. Although the exposure to new music in Paris was an education in itself for the son of a conservative orchestra conductor, Boulanger herself supplied the missing ingredient that gave these musical experiences meaning. The master pedagogue guided Lockwood through a strict and disciplined study of classics such as the cantatas of Bach and the Beethoven string quartets, as well as various contemporary composers. Her biographer, Léonie Rosenstiel, provides a comprehensive list of composers Boulanger covered that includes Wagner, Schmitt, Dupré, Prokofiev, Bartók, Bloch, Dukas, Debussy, Auric, Poulenc, Honegger, Ravel, and Fauré.[5] While Stravinsky's works were prominent in the Boulanger studio, Lockwood remembers that they were "not to be imitated beyond what simply seeped into the veins. And why not that? As far as I know, Beethoven never made any apologies over Haydn."[6] With these musical models, Boulanger created the framework against which her students could develop individual styles, as she remarked, "You need an established language and then, within that established language, the liberty to be yourself."[7]

Lockwood has often reflected upon Boulanger's pedagogical gifts:

> Boulanger was a teacher if there ever was one. . . . She had what I'd call perspective. She could spot what was unique in a student; she was the first person to give me a point of view on myself and my own work. When the breakthrough to my own language finally came, it was with a little piece. I took a poem by Whitman and set it for tenor, flute, and alto flute.[8]

---

4. Normand Lockwood, interview by Kay Norton in Denver, 4 September 1989.

5. Léonie Rosenstiel, *Nadia Boulanger: A Life in Music* (New York: Norton, 1982), 207-08.

6. Lockwood, Denver, letter to Kay Norton, Boulder, 7 September 1989.

7. Monsaingeon, 53.

8. Wes Blomster, "A Tribute to Lockwood, Who Earned It," *Boulder Sunday Camera,* 24 November 1985: section D, 1 and 4.

This "little piece" was soon performed for the International Society for Contemporary Music in Paris. Entitled *When Lilacs Last in the Dooryard Bloom'd*, its harmonic simplicity belies its importance in Lockwood's later career. Not only is this version of "Memories of President Lincoln" Lockwood's first setting of Walt Whitman's poetry, the compositional language Lockwood mentions is one he consistently employed in numerous choral and vocal settings of the poet's work throughout his career. Testifying to the success of Boulanger's primary teaching philosophy, Lockwood had assimilated the musical languages around him and created one that was wholly his own.

Lockwood's private composition lessons took place every week, at the cost of about ten dollars per hour. Rosenstiel elaborated on the finances of several Boulanger students at the time, including Lockwood:

> Americans who went to Paris to study with Nadia generally expected to stay for about three years. That was how long Virgil Thomson, Aaron Copland, and Melville Smith remained with her, and most students who could manage to scrape together the money tried to maintain themselves in Paris for that long. Claire Leonard, a young M. A. from Harvard, was able to stay for almost four years on a Paine Traveling Fellowship. But Normand Lockwood was on his own, as was Illinois-born organist Barrett Spach who, fortunately, could look to his family for help.[9]

Boulanger saw a great many students in the 1920s, teaching both privately and in classes at the American Conservatory in Fontainebleau, the École Normale, her Paris apartment, and at her summer home in Gargenville. In addition to private composition lessons that focused on strict species counterpoint, Lockwood attended her École Normale class on the Beethoven quartets. In composition lessons, Boulanger often criticized his works quite sharply, and "she wouldn't palaver about it . . . she could see what was extraneous and what was essential. She would say, 'This is not right,' and prove it with some structural reason."[10] Regarding his own self-discipline, Lockwood related

> She gave me "the works" and I studied hard. I owe her one of the most impor-tant things. She taught me discipline, not just from the outside, doing what you're told, but also from the inside, selecting what you are going to do and doing it.[11]

As a result of his study with this exacting individual, the lack of focus so present in Lockwood's youth soon disappeared. With regard to internal discipline, he must have learned her lessons well. Lockwood has composed continuously, beginning with his appointment at Oberlin, and including one period in the 1950s when he did not hold an academic position, as well as during the years since his retirement from the University of Denver.

In addition to their 1920s interaction, Lockwood adopted the role of student twice more with Boulanger after she came to the United States in 1937. One meeting is

---

9. Rosenstiel, 208.

10. Lockwood interview, 4 September 1989.

11. Peggy Scott, "Composer-in-Residence Helps Unlock Student Musical Ability," *Southeast Missourian* (Cape Girardeau), 19 March 1989, 7A.

commemorated by a photograph of the two. Still displayed in Lockwood's studio, it commemorates the change in their relationship. By that time, he had been on the Oberlin faculty for five years. In those later sessions with Boulanger, he realized he had learned all he could from her: "She had begun to repeat herself a bit."[12] She had supplied a great need in the 1920s, but from the time of his appointment to the Oberlin faculty, he relied on his own internal discipline to achieve professional success.

Applications

At Oberlin College, Lockwood was required to adhere to the rigors of institutional discipline for the first time since 1924. Teaching the most architectonic of musical topics—theory, harmony, and counterpoint—forced him to draw on his internal powers of organization. Although he recalls, "I acquired ways of teaching as I went,"[13] many of these ways of teaching bear a striking resemblance to those of his mentor. Boulanger's impact therefore did not stop with Lockwood the composer, but continued through his unconscious emulation of some of her pedagogical ideas.

At the outset of Lockwood's teaching career, Boulanger and he were similarly perceived in their respective musical arenas. Boulanger's most famous 1920s student, Aaron Copland, related that

> She knew about contemporary music in the 1920s. That was a very radical time in music, and so not all teachers felt at home with the new idiom. I remember my teacher back in New York, knew very little about the newer things. His revolutionary was Richard Wagner, but Nadia Boulanger was "au courant," we used to say, "à la page"—up to the minute, ready with all the answers, even about the most contemporary expressions in music.[14]

Lockwood's early years at Oberlin are characterized in the words of Oberlin historian Willard Warch:

> The theory course of 1936 seems from the catalogue description to have been little changed from that of 1916. But Mr. [Arthur E.] Heacox, who was a strong teacher and department head, had just retired, and the old Leipzig-style approach to theory teaching was about to give way to the integrated teaching of sight-singing, ear-training, keyboard work, analysis, and written work. The composition teacher, Mr. Normand Lockwood, an ardent disciple of Nadia Boulanger, was upsetting some of the older faculty conservatives by writing in the then-modern Stravinsky-Hindemith vein of neo-classicism, and was prodding individuals and organizations into performing works of this style.[15]

---

12. Lockwood interview, 4 September 1989.

13. Ibid.

14. Aaron Copland, recorded reminiscence on *The Influence of Nadia Boulanger: A Discussion of the Teaching Techniques of a Musical Giant* (cassette 001-532-OU, Music Concepts, 1969).

15. Willard Warch, *Our First 100 Years: A Brief History of the Oberlin College Conservatory of Music* (Oberlin: Oberlin College Conservatory of Music, 1967), 45-46.

Evidently Lockwood's European study made him somewhat of a champion of new music at Oberlin, a role Boulanger had played in Paris during the previous decade. From the student perspective, Lockwood's interest in contemporary music is remembered by William Hoskins, professor and Composer Laureate at Jacksonville University:

> Lockwood liked to see to it that his student composers were exposed to unusual, good music. He took several of us to Cleveland on one occasion to hear Hindemith give a recital of his own viola works.[16]

Lockwood had studied Hindemith's music first with Boulanger, who admired the German composer enough to consider translating his treatise *The Craft of Musical Composition* into French. Whether thwarted by Hindemith's flight from the Nazi regime in 1937, or her stipulated foreword which would have stated her objections to the book, the idea never came to fruition.[17]

While Lockwood remained a reticent individual and Boulanger was an ardent self-promoter to her death, the two shared an intelligence about human nature that enhanced their teaching styles. In 1969, Virgil Thomson remembered one particularly motivating manifestation of this quality in Boulanger:

> Mademoiselle Boulanger always gave her students—I suppose she still does—the impression that she had absolutely nothing in the world to do for that hour but to occupy herself in a concentrated and thoroughly interested manner with you. That is a compliment that is practically irresistible, and it gets awfully good work out of people.[18]

At Oberlin, Lockwood used the particulars of his situation to form a similar bond with his composition students. Close to them in age, and an active composer himself, he was able to share their compositional processes in an intimate way. He was, therefore, a "first among equals" in his studio, creating a learning situation that was doubtless very dynamic. One of Lockwood's students at Oberlin was Paul Christiansen, heir to a strong family tradition in choral music fostered by his father, F. Melius Christiansen. From his position as director of the Concordia (Minnesota) College Choir, the younger Christiansen wrote to Lockwood in 1971:

> I shall always be deeply grateful to you for many things. . . . I shall always value your personal friendship and interest, even from my student days at Oberlin, when you as a faculty member invited me to your home. Your help in getting some of my music performed will also be appreciated always.[19]

Former Oberlin student Ludwig Lenel, a composer now retired from Muhlenberg College in Allentown, Pennsylvania, found Lockwood to be very helpful in identifying his

---

16. William Hoskins, Jacksonville, Fla., letter to Kay Norton, Kansas City, 8 August 1991.

17. Rosenstiel, 282.

18. Virgil Thomson, recorded reminiscence, *Influence of Nadia Boulanger*.

19. Paul Christiansen, Moorhead, Minn., letter to Lockwood, Denver, April 1971. Normand Lockwood Archive (hereafter NLA), American Music Research Center, University of Colorado at Boulder.

compositional voice. His description of Lockwood's teaching style is strikingly similar to Lockwood's assessment of Boulanger's gifts:

> One outstanding trait was Normand's ability to rather quickly seize upon a student's compositional talent and his potential for growth. He tried to develop compositional skills which were as yet undeveloped, but within reach of the student—without ever imposing his personal style. He very quickly saw weak passages and suggested how to improve them. . . . All this was accompanied by an ever-present positive attitude (although he could be quite outspoken at times, but never hurtful), by pushing a student forward at his own pace.[20]

Lockwood's gift of insight has also guided his own compositions, in works that are unfailingly idiomatic for performer, instrument, text, and performance environment.

The Boulanger attribute mentioned most often by her former students was her desire to allow students the experience of self-discovery instead of imposing upon them a pre-ordained compositional style. She stated:

> As a teacher, my whole life is based on understanding others, not on making them understand me. What the student thinks, what he wants to do—that is the important thing. I must try to make him express himself and prepare him to do that for which he is best fitted.[21]

She illustrated the extent of her commitment to this belief in an interview with Bruno Monsaingeon:

> I have a student who is very nice, but frightened. He wants to please me, he wants me to like his harmony. He plays and then turns toward me, desperately anxious: "Is that how it should be?" I say, "But I've no idea, I don't know what you want. As long as I don't know what you want, musically you don't exist for me."[22]

Boulanger was uniquely qualified to approach composition in a manner free from her own artistic needs; she had abandoned composition in 1918 when her sister and fellow composer, Lili, had died. At that point she determined that her most lasting gift to the musical world would be her teaching. She viewed teaching as a high calling and drew upon the words of one of her favorite philosophers, Henri Bergson, to describe the discovery of her life's work:

> Nature gives us a sign when an individual discovers his own destiny. This sign is joy. The man who has made a factory work, the woman who has given birth to a child, the man who has perfected a work—they all know a joy which may only be qualified by one phrase, "joie d'origine, d'essence divine" [joy of origin, divine essence].[23]

Teaching composition without imposing strongly held ideals was a challenging legacy for Lockwood, a working composer who was constantly concerned with solving his own compositional riddles. To his credit, however, he managed to keep his own music out

---

20. Ludwig Lenel, Orefield, Pa., letter to Kay Norton, Kansas City, 12 July 1991.

21. Don G. Campbell, *Master Teacher: Nadia Boulanger* (Washington, D.C.: Pastoral Press, 1984), 65.

22. Monsaingeon, 55.

23. Walters, 358.

of the composition studio, as remembered by composer Austin C. Lovelace, one of Lockwood's students at Union Theological Seminary. A prolific composer who has since published some 650 works, Lovelace recalls:

> Normand didn't require writing in any particular style, but insisted that styles not be mixed in a single work. He gave a lot of freedom, and his comments were always on target. I found him a great teacher.[24]

Robert Washburn, dean emeritus and Senior Fellow at Potsdam College of the State University of New York, was a Lockwood student at Trinity University. He remembers:

> I was most impressed by his professionalism, his concern for even the tiniest detail in the compositional process (quite likely a Boulanger carry-over) and, even though he could be thoroughly and honestly "academic" it was never the principal impact of his teaching. I believe he has a unique combination of stressing the importance of discipline and at the same time letting the creative imagination be the most important factor.[25]

Lockwood's combination of discipline and imagination echoes Boulanger's concern for the establishment of a musical language, balanced with artistic liberty.

Washburn also mentions another Lockwood trait, his attention to detail, that is seconded by choral conductor Daniel Moe, professor emeritus at Oberlin Conservatory. Moe was hired by the University of Denver as choral director in 1953 and met Lockwood several years later:

> I was still wet behind the ears when I met Normand Lockwood at the home of George Lynn in Denver. In the course of the evening, one of us suggested that the three of us should get together to talk about our compositions on a somewhat regular basis, to which we all agreed. We subsequently met in George Lynn's studio, and on one occasion I brought a new work of mine, *Hosanna to the Son of David*. Normand suggested a rhythmic change of one tiny note, adding a syncopation on the word "the" in measure seven. Without it, the work might have been a very boring piece, but as it is, it has sold over 200,000 copies.
>
> That's the essence of what I gained from knowing Normand Lockwood. As a young composer, I thought that when I wrote a double bar, the piece was finished. Normand showed me the value of continuous revision.[26]

Whether the process is called continuous revision or a meticulous attention to detail, Lockwood has valued the editing of his work, always looking for the perfect expression of his musical inspiration. This attitude of constant searching is reminiscent of Raïssa Boulanger's question that became a guiding force to her young daughter, "Are you certain that you did *all* that you could?"[27] Boulanger conducted her entire life in response to this inquiry, and doubtless transferred it to many students.

---

24. Austin C. Lovelace, Denver, to Kay Norton, Kansas City, 17 July 1991.

25. Robert Washburn, Potsdam, N.Y., letter to Kay Norton, Kansas City, 15 July 1991.

26. Daniel Moe, Oberlin, phone interview by Kay Norton, 12 September 1991. *Hosanna to the Son of David* was published in 1956 by Mercury Music Corporation, a division of Theodore Presser Company, in "The Green Lake Choral Series." George Lynn was the editor of the series.

Departures

Just as Lockwood and countless other Americans composers personalized the dodecaphonic precepts of Arnold Schoenberg, so did they adapt Boulanger's teaching methods, retaining only the most useful elements of her style. A most striking contrast between Boulanger and Lockwood lies in their approaches to students. Boulanger imparted knowledge with a force that bordered on fanaticism in her later life, while Lockwood has maintained an unobtrusive teaching style. Once a student of Lockwood at the University of Oregon, William Wood is composer-in-residence at the University of New Mexico. He remembers

> Normand's teaching style was quite simple; while you were with him in the studio you weren't *aware* that he was "teaching." He would suggest several ways with which to solve a particular compositional problem—leaving the final choices to you. You began to "see" what you were doing and to *hear* the page. He made sure that *you were sure* of the results . . . that it was *exactly* what you wanted. You gradually realized that you were writing *your own* music—not what someone else tells you to put down. . . . You find out what composing is about with this kind of guidance.[28]

While years of experience must surely have modified Lockwood's teaching style, his approach to students seemed always to revolve around a sincere respect for their innate compositional impulses. Former University of Denver student Kevin Kennedy, chair of the music department at Arapahoe Community College, commented on Lockwood's teaching at his final academic position:

> [Of all my composition teachers], none seemed so egoless, so selfless, so genuinely interested in the student as Normand. Never did his past accomplishments or present projects intrude on the time he was dedicating to his students in class. Never did he seem interested in anything but the business at hand, that business being to move his students from the level they had reached to some higher level based on their respective talents and individual musical language.[29]

Motivation is another distinguishing factor between Lockwood and his mentor. Boulanger, like so many other successful artists, seemed always driven to pursue greater notoriety in the musical community, often creating opportunities for herself through the achievements of her students. In contrast, Lockwood has pursued composition and teaching steadfastly and often quietly, within and outside the realm of the public eye. Some of his finest works are unsolicited, and many have never been performed. His wealth of experiences, including both successes and failures, has taught him that popular art music is not necessarily good art music, and he is quite content with that maxim. As he stated in 1979,

---

27. Rosenstiel, 44. Boulanger also refers to her mother's comment on *The Influence of Nadia Boulanger*.

28. William Wood, Albuquerque, N.M., letter to Kay Norton, Kansas City, 5 July 1991. Emphases original.

29. Kevin Kennedy, Denver, letter to Kay Norton, Kansas City, 18 July 1991.

> I write for the shelf—that's a good place. Some works emerge from the shelf and get performed. Some please and some don't. But that doesn't have anything to do with quality: some lousy things are popular and so are some good things.[30]

Lockwood's innate shyness may have fundamentally affected his career in another way that Nadia Boulanger never experienced. Former Oberlin student William Hoskins offered one negative appraisal of the composition teacher he otherwise admired:

> There were some . . . Lockwoodian traits which it would have been better not to have learned. His attitudes reinforced my own publicity-shyness; I could never bear to become the self-promoting salesman which a successful American composer almost has to be—and in that, I was a true disciple of N. L. He was always shy and tentative in putting forward his own compositions, and this attitude could not have helped but cost him some career opportunities along the way.[31]

Many of Boulanger's associates have commented upon her exhaustless promotion of herself. As Lockwood remarked, "Why, [self-promotion] was such second nature to her that one did not notice it after a while."[32] While this quality was sometimes difficult to negotiate for those around her, she believed it to be an essential ingredient of a career based on public acclaim.

One of the most important lessons Lockwood learned from his contact with Boulanger was to avoid her dogmatism. As opposed to Boulanger's rather single-minded rejection of dodecaphony, Lockwood has exhibited a flexibility and tolerance of differing compositional methods that has allowed him to remain vital and fascinated with composition to this day. Lockwood stated his opinion regarding systematic compositional systems in 1991:

> There have been a great many fashions—"isms." I never hooked on any, but I was interested, of course. There is a big differentiation between what interests me and what I necessarily like. Twelve-tone writing draws me itself, not the idea that I have to do it. With anything, there is a danger of getting too pedantic.[33]

The adoption of this belief might have benefitted Boulanger on many levels—her championing of neoclassicism after World War II, well after its initial popularity had faded, along with her rejection of dodecaphonic practices, contributed greatly to her relegation to the musical "old guard" in the 1950s and beyond.

---

30. Barbara Haddad Ryan, "World Premieres Top Concert List," *Rocky Mountain News*, 4 March 1979, 36.

31. Hoskins letter, 8 August 1991.

32. Lockwood, interview by Kay Norton in Milwaukee, Wis., 4 April 1992.

33. Lockwood, interview by Kay Norton in Denver, 2 June 1991.

Reflections

Although the teacher-student relationship between Nadia Boulanger and Normand Lockwood changed with Lockwood's appointment to Oberlin, they maintained their liaison through periodic correspondence. The friendship was one that the composer cherished for many decades, keeping a file of her letters, reread many times, among his personal papers. The feeling was apparently mutual, as evident in these letters, as well as in a story concerning one of Lockwood's Denver students, John Ryan. In 1925, the very young Lockwood had been embarrassed to tell his composition teacher his correct age, and had added four years to the total. As the story goes, the next year he forgot what he had said the previous year, and told her, again, that he was twenty-three. Whether or not he compounded the exaggeration by stating the same age the third year is unknown, but when Ryan gave her Lockwood's greeting nearly five decades later, she remarked, "Oh, is Lockwood still twenty-three?"[34]

In her fourteen extant letters to Lockwood, Boulanger wrote of many things: composition, politics, even life and death. In December of 1940, her thoughts reflected upon world events that moved her celebration of Christmas from France to Cambridge, Massachusetts.

> [I write] only to send you my deepest wishes for Christmas. No one, since my birth, has been as serious as this one: the world we loved, may have disappeared—and, we have to concentrate in order to find the new path. For you, still young, it is a great opportunity. But . . . What will be your to-morrow?
>
> I know one thing only: how deeply my thoughts are with you—how I wish you to escape the conflict which has brought to light the ultimate and discouraging cruelty and blindness men can reach. Only fair to say that the same events have also created greatness. But, at what price?[35]

On another occasion, Boulanger expressed a continuing interest in Lockwood's music:

> I keep the early confidence I had musically in you, entire, faithful—and that it is a true joy being able to see now that this confidence is justified by the works you have written—and are to write.[36]

Another Boulanger letter hints at the origin of Lockwood's lifelong focus on individual textures and timbres, as opposed to always subordinating them in a larger context:

> If musicians had truly the clear perfect feeling for "sound" as such, as precise fact, than for succession, for superposition [sic] of sound from simple intervals to complex chords—and the same with all the elements of music how everything would become simple and fruitful![37]

---

34. Vona (Mrs. Normand) Lockwood, interview by Kay Norton in Denver, 4 September 1989.

35. Boulanger, Cambridge, Mass., letter to Normand Lockwood and family, Oberlin, 16 December 1940, NLA.

36. Boulanger, Paris, letter to Lockwood, Oberlin, 28 April 1932, NLA.

37. Boulanger, Gargenville, France, to Lockwood, Oberlin, 9 September 1932, NLA.

The choral piece *Out of the Cradle Endlessly Rocking* (1938) shows Lockwood's interpretation of Boulanger's comments on isolated sonorities, manifesting the expressive chordal pattern that he first discovered as a result of his study with her. Lockwood sent that piece and others to her in 1938. By that time Lockwood had turned to the independent pursuit of his musical style, but he still valued her comments enough to accept her suggestions.

> I received your choruses—and am very impressed with them . . . they are moving, beautiful, and must sound so well. I am happy to think that soon I will see them with you, to express my deep appreciation—and also to discuss some details.
>
> But how you progress, in freedom of technic of expression, is a true joy for me.[38]

Boulanger's presence endured in Lockwood's life far beyond his compositional interaction with her. Communicating a similar sentiment in 1971, Lockwood's former Yale graduate assistant, Robert MacKinnon, wrote Lockwood from his faculty position at Stanford University,

> To recite the many ways you have influenced my musical life would take pages. Suffice it to say that you were, and still are, a guide-line kind of "presence" that is always hanging around to pester me whenever I write or arrange music. All I have to do is think how delighted you would be or how disgusted you would be, and I automatically leave it in or tear it all up and start over. If it is the latter, I curse you up and down for being such a fuss-pot. Then later I fall in love with the finished product, and of course forgive you with great magnanimity.[39]

Conclusions

The artistic empathy that continued between Boulanger and Lockwood in later life is illustrated in a story Lockwood related in 1989. By the age of eighty-three, he was more a peer than a pupil of Boulanger, who had died a decade earlier. At that point, they were united by their association in the 1920s, and by a similarity of perspective that age had brought. Lockwood's story begins with an experience that took place in Cape Girardeau, Missouri:

> A dear young girl sitting in the front row of a class meeting of fifty or sixty students at Southeast Missouri State asked, "Where do you get your inspiration?" Now, six months later, I haven't the vaguest recollection of how I may have answered that one? Of course I haven't found the answer—not any more than I had an answer to my father at age fifteen. I might have liked to say in both instances, "Composing is an obsession." That's akin to what Nadia Boulanger said to me: "Zee musique, she must be like a seekness." (I'm sure Nadia wasn't aware of the excellent pun.)[40]

38. Boulanger, Paris, to Lockwood, Oberlin, 16 October 1938, NLA.

39. Robert MacKinnon, Stanford, Calif., letter to Lockwood, Denver, 20 April 1971, NLA.

40. Lockwood, Denver, letter to Kay Norton, Boulder, 1 October 1989.

Lockwood is not alone in his inability to capture the essence of artistic inspiration in words; the definition provides the aesthetic world with endless avenues of inquiry. And yet, while its precise meaning is elusive, the presence of inspiration in Nadia Boulanger's studio is proven by the continuing impact she made upon Normand Lockwood and his life as a composer. In turn, he has transferred his version of the same gift to many other students in this country. Artistic inspiration may yet remain a mystery, but the endowment of its ineffable truth from teacher to pupil stands as an affirmation of its presence. Indeed, the studio of a master teacher is one of the few places in which the pursuit of discipline, technique, and individual expression can result in that precious human commodity: artistic creation.

25

Nocturne

John Milton
Paradise Lost, book 4

Richard Toensing

Boulder, Colo. 8/28/92

26

Old World Origins of the Matachines Dance

Brenda M. Romero

Because traditional New Mexicans—*Nuevomejicanos*, or *Mejicanos*—know so little about the eight hundred years rule of the Moors in Spain, we are fascinated with the Old World touches of Moorish culture in the matachines dance. Of particular interest are the fringed masks over the eyes of the dancers and the tall coronas which resemble the ceremonial hats of desert peoples of North Africa. Succumbing to the natural curiosity to know one's own roots, this essay specifically addresses questions of the Old World origins of the matachines; it focuses in particular on Moorish origins of the dance by tracing elements of the ritual to the Roman occupation of North Africa, and from there to Moorish Spain. By focusing on these Old World layers, this investigation of Latino music and culture will also further an understanding into the richness of its roots. Additionally, it will explore the long-forgotten meanings of ancient gestures, and other aspects of the music and dance. Because it is difficult to organize this diverse collection of overlapping information, I will first offer a critical examination of scholarly contributions by others who have been concerned with the question of the Old World origins of the matachines. From there I will gather the many threads of my own research in an effort to shed some light on the multi-faceted question of where matachines came from. Due to space limitations, I will not discuss the indigenous New World layer that was added to the Old World dance.[1]

---

1. A comprehensive discussion of both Old and New World origins is found in chapter 1 of my dissertation "The Matachines Music and Dance in San Juan Pueblo and Alcalde, New Mexico: Contexts and Meanings" (Ph.D. diss., University of California, Los Angeles, 1993).

The Matachines Dance of New Mexico

Los matachines refers to a pantomimed ritual dance-drama, a morality play brought by the Spanish and superimposed on indigenous rituals as a means of evangelization during colonial times.[2] The dance ritual survives in the southwestern United States in various Mejicano and Indian communities, and is still a strong tradition throughout Mexico, especially in the north.[3] In all geographical locations, the dance represents the syncretism[4] of Old and New World elements; it is usually performed on important Catholic feast days, and many elements vary from place to place. This paper focuses only on the matachines of New Mexico, where the so-called "Spanish" version is accompanied by violin and guitar, and the "Drum" version, performed in some Pueblos, features the traditional format of a drum-accompanied male chorus. The Pueblos mostly refer to the dance as *matachina;* it is the only Pueblo ceremonial dance which uses European instruments and music.

Although there are many variations from place to place, the matachines drama takes place between two lines of dancers, after whom the dance is named. It is here that the *monarca* (the monarch) dances, in similar dress to the matachines, but wearing a king's crown rather than matachine *coronas* (crowns); all are nonetheless generically called *coronas* in most Mejicano villages. In the space between the two lines of dancers the matachines protect the *malinche,* the young girl in white communion dress,[5] from the lower nature represented by a young *toro,* or bull. Here the *abuelos,* or grandfathers, who double as clowns, eventually subdue, symbolically kill, or castrate the *toro,* depending on where the dance is held. In Mejicano contexts and in some Pueblos one of the grandparents is a man dressed as a woman, called the *abuela* (grandmother), who engages in bawdy behavior with the *abuelo,* sometimes imitating a nun who might give birth to a baby while the dance is taking place. In some Pueblos, notably the Pueblo of Jemez, the *abuela* is genderless and does not dress as a woman, but wears a mask with traditional trickster associations and dances the entire time, directing the dancers in the complicated interwoven formations required by the ritual, and cuing the musicians. He is also a central figure in the *monarca's* dance, where he symbolizes spiritual struggle. The other *abuelo* or

---

2. The Matachines should not be confused with the tradition of mock dramatic conflicts between the Moors and the Christians, the genre of *Los Moros y los Cristianos*, which involves recitation in addition to music and dance. Flavia Champe, in *The Matachines Dance of the Upper Rio Grande: History, Music, and Choreography* (Lincoln: University of Nebraska Press, 1983), 3, cites "The Comanches and the Spanish Soldiers," a ritual play on horseback, as one variant of *Los Moros*. It is performed in Alcalde, New Mexico, right after the Matachines on December 27.

3. In Mexico the dance is sometimes a variant of the matachines without reference to the term "matachine," but including the same or similar charcters, perhaps with Nahuatl names. These variants include the *Santiago, Santiaguitos,* and *Negritos* dances. See Gertrude P. Kurath and Antonio Garcia, *Music and Dance of the Tewa Pueblos* (Santa Fe: Museum of New Mexico Press, 1970).

4. "Syncretism," as used in anthropology and ethnomusicology, refers to the merging of cultural elements of diverse origins into a new form which reflects the characteristics of its origins.

5. The *malinche* does not have the same connotations of innocence in Mexican folklore, where she is condemned as the traitoress of Mexican indigenous culture. This points to a very different socio-cultural environment for *Nuevomejicanos* and Mexican nationals following Americanization in the mid-nineteenth century of the lands now referred to as the southwestern United States.

abuelos circumambulate the dance area, keeping out dogs and little children, or picking up children and otherwise creating laughter. They will also sometimes solicit money from the audience for the dancers and musicians, but mostly they entertain the audience by chasing after the bull, who is always butting them when their backs are turned.

The music is a set of dances[6] performed on violin and guitar in the Spanish version. In both Mejicano and Pueblo settings all the dancers except the *abuelos* hold gourd rattles or maracas upside down, usually under a scarf, in the right hand. In some Pueblos the dancers also wear bell or shell rattles around the waist. The meters of the songs are usually simple or compound duple (mostly 6/8), although John Donald Robb documented many regional deviations from regular rhythmic groupings.[7] The dances are nowadays often simply titled by the character who is featured in that dance *(monarca, malinche, toro)*, or with the dance formation or part of the dance, such as *cruz* (cross), or *entrada* (entrance).

Scholarly Contributions to Old World Origins Theories: Arabic Origins Theories

Modern Spanish encyclopedia entries define the matachines as a dance of the sixteenth and seventeenth centuries that parodied the ancient war dances.[8] One line of dancers carried swords and the other line of dancers carried bovine bladders filled with air; they struck at each other with either sword or bladder, defending themselves with shields, all to the beat of the music.[9]

The anthropologist Gertrude P. Kurath was the first to link the matachines with Moorish culture by ascribing to the name an Arabic derivation:

> The meaning of the term *Matachin* was divulged by the scholar William Worrell, who puzzled with me over the dance. The name is probably derived from the Arabic *mudawajjihin* (pl., *mudawajjihen*), which can mean "those who put on a face" or else "those who face each other." The *Supplement aux Dictionnaires Arabes* and *Webster's International Dictionary* give similar meanings. Either meaning is applicable to the earliest *Matachin* on record and also to most of the modern *Matachines*.[10]

6. The number of dances and their melodies differ in the different locations.

7. John D. Robb, *Hispanic Folk Music of New Mexico and the Southwest* (Norman: University of Oklahoma Press, 1980). Robb collected a large number of matachines recordings in the 1950s and 1960s; eighty-seven of them are transcribed in his volume. They form the basis for a regional comparison of *matachines* melodies in my dissertation.

8. One example is the *Gran Enciclopedia Larousse*, 24 vols. (Barcelona: Editorial Planeta, 1967), 7:35.

9. Spanish religious processions in various places still have vestiges of this parody among the *cabezudos* (the stubborn ones), who nowadays carry water balloons that they toss around. I witnessed these at the Corpus Christi parade in Granada, Spain, in June 1990; the tradition is said to date back to the 14th century. See Francisco de Paula Valladar, *Fiestas del Corpus en Granada, escrito por acuerdo del Municipio para conmemorar las que se celebraron en 1886* (Granada: Imprenta de la Lealtad á carge de J. G. Garrido, 1886).

10. Gertrude P. Kurath, "Mexican Moriscas: A Problem in Dance Acculturation," *Journal of American Folklore* 62 (1949): 224.

Her early articles provide valuable information on the origins of the dance in the Old World,[11] and of its meaning and distribution as "part of a large and popular family of ritual dances" in New World contexts.[12] Kurath introduces the idea that oppositions in sword dances from which the matachines derive are symbolic remnants of fertility rituals or vegetation rites,[13] but she does not develop the idea of a Moorish connection in these or later publications.

John Robb cites evidence of the relationship between the English Morris dances and the New World matachines, emphasizing their common origins in the "morisca, or moresca (from which *morris* derives), a pantomimic dance of the fifteenth and sixteenth centuries that was executed in Moorish costumes and other grotesque disguises, the dancers having small bells attached to their legs." These occurred "in two types, a solo dance and as a dance between two groups representing a sword fight between Christians and Mohammedans."[14]

Aurora White Lea, quoting from the *Dictionary of Folklore, Mythology and Legend*, reiterates Kurath's suggestion that "the word *matachin* comes from the Arabic . . . [and] that a form of Morisca dance was widespread in Renaissance Europe."[15] In his *Morris and Matachin*, John Forrest traces the Arabic etymology of the word to the *Glossaire des mots espagnols et portugais dérivés de l'Arabe* (1869):[16]

> He [Dozy] suggested that the term was derived from the Arabic word *mutawajjihin* 'maskers', the present participle plural of *tawajjaha* 'to assume a mask', a denominative verb from *wajh* 'face'. From Arabic it passed into Spanish and thence to Italian and French.[17]

Forrest believes this derivation to have been invented by Dozy, and this may have been the case. According to my colleague Frederick Denny, an Islamic religious studies scholar, one can invent words in Arabic. Denny also points out that the third form of *tawajjaha*, "to face each other," is *muwajahatan*, meaning "face to face." The rarely used sixth form would be *mutawajjihin*, that could be translated as "those who put on a face"—one of the meanings that Kurath has suggested—but a more likely translation, that she has also suggested, would be "those who face each other." The word for "to mask" or "to veil" is *al-mutanakkara*, that literally means "incognito" or "in disguise."

Given the different words used for "mask," the extension of *mutawajjahin* to mean "maskers" seems far fetched, if grammatically possible. When spoken by a native speaker

---

11. Kurath, "Mexican Moriscas," and "The Origin of the Pueblo Indian Matachines," *El Palacio* 64, nos. 9-10 (September-October 1957).

12. Kurath, "Mexican Moriscas," 88.

13. Kurath, "Origin," 263.

14. John D. Robb, "The Matachines Dance—A Ritual Folk Dance," *Western Folklore* 20 (1961): 88-89.

15. Aurora White Lea, "More About the Matachines," *New Mexico Folklore Record* 9 (1963-64): 7.

16. *Glossaire des mots espagnols et portugais dérivés de l'Arabe*, ed. Reinhart Dozy and W. H. Engelmann (Leyde: E. J. Brill, 1869).

17. John Forrest, *Morris and Matachin, A Study in Comparative Choreography* (Sheffield: Centre for English Cultural Tradition and Language, University of Sheffield, 1984).

of Arabic today, the pronunciation is very close to the Spanish pronunciation of the word *matachine,* but the pronunciation of *wajh* (face) in medieval Spanish dialect was *ujj,* which would alter the spelling to *mutawujjihin.*[18] This fact further challenges the hypothesis that *matachine* is a corruption of the Arabic *mutawajjahin.* Finally, although the Moors tolerated Christians as second-rate citizens, and many Arabic words found their way into the Spanish language over almost eight hundred years of Moorish dominance in Spain, would not in itself suggest that the matachines dance was derived from the Moors. It is doubtful that the Spanish would have copied a Moorish dance during the 400-year war preceeding the expulsion of the Moors to North Africa, except to symbolize a Christian victory over the "infidel."

European Origins Theories

In addition to suggesting possible New World indigenous origins (Nahuatl, or Aztecan), Lea offers an alternative Old World derivation: "For those who think the Arabic origin debatable there is also the theory that its ancestry might be traceable to the Strolling, Medieval Buffoon Dancers, ultimately the Pantomimi of Rome, in a blend with ritual fools of pre-Christian Europe."[19] Champe disregards the possibility of a Nahuatl origin for the term *matachine* and, quoting the *Oxford Dictionary,* also casts doubt on Kurath's Arabic derivation: "It is true this [*mutawajjihin*] could apply to the present-day New Mexican Matachines, since the dancers have their faces covered, or masked, and, from time to time, face their partners. But over the centuries it has not been customary for all Matachines to be masked at all times."[20] She suggests that the term was coined in Italy, the dance having followed a path "from the Orient, to Greece, and then to Italy and Spain." She suggests the possibility that in Italy the dance was originally a satirical parody at Marco Polo's expense, and cites the usual Spanish dictionary synonyms for *matachin* as "scoundrel," "harlequin," "puppet-player," "indecent," and the like.[21] To strengthen this connection, Champe relies on Arbeau's explanation of the *bouffons* or *mattachins* sword dances derived from the Roman *salii* (dancers) or the Greek weapons dance called the *Pyrrhic.* The *salii* were appointed

> by King Numa, to the number of twelve, to celebrate the sacred festivals of Mars, being dressed in painted robes with rich baldrics and pointed caps, swords at their sides, little sticks in their right hands and bucklers in their left (of which one was said to have come down from Heaven) danced to the sound of *tibiae* and made martial gestures, sometimes successively, sometimes all together.[22]

She is correct that Arbeau never refers to the *mattachins* (or *bouffons*) as Moorish dances, having made this connection with the *morisque* and the Morris dance of

---

18. Special thanks to Professor Denny for checking various Arabic language dictionaries and sources and providing this information.

19. Lea, 7.

20. Champe, 1.

21. Ibid., 2.

22. Thoinot Arbeau, *Orchesography* (Paris, 1583; reprints, London: Cyril W. Beaumont, 1925, and New York: Dover, 1967), 153.

England.[23] Champe cites Sharp's early position that "the Morris dance has a Moorish kinship and may have been introduced into England in the fourteenth century at the time of Edward III, when John of Gaunt returned from Spain."[24] If Morris and the New Mexican matachines can be said to have had common roots, the same music may have been used with both Morris and *buffons* dances, for it is Arbeau's *buffons* melody that is still in evidence in the New Mexican matachines repertories.

Musical Evidence

Arbeau's transcription of the *buffons* melody is stylistically reminiscent of matachines melodies and two of his *morisque* airs[25] bear a striking resemblance to a New Mexican matachines melody one frequently hears in many variations. Arbeau's *bouffons* melodies are all the same, with negligible variation (quarter note substituting for two eighth notes or vice-versa), to accompany each dance, although the dances themselves have differentiating titles.[26] Perhaps the choreography changed with the titles, as occurs with the matachines, but I know of no matachines in which fewer than six melodies are employed throughout the entire dance ritual, although some melodies may be repeated for more than one dance section of the entire ritual. Ex.26.1a features Arbeau's *bouffons* melody as an example of the simple rhythms and gestures also typical of matachines melodies. Exx. 26.1b and 26.1c compare Arbeau's *morisque* melody with matachines melodies from New Mexico.

The similarity of motives defined by rhythm and pitch between the different melodies of exx. 26.1b and 26.1c is apparent, and is instantly recognizable once one is familiar with the melodies. While the skeptic might hold that the melodies are basically developed from triads and therefore the identities are not surprising, it is the characteristic gestures (motives) of the combined rhythm and pitch that so closely resemble matachines. During the course of this study, I compared the folk music styles of many regions of Spain with the matachines style and found only one (from old Castilla) in which both melodic and rhythmic combinations resembled the matachines.[28] Perhaps these similarities hold greater significance than would be the case if song repetition were not such a prominent feature of the *matachines* (as it was with Arbeau's sword dances). The comparisons of

Example 26.1a: Arbeau's *bouffons* melody,[27] in the key of C.

23. Ibid., 149.

24. Champe, 2.

25. Arbeau, 149-50.

26. Ibid., 156-62.

27. Ibid., 156.

28. See chapter 1 of my dissertation.

Example 26.1b: La Malinche, San Juan Pueblo and Alcalde, compared to Arbeau's *morisque.*

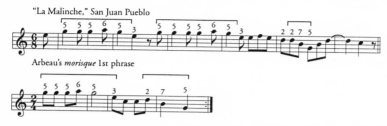

Example 26.1c: *Cerrada* (closing), San Juan Pueblo and Alcalde, compared to Arbeau's *morisque.*

Arbeau's *morisque* melody with the San Pueblo/Alcalde *matachines* melody in ex. 26.1a illustrates similarity of melodic combinations, while ex. 26.1b illustrates similarities in both rhythmic combinations (1) and melodic contours (2). The repetition of motives within phrases is another characterizing feature of many of the *matachines* melodies of New Mexico, and can easily be seen throughout Arbeau's *bouffons* in ex. 26.1c.

Old World Contexts

Forrest's *Morris and Matachin* presents significant Old World parallels to the development of the dance in the New World. In the process of uncovering sources to document the links that exist between the Morris and matachines dances, he illuminates the medieval European contexts of which the matachines were a part. With regard to origins of the dance, Forrest first cites Francis Douce's "A Dissertation on the Ancient Morris Dance," an appendix to the author's *Illustrations of Shakespeare.*[29] Among Forrest's summarized list of contributions supplied by Douce to the information on origins, he mentions that there are remnants of the ancient Pyrric dance in the Morris dance, but that "the *Pyrrhica Saltatio* that former authors had referred to goes under the name *Matachins* in France and Italy and was brought to England at one time. But, this dance differs from the *common morris.*" Forrest also notes that Douce discounts the theory that John Gaunt brought the dance to Spain at the time of Edward III, "since no trace of it can be found in England prior to the time of Henry VII."[30]

---

29. Francis Douce, *Illustrations of Shakespeare:* Gesta Romanorum; *and on the English Morris Dance* (1839; reprint, New York: B. Franklin, 1968).

30. Forrest, 2. Edward III lived from 1312 to 1377; Henry VII lived from 1457 to 1509.

Addressing the question of the dance's origins in ancient fertility rites, which Sharp and others have proposed, Forrest quotes from Sir Edmund Chambers's 1903 book *The Medieval Stage*, in which the connection between ancient ritual and folk dance is explored:

> The customs of the village festival gave rise by natural development to two types of dance. There was the processional dance of the band of worshippers in progress round the boundaries and from field to field, from house to house, from well to well of the village.[31]

In San Juan Pueblo, where the Spanish Europeans exerted their earliest influence in what is now New Mexico, the matachines still make a circuit to the houses of the important dancers in the matachines ritual, where they perform the entire dance. This practice differs from traditional Pueblo practices and may have been introduced with the matachines. Forrest himself later discredits the idea that the Morris or matachin dances originated in fertility rites as Sharp proposed, because the dances were calendric rather than life-cycle rituals, and because their context was in or around the courts all through the first half of the sixteenth century.[32]

Forrest notes that Chambers also suggested that the name "Morris" derives from spectators who thought that the dancers were Moorish because they blackened their faces in imitation of Moors. Because of an old "custom of smearing the face with the beneficent ashes of the festival fire,"[33] however, the black-faced dancers were probably thought to be Moors.[34] Nonetheless, Forrest finds no evidence that the early Morris dancers ever blackened their faces, and concluded that Chambers mistook mummers for Morris dancers, although there is no connection between them.[35] Heath-Coleman mentions that English Molly dancers, often dancing in the same contexts as Morris dancers, always blacken their faces.[36] There is no proof, however, that the dancers were imitating Moors; more likely they were participating in a religious rite, perhaps one related to fertility.

Forrest also cites another influential work, *The Morris Book*, in which Cecil Sharp replaces his earlier hypothesis that the Morris dance was originally Moorish with a new one that postulates "that the morris dance is a development of a pan-European, or even more widely extended custom," rather than "that the European customs [could] have been *contaminated* [emphasis mine] very generally by Moorish influence."[37] Forrest

---

31. Ibid., 2.

32. Ibid., 23.

33. Ibid., 5.

34. Kurath, "Mexican Moriscas," 99, credits Cecil Sharp with making this distinction in his 1912 publication: Cecil James Sharp and Herbert C. Macilwaine, *The Morris Book,* 2nd ed., 3 vols. (London: Novello, 1912, 1919, and 1924).

35. Forrest, 18.

36. Philip Heath-Coleman, "Forrest and Matachin: An Assessment of John Forrest's 'Morris and Matachin,'" *Folk Music Journal* 5 (1985): 95.

37. Sharp's choice of words here probably reflects an understanding of the severity with which all things Islamic were kept separate from all things European in medieval times, culminating with the Inquisition.

discusses Sharp's influence on other well-known scholars of the time, including Violet Alford and Rodney Gallop; all emphasized the commonality of dances celebrating the expulsion of the Moors from Europe in the Middle Ages.[38] Such dances were then superimposed on pre-existing fertility dances, which often included animal sacrifice. Forrest notes that Sir James George Frazer, in *The Golden Bough*,[39] theorized that the dancers' bells were probably a means of dispelling "the demons who might hinder the growth of the corn, or to waken the spirits of vegetation from their long winter sleep."[40] The San Juan Pueblo matachines dancers sometimes wear bells, which arrived with the Spanish Europeans, around their ankles; one wonders if the bells did not accompany the introduction of the matachines dance.

According to Forrest, the first references to the matachines are found in Italy. I concur that the likelihood is indeed much greater that the real derivation of matachines is the Italian word *mattaccino,* meaning "charlatan, jester, mimic, odd fellow; strolling player."[41] The root of the word is *matto,* "mad" or "fool," and it derives from the Latin *mattus* or *matus,*[42] from the Sanskrit for "mad" or "to be drunk." Among the Romans it meant "drunk," "intoxicated."[43] The profane processional contexts of matachines and similar dances carried connotations of uncontrolled, presumably humorous, behavior suitable for the celebratory occasions in which the dances appeared. If one can judge from contemporary matachines village contexts in New Mexico, much of the uncontrolled behavior was featured in burlesques which accompanied the dancing.

Possible Headdress and Mask Origins

Most citations mention the use of masks, which came to be associated with the matachines in the way that bells came to be associated with the Morris dancers, who do not wear masks. The matachines also wore bells, however. The idea of the English masque and antimasque originates in a custom of "disguisings," which were an important part of Christmas and Shrovetide (the three days before Ash Wednesday) festivities in the English royal court during the fourteenth century. It is interesting to note that the word *masque* itself is derived from the Arabic word for mask, *maskhara,* which was associated with clowns and buffoonery,[44] and came to England via France in the early sixteenth century.[45]

---

38. Forrest, 6.

39. Sir James George Frazer, *The Golden Bough: A Study in Magic and Religion* (New York: Macmillan, 1900).

40. Forrest, 7. This makes one wonder why medieval jesters wore bells; perhaps it was not only simply a way of creating a cheerful atmosphere. Among the Pueblos, the clowns are most sacred in part because they insure the "right heart" essential to a ritual's efficacy. Jill D. Sweet, *Dances of the Tewa Pueblo Indians* (Santa Fe: School of American Research Press, 1985).

41. *Cassell's Italian Dictionary,* comp. Piero Rebora, with Francis M. Guercio and Arthur L. Hayward (New York: Macmillan, 1979).

42. Forrest, 34.

43. *A Latin Dictionary,* comp. Charleton T. Lewis and Charles Short (Oxford: Clarendon Press, 1962).

44. *Webster's New World Dictionary of the American Language,* 2nd ed., ed. David B. Guralnick (Cleveland: William Collins and World Publishing Co., 1972).

45. Herbert Arthur Evans, *English Masques* (New York: Books for Libraries Press, 1971), xii.

Although the English spelling "mask" or "maske" was used at first, by the end of the century the English preferred the French spelling.[46] In England the word "viser" was previously used to denote a mask, and the early use of the term maske referred to an entertainment, the "disguise" of former times.

I note elsewhere that the English may have imitated the Spanish fringed mask during the period that the matachines was first introduced in England. It is questionable, however, whether the Italians ever used the fringed masks in the street and popular theater entertainments of the day. The Italian masks associated with the *mattacino* jester dances are mostly half masks covering the eyes and nose; they are anthropomorphic and realistic, if satirically exaggerated. The nose in particular is often long and exaggerated to suggest pomposity and deceit. It is more significant that the word *mattacino* is merely an Italian translation of the Spanish-Arabic word for mask, in the context of clowns or buffoonery. It was probably the French, as close neighbors to the Spanish, who first coined the Arabic term that was probably commonly used in Spain by the sixteenth century. That the Italian term *mattacino* survived in the New World is most likely a reflection of the dominance of the Church and Roman Papal authority in Spanish culture during and after the reconquest of Spain.[47] Italians currently use the word *maschera* to mean mask, masked figure at a dance, masked man, disguise, masque, death mask, (theater) attendant, or (fencing) faceguard.[48] The term does not imply the buffoonery of the term *mattacino*.

The most suggestive Moorish element of the dress, a fringe over the eyes, may have originated in the desert hat with beaded fringe that is still found among some mountain peoples of the Sahara region. Evidence in support of an Old World provenance of the fringe is a hat that resembles the Saharan one described above, currently used by the Chinelo Carnival dancers in Mexico for pre-Lenten festivities. The hat features a fringe and beaded loops dangling over the face. Such a hat can only be interpreted as a surviving remnant from colonial times; in addition to the elaborate beaded hats, the Chinelo dancers also wear lavish velvet costumes such as those worn in Old World processions.[49] Such extravagance was common and somewhat worrisome to the Church in Spain:

> Once more these theatrical representations gradually took on such a character of profane fiestas, that neither the Councils nor the pragmatic nobility could contain the abuses throughout the fifteenth century. The arch priest of Talavera, in his *Condemnation of Mundane Love (Sacred Spain, The Geographic-Historic Church Theater of Spain*, vol. 45) reveals the luxury with which damas and caballeros attended these fiestas, "showing not only rouge but also solimán [a volatile white substance made up of two parts bleach and one part mercury (*Encyclopedia del Idioma*, 1958)] and perfumes with which they made up their faces, in the mouth they carried cinnamon, tropical cloves and other equally fragrant herbs, with which they excited the senses more than the devotion of their lovers. On the other hand,

---

46. Ibid., xv.

47. For example, severe punishment accompanied even the finding of a book written in Arabic during the Inquisition.

48. *Cassell's Italian Dictionary.*

49. Donald Cordry, *Mexican Masks* (Austin: University of Texas Press, 1980), 74.

they rushed to add to their costumes whatever had most recently been invented by the refinement of an excessivley effeminate epoch.[50]

Contradictory evidence in support of Old World origins of the fringe is manifest in Zuni Pueblo face masks, which feature human or horse hair fringe hanging over the eyes, but it is equally possible that such masks resulted from matachines influence.

The matachines headdress is characterized by tall decorated hats from which multi-colored ribbons fall, with scarves covering the mouth, neck, and back, and with a bead or cloth fringe covering the eyes. The combination evokes the image of a Near Eastern desert tribal costume and, as previously stated, it is the headdress that has most stimulated discussion of the possible Arabic derivation of the dance itself. Champe distinguishes between "three possible interpretations: Spanish-Arabic, Aztecan, and Catholic," stating a strong argument in favor of the Aztecan origins, on the basis of the similarity of construction between the matachines headdress and the crown worn by Aztec lords and high officials.[51] In New Mexico the hat appears to be most closely related to Old World bishops' miter hats, the front of which were embroidered or otherwise decorated, sometimes with precious jewels, but the shape and style is also very similar to that of traditional ceremonial hats worn by the Tuareg men who inhabit the Moroccan desert.[52]

Original Research on Old World Origins

Very little has been written about the matachines dances in Spain. As demonstrated above, several scholars have speculated that they derived from the antique mimes of the Italian *commedia dell'arte,* having reached Spain via France. While this derivation seems logical on the basis of the Italian origins of the word *mattachino,* a close examination of the Italian comedies reveals a highly developed theatrical genre, which introduced to the Spanish the classic Italian characters "Arlequino (Harlequin), del Pantalone, y del Dotore."[53] If one is to accept an Italian origin of the matachines, it has to be from one of the later theatrical genres, and not from the dance that became the New World matachines. In Spain, a play version of the matachines or other such genres was sometimes incorporated into theatrical settings as an *entremés* (literally "side dish"), a kind of theatrical interlude.[54] The *entremés* was a brief comic scene usually associated with

---

50. Valladar, 33-34; my translation.

51. Champe, 5. I consider the Aztec headdress an aspect that encouraged acceptance of the matachines in New World contexts within a broader process of syncretism, but I discount the idea that Aztec hats were the prototype for the New Mexican matachines headdress. I base my opinion on a general familiarity with Aztec ceremonial headdresses and on the more striking matachines resemblance to other headress types.

52. Henri Lhote, *Les Touaregs du Hoggar* (Paris: Bibliothèque Scientifique, 1955), 305. Originally the matachines probably represented subdued Moslems; perhaps in modern-day New Mexico the matachines subconsciously imitate church authority figures who wear the miter hat. If so, this is an example of the ways change in meaning can occur over time and place for folk idioms in general.

53. Hugo Albert Rennert, *Spanish Stage in the Time of Lope de Vega* (1909; reprint, New York: Dover, 1963), 30.

54. The theatrical interlude was common practice in Europe, as evidenced by the early use of opera buffa between the acts of more serious theatrical pieces.

commoners and low social status; it was a one-act farce characterized in some fashion by ridicule, be it of incompetence, adultery, effeminate men, hypocrisy, and so forth.[55] The profane dance called the matachines is characterized by Covarrubias thus:

> The matachines dance is very similar to that which the Thracians used in ancient times, who, armed with snares and light leather infantry vests (*Encyclopedia del idioma,* 1958) with bare arms and legs, with shields and big pans to the sound of the flutes, went out leaping (skipping) and dancing and to the beat, gave each other such awful blows that spectators were afraid. . . . Some fell on the ground and the victors despoiled them. And because of this apparent havoc, in which they appear to kill each other we can call them matachines.[56]

The Thracian dances may be a reference to the Pyrrhic dances previously mentioned, which were called *matachin* in Italy and France.

Dances such as the matachines, that could function as vehicles of social protest through satire, were likely to choose authority figures as objects of contempt, as is still encountered in New Mexico.[57] Such profane dances were outlawed in processions by the Church in the sixteenth century.[58] The prohibition no doubt led to a decline in street performances, especially during the Inquisition, and coincided with their slightly greater prominence in the theater. How then, does one explain the survival of such dances in places such as Palencia in Castilla, and in the New World? The *auto* (literally "act"), a religious play, that included music and dance in all phases of its development,[59] was eventually associated with the Corpus Christi festival (instituted in Spain in 1264), producing the *auto sacramental,* "a dramatized exposition of the Mystery of the Blessed Eucharist."[60] Aurelio Capmany's description of a *danza sacramental* (for the Corpus Christi feast) dates back to 1508 in Sevilla:

> . . . the ten boys appear barefoot between the bench pews, forming two lines, some in front of others, with their hats under their arms and the castañuelas in their hands. The four boys who are the tallest, situated at the ends of the two lines, are called the "tip," or "point"; the four immediately next to them are called "seconds," and the two in both centers are called "trancos."[61]

55. Gaspar Merino-Quijano, "Los bailes dramaticos del siglo XVII, tomo I" (tesis doctoral, Departamento de Literatura Española, Sección de Filología, Facultad de Filología, Universidad Complutense de Madrid, 1981), 107-08.

56. Ibid., 120. *Tesoro de la lengua castellana or española: Compuesto por Sebastian de Covarruvias Orozco* (Madrid: Turner, 1977). My translation.

57. Sylvia Rodriguez, an anthropologist at the University of New Mexico, pointed this out to me in a video of a recent matachines dance in Arroyo Seco, where the *abuelos* dressed like the priest and characterized priestly excesses.

58. Valladar, 34.

59. The term originally applied to plays in general but came to apply to religious plays (Rennert, 67). In other non-theatrical contexts, the term auto is primarily a legalistic term, meaning decree, edict, etc.

60. Valladar, 48.

61. Josep Crivillé i Bargalló, *Historia de la música española* (Madrid: Alianza Música, 1988), 199. "Trancos" refers to a not very graceful long step. My translation.

The variety of early dances from which matachines developed included basic formats, such as *danzas de cascabel* (dances in which the dancers wore bells), and *danzas de espada* (sword dances), on which many scenarios could be superimposed, depending on the religious occasion. During the Inquisition such sacred contexts no doubt assured the survival of a New World matachines whose religious significance, among traditional Mejicanos, is closely related to colonial Catholic ideology.

Related North African Survivals

Extending this investigation of early origins of the matachines to North Africa, one finds that similar dances were still performed at festivals there at the turn of the century. Among the Tuaregs of today, there is still a masked "warrior's dance" in which the men carry swords and wear the tall decorated ceremonial hats from which a cloth fringe falls around the head. The faces are veiled, although this in itself is normal for Tuareg men, who wear veils at all times even though the women do not wear them.[62] They are described as performing "leaps and wild gestures, swinging their swords, and executing a war dance, and then another."[63] Because dance is not common among Tuareg traditions, the syncopated sword dance is likely to have come from the Arabic speaking groups further south of Tuareg territory.[64] The headdress is strikingly similar to the one used in the New World matachines. One wonders whether the fringe hanging from the top may be an old association with Old World rain-bringing traditions such as those in which hair served as a metaphor for rain.[65] Another association, perhaps more remote, is a North African tradition that attaches to a tuft of hair at the top of the head a *hámsa*, consisting of "glass beads threaded on strings in such a manner as to resemble the five fingers of a hand, as a charm against the evil eye."[66]

At the turn of the century there were North African masked dance traditions that served as part of rain-petitioning rituals. Westermarck cites a ritual in which bizarre costumes and masks were worn by men dressed as women who danced women's dances to the music of a flute and tambourine. In other dances most of the dancers covered their faces with soot or fat, and wound around the old tents.[67] Women participated in rain rituals; "the fluttering of the loosened hair [was] also believed to produce rain," and they were required to stay outdoors until the drought had ended.[68]

Westermarck has some evidence that the ancient Libyans may have had "ceremonial combats for the purpose of producing rain"; such combats may have been due to the influence of the ancient Phoenicians, as a goddess called Athena is featured in at least one

---

62. René Gardi, Karl Suter, Alexander Wandeler, and Hans Rhotert, *Sahara* (London: George G. Harrap & Co., 1970), 71-73.

63. Ibid., 143.

64. Francis Rennell Rodd, *People of the Veil* (London: Macmillan, 1926), 272.

65. Edward Westermarck, *Ritual and Belief in Morocco*, 2 vols. (London: Macmillan, 1926), 2:262.

66. Ibid., 418.

67. Ibid., 258.

68. Ibid., 262.

of these combats[69] that act out the "strife between drought and rain."[70] In addition, there were various times when processions featured masquerades.

Among the characters portrayed in the Moroccan dances were some that are also found in the New Mexican matachines, but do not usually appear in historical references to the Spanish dances. This difference suggests that such burlesques were censured in Spain. One Moroccan character is a woman who "gives birth to a child with shrieks of agony when a performance is made in a house." That woman is a man dressed up as a Jewess.[71] In New Mexico a man often dresses up as an old woman (but without reference to any ethnicity or religious affiliation). There is also a Moroccan custom in which the various characters in masquerade include an old man and an old woman. "They sing and play, their talk is most lascivious, and the behaviour of the old couple in particular is as indecent as it could be."[72] Among one tribe, the couple is supposed to be an old Jew and his wife who are encouraged and pretend to have intercourse on the ground.[73] In New Mexico the indecent old couple is a regular aspect of the Alcalde matachines, and the birth of a child from the transvestite is a regular feature of the Taos Pueblo matachines as well as others.[74]

Among the mountain tribes of northern Morocco, the Great Feast Carnival at the turn of the century featured another character similar to one in the New Mexican matachines; it is a man dressed in the skin of a sacrificed animal who was both mocked and ridiculed, and held to possess healing powers. The part was played by a man with a skin disease of some kind, in order to be cured by the sacrificial skins.[75] Typically he was a poor man who received food and money collected when a procession went from house to house.[76] An old man was featured in this festival as well, symbolizing the Old Year as an object of ridicule and mockery.[77] Another man or boy was dressed as a woman and played the wife of either the man in the skin, or of the old man. Alternatively, the man in the skin and the old man fought over the "young woman." Others dressed up as Jews or Christians; all sang, danced, and acted, walking from house to house or tent to tent.[78]

Another interesting detail which one sees also in New Mexico is described in a Berber version of the feast: "a man is made to represent a ram or a he-goat by being

---

69. The ancient presence of the Phoenicians in the south of Spain is documented by the Archeology Museum in Granada, in a display of a Phoenician cave tomb with the remains of an entire group of Phoenicians.

70. Westermarck, 2:272.

71. Ibid., 82.

72. Ibid., 84.

73. Ibid., 138.

74. Sylvia Rodriguez, *The Matachines Dance: Ritual Symbolism and Interethnic Relations in the Rio Grande Valley* (Albuquerque: University of New Mexico Press, 1996).

75. Westermarck, 2:147.

76. Ibid., 136. In Spanish, *baraka* translates as *bendición,* or blessing. Among the plains Arabs, people believed that being beaten with the skins of the sacrificed animals could heal illness because "there is *baraka,* holiness, in this beating."

77. Ibid., 85.

78. Ibid., 133.

dressed in the skins of sacrificed sheep or goats, and holding in either hand a short stick, which gives him the appearance of walking on four legs."[79] Among the Pueblos the sticks held in order to more closely resemble the animal is seen not only in the matachines but in game dances as well. This is not seen among other North American Indian groups, possibly suggesting an Old World matachines influence.[80] In the old Moroccan dances the dancer beat the spectators with the sticks to heal them by expelling evil.[81] These Moorish masquerades were essentially purificatory and the participants in the spectacle were given food and money. It can be said that the use of bawdy behavior in the burlesques is purificatory in that those aspects of humanity that hide themselves, especially sexual or erotic concerns, are aired and their psychological power is thus diffused in laughter. In this fashion obscenity is a symbolic reversal, teaching about "correct" behavior in an indirect fashion. Here it is a way of attributing such behavior to members of other religions and cultures, Christians and Jews, the ancient historical enemies of Islam, thereby both making fun of those cultures and discouraging that behavior among Moslems.

Westermarck believes that since obscenity as an element of ritual is pre-Islamic in North Africa, it is also likely to have initially expressed opposition to Islam. This suggests that the burlesques, many elements of which have survived in New Mexico, are older than the Islamic presence in North Africa and Spain. That these rituals are not found in the Mashriqi (the Arab countries of the East)[82] suggests a connection with Europe, perhaps with the early, pre-Christian Romans, who also struck people, mostly infertile women, with the strips of hide from the sacrificed animal. Westermarck notes various other reasons that indicate the Moorish carnivals were related to the early Roman festivals, although he mentions similar animal masquerades among the Celtic peoples and in paleolithic drawings in Spain, in the south of France, and among the Berbers.[83]

These descriptions of ancient Moroccan dances from the turn of the century demonstrate the persistence of profanity in celebratory rituals from North Africa, to Spain, and to the New World. Since the Church censured such profanity, descriptions such as Westermarck's do not survive in most Spanish sources, although evidence of the popularity of such profanity is clearly seen in some of the surviving forms of the New World matachines. It is impossible to know the degree to which the historical antagonism between Christianity and Islam has censured the Moorish connections in literature of the past.

---

79. Ibid., 139.

80. Among the Creeks in the Southeast, ball game participants hold their game sticks racket-side up for dances. The sticks are three feet long and the dancers do not wear animal costumes (Charlotte Heth, personal communication, 1991), although they are apparently identified with animals in other ways. This is different from the Pueblos' use of sticks.

81. Westermarck, 2:147.

82. Ibid., 149.

83. Ibid., 156-58.

Matachines from Old to New World

Because of the Church's role in censuring profane displays in Spain, they probably declined quickly after their prohibition in Church processions in 1780.[84] It was not the first time such displays had been prohibited by the Church; that they survived at all in Spain and to the extent that they did in the New World is because not all of the dances were profane nor were all contexts prohibited; the *danza sacramental* is one example.

In Spain the choreographies, the circumstances for their performance, and the places of performance all imply that some of the dances were associated with rituals of well-being and prosperity, and others with rain rituals. There were also obvious links between fertility rites and sword dances as prophylactics against psychic harm and physical ailments.[85] Some aspects of the burlesque seem to have been maintained only in Moorish Spain and survived in the New World as they were originally introduced in the early years of the Conquest. That the fringe over the eyes has been preserved in New Mexico and Mexico suggests a syncretism with New World mask traditions in which there was an attendant supernatural association, such as rain-bringing power or warding off the evil eye, with this element of the costume.

Those who insist that the matachines originated in the equestrian, narrated dances of the Moors and Christians ignore the great capacity for fantasy that the Spanish exemplified in their emphasis on dance, music, and acting. As evidenced by the following, the matachines were always pantomimed:

> *Matachines.* A grotesque dance which in Spain served primarily to end mojigangas. The characteristic feature of mojiganga dancers was the extravagant costume, which was not determined by any particular idea , at times of a savage, and the movements immodest and exaggerated, even if always rhythmic and coordinated. In addition to the dance, it was a kind of pantomime.[86]

Mimed dances or their remnants, of a Spanish origin (or perhaps Spanish-influenced), are still found in Mexico. For example, a dance that survives in different versions in Mexico is called the *vaquero,* or Cowboy Dance. All versions feature a central scene in which a bull is captured; in the old days it was a real bull that was then killed. There are two groups of dancers, each with its own captain (*capitan*) who engages in dialogue with the other captain, while both perform "tactical movements with their men."[87] Among the New Mexicans, the matachines at the front and end of the lines are often called "capitanes." The essence of the *mojiganga* in Spain was the mask (often in animal shapes), the unusual costumes (both ridiculous and extravagant, including bells and wooden swords which might carry cow's bladders), the movement, tumult and disorder, and the dancing. The *mojiganga* survives in some Mexican contexts as a procession mask made of a cow's pelvis, with cloth covering the head and face underneath

---

84. Valladar, 102.

85. Crivillé i Bargalló, 99.

86. *Diccionario de la música labor,* iniciado por Joaquin Pena, continuado por Higinio Anglés, Pbro, 2 vols. (Madrid: Editorial Labor, S. A., 1954), 2:1494. My translation.

87. Cordry, 238.

the pelvic bone, and held on by tying a rope around mask and head. The person who wears the mask is a musician playing a drum or shaking a noisemaker that lets the townspeople know that the fiesta is about to begin.[88] In the mountain regions of south Mexico the *mojiganga* is a devil character in the Devil Dance.[89]

Arturo Warman speculates that the matachines became important in the colonization of the northern frontier, and that the Franciscans brought and utilized the dance to further indoctrination after the eighteenth century.[90] When the theocracy, both Church and state, failed to find the seven cities of gold, the powerful left this northern area of New Spain, and consequently it was the heavily male dominated Church societies that attended to the preservation of Catholicism. Warman's thesis undermines the faith and independence of the early Spanish colonists, whose isolation in the north prevented written accounts of that developing culture for nearly 150 years before the eighteenth century. The early colonists could and probably did preserve an early matachines in their isolation from Church authority, as a form of religious observance and entertainment. They probably added aspects of various other remembered dances (such as the *vaqueros* dance mentioned above) in the eclectic, creative manner they knew, to create what we now know as the New Mexican matachines. The dance was colorful and ceremonial, and the music was repetitive. No doubt the Spanish soldiers saw its great potential for attracting or perhaps subduing the *indigenes*, but clearly it was important to the Spanish for purely cultural reasons.

Indigenous ritual practices must have reinforced the kinds of performance contexts that were transplanted, and had flourished in Spain prior to the seventeenth century. Because the Indians tended to perform rituals as they were received (sometimes with grave penalties for making mistakes), and because the Franciscans allowed various choreographic elements of indigenous rituals to be retained, the survival of the matachines in the New World was ensured.

The dances continued to be accompanied by medieval dance tunes that changed gradually and to which new melodies were sometimes added. Adrian Treviño suggests that the dances were originally representations of martial formations and maneuvers.[91] Others concur that the music is old Spanish martial music.[92] The melodies do not sound typically Spanish, but there can be little doubt that they originated in Europe; the ornamentation has more in common with Arabic ornamentation than with notated Western European medieval practices.

---

88. Ibid., 81, 112.

89. Juan Guillermo Contreras Arias, class lecture, Albuquerque, N.M., July 1995.

90. Arturo Warman, *La danza de Moros y Cristianos* (Mexico City: Instituto Nacional de Antropología e Historia, 1972), 129.

91. Adrian Treviño, personal communication, December 1988.

92. Aurelio M. Espinosa, *The Folklore of Spain in the American Southwest* (Norman: University of Oklahoma Press, 1985), 226.

Conclusions

In an encompassing glimpse of the past, then, one sees various historical and simultaneous influences on the matachines, including those of ancient European and pre-Islamic North African fertility rites, of Roman sword dances with symbolic content, of possible Islamic influences on the headdress and musical ornamentation, and of European folk music as well as of theatricals and social parody. All of these and many other connections speak to the timeless dimension of the human recognition of ritual for self-empowerment over natural elements and within the social order. This more than anything else is the contemporary spirit of matachines performance in New Mexico. Essentially an act of faith, the ritual is also an expression of resistance to cultural hegemony, both by design and through its persistence. In coming to know the Old World layers of the matachines, Latinos themselves might better understand the richness of the roots of their own culture and therein find empowerment. *Los Matachines* persists in part because of its classical elements of form, symmetry, and allusions to the "Unknowable." The fringed mask plays no small part, with regard to these allusions.

27

New World Inspiration and
Peggy Glanville-Hicks's Opera *Nausicaa*

Deborah Hayes

Peggy Glanville-Hicks's fourth opera, *Nausicaa,* set in ancient Greece, received its first performance in modern Greece at the 1961 Athens Festival of Drama and Music. Glanville-Hicks (1912-90), an Australian by birth, a New York City resident since the 1940s, and an American citizen since 1948, based the opera on Robert Graves's 1954 novel *Homer's Daughter.* Set in the seventh century B.C., the novel tells of the young princess Nausicaa, who is aided by a foreign prince, Aethon, to defend the palace from would-be usurpers pretending to be her suitors. Nausicaa now instructs the court bard to remove from his repertory an old story of Penelope and her fifty lovers and to sing instead the story of the *Odyssey* that we now attribute to Homer, in which Penelope remains faithful to her husband Odysseus while she awaits his return from the Trojan War. Glanville-Hicks made extensive preparations for the composition of *Nausicaa,* collecting traditional and "demotic" or popular music from archival recordings and from various locations in Greece so that her music would reflect Greek music's essential melodic and rhythmic features.

The three performances of *Nausicaa* in the restored outdoor theater of Herodus Atticus in late August and early September attracted international audiences and virtually world-wide critical attention. The production was international as well. The director/ choreographer was the noted American choreographer John Butler, while the set and costume designer was a Greek, Andreas Nomikos. The principal roles were sung by young Americans of Greek heritage who had attracted Glanville-Hicks's notice in New York, including the Canadian soprano Teresa Stratas in the title role and John Modenos as Aethon. The chorus and orchestra were Greek and rehearsed in Greece; the chorus sang in modern Greek. The principals sang in English; conductor Carlos Surinach rehearsed them in New York, and then they all sailed to Athens to join forces with the local chorus and orchestra. Glanville-Hicks, a distinguished critic and experienced concert producer as well as a composer, supervised every phase of the production and wrote the publicity material and informative program notes.

In December, she published a lengthy discussion of *Nausicaa,* titled "At the Source," in *Opera News.* The next year, she published excerpts from the reviews and a small part of the *Opera News* article in the *American Composers Alliance Bulletin.* A recording of the Athens production, released on the CRI label around 1964, contains excerpts totaling about one hour of music, or about half of the two-hour opera; the recording comes with a copy of the complete libretto, notes by the composer, and excerpts from reviews.[1]

American Inspiration

A review of the circumstances and ideas that led Glanville-Hicks to write a Greek opera in New York must begin with her student years. She began to acquire experience in opera production and a fondness for music theater at the Melbourne Conservatorium, principally from her studies with Fritz Hart (1874-1949), the English conductor and composer of over twenty operas. In the 1930s she studied at the Royal College in London with Ralph Vaughan Williams and others, and later, for a short time, with Nadia Boulanger in France. From Vaughan Williams she acquired her high regard for folk song; she began to conceive of folk song as an international, largely unconscious, source of musical material, which composers needed to "integrate" into their musical consciousness if they were to write good authentic music.

As she recalled in later years, coming to the U.S. in the early 1940s after the "old world" of Europe was an important part of her musical growth. "Going to New York was like coming home! Having come [originally] from the 'new world' [of Australia], it was my cup of tea."[2] Further, she already knew many Americans from her time at the "Boulangerie."[3] She became active in many phases of New York musical life. She wrote hundreds of concert reviews, signed "P. G-H.," for the *New York Herald Tribune,* beginning with the 1947-48 season, and wrote extensively about new music for American periodicals. She managed the Composers Forum series and produced numerous other concerts as well. She was in charge of updating the American material for the fifth edition (1954) of *Grove's Dictionary of Music and Musicians* and wrote almost one hundred of the American composer entries, mostly of composers of her generation and younger.

---

1. Composers Recordings Inc. (New York), CRI 175. There are some differences in the recorded performance from the piano-vocal score in the composer's hand now held by the Library of Congress, which is the source of exx. 27.1 and 27.2 below. This recording is now available on CD 695.

2. From the documentary film/video *P. G-H.: A Modern Odyssey* (Sydney: Juniper Films, 1990).

3. In French, *boulanger* is "baker" and *boulangerie* is "bakery." The punning humor in calling a collection of Boulanger's students a *boulangerie* also results from the general rule that the *-ie* suffix creates a collective noun (for example, *oranger* = orange tree, *orangerie* = orange grove).

Like many of her American composer colleagues, she sought stylistic innovation, and as a critic she frequently theorized about the creation of an enduring new style. For her, the true American direction was independent from the predominant European directions such as atonalism and neoclassicism. She looked for more authentic roots of music, she said, both in historical sources and in individual, spiritual sources within each composer. While her writings show that she admired many American composers whose work "integrated" the essence of American folk and popular idioms, she did not try to develop an American sound herself, but rather an international sound. In the works of the 1950s she adapted traditional melodies and rhythms of several parts of the world: Spain (in the Sonata for Harp, 1950-51), central Africa (Sonata for Piano and Percussion, 1951), India (*The Transposed Heads*, 1952-53), North Africa (*Letters from Morocco*, 1952), ancient Etruria on the Italian peninsula (*Etruscan Concerto*, 1954), ancient Rome *(Concertino antico*, 1955), and South America (*Prelude and Presto for Ancient American Instruments*, 1957). She became increasingly interested in ancient, pre-Christian cultures as authentic sources of music; Etruscan civilization intrigued her for its "mystery, intelligence," and matrilineal systems.[4]

For the music of *Nausicaa* Glanville-Hicks built on her famous Asian-influenced "melody-rhythm" structure, first devised in the early 1950s as an alternative to the contrapuntal complexity and harmonic density of the European tradition. In her works from this period, melodies are scored for a few strings, single winds and brass, and sometimes piano and xylophone, with lots of percussion for rhythmic accompaniment: gongs and cymbals for sustained sound, punctuated with timpani, bass drum, snare drum, tom-tom, and triangle. She wrote five-note or six-note melodies based on the gapped scales of folk music, the beauty of which, she frequently observed, depends on the concept of restricted means.

By the time of *Nausicaa,* composed in 1959-60, she had modified the melody-rhythm structure to achieve a more romantic sound, as though her original English training had matured and resurfaced. Works from the mid-1950s contain "vertical blocks" of sound, as the composer described the texture of the *Concerto romantico* (1956) for viola and orchestra—she rarely used the old-fashioned word "chords"—and orchestration is more traditional or romantic. *Nausicaa* calls for an orchestra of fifty-five to sixty players: two flutes, oboe, three clarinets (and bass clarinet), two bassoons (and contrabassoon), pairs of horns and trumpets, one trombone, her standard percussion as listed above, two harps, piano, and strings.

In keeping with the ancient Greek setting, *Nausicaa* contains some classical dramatic devices, including a prologue to preview the plot and a Greek chorus for commentary. As Glanville-Hicks wrote in *Opera News*, "The composition and production of *Nausicaa* followed a kind of artistic journey to the source of the river, both in musical idioms and in forms."[5] The composer also adopted operatic devices from the nineteenth century, including arias, extended scenes for a principal character, recitative and arioso textures,

---

4. Wendy Beckett, *Peggy Glanville-Hicks* (Sydney: CollinsAngus & Robertson, 1992), 129. The biography is based largely on the composer's recollections during the last few years of her life.

5. Glanville-Hicks, "At the Source," *Opera News* 26, no. 5 (December 1961): 8-13.

orchestral interludes, and characteristic motives associated with certain characters and ideas, somewhat like a *leitmotiv* structure. *Nausicaa* has a "symphonic form," she wrote, modelled after Berg's *Wozzeck* but without the atonalism. The music of *Nausicaa* is perhaps best described as thoroughly-researched "exotic" 1960s neo-romantic opera.

A Greek Opera

During the 1950s Glanville-Hicks had searched for some time for a Greek story to serve as a basis for an opera. Her first idea was to use *The Women of Andros* by the American writer Thornton Wilder (1897-1975), and by 1955 she had written a libretto, but Wilder refused to give her permission to use his novel. When Graves's new book *Homer's Daughter* appeared, she wrote to the renowned English classical scholar and poet for permission to adapt it, and he was agreeable. Late in the summer of 1956, she traveled to Mallorca to the sleepy village of Deyá where Graves lived. As she noted in *Opera News,* she "emerged from a summer in Mallorca with the first draft of a libretto for *Nausicaa.*"

Graves had revived a theory that had been proposed in 1896 by Samuel Butler—and dismissed as a huge joke—that the *Odyssey* was not part of the Homeric tradition of the *Iliad,* a story sung by bards known as the "sons of Homer," but of a female tradition, sung by the "daughters of Homer." Graves thought it might be true. In the novel, Nausicaa is a "daughter of Homer"—that is, a storyteller. In a "Historical Note," Graves explained that in an earlier version of the *Odyssey,* Odysseus returned to Ithaca, killed his wife Penelope's fifty lovers, who were "living riotously" together in his absence, and sent Penelope home to her father in disgrace. Odysseus was then accidentally transfixed by a sting-ray spear by his long-lost son Telemachus, who had arrived unannounced and did not recognize him. In the version attributed to Homer, however, Penelope remains a faithful wife. Graves concluded that the *Odyssey* is, despite its male hero, "a poem about and for women." Interviewed with Glanville-Hicks in Athens at the time of the opera production, he explained further that the story is full of details of domestic life, and the information about ships is not accurate because women were not allowed on ancient Greek ships.[6]

Although several reviews named Graves as the librettist, Glanville-Hicks was intentionally ambiguous. The opera "has been arranged from the novel *Homer's Daughter* by Robert Graves," she wrote. Though most of the text is from Graves's book, the libretto was actually prepared by Alastair Reid, whose name even now seldom appears in connection with the opera.[7] My first inkling of Reid's role came from a 1974 article in

---

6. Winifred Carr, "Opera at the Foot of the Acropolis," *Daily Telegraph and Morning Post* (London), 7 September 1961, 11. In the *Odyssey,* book 6, Nausicaa is the name of the princess whom Odysseus, shipwrecked in the last year of his ten-year voyage, first sees washing clothes and bathing in the river with her servant women. She invites him to her father's palace where he recounts his adventures, which continue into book 13—his encounters with the Lotus-Eaters, the Cyclops, the Sirens, Calypso, and others. His hosts supply him with food, clothes, and fine gifts, and deliver him by ship to his own country.

7. A rare listing of Reid as the *Nausicaa* librettist is in Cameron Northouse, *Twentieth-Century Opera in England and the U.S.* (Boston: G.K. Hall, 1976). On the title page of the piano-vocal score the composer has written "Libretto arranged by Robert Graves." The CRI recording cover reads "*Nausicaa . . .* by Peggy Glanville-Hicks and Robert Graves."

the journal *Focus on Robert Graves*.[8] In 1988, wishing further information, I contacted Reid, who told me that in 1956 his close friend Graves passed Glanville-Hicks's letter on to him and asked him to prepare the libretto. Reid almost certainly collaborated on a first draft.[9] Glanville-Hicks probably made strong contributions as well, based on her experience as an operatic composer. She may even have prepared an outline of scenes in New York before the Mallorca trip,[10] perhaps with the help of Reid, who recalls that he had received some ideas from Graves about dramatic structure.

Reid prepared the libretto without charge; he had been in Deyá for part of each year during the time when Graves was writing *Homer's Daughter,* and it remains his favorite of Graves's books. While Glanville-Hicks wrote in her program note that the libretto was complete in 1957, Reid recalls completing the libretto over the summer of 1958 and visiting Glanville-Hicks in New York in December. Both composer and librettist refer to text changes that she made in the course of composing the opera—changes in the connecting lines, not in the main text which is taken from Graves's book. Shortly after the December 1958 meeting, Reid heard the composer speaking on the radio about working line-by-line with Robert Graves, a complete fabrication. She referred to Graves's work on the libretto, even in private correspondence: "Robert and Alastair are re-writing the second and third acts in line with my now crystallised form," she had written to Virgil Thomson in September 1958. Eventually, Reid asked for his name to be removed from any notices about the opera, and she complied. Graves, too, was uncomfortable with being named as librettist, he wrote to her, but decided not to make an issue of it.

The story of Glanville-Hicks's dealings with Reid illustrates several facets of her method of working. Robert Graves was, of course, a famous name in matters of ancient Greek history, and Glanville-Hicks always chose carefully the people with whom she would work. Further, there was an impatient, perhaps desperate quality to many of her dealings at this time, not just with Reid. The four years from 1956 to 1960, when she worked on *Nausicaa* "intermittently," as *Time* magazine reported,[11] was one of intense effort. She was increasingly anxious to accumulate a sizable body of works and sufficient funds to move permanently to Greece, where she could live less expensively than in New York and have more time to compose music. She also was experiencing severe headaches

8. Alan M. Cohn, "Glanville-Hicks's *Nausicaa* and Graves," *Focus on Robert Graves* 4 (June 1974): 71-73. Cohn discovered in the Southern Illinois University manuscript collection five pages of material seemingly from *Homer's Daughter* in Graves's hand, with a note "to Alastair" requesting, "Please revise *Nausicaa*." Cohn identified Alastair as Alastair Reid, and once he located the *Nausicaa* libretto, which is published with the CRI recording, he identified the pages as early drafts of the *Nausicaa* prologue.

9. Reid has photos of himself, Graves, and Glanville-Hicks around a well in Deyá. Glanville-Hicks in publicity and biographical material used only photos showing herself with Graves alone. This and the following information come from Reid's letter to me of January 1989 and a telephone conversation a short time later. Reid, now resident in the Dominican Republic, is the author of several books and a contributor to the *New Yorker* magazine; critics have praised his recent English translation of Fernando Savater's *Amador* (1994).

10. This was her method in *The Transposed Heads*. She prepared the libretto by quoting verbatim from Thomas Mann's story of the same name and cutting descriptive material as necessary for a one-hour opera.

11. "Robert Graves and Opera," *Time,* 1 September 1961, 55.

and failing eyesight, which, *Time* reported, she thought were merely the results of overwork. Her friends found her impatient and short-tempered.[12]

Attributing her state of mind to overwork would seem plausible. In May 1956, in Germany before travelling to Mallorca, she finished the *Concerto romantico,* a major work; she organized its premiere in January 1957 and a recording on the MGM label. She saw her opera *The Transposed Heads* through its New York premiere in February 1958. She published a major article in the *Juilliard Review* on the aesthetics of music and composing.[13] Based in Greece from April to October of 1958, the composer travelled to Spoleto in June to attend performances of her ballets *Masque of the Wild Man* and *Triad,* choreographed by John Butler; he returned with her to Athens to begin planning *Nausicaa.* She finished a short "curtain raiser" opera, *The Glittering Gate,* and produced its premiere in New York in May 1959. She wrote music for a ballet, *Saul and the Witch of Endor,* for CBS television, with choreography again by Butler. Besides the pressures of intense work, in 1959 she was thrown into a state of utter grief when her ex-husband, the English pianist and composer Stanley Bate, committed suicide.[14] Perhaps more anxious than ever to change her surroundings, she purchased a house in Athens near the Acropolis and the Herodus Atticus theater. Yet New York continued to be her home; the *Nausicaa* score is inscribed at the end, "N. Y. C., April 1960."

The Story of Nausicaa

The libretto for *Nausicaa* meets one of Glanville-Hicks's principal requirements, which is that it be very short. "One page of text can make a two-hour opera," she often observed. This libretto is more than one page long, but still miniscule in comparison to the novel that was its source. The wealth of detail of the book is reduced to a prologue and six scenes, arranged in three acts: three scenes in the first act, two in the second, and one in the third. The prologue, in the tradition of classical drama, previews the plot. Phemius, the old court bard (tenor), sings of the hard fate of the Greek hero Odysseus, "cast by Alien Seas far from his native Ithaca" and betrayed by a faithless wife, Penelope, in his absence. Princess Nausicaa interrupts to reprimand him: "Such tales of faithless Penelope are an insult to women, and bad for their ears. I forbid you to sing of such ribald behavior in this palace!" He refuses to change the story: "We sons of Homer take no orders from women; our stories are sacred and unchangeable! The bow of Philoctetes hangs in this Palace." According to the legend, the true hero will be able to bend this bow, to string it, and win Nausicaa's hand in marriage.

In the first scene, King Alcinous, Nausicaa's father (bass), announces his departure on a voyage to find his elder son, Laodamus. As shown in ex. 27.1, the king sings a simple but memorable "tune" or *leitmotiv,* that will recur near the end of the opera when he returns. The passage illustrates the "melody-rhythm structure"—that is, a tune with

---

12. Beckett, 156-58.

13. Glanville-Hicks, "Technique and Inspiration," *Juilliard Review* 5 (spring 1958): 3-11.

14. Beckett, 113. Although they had been divorced for ten years, and had lived apart for several years before that, her attachment and loyalty continued to be strong.

Example 27.1. *Nausicaa*, act 1, scene 1, piano-vocal score, p. 8.

rhythm accompaniment and a counter-melody, but no real harmony in the European sense.

Example 27.2, also from scene 1, is from the first aria of Nausicaa (soprano). The text essentially summarizes several long, beautifully poetic scenes in Graves's novel in which the goddess Athena sends signs and prophesies to tell Nausicaa her destiny. The melody lingers on the main motive, with its exotic augmented-second interval; the note A seems to be the tonal center, even though at first we wait for it to resolve to D. Glanville-Hicks was especially attracted to this aspect of modal melody, its "malleability," as she called it in the program notes—that is, its ability to take many directions without abandoning the mode, as when a melody "modulates" out of a "key." The aria unfolds

Example 27.2. Nausicaa's aria, act 1, scene 1, piano-vocal score, p. 26.

slowly and expansively. The music moves slowly to a new harmonic or melodic "color," which is likewise developed slowly. Queen Arete, Nausicaa's mother, enters and there is dialogue in recitative and arioso, and finally Nausicaa returns to this opening melody of her aria to conclude her thoughts and round off the scene. The construction, in other words, is modelled on the *scena* of traditional opera.

A stranger arrives, identifying himself as Aethon (baritone), a nobleman of Crete, shipwrecked in a storm. Nausicaa recognizes her predestined husband whom Athena has told her about in dreams and signs. The false suitors suspect nothing. Nausicaa helps Aethon disguise himself as a beggar and swears her servant women to secrecy. Another confrontation ensues between Nausicaa and Phemius, the old court bard. Now the false suitors are egging him on in their drunken revels. Nausicaa instructs Phemius, "Tell, instead, of the fifty lovers, recite the list of their infamous names and tell how Odysseus with Apollo's bow slaughtered them all, redeeming his loss with avenging arrows!"

Scene 5 begins with a love duet for Nausicaa and Aethon. The Queen enters and Aethon pledges his loyalty and his willingness to aid Nausicaa in her revenge. Phemius is summoned and reports that all signs are that Aethon alone will be able to bend the great bow. The wedding of Nausicaa and Aethon takes place immediately, "a wedding by night, to save the day," says Phemius. The wedding scene is subdued, portrayed as a brief masque; a solemn torchlight procession and a traditional Greek bride's dance are presented to orchestral accompaniment.

In the last scene, the false suitors, though full of confidence, are nevertheless unable to bend the bow and win Nausicaa's hand in marriage, as Nausicaa already knew would happen even before the contest took place. After two men fail, Aethon, no longer disguised as a beggar but revealed to be a prince, steps forward and strings the bow. In a triumphant, seven-beat melody—Glanville-Hicks often wrote that she found extraordinary rhythmic energy in five-beat and seven-beat meters—the Queen and Nausicaa's younger brother Clytoneus celebrate the revealing of Aethon as her true husband. Aethon proceeds to use the bow to kill the false suitors. But Nausicaa commands that Phemius's life be spared: obnoxious as he has been, his death would destroy history and thus civilization. "A Son of Homer is sacred to Apollo!" she warns. "Slay a minstrel and the wrath of all the gods will surely fall upon this House!" The King's *leitmotiv* announces his return; having heard what has transpired, he blesses the "immortal gods" for the happy outcome. In the last scene, Phemius, in return for Nausicaa's having spared his life, agrees to tell *her* story of a faithful Penelope; she commands him to attribute it to Homer, as "no one would listen to a poem by a woman's hand." A final chorus ends the opera.

Clearly, the story of *Nausicaa* is significantly different from the *Odyssey* legend itself. In *Odyssey*, as in Monteverdi's opera *Il ritorno d'Ulisse in patria*, based on that legend, no wedding takes place because Odysseus and Penelope are already married. There, however, the bow-stringing contest and the killing of the false suitors are not enough to prove that the stranger is really Penelope's long-lost husband Odysseus/Ulysses; she is convinced only after the old family nurse sees him in his bath and recognizes an old scar, and after Odysseus is able to describe to Penelope the coverlet on their bed, which only he would know. Nausicaa, by contrast, already knows Aethon's identity from Athena's signs and portents. The main focus of the Nausicaa story, then, is not on a woman's faithfulness, but rather on the struggle of Nausicaa and Phemius over what form of the story will be transmitted through history. Phemius's importance derives from the sacredness of the history he sings; his importance is corroborated by his voice range, as the tenor role is traditionally the operatic hero. Nausicaa, for her part, is endowed with spiritual gifts that enable her to read Athena's signs. Finally, just as Nausicaa assigns Phemius, a man, the authoritative telling of the women's story, so Glanville-Hicks attributed Nausicaa's story to the authoritative voice of Robert Graves, as she had found many times during her career that there can be trouble in store for an opera "by a woman's hand."

The Opera's Reception

Reviews of *Nausicaa* in 1961, published in Athens, New York, London, Paris, Frankfurt, Belgrade, Vienna, Zagreb, Mexico City, Toronto, and Melbourne, were generally favorable and in some cases enthusiastic.[15] The *Athens News* reported a "splendid production"; the music "recaptures some of the noble vigour of Greece," wrote the critic, while the "audacious libretto" by Robert Graves takes creative liberties with the original *Odyssey* legend. The idea, "probably sacreligious" to historians, that a woman might have "written" *Odyssey*, "has a certain fascination" as well as appeal to a lover of the opera and theater. The reviewer for *Le Messager d'Athenes* found that the action "fell in with the ancient Greek tradition" and that the dances by John Butler gave the work "a particular character." The *Athens Daily Post* reported that all 3,200 fans who attended were impressed, in spite of the young unknown singers and the libretto that "alters" ancient Greek history.

In New York, *Variety* reported a ten-minute standing ovation and eight curtain calls for the cast of 150, from the "capacity crowd of 4,800 which overflowed the aisles and represented the cream of Athens society," including many international figures. Peter Gradenwitz in the *New York Times* estimated the crowd at 3,800 and praised the chorus for bringing the music to dramatic heights. *Time* magazine reported that Glanville-Hicks "wrapped the story in sinewy, astringent music," using the metric cadence of Greek folk song. Trudy Goth in *Opera News* praised the production details, "from John Butler's fluid staging to Andreas Nomikos' elegant sets and costumes." In *Musical America* she commented that this "was the first time in the history of a new European music festival that an American opera has been premiered," and "probably the first time too that an American composer wrote, cast, rehearsed and launched her own work."

In England, the *Guardian* reported a "successful adaptation to the Western tradition of the classical modes that still live between Greece and India." The London *Times* correspondent, reporting an audience of 4,500, discussed Greek reception of the two major elements of controversy—the libretto and the music, "each trying to present some

---

15. For complete citations see Deborah Hayes, *Peggy Glanville-Hicks: A Bio-Bibliography* (Westport, Conn.: Greenwood, 1990). Listings on p. 58 of the book include a performance of excerpts from the opera in New York City on 13 March 1979 by Janet Steele, soprano, Patrick Mason, baritone (now a faculty member at the University of Colorado), and Michael Fardink, pianist.

theory novel to the Greeks." Glanville-Hicks's analysis of Greek folk melody shows that it "belongs to the common ancient classicism that prevails in remnants throughout the Middle and Far East," the critic reported (quoting the composer's program notes), and that in India "the system handed down in unbroken tradition is still in use," as her opera score tries to demonstrate. Jean Demos in the English periodical *Opera* credited Kimon Vourloumis, director of the Athens Festival, with the decision to mount the "difficult and controversial" *Nausicaa*. Controversy begins with the libretto, she noted, which exceeds the limits a poet may take with legend and results in disunity of the plot. Is this about Odysseus and his wife Penelope, she wondered, or about Nausicaa and Aethon? And why does Aethon marry Nausicaa *before* winning the bow-stringing contest and slaughtering the suitors? Also controversial, she continued, is Glanville-Hicks's articulate explanation of an assumed connection, "surely more mystical than scientific," between ancient and modern folk music. Yet the music itself is "original, consistent and often exciting."

Opera and Autobiography

Several critics, as even these brief excerpts show, had been left a bit confused by the composer's explanations of the music and even more about the plot. The unpublished correspondence indicates some of her intentions.[16] "Be provocative," a public relations expert advised her. Play up the uniqueness of the "woman composer" of opera, he urged, and the controversial theory that the *Odyssey* is a women's story. This advice may have disturbed Glanville-Hicks, who had always avoided associating with women composers and women's organizations, and had never before chosen a story or text that depicted female heroism. She took the advice; she was indeed provocative. As the premiere approached, the festival director, Vourloumis, took to addressing her as "Nausicaa" in his letters, and she did not object to the name. But in her public utterances she deflected attention away from her interest in her opera's important main character and talked about Robert Graves and his controversial theory instead.

Perhaps because the composer provided so much information, few critics and commentators explored the opera much further. Glanville-Hicks was a formidable figure, well connected in the musical world; she wrote with skill and authority. A closer examination of the opera, however, suggests that her extraordinary efforts to write *Nausicaa* and see it produced were due to a feeling of kinship with the character of Nausicaa, not just as a woman but as a composer, particularly a composer in the "new world." Yet she did not make these connections in print. "The characters of Penelope and Nausicaa become merged into one," she wrote in the program notes, thereby confusing the issue. For Nausicaa is not Penelope, but rather the woman who determines how history and legend will be sung.

Although *Nausicaa* has often been casually summarized as representing the *Odyssey* as a woman's story, it really focuses on the importance of history and historical song to a culture, and on the sacredness of legend and song—important topics, certainly, for Robert Graves as a classical scholar, for Alastair Reid as a writer, and for Peggy Glanville-Hicks as a musician. In its celebration of the power of song, the story resembles the

16. Letters are in the Yale University library, the Library of Congress, and the State Library in Melbourne.

Orpheus legend, such a favorite of composers. It is not surprising that Glanville-Hicks was attracted to this story and gave it her best efforts in every regard. It is surprising, however, that, unlike the Orpheus legend, the story of *Nausicaa,* "Homer's daughter," has so far been set only once.

After Athens

After *Nausicaa* Glanville-Hicks remained in Greece for a year of "total rest" and recuperation from the opera production. In 1963 she completed another big opera, *Sappho,* for the San Francisco Opera Company, but so far its only performances have been of excerpts in concert version. In 1967, on a visit to New York to attend the premiere of a new ballet she had composed, Glanville-Hicks suddenly became almost totally blind and was hospitalized for surgery to remove a brain tumor—the apparent cause of the many years of severe headaches, and of what had seemed to be eyestrain. The surgery was successful and she returned to Athens, but she composed little music after that. Her active career had really ended, then, at age 54. Within a few years she returned to Australia. In the 1970s and 1980s, living in semi-retirement in Sydney, she enjoyed many performances of the music from her American years, including revivals of the operas *The Glittering Gate* and *The Transposed Heads.* A revival of *Nausicaa* is still being discussed.

Index

List of Contributors

Allen P. Britton has served as president of the Music Educators National Conference and the Sonneck Society for American Music. He is the founding editor of the *Journal of Research in Music Education* and *American Music*. He has served as Professor, Associate Dean for graduate studies, and Dean of the School of Music of the University of Michigan. He is the author of more than 100 articles and reviews, including his major opus, *American Sacred Music Imprints, 1698- 1819: A Bibliography*, written jointly with Irving Lowens and completed with an introduction by Richard Crawford.

Wilma Reid Cipolla is Librarian emerita at the University of Buffalo. Her writings include *A Catalog of the Works of Arthur Foote*, an introduction and notes for *Arthur Foote: An Autobiography*, and articles and essays for numerous publications.

J. Bunker Clark is Professor emeritus of music history at the University of Kansas. He has published extensively on American music; his publications include of "The Dawning of American Keyboard Music" and the recently prepared reprint edition of Anthony Philip Heinrich's "The Sylviad" (1823-36).

Walter Collins was Associate Dean for Graduate Studies at the University of Colorado. He served as President of the College Music Society and of the American Choral Directors Association and as Secretary-General of the International Federation for Choral Music. He was co-author of three books, including volume 23 of *Musica Britannica*, "The Anthems of Thomas Weelkes."

Mary DuPree is Professor of Music at the University of Idaho Hampton School of Music and co-director of the University's American Studies Program. Her essay on bands in Pocatello is part of an ongoing study of town bands in Idaho; her research on various aspects of American music has been published in various journals.

Linda Davenport has taught at Mesa State College in Grand Junction, Colorado, and at Lewis and Clark Community College in Godfrey, Illinois. She has recently published a book on Maine psalmody and edited the collected works of Maine psalmodist Supply Belcher.

Charles Eakin is a bassist and composer who taught theory and composition at the University of Colorado at Boulder. He has written many works in a large variety of genres, among them capriccios, operas, symphonies, jazz, string quartets. He currently lives in La Veta and continuing to compose.

Robert R. Fink is Professor of Music and Dean emeritus at the University of Colorado College of Music at Boulder. He served as Dean from 1978 to 1993 and then taught full-time until his retirement in 1994. He is the author of *The Language of Twentieth Century Music: A Dictionary of Terms*, and has written numerous articles and compositions.

John Graziano is Professor of Music at the City College and Graduate Center, City University of New York. He has co-authored an edition of chamber music for strings by the little-known nineteenth-century American composer, Charles Hommann, and has written numerous articles on American topics. He also served as Editor of *American Music.*

Deborah Hayes is Professor of Music and Associate Dean for Graduate Studies at the University of Colorado at Boulder. Her publications include studies of the theoretical writings of Jean-Philippe Rameau, editions of Classic keyboard sonatas by Francesca LeBrun and Marie-Emmanuelle Bayon Louis, and bio-bibliographies of Peggy Glanville-Hicks and Peter Sculthorpe.

Daniel C. L. Jones teaches Humanities, Western Classical Music, American Folk and Popular Musics, and World Musics at the University of Colorado at Boulder. His areas of interest, research, and publication include early American psalmody, country music, jazz, music education, and music theory.

Kate Van Winkle Keller is Executive Director of The Sonneck Society for American Music. She is the author of bibliographies and studies of eighteenth-century popular music and social dance, and is the co-director of the National Endowment for the Humanities supported projects, *National Tune Index: 18th-Century Secular Music* and *The Performing Arts in Colonial American Newspapers, 1690-1783.*

Dan Kingman is Professor emeritus at the University of California, Sacramento. He is a composer who was seduced into authorship (*American Music: A Panorama*) by a consuming interest in all aspects of the music of his native land. He likes to imagine *Mountain Calls* echoing from the canyon walls and resounding from the glacial peaks of the mountains that Bill Kearns knows and loves so well.

Karl Kroeger is Professor emeritus at the University of Colorado at Boulder. He is active as a composer, writer, and editor. His publications include *The Complete Works of William Billings*, and a series of twelve volumes on early American anthems of the first New England school.

Normand Lockwood is often asked what characterizes American music. Not brave enough to admit being stumped, he points out that a lot of our heritage worthy of emulation and found in song and text in nineteenth-century New England and still extant, is *humor*, such as nonsense- singing at mealtime at the Putnam Camp at St. Hubert's , New York, and on into the South with such songs as the hilarious ballad-like "Sam Johnson" or the melodramatic "Carmen Possum."

Anne Dhu McLucas is Dean and Professor of Music at the University of Oregon. Her scholarly work in the areas of British-Celtic-American folksong, British and American theater music, and Native-American music has been published in many of the major music journals and in various dictionaries.

Gordon Myers is Professor emeritus at Trenton State College. He has appeared as King Darius in Noah Greenberg's New York Pro Musica production of *The Play of Daniel*, and has presented his one-man concert, *The Art of Belly Canto*, for many audiences. His setting of James Weldon Johnson's *God's Trombones* is for baritone solo, chorus, and brass ensemble.

Kay Norton is Associate Professor of Music History at the Conservatory of Music, University of Missouri-Kansas City. Her publications include a life-and-works monograph on Normand Lockwood and articles in various journals. She is currently investigating eighteenth-century hymnody in Georgia.

Nancy Ping-Robbins is currently performing as one-half of a piano duo, the Chekker Ensemble. She has recently published a monograph on Scott Joplin in the Resource Manual in Composer series. Her recent compositions include an orchestral work, Alabama Summer Morning" and choral music.

Susan L. Porter was Professor of Music History at the Lima campus of The Ohio State University. She was the author of *With an Air Debonair: Musical Theatre in America, 1785- 1815*, as well as numerous articles and reviews, and edited a critical edition of the Samuel Arnold opera, *Children of the Wood.* She also served as Editor of the Sonneck Society Bulletin.

Brenda M. Romero is on the Musicology faculty at the University of Colorado in Boulder. Her research focus is on New Mexican folk music genres that reflect both Spanish and Indian origins. She is the author of "Cultural Interaction in New Mexico as Illustrated by the Matachines Dance," a chapter in *Musics in Multicultural America,* published by Schirmer in 1997. She frequently gives local and regional lecture/recitals on the older folk music of New Mexico and southern Colorado.

Deane L. Root is Curator of the Center for American Music at the University of Pittsburgh's Stephen Foster Memorial and a member of the faculty at the University of Pittsburgh. He has served as an author and editor for the *New Grove Dictionary of Music and Musicians,* and was General Editor for a sixteen-volume series of *Nineteenth-Century American Musical Theater.*

Randall Schinn was born in Oklahoma, 1944, where he learned to play the horn, and decided to pursue music. He received an MA in performance at University of Colorado and began composing during his four years in the Air Force in Vietnam. After teaching at the University of New Orleans for three years, he is now at Arizona State University in Tempe.

Murl Sickburt is Music and General Reference Librarian at Hardin-Simmons University in Abilene, Texas. He is currently at work on a number of research projects, which includes a performing edition of a Mozart *Credo* fragment and a book on the late eighteenth-century chaconne. He directs five choirs at Zion Lutheran Church.

Nicholas Tawa is Professor emeritus at the University of Massachusetts at Boston. He is the author of numerous books and articles on music in the United States. Among these are *The Coming of Age of American Art Music* and *Arthur Foote: A Composer in the Frame of Time and Place.*

Richard Toensing is Professor of composition and Chair of the compositional theory faculty at the University of Colorado at Boulder. His works are published by Carl Fischer and H. W. Gray, and appear on OWL, Golden Crest, and North/South recordings. He writes serious concert music in all genres.

Paul F. Wells is Director of the Center for Popular Music and Associate Professor of Music at Middle Tennessee State University. His research interests include fiddling and fiddle tunes, country music, the interchange between white and black traditions in southern rural musics, relationships between folk and popular musics, and Irish traditional music. He has published articles and reviews in numerous scholarly and popular journals.

Larry Worster studied musicology at the University of Colorado at Boulder and currently teaches music history, world musics, and music technology at The Metropolitan State College of Denver. He played for ten years in the Irish ensemble Colcannon. He has published one book: *Cecil Effinger: A Colorado Composer.*